BELLS & MORTARS

Catalogue of Italian Bronzes
in the Victoria and Albert Museum

BELLS & MORTARS
AND RELATED UTENSILS

ഇരു

PETA MOTTURE

Scientific programme by Graham Martin

V&A Publications
Distributed by Harry N. Abrams, Inc., Publishers

In memory of my mother and father

This publication would not have been possible
without the generous support of Daniel Katz

First published by V&A Publications, 2001
V&A Publications
160 Brompton Road
London SW3 1HW

Distributed in North America by Harry N. Abrams, Incorporated,
New York
ISBN: 0-8109-6582-8 (Harry N. Abrams, Inc.)

Designed by Yvonne Dedman
V&A photography by Stan Eost and Christine Smith
Line artwork by Technical Arts Services

Printed and bound in Italy

*Half title: Mortar made for Giovanni de
Pancioni, physician to Cardinal Latino
Orsini, attributed to the workshop of
Guidoccio di Francesco da Fabriano
(March of Ancona); dated 16 August
1465 (cat. no. 4).*

*Frontispiece: Footed bowl by the
Alberghetti foundry (Venice); probably
1550–1600 (cat. no. 18).*

*Front jacket: Detail of hand-bell by
Giuseppe de Levis (Verona); signed and
dated 1583 (cat. no. 50).*

*Back jacket: Detail of An alchemist's
laboratory by Philip Galle. Engraving
after a painting by Giovanni Stradano
(fig. 11, p. 45).*

*Images © The National Art Library,
Victoria and Albert Museum: figs 1, 2, 7,
10, 11.*

HARRY N. ABRAMS, Inc.
100 Fifth Avenue
New York, N.Y. 10011
www.abramsbooks.com

Contents

ನಲ

Foreword

ৎৎ

The study of Italian bronzes has been one of the most active areas of sculpture scholarship in the last 30 years. As Peta Motture explains in her preface, much of this work has taken the form of catalogue entries, and there is still much to do in the way of making the basic corpus of works available to a wide public. Inevitably and increasingly this material will become accessible electronically, as museums open up their holdings on the Internet. There remains a need, however, for authoritative handbooks that place significant parts of museum collections in context, and for the purposes of publishing we have endeavoured to divide the unparalleled collection of Italian bronzes at South Kensington into logical groups that will be of use to both specialist and general audiences. Following the present volume on bells and mortars, it is the intention to publish the other functional bronzes (including andirons, candlesticks, door-knockers, and so on), the statuettes and finally the busts and reliefs.

The Italian bells and mortars were an especially appropriate choice with which to begin. Many of the pieces have not been published before and several of them carry inscriptions that shed valuable light on the circumstances of production and consumption in the Renaissance. Because the Museum is fortunate to hold one of the most comprehensive collections of Italian bells and mortars in the world, it is to be hoped that this volume will serve not only as a catalogue of our holdings, but also as a convenient introduction to the subject.

Paul Williamson
Chief Curator of Sculpture

Preface

ରୀ

The collection of Italian bronzes in the Victoria and Albert Museum is the most extensive ever assembled. It numbers approximately 620 objects (excluding medals and plaquettes), around 360 of which are sculptural – statuettes, groups, busts, reliefs – with the remaining 260 being functional pieces, such as candlesticks, lamps, andirons, door-knockers, ink-stands, bells and mortars. Due to the systematic approach to collecting that has been peculiar to the Museum from its earliest years, the collection is unique in its size, variety and scope. The functional bronzes in particular include an unusually high proportion of pieces inscribed with names, locations and dates.

The study of bronzes as a separate subject within the history of sculpture was pioneered at the end of the nineteenth and the beginning of the twentieth centuries by such scholars as C. D. E. Fortnum (1820–99) and Wilhelm von Bode (1845–1929). Somewhat surprisingly, Fortnum's 1876 catalogue of European bronzes in the V&A (then the South Kensington Museum) remains the only published survey of the collection, including 194 bronzes then considered to be Italian in origin. Since then the Museum has benefited from the important bequests of George Salting in 1910 and Dr W. L. Hildburgh in 1956, and consequently the collection has grown significantly.

After the addition of 124 pieces to the collection with the Salting Bequest, work on a new catalogue was started by Eric (later Sir Eric) Maclagan, Keeper of the Department of Architecture and Sculpture from 1921 to 1924 and then Director. Perhaps due to the onerous duties of Maclagan's position, the catalogue remained unfinished at his retirement in 1944.

The study of bronzes has subsequently been transformed. The staff of the Museum have played an important role in this, largely through research on the collection and through their involvement in international exhibitions, two of which were held at the V&A. The first, on Italian bronze statuettes, was organized by John (later Sir John) Pope-Hennessy (Keeper of Architecture and Sculpture 1954–67, then Director until 1973) in 1961; it was shown also in Florence and Amsterdam. The benefit of seeing various pieces together for the first time allowed new connections to be made based on facture, and by the time of the showing in Amsterdam it was possible to include some modifications in the Dutch catalogue. The second was the great Giambologna exhibition of 1978, also shown in Edinburgh and Vienna. Organized by Anthony Radcliffe and Charles Avery, Assistant and Deputy Keepers in the Sculpture Department, with Manfred Leithe-Jasper of the Kunsthistorisches Museum in Vienna, it provided an opportunity to develop a scientific approach to the study of bronzes by use of radiographs, establishing methods of facture not visible to the naked eye. X-rays were taken of many of the bronzes in the exhibition by Jonathan Ashley-Smith of the V&A Conservation Department, and these have formed the basis of studies beyond those carried out within the Museum itself. Numerous publications have been produced on various aspects of the bronzes collection, notably the works of Charles Avery, who left the Museum in 1979, and of Anthony Radcliffe (Keeper of Sculpture 1979–89), who retired from the Museum in 1993.

The growing interest in the subject has highlighted the invaluable nature of the collection as a great resource for both the art-historical and technical study of bronzes. It was therefore decided to produce a series of volumes on Italian bronzes, which, in addition to the information traditionally covered in such publications, would also contain technical data, gathered using a variety of methods. The combination of art-historical and scientific research is becoming the standard approach for the study of bronzes. Radiography is expected to play an important role in the examination of objects contained in the later volumes, as it is essential for revealing the structure of hollow-cast bronzes. It is less useful for bells and mortars, for several reasons: the interiors are visible; they are often so thickly cast that only very powerful X-rays can penetrate them; and the decoration applied to the circular shape makes them difficult to interpret. However, a number of the radiographs that were taken have provided some key information (see cat. nos 41 and 50 (pl. 41b and 50c), for example). For this first volume, the principal scientific technique employed has been elemental analysis by Energy Dispersive X-Ray Fluorescence spectrometry (EDXRF). The science programme has been carried out by the Head of Science and Information Section, Graham Martin, whose essay on alloy analysis (see pp. 51–2) outlines the methodology, the benefits and limitations of this technique.

The literature for bells and mortars, notably those of Italian origin, is somewhat scattered. Among the standard works on mortars are Lise and Bearzi's *Antichi mortai di farmacia* (1975) and Middeldorf's *Fifty Mortars* (1981), as well as Launert's more recent survey of European mortars, *Der Mörser* (1990), but much useful information is contained in articles published in a variety of journals. Similarly, there are a number of books devoted to the subject of bells, particularly in England, such as those by Ellacombe (1872), Walters (1912) and Jennings (1987). Lange's *Europäische Tischglocken* (1981), Schilling's *Glocken und Glockenspiele* (1985) and *Glocken: Gestalt Klang und Zier* (1988) provide detailed studies

that concentrate primarily on German examples. For Italy, major works include the catalogues of two exhibitions of bells held in Verona (1979) and Padua (1986), a series of articles by Blagg (notably 1974 and 1978), and Avery's studies of Giuseppe de Levis (republished in 1981).

In the case of both bells and mortars, catalogue entries have tended to be quite summary, with the objects being treated alongside other bronzes to which, in general, more attention is paid. There are exceptions to this rule, including Pechstein's catalogue of the collection at the Kunstgewerbemuseum in Berlin (1968) and – to some extent – Pope-Hennessy's Kress Collection catalogue (1965). The most significant contributions, however, have been the entries by Radcliffe in the catalogues of the Thyssen-Bornemisza (1992) and Robert H. Smith (1994) collections, which provide model prototypes.

The broader context of bells and mortars is provided by a series of introductory essays, which serve in part for the collection of bronzes as a whole. Those specific to this book focus primarily on Italy in the Renaissance to reflect the contents of the volume. The entries attempt to resolve a number of issues arising from these objects, although – as is so often the case – this can result in more questions being raised than answered. In some instances it has been possible to identify workshops or to attribute works to a particular area, but unless there is sufficient evidence to do so, the question of their origin has been acknowledged as uncertain. It is the hope that the publication of these pieces will prompt further information to emerge.

Peta Motture
June 2000

Acknowledgements

A catalogue of this nature involves considerable collaboration and support to bring it to completion. Any errors and omissions are, of course, my own, but my thanks go to all who have contributed.

Acknowledgement goes firstly to those colleagues who have made a special contribution over the years, and whose enthusiasm and helpful suggestions have been invaluable. Diane Bilbey has been involved from the outset, and in addition to providing excellent secretarial support, she undertook various aspects of the research, including gathering information on collectors and dated bells and mortars. Fiona Leslie was responsible not only for so ably organizing the greater part of the photography and science programmes, but also for assisting in the research, notably identification of heraldry. During the last year Jemma Street kindly checked and investigated many references. In addition to Graham Martin's technical expertise, I have enjoyed his unfailing good humour and patience in responding to my queries.

A period in 1996/7 was largely devoted to this project, with the assistance of my colleagues in the Sculpture Department, who covered the majority of my duties. I am especially grateful to Paul Williamson, most particularly for his insightful comments and suggestions on the text. A significant debt is due to Marjorie Trusted, Wendy Fisher, Norbert Jopek and Lucy Cullen for their constant support and assistance on specific issues, and to Chloë Archer and Alexandra Corney, along with my other Sculpture colleagues over the years, named below.

I benefited from a travel grant from the Research Department, to which Graham Martin was seconded for six weeks during the initial stages of the scientific analysis programme. We are grateful to Paul Greenhalgh, Malcolm Baker and Jonathan Ashley-Smith for their support; to Boris Pretzel, David Ford, Paula Mills and Brenda Keneghan for their assistance with the scientific programme; and to Paul Robins, who carried out the X-radiography programme. The volume is enhanced by photographs taken by Stanley Eost and Christine Smith.

I am also grateful to Diana Heath and Kenneth Turner for their comments on facture, to John Meriton for blazoning the majority of the arms, Ken Jackson for advising on photography and Peter Ford for his essential computer back-up. Mary Butler, Miranda Harrison, Mary Wessel and Mandy Greenfield helped greatly with the production of the volume, which has been designed with great flair by Yvonne Dedman.

Other Museum colleagues, both past and present, who have contributed in a variety of ways include Marta Ajmar, Rachel Akpabio, Nicholas Barnard, Julia Bigham, John Boniface, Marian Campbell, Neil Carleton, Michael Clark, Helen Clifford, Carlo Dumontet, Mark Evans, Alun Graves, William Greenwood, John Guy, Anna Hamilton, Emma Hardy, Wendy Hefford, Sarah Herring, Jo Hodden-Brown, Louise Hofman, Jim Honey, the late George Jackson, Sally Korman, Reino Liefkes, Keith Marks, Elizabeth Miller, Maureen Mulvanny, Rebecca Naylor, Anthony North, Paul Ruskin, Anthony Ryan, Pippa Shirley, Deborah Sinfield, Sue Stronge, Claire Sussums, Katie Swann, Eleanor Townsend and James Yorke. The late Clive Wainwright generously provided information on the history of collecting. Sadly, his offer to read the relevant essay was unfulfilled, and his enthusiastic encouragement is greatly missed.

In addition to those specifically referred to in the notes, many friends and colleagues from outside the Museum have provided advice, information, access to collections or enlightening discussions. These include Francesca Bewer, who made invaluable suggestions on the materials and techniques; Jo Castle, who gave essential advice on pharmaceutical history; David Rundle, who checked and advised on the translations of Latin inscriptions; Luke Syson, whose various comments were most helpful; Susan Bradley, Richard Kibrya and David Thickett of Conservation Research at the British Museum, who carried out XRD analysis; Robert Bracegirdle and Andrew Higson at the Taylor Bellfoundry and Museum at Loughborough; Richard Brewis, Arthur Cuthbert, Peter

Harrison, Peter Trick, Nick Davidson and Danny Matholus at the Whitechapel Bellfoundry; and Daciano Colbacchini and Luigi Cavadini at their respective foundries in Padua and Verona; as well as: Renzo Alidosi, Luisella Angiari, Irene Ariano, Philip Attwood, Fabienne Audebrand, Charles Avery, Victoria Avery, Gordon Balderston, Davide Banzato, Sophie Baratte, R. and A.-M. Bautier, Thomas Blagg, Monique Blanc, Antonia Boström, Vince Bridgman, Lia Carmerlengo, Patrizia Catellani, John Cherry, Howard Coutts, Thierry Crépin-Leblond, Robin Crighton, Laura Dal Prà, Alan Darr, Isabel de Dauw, Nicholas Davidson, Cara Denison, Gerhard Dietrich, James Draper, Bruce Edelstein, Godfrey Evans, Peter Fusco, Giancarlo Gentilini, Cristiano Giometti, Bernhard Heitmann, Igor Jenzen, Donald Johnston, Lorraine Jones, Jutta Kappel, Daniel Katz, Michael Knuth, Volker Krahn, Michael Lea, Douglas Lewis, Domenico Lini, Stuart Lochhead, Elena Lucchese Ragni, Maurizio Mondini, Jennifer Montagu, Susanne Netzer, Enrica Pagella, Beatrice Paolozzi Strozzi, Nicola Perrin, Bruno Pessamani, Angelo Piazza, Frau Prahs, Carmen Ravanelli Guidotti, Caroline Reed, Joseph Reinis, Luciano Rognini, Giandomenico Romanelli, Corrado Rossini, Nicolas Sainte Fare Garnot, Claudio Salsi, Gian Carlo Signore, Richard Stone, Mary Sullivan, Göran Tegnér, J. R. Ter Molen, Anna-Elisabeth Theuerkauff, Christian Theuerkauff, Dora Thornton, Camillo Tonini, Kevin Tucker, Susan Urbach, Jeremy Warren, Evelyn Welch, Jean-Marie Welter, Patricia Wengraf, Robert Wenley, Pamela Willis, Elizabeth Wilson, Timothy Wilson and Annalisa Zanni.

My particular gratitude goes to Anthony Radcliffe, who must be singled out for his unique role. While keeping a discreet distance to allow me to find my own way, Tony Radcliffe has remained an encouraging influence, providing comparative material, willingly discussing particular problems and raising pertinent questions, and ultimately making telling comments on the text.

Finally, my most special thanks go to my partner Alistair McFarlane for his wholehearted support, helpful suggestions and unfailing interest.

INTRODUCTION

෨෬

Collecting and Collectors

The Collection's history begins with the Museum of Ornamental Art, which was set up at Marlborough House in 1844.[1] In 1857 the collections moved and became part of the South Kensington Museum, before it was radically reformed and changed its name to the Victoria and Albert Museum in 1899. The guiding principle of the original acquisitions policy was to encourage excellence in contemporary design and manufacturing through the study of exemplary pieces from both the present and earlier periods. Acquisitions were justified by their importance as exemplars of techniques, rather than as works of art, and this policy was strengthened with implicit reference to the sculpture holdings in a Minute of 13 June 1863. This ordered that 'future purchases be confined to objects wherein fine art is applied to some purpose of utility; and that works of fine art not so applied should only be admitted as exceptions and so far as they may tend directly to improve art applied to objects of utility'.[2] It is therefore not surprising to find bronze utensils that were bought as Italian among the earliest acquisitions, including bells (Appendix 3, nos 1 and 2) and mortars (cat. nos 8, 10 and 75), as well as a footed bowl or tazza (cat. no. 19).

In 1909 the Museum underwent a further major reorganization, being divided into eight curatorial departments, including Architecture and Sculpture (renamed Sculpture in 1979) and Metalwork.[3] Functional bronzes were generally viewed as metalwork, and purely artistic pieces as sculpture, although it would seem that admission to the existence of the latter category was questionable in light of the Museum's stated mission. Moreover, these criteria led to the rather odd situation whereby medieval bronzes were considered utilitarian, and therefore assigned to Metalwork, whereas similar post-medieval pieces were lodged with Sculpture.[4] Even this approach was not strictly adhered to, with candlesticks being variously assigned, depending in part on their form. A notable oddity was the allocation of a group of salt cellars, all from the Soulages Collection, in the form of a kneeling man supporting a shell, which was divided between the two departments.[5] The result was, therefore, a rather anomalous arrangement, which in time was supplanted by a more pragmatic solution that reflected the nature of Italian bronzes scholarship. While remaining formally under Metalwork's charge, many of the utilitarian bronzes were for a number of years displayed and stored with the other Italian bronzes in the Sculpture Department and caretaken by successive curators there. A formal transfer of the material was instigated in 1992. While on the surface appearing to be a rationalization of the collection, it has been applied only to the Italian pieces, with virtually all other European 'bronzes' remaining in Metalwork, including substantial holdings of bells and mortars.

The confusion about the status and context of these pieces highlights the often misleading distinction between the so-called 'fine' and 'decorative' arts. While bells and mortars were indeed functional, they were produced both by specialists and, on occasion, by individual sculptors. At the same time, bell and artillery foundries were often employed by sculptors to cast bronze statuary.

While their functions are very different, bronze bells and mortars are closely related by their method of facture, and often by alloy. They are, however, both produced in other materials. Bells may be ceramic, glass and even terracotta, while mortars have been made of such diverse materials as stone, marble, wood, terracotta, maiolica and ivory. These objects therefore appeal to a variety of collectors, some of whom are represented here.

Unfortunately, the provenance of many of the early acquisitions was not recorded in the Museum's registers, and whatever correspondence existed has subsequently been lost or 'weeded'.[6] The earliest acquisition for which there is any information is a vase bought in 1865 from John Webb (1799–1880), the details of which were removed during an external audit (cat. no. 26).[7] A cabinet-maker and upholsterer based in Old Bond Street, London, Webb also dealt in antiquities. He was a great friend to the South Kensington Museum, often acting as agent on such important matters as the sale of the collection belonging to the French writer Eugène Piot (1812–90) in 1864.[8] Piot inherited a substantial sum from his father in 1832, much of which was spent enjoying life with his friends, indulging his interests in art and music, and buying old books and prints. He founded a periodical aimed at collectors in 1842 (*Cabinet de l'amateur et de l'antiquaire*), but it was a financial failure and soon closed, being revived briefly in 1861–3. The Fondation Eugène Piot, however, still produces a periodical entitled *Monuments et Mémoires*.

Piot travelled extensively, frequently making acquisitions en route. Much of his collection was dispersed in sales in 1847–8, 1864 and following his death in 1890, but some key pieces were donated to the Louvre. In 1877 he lent (for a fee) a substantial collection of antique glass to the South Kensington Museum, some of which was purchased in 1879. However, most significant is the Piot collection of books on pageantry, purchased by the Museum in 1880–1, which he had collected over a period of 25 years. His varied posses-

sions also included paintings, prints, furniture, arms, ceramics and sculpture (notably medals, plaquettes and small bronzes).

In a report on the 1864 sale produced by John Charles (later Sir Charles) Robinson (1824–1913), formerly Superintendent of the Art Collections at South Kensington but then an Art Referee, he stated:

> The bronzes are very important, and in this section we are as yet comparatively poor. The fine specimens are likely on this occasion to command much higher prices than such works have ever realized before. My own acquisitions in past years for the Museum in the category of Italian sculpture have been mainly the cause of this and many objects are likely now to sell for as many pounds as similar ones have been purchased by me in Italy for shillings – such works, however, will still run very much higher in the scale of pecuniary value, and for this reason I think an effort should be made at the sale to secure all the objects really desirable.[9]

Robinson's recommendations were rejected and his pique at this decision, coupled with the terms of the 1863 Minute, was evident in his assessment of Baron Mattei of Naples' collection the following month, when he reported that 'considering…the purchase of the sculptures from the Piot sale has just been declined by the Board, I do not see how I could directly recommend my Lords to entertain the purchase of objects such as these on an exceptional footing, they being in every respect beyond comparison less important than the Piot sculptures'.[10]

He did manage to secure the *Winged Putto with a Fantastic Fish*, attributed to Donatello, at the Piot sale.[11] The vase cited above (cat. no. 26) was one of the items bought by Webb and subsequently offered to the Museum, a practice he regularly undertook, often placing the objects on loan until the Museum could pay.[12] Piot owned just a few other bowls, bells and mortars.[13] Another large footed bowl or wine cooler was bought by George Salting at the 1890 sale, and was later bequeathed to the V&A (cat. no. 27).

Webb was also involved in the acquisition of the Soulages Collection, which was bought for the nation by a number of subscribers in 1856 and subsequently purchased in instalments up to 1865. Not only was Webb the assessor of the collection, but also a subscriber. Jules Soulages (d. 1857)[14] was a lawyer and antiquary whose extensive and varied collection was built up while he was living in Paris during the 1830s and '40s, largely through regular excursions to Italy. It was subsequently moved to his native Toulouse. The collection included furniture, textiles, tapestries, enamels, porcelain and, of course, bronzes, some of which beg further consideration.[15] His aggressive collecting policy led to his being described by Italian writers as 'one of the most successful and untiring ravishers of the art treasures of their country'.[16] Two bells were among the objects acquired in 1865 (cat. nos 40 and 46).

In 1869 two mortars from the Tordelli (sometimes referred to as Toretelli) Collection in Spoleto were bought from Giuseppe Baslini (sometimes referred to as Basilini) of Milan. Tordelli's palace in Spoleto was described as being full of a variety of antiquities and works of art, freely available for curious visitors of all nationalities to visit. His important collection of maiolica was, like so many other collections at the time, taken to Paris for sale in May 1870.[17] Baslini was a dealer in Milan, from whom the Museum purchased the *Lamentation* relief by Bartolommeo Bellano.[18] According to Nobili, 'Some of the best art connoisseurs, those of the surest touch, come from an ignorant class of workers, such as the celebrated Couvreur of Paris or the Milanese Basilini, a former carter who was often consulted by Morelli, the Italian art critic and inventor of the analytical method, a connoisseur of undisputed merit.'[19]

Another great nineteenth-century collector was Alessandro Castellani (1823–83).[20] A prominent member of the Italian family of jewellers, writers and collectors, he suffered political exile from Rome in 1859, subsequently establishing premises in Paris, London and Naples. He was a noted antiquarian, widely consulted for his expertise in jewellery. However, Castellani also produced copies of ancient works – the South Kensington Museum (as it then was) ordered bronze reproductions of Pompeian

objects from him in 1869 – and he made fakes.[21] In 1870 he wrote to the Secretary of the Science and Art Department and Director of the Museum, Henry Cole:

> I just arrive from Rome, whence I had been banished eleven years ago, and where I entered on the 20th of September last with the Italian army on the ruins of the temporal powers of the Popes…
>
> At last I am free to dispose as I like of my large Collection of ancient [*sic*] gold ornaments, gems, bronzes and other antiquities, the Italian Government being unable to find the money to purchase it.[22]

The intention was that the collection be placed on loan at the Museum with a view to purchase, and with the British government providing passage in a naval vessel. After much debate, the collection arrived and was instead deposited at the British Museum. In 1881 a proposal was put forward that the two museums jointly acquire the collection. This was enthusiastically supported by the four advisers, whose opinions differed mainly on the valuation. The proposition faltered, perhaps because the parties could not agree on the price, with the British Museum declining to meet Castellani's figure of £18,000 (reduced from £20,000).

At some stage in the following two years the collection must have returned to Rome, where it was auctioned in March and April 1884. In a report on the forthcoming sale, the great connoisseur, collector and bronzes expert, C. D. E. Fortnum, highlighted Castellani's 'unrivalled knowledge and opportunities [which] enabled him to form this collection, perhaps the most important, both in regard to the exceptional excellence of the greater number of the objects, and the representation of artistic production in every branch, that has been dispersed during the last quarter of a century'.[23] Objects were suggested for several museums and the subsequent bidding was made by Fortnum, who also made purchases for his own collection. Among the acquisitions were several ceramic objects and three ivories, including the outstanding Byzantine statuette of the *Virgin Hodegetria*,[24] but only one bronze – a bell (cat. no. 54), which had not originally been selected.

A group of 20 mortars was bought from Michelangelo Guggenheim (1837–1914)[25] of Venice in 1889, 19 of which are Italian and form a large proportion of the Museum's total collection of 48. In 1857 he set up the Stabilimento Guggenheim for the production of decorative and industrial arts (furniture, bronzes and stonework), which continued to operate until 1910. Its output consisted of both new designs and reproductions of traditional works, including, for example, a reduced version of the bronze wellhead in the Palazzo Ducale, Venice, by the Alberghetti foundry, of 1559.[26] Guggenheim was also active in developing a programme for museums, publishing various papers and receiving honours for his contributions to the life of Venice. He wrote a few small books and pamphlets, including one on Renaissance frames. His own collection contained a wide variety of pieces, among which were several bells, mortars and other bronzes. Guggenheim made various offers to the Museum, but the main purchases made were the mortars,[27] all acquired as of Renaissance date (apart from cat. no. 68, which is a rare survival, datable to the early fourteenth century). However, close examination suggests that some are not old (see, for example, cat. nos 64 and 66).

Another major figure of the time was the Florentine painter, dealer and restorer, Stefano Bardini (1836–1922).[28] He was a notable connoisseur, whose palace and much of its contents were eventually acquired by the Italian State (now forming the Museo Bardini). The Museum purchased a number of objects from him in the 1880s and '90s. A fascinating letter written from Florence by the artist Frederick (Lord) Leighton (then an Art Referee) points out that Wilhelm Bode was making regular visits to Bardini. He urged the Museum to do the same, stressing that 'Now competition is very keen *and very intelligent*, and on the other hand everything in Italy goes to Bardini's and whoever *goes there oftenest* has an immeasurable advantage over the others'.[29] A large proportion of the artworks in his possession consisted of sculptural objects, including bronze statuettes, some of which are now in the Frick Collection in New York.[30] The Museum bought two bells (one now lost)[31] from one of the Bardini sales

held in London (see cat. no. 48), and subsequently acquired a bell (cat. no. 37) and a mortar (cat. no. 28) with the Salting Bequest.

George Salting (1835–1909) was born in Sydney, Australia, of Danish parents, who eventually settled in England.[32] He inherited a fortune on the death of his father in 1865 and embarked on what was to become his career as a serious collector. His initial interest was in Chinese porcelain, of which he amassed a huge collection, and he gradually expanded this to include metalwork, ceramics, enamels, lacquered furniture, illuminated manuscripts, miniatures, paintings, prints, drawings and small-scale sculpture. His bronzes represent a significant proportion of his extensive possessions, which he began depositing at the Museum in 1874, and which he finally bequeathed.

Most of his acquisitions were made through dealers, such as George Durlacher (1856?–1942) and Murray Marks (1840?–1918), from whom the Museum bought a footed bowl (cat. no. 18), but Salting also attended many important sales, at which he usually bid for himself. Fourteen bells, mortars, vases and bowls are included in this volume; at least seven have illustrious earlier provenances. Piot has already been mentioned. Another significant collection was that of Sir Thomas Gibson Carmichael (1859–1926),[33] from which Salting bought two impressive mortars, presumably from the different dealers who purchased them at the sale, Stettiner and Durlacher (cat. nos. 4 and 11). The latter bid for a few objects at the sale on behalf of the Museum, among them a carved bone pastoral staff (inv. no. 604-1902).[34] Gibson Carmichael was another prolific collector of bronzes, ivories, enamels, porcelain and other objects. He loaned many of his pieces to the Museum, and gave one sculpture.[35]

Another sizeable group of objects in this volume came from the Alfred Williams Hearn Collection. Both the gift (1923) and the later bequest (1931) were actually made by his widow,[36] who had continued to collect beyond her husband's death in 1904; therefore a good proportion (if not all) was never actually in his possession. Alfred Hearn seems to have collected a variety of objects, primarily metalwork (notably pewter), of which he was particularly proud.[37] The list included English, continental and Oriental porcelain, a substantial amount of furniture (much of which had been severely altered) and various metalwork and sculpture items, including wood sculpture, ivories and bronzes. Mrs Hearn bought many objects through the dealer Thomas Sutton of Eastbourne, who acted as her agent, as he had done for her husband. Hearn had apparently intended to leave his works of art to the Museum for 'the public good', and his widow continued to collect with the express view of augmenting his collection in a worthy fashion for this purpose. Like her husband, she bought at good sales, as well as at the main London auctions. She was keen for the collection to be displayed together, but there was evident concern to avoid the restrictions of this request (already experienced with the Ionides and Jones Collections) when the future bequest was under discussion in 1904–5. It is therefore interesting that the Salting Bequest was accepted on this very basis in 1910, although the stipulation was only honoured for a while after the collection was first displayed.

After Mrs Hearn's death in 1931 there were 105 objects stored at the Museum on her behalf, and a selection of the remainder at her villa in Menton in France was to be made by the Museum. Sutton, who was an executor of her will but had fallen out with the remaining family, wrote three urgent and concerned letters from his hotel in Sicily within five days, entreating the Director, Eric Maclagan, to meet him at Menton to go through the collection. The bequest was finally settled, and among the objects chosen from the villa was the 'large bronze mortar (Ignatius Loyala [*sic*] from Rome)' that stood outside the library (cat. no. 16).[38] Sadly, another 'remarkable' mortar inscribed 'LIBORIA BARAGLI L'ANNO 1520' was apparently overlooked or rejected, and was subsequently bought by a pharmacist at a Sotheby's sale.[39]

A better-known and major benefactor was Dr Walter Leo Hildburgh, FSA (1876–1955), the American collector and art historian who settled in London in 1912.[40] Hildburgh was a scientist by training and considered his objects as 'specimens' to be comprehen-

sively collected. He began donating as early as 1912, his first gift being a wafer iron plate. For more than 40 years the Museum benefited from his loans and gifts. He often gave in January (thereby ensuring that in most years the first number of the annual inventory was a Hildburgh gift) and on his birthday in March. On his 70th birthday in 1946 Hildburgh gave his outstanding collection of English medieval alabaster carvings – 260 in all. His magnificent bequest, consisting largely of metalwork and sculpture, was registered in 1956. Hildburgh's scholarly output included several articles on sculptors. Notable in connection with this catalogue are the articles on Italian wafer irons and pastiglia boxes, the decoration of which can be related to ornamented motifs used on bronze utensils (see p. 49). Fifteen bells and mortars from Hildburgh appear in this volume, as well as one of only two surviving pestles (cat. no. 59). Surprisingly, none entered the collection after 1938, when he gave a total of 35 mortars of various nationalities.[41]

The remaining objects came from a variety of sources. The hand bell by Giovanni Alberghetti (cat. no. 17) was bought in 1886 from Cavaliere Attilio Simonetti in Rome. A fascinating mortar, possibly with alchemical associations (cat. no. 73), was acquired in 1901 by transfer from the Museum of Practical Geology in Jermyn Street, when recommendations were made to redistribute much of its material. Among this was 'a collection of statuettes, vases etc., illustrating the casting and chasing of metals',[42] which presumably incorporated the various bronzes (including Oriental pieces) that formed part of the transfer, together with the substantial ceramics collection. Among these was another mortar, signed and dated 1558 by the Flemish bell-founder, Peter I van den Gheyn (d. 1561) now in the Metalwork collection (inv. no. 5446-1901), and an Italian bronze statuette of a male anatomical figure (inv. no. 5438-1901).[43]

Two other important pieces were given by donors about whom nothing is known – N. Bear of London, from whom the Melfi mortar was bought in 1903 (cat. no. 69), and Signora Ada Cardinale of London and Rome, who gave the sanctus bell from Teglio in 1925 (cat. no. 60). Another mortar, received in 1926 (cat. no. 13), came from the bequest of Lt Col G. B. Croft-Lyons, whose collection had been on loan, and which included a number of English mortars acquired at the same time.

In virtually all the cases here, the bells and mortars formed part of broader collections, or were acquired from dealers who specialized in a range of objects. One such was Arthur Davidson, who dealt primarily in objects for interior decoration. The distinctive mortar cast by Ambrogio Lucenti (cat. no. 15) was the only object that the Museum purchased from him (in 1974). He subsequently sold his business in Jermyn Street and moved abroad. More recently the Museum has benefited from the generosity of Daniel Katz, the prominent art dealer and collector with a well-known penchant for – and considerable expertise in – small bronzes, whose gallery is also based in Jermyn Street.[44] He has donated a bell by Giuseppe de Levis (cat. no. 50) and an important French mortar (inv. no. A.2-1999).[45]

Despite their functional origins, bells and mortars have formed part of many of the most important art collections of the nineteenth and twentieth centuries. In addition to those so far mentioned, other collectors included Castiglione, Figdor, Dreyfus, Simon and Pierpont Morgan. The Pierpont Morgan Collection was on loan to the Victoria and Albert Museum at the same time as that of Salting, and it was hoped that it too would be donated. In his introduction to the catalogue of Morgan's bronzes, Bode describes him as 'the greatest collector of our time'.[46] His collecting style was characterized as one of 'utmost completeness' over a broad range of objects from all periods, but a high point was his 'predilection for plastic art in bronze'.[47] He was said to have owned 'the most comprehensive and probably the most important collection of bronzes to be found in private possession, a collection moreover exceptionally rich in Italian small bronzes of the Renaissance'.[48] It contained only a few bells, mortars and related utensils. Two bronzes with a Morgan provenance did eventually find their way into the V&A's collection,[49] but most of the remainder came to rest in the Frick Collection and the Metropolitan Museum of Art in New York, and the Frick Art Museum in Pittsburgh, Pennsylvania.[50]

Surprisingly, there appears to be only one anomalous collector represented here, certainly in terms of the Italian material. Dr Anselm Lange's interests lay in bells of all materials, rather than in bronzes or decorative art. There were also notable specialist mortar collections, including those of Hemming and Wellcome, which often ended up, instead, in science or medical history museums. The same is true of drug jars, which are variously viewed as artistic or practical exemplars of a scientific application, and specialists continue to collect according to their specific interests.[51]

ॐ

The Materials

Bronze is an alloy of copper and tin, but the term is applied to a wide variety of copper-tin alloys, which frequently contain other elements.[1] In ancient civilizations there was generally only one word that covered copper and its alloys – the Greek term being *khalkos* and the Latin *aes*.[2]

The term *bronzo* seems first to have appeared in Italy in the fifteenth century, when it was used to refer to the metal of the antique artefacts that were at that time regularly being excavated.

Copper minerals exist in different forms, the most abundant of which, copper pyrites, are double sulphurets of copper and iron. They are extracted by a series of processes, including grinding, washing and roasting in a furnace, during which lengthy process the sulphur is burnt off and the iron is separated as slag. The remaining copper oxide must be further reduced by burning with charcoal, leaving the pure copper with some impurities, which can be removed by refining.[3]

Copper, which has been in use since the Neolithic period (8000–7000 BC), is fairly soft and malleable, easily shaped by hammering, but not hard enough to take the good edge desirable for tools and weapons. It can be difficult to pour when molten,[4] which occurs at 1083 °C, having a tendency to 'gas', and therefore producing a porous cast. The addition of other elements improved the limitations of using pure copper, and by the end of the fourth millennium BC harder copper-arsenic alloys appeared – a development that probably occurred initially by accident, due to the frequent proximity of arsenical minerals and copper ores. Tin deposits, on the other hand, are rare and usually quite separate from those of copper (see p. 21). Analysis of objects dating from ancient dynasties at Ur (about 6000–5000 BC) and Sumer (about 5000–3000 BC), both now in modern Iraq, indicates that many artefacts usually referred to as copper were, in fact, copper-tin alloys.[5] These would have been made by combining copper ore with tin ore. This material did not 'gas' in the way that pure copper did, and could therefore be poured into closed moulds; it was more easily controlled than arsenic-copper alloys.[6]

The next stage of the development of bronze production was to heat tin oxide, metallic copper and charcoal together to create the alloy. Finally, in about 1700–1500 BC true bronze was made by combining metallic copper with metallic tin, which had been separately reduced from the tin-ore by burning with charcoal. It is difficult to say exactly when tin was isolated as a separate metal as the evidence is both scant and inconclusive, but during antiquity tin was used virtually exclusively to produce bronzes.

In addition to tin, bronzes frequently contain other elements, either by design or accident, including lead, zinc, nickel, arsenic and antimony. Many of these exist as trace elements, while others have a significant effect on both the properties and the appearance of the alloy. The more tin, the harder and more brittle the metal, and with over 15 per cent tin it becomes impossible to work when cold, although it can still be hammered out when red-hot. High-tin bronzes are sonorous, making them ideal for bells, which contain 20–23 per cent tin, but their comparative fragility means that they must be carefully designed to avoid cracking when they are struck. At over 25 per cent tin they become much more easily damaged. These alloys are often referred to as bell-metal, for obvious reasons, or in some cases simply as 'metal'.[7]

The addition of lead to make a ternary alloy (often called leaded bronze) has the effect of lowering the melting point, thus making the metal easier to cast.[8] Although it flows more easily, details will be softened. It is also less suitable for bells, where a musical tone is required, as lead has the effect of dulling sound.

Some so-called bronzes are actually brass (also known as latten or maslin) – a copper-zinc alloy – which was commonly used in the medieval period and particularly in northern Europe, but also in Renaissance Italy. Brass is more malleable and usually has a lower melting range than bronze. Being softer, it will also withstand damage more easily than tin-bronzes. The earliest known objects with any significant amount of zinc date from about 1400–1200 BC, although it was not commonly used until the end of the Roman period. Metallic zinc was not recognized in the West until the sixteenth century and was not produced commercially until the eighteenth; brass was not generally made by combining the two metallic elements until the early part of the nineteenth century.[9] Previously it was achieved by heating calamine (zinc carbonate, which may be roasted to become zinc oxide) with charcoal and copper. Experiments indicate that brass made by the calamine method contains no more than 28 per cent zinc, but when copper and zinc are alloyed the mixture can contain as much as 30–40 per cent.[10]

Just as copper and its alloys were at times referred to as 'bronze', so the same materials were known as 'brass', notably in England until about the seventeenth or eighteenth century. A common term was applied, for example, to any such alloy used for artillery, regardless of its content, throughout the fifteenth to eighteenth centuries.[11] Today the terms are still used loosely, with bronze being particularly associated with artwork and related pieces, and brass with more utilitarian objects, except when it comes to Italy, where the term 'bronze' predominates. In fact, some statuettes, such as the *Venus and Adonis* (inv. no. A.58-1956) by the Anglo-Italian sculptor Francesco Fanelli (b. 1577, last documented 1641) are brasses.[12]

In his *Natural History*, Pliny the Elder (AD 23–79) uses the term *aurichalcum*, translated as 'gold-copper' or 'mountain-copper', when referring to yellow copper ore and brass.[13] The Sienese metallurgist Vannoccio Biringuccio (1480–1539) makes reference to this in his treatise *De la Pirotechnia*, published in Venice in 1540, where he outlines the method of brass production that he had seen in Milan. But for Biringuccio brass was copper coloured yellow. He considered this 'a splendid discovery, for which we must praise the alchemists, although perhaps whoever discovered it was deceived, thinking that he had made gold for copper'.[14]

The appearance of an alloy was largely (though not entirely) determined by its ingredients, and in antiquity distinctions were often made on the basis of colour, as is evident, for example, in Pliny's discourse on the various types of bronze, which included a discussion of where they were made and how they were used. For Corinthian bronze, which was used for coinage and 'valued before silver and almost even before gold',[15] Pliny mentions four types – a white variety, where silver predominates; another where the 'yellow quality of gold predominates'; and one where the metals are blended in equal proportion, which is not described by colour. Perhaps the most interesting, however, is the fourth kind, for which he says he cannot give a formula, 'although it is man's handiwork:...the bronze valued in portrait statues and others for its peculiar colour, approaching the appearance of liver...is a blend produced by luck...'[16]

Equally, the question of colour was not lost on the post-medieval European bronze casters. The scholar Pomponius Gauricus (*c.*1480–1530), for example, specifically mentions the diversity of the hue of bronze in his treatise on sculpture, and, to some extent, how to achieve it.[17] The contract for the equestrian statue of *Charles I* (signed and dated 1633) by the Anglo-French sculptor Hubert Le Sueur (active 1602–58), now in Trafalgar Square, London, for example, calls for the 'best yealouw [*sic*] and red copper' to be used, demonstrating the concern with both quality and appearance.[18]

In 1561, when Daniele da Volterra was preparing to cast the equestrian statue of Henry II of France, a similar interest was evident, when he stated that the addition of brass to the copper-tin alloy would give a 'more beautiful colour and softer material'.[19] As well as demonstrating his understanding of brass, Biringuccio describes the transition of copper to bell-metal by the addition of tin not only in terms of its properties but also its colour, 'changing from red, which is the colour of copper, it becomes white; from soft and flexible it becomes hard and brittle as glass'.[20]

Sources of metals

The main sources of copper during the Renaissance were the mines in Austria and Hungary. During the 1490s the wealthy merchant Jakob Fugger of Augsburg, banker to the Emperor Maximilian, negotiated concessions to the copper mines in exchange for loans. He then controlled the majority of the copper trade, and the great demand was met by improved output brought about by Fugger's investment in the best available mining equipment. Daniele da Volterra was advised to obtain the copper from the Fugger mine near Vienna for his *Henry II*. This metal could be bought more cheaply in Antwerp than Venice, which by then had been superseded by the northern port as the most important metal market in Europe. Daniele had been told that the best copper imported into Venice was the *pelosi*. This was rosette copper, referred to as *rame peloso* or 'hairy copper' by Biringuccio. It was formed by scraping the crusts of copper from refined metal as it solidified, and was sold in cakes (or *migliacci*) by copper dealers, including the Fuggers.[21]

According to Biringuccio, who discussed the location, origin and nature of ores and minerals, copper was plentiful in Italy. Despite this, he notes that 'very little is mined there, perhaps because of the cowardly Italian avarice',[22] which made them lazy or only interested in projects where the outcome was assured. He further castigates his countrymen by claiming that they are concerned that they will be called fools and that 'it seems better to them to be praised for becoming rich through usury and by many other infamous and illicit methods than to lay themselves open to danger of censure…'[23] Nevertheless, he refers to the many mines (mostly of copper, though some of silver) in Venice, Carnia and other places, outlining a proposed enterprise to develop a (silver?) mine around Friuli and Carnia (in north-east Italy), which was finally halted due to the war between Venice and the Emperor Maximilian (1508–11).[24]

Copper was, of course, particularly valuable because, following the change from iron cannon to bronze in the fifteenth century, it was a principal ingredient in the facture of arms.[25] It was also used as currency in the spice trade with the East, particularly by the Venetian and Ottoman merchants.[26] The control of this highly valued and versatile commodity was therefore of considerable importance. The expense involved in obtaining imported copper led to the reuse of metal utensils, such as kettles, bowls and even mortars. Such objects were among those melted down for casting the sacristy doors of Florence Cathedral.[27] However, Biringuccio stresses that reused copper should be added to molten alloy, as it would otherwise be extremely difficult to melt.[28]

The main source of European tin was England, where tin mining flourished in Cornwall through to the early twentieth century; the last commercial tin mine was closed as recently as 1998.[29] Biringuccio considered English tin (which was also produced in cakes) to be 'much more beautiful and better in all works than is that made in Venice'.[30] He had not seen the ore, and chose not to list all the places where it was found, due to the strangeness of their names. Nevertheless, he cited Flanders, Bohemia and Bavaria as other sources.[31]

Lead was comparatively plentiful and widely spread. One significant property is its ability to be separated from the metals (other than tin) to which it is alloyed. Lead was the medium by which silver and gold could be extracted from copper.[32]

Bronze recipes[33]

As has been seen, despite the difficulties with terminology, Pliny gave some indication as to which bronze was used for which purpose. A variety of such recipes survive from the medieval and early modern period. The earliest description of casting is given by Theophilus (identified as the Benedictine monk and metalworker, Roger of Helmarshausen) in his *De diversis artibus* (*On the Various Arts*), written in about 1100–40. He outlines how to make brass and cast brass censers, as well as tin-bronze bells. In Italy in the fifteenth and sixteenth centuries, the period in which most of the objects in the collection were made, several texts addressed this issue. Most significant were those of the goldsmith and sculptor Benvenuto Cellini (1500–71), the painter and biographer Giorgio Vasari (1511–74) and, of course, Vannoccio Biringuccio, as well as Pomponius Gauricus and Leonardo da Vinci (1452–1519).[34]

Statuary bronze

Despite his assertion that statuary bronze is created 'by luck', Pliny went on to claim that the 'proper blend' for making statues is smelted copper ore to which is added one-third of scrap copper ('bought up after use'). He considered that this alloy contained a 'peculiar seasoned quality of brilliance that has been subdued by friction and so to speak tamed by habitual use'. Twelve and a half pounds (lbs) (5.67 kg.) of silver-lead (that is, tin and lead mixed in equal parts) was added to every 100 lbs (45.36 kg.) of the fused metal.[35] This would produce a copper-tin-lead mixture of about 89/5.5/5.5 per cent.

Gauricus clearly knew Pliny's writings when he set out his recipe in *De Sculptura* (1504). He separates the alloys of bell-founders and sculptors, providing different mixtures for statues, plaquettes and seals. For statues, the recipe he recommends consists of 12 lbs

(5.44 kg.) of tin to 100 lbs (45.36 kg.) of copper, of which one-third is recovered – that is, reused by melting down other objects (a copper-tin mix of about 89.3/10.7 per cent, depending on the quality of the recovered copper). He states that lead itself is not mixed with the copper, but is added during the process for coloration. He gives the proportions as one-tenth of 'black' lead, and one-twentieth of 'argentarium' (that is, tin and 'black' lead mixed in equal parts) for a 'Greek' colour (giving copper-lead-tin of 85/12.5/2.5 per cent). However, for a purple colour, one-twelfth of 'black' lead is added to Cyprian copper (copper-lead: 92/8 per cent).[36]

For statuettes, he recommended casting used copper with brass in equal quantities, adding to each 1 lb. (450 g.) 2 ounces (oz.) (56.7 g.) of tin, or – if a reddish 'lustre' was required – calamine. For bronze that is 'white like silver', the remains of purified copper was melted, and 3 oz. (85.05 g.) of arsenic and saltpetre passed by a *bain de vapeur* was gradually added to every 2 lbs (907 g.). The metal was cooked in a closed vessel and finally poured into the mould.[37] This recipe varies considerably from the traditional view of a statuary bronze alloy.

In his treatise on sculpture in the preface to the *Lives*, Vasari gives two-thirds copper and one of brass as the Italian alloy for statuary bronze, further stating that the Egyptians used the same materials but reversed the proportions.[38] If by 'brass' he was referring to a copper-zinc alloy, then Vasari's recipe technically produces a brass, rather than a bronze. Unlike Gauricus, he makes no mention of lead, although analysis has shown that many fifteenth- and sixteenth-century bronzes are leaded, based on a copper-tin as opposed to copper-zinc alloy.[39]

Bombard bronze

The recipe Vasari gave for bombard bronze, or that used by founders of artillery (also referred to as 'cannon' or 'ordnance'), consists of a copper-tin ratio of 90/10.[40] Biringuccio supports the notion that different alloys are required for statues and artillery, but fails to be specific, stating that 'eight, nine, ten, up to twelve

pounds of tin are put with every hundred pounds of copper'. Despite this, it is clear that some founders did use what Vasari termed 'bombard bronze' for casting statuary.[41] Mixtures recommended by other writers include latten (or brass), as well as lead.[42] Leonardo states that gun metal must be made with 6 or 8 per cent of tin (given as 6 lbs (2.72 kg.) of tin to 100 lbs (45.36 kg.) of copper), asserting that less tin makes for a stronger cannon.[43]

Bell-metal

Bells were, of course, made in a variety of metals, including iron, but the term 'bell-metal' generally refers to high-tin/copper alloys. In contrast to the alloy variations seen above, the recipes for bell-metal are, not surprisingly, virtually identical, as the ability to produce a musical tone is governed by the tin content. Although at least one bell-metal recipe includes lead as the third alloy,[44] this was said by Biringuccio not only to make the casting 'ugly', but also to impair the tone.[45]

Theophilus describes smelting copper ore with charcoal and adding 'a fifth part of tin' to the copper produced, giving a copper-tin alloy of 80/20 per cent.[46] Gauricus says that bell-founders use 20 lbs (9.07 kg.) or, according to the nature of the copper, 30 lbs (13.61 kg.) of tin to 100 lbs (45.36 kg.) of copper (c.83.4/16.6 per cent or c.77/23 per cent, depending on how this is interpreted).[47] Biringuccio groups 'bells, mortars, basins, and similar cast objects' together (as opposed to statues and artillery), saying that bell-makers use 23, 24, 25 or 26 lbs (between 10.43 and 11.79 kg.) of tin with 100 lbs (45.36 kg.) of copper, depending on the size of the bell and the required tone, a subject to which we will return.[48]

The content of modern bell-metal is fairly standardized and controlled, being provided in ingots of the alloy. Today bell-foundries use 22 or 23 per cent tin for large bells.[49] Smaller bells are more susceptible to damage. The thinner walls have less latent heat and therefore cool more quickly. As the crystalline structure can be influenced by the rate of cooling, and a higher tin content makes the metal more brittle, hand bells are today made with 20 per cent tin instead.

Bronze mortars are frequently referred to as 'bell-metal mortars', particularly in connection with northern Europe. Both Theophilus and Biringuccio provide slightly different high-tin bronze recipes for mortars and bells. In his description of how to make a mill for grinding gold, which basically took the form of a mortar and pestle, Theophilus gives the recipe for the alloy as 'three parts of pure copper to a fourth part of lead-free tin', that is 75/25 per cent.[50] Biringuccio simply states that mortars are made of 'bronze', having distinguished 'metal' on the basis of higher tin content alone.[51] This is an apparent contradiction of his earlier distinction between alloys, cited above.[52] The exact meaning behind his choice of terminology is unclear, in light of his statement that 'in short, "bronze" and "metal" are the same thing, but they are called thus in order to distinguish the differences according to the works'.[53] He further asserts that basins and mortars are made of bronze, rather than copper, because they should not contaminate the contents with taste, smell or 'unpleasant green colour' (verdigris), which is prevented by adding tin.[54] It has been suggested that in England bell-metal was used to make mortars until about 1700, after which brass gradually took over as the favoured material.[55] Analysis of the mortars in this volume, however, indicates that a variety of alloys were used (see p. 52 and Appendix 1).

It is clear from the variations in the recipes referred to above that they merely provided a guideline, and that the knowledge and experience of the founder formed a key part of the process. This can also be deduced from different descriptions of how to prepare the metal for pouring and how to tell when it is ready. Gauricus, for instance, who did not have first-hand knowledge of the processes, recounts how the foundrymen themselves stressed the need to understand the nature of the metals, how they flow in the mould and when they become liquid or boil.[56] Similarly, Leonardo advises not to trust a dull, smoking flame, particularly when the flux metal is almost fluid, and that tin should be added to the copper when the latter is molten.[57] It is also evident that foundries often developed their own favoured alloys and ways of doing things, which were frequently kept secret.[58] Mortars were made not only in the same foundries as bells, but also in artillery foundries.[59] Many of the Italian foundries made other utensils, and even sculpture, and would therefore be expected to vary the alloy as appropriate, particularly bearing in mind the comparative cost and fragility of high-tin bronze. However, analyses have shown that occasionally bell-metal was used for utensils, perhaps due to the experience of the founder or the ready availability of the material (see, for example, cat. no. 67).

Bronze is an expensive material, and it is not therefore surprising that melting down bronze objects (as well as those in precious metals) was a common practice. Sometimes the metal was directly recycled, making a replacement from the original bell or cannon, for example.[60] Alternatively, it was reused for other purposes, often due to military or political reasons. Probably the most famous account of this practice is the recasting of Michelangelo's monumental bronze statue of Pope Julius II, unveiled at Bologna in March 1508 and destroyed by the citizens barely four years after its completion. The bronze was reused to make a cannon, christened the *Giulia*.[61] One source describes how a Spanish apothecary melted down a collection of medals to make a mortar for his shop.[62] This practice continued over the centuries, as the need arose. For example, a vast number of mortars were also destroyed in Italy in 1936 to make a bell for a hospital in Addis Ababa,[63] and German mortars were melted down during the Second World War to make parts for U-boats.[64] The recycling of metals meant that, in spite of the guidelines provided by the treatises, alloy calculations during the Renaissance were not always as precise as they can be today.

Facture and Foundries

The facture of bells and mortars follows the same principles, and varies only due to the restrictions imposed by the differences in shape. The *cire-perdue* or lost-wax method for casting bells was initially described in great detail in the twelfth century by Theophilus, who had first-hand experience of the process. He concentrated on large bells, but also provided some information on how to make sets of small musical ones.[1] Four centuries later Biringuccio set out his detailed description. He benefited from direct experience, having recast a bell at Castel Sant'Angelo during Paul III's pontificate (1534–9). Biringuccio focused on a technique using clay and wax, but also referred to brass bells made by hammering and casting, and briefly outlined how to sand-cast small bells (fig. 1).[2] Modern musical hand bells are made in a very similar manner.[3] Another primary source from the Italian Renaissance is a manuscript by Vittorio Ghiberti (1418–96), the son of Lorenzo, the sculptor responsible for two of the sets of bronze doors for the Baptistery in Florence. It includes drawings showing designs, a bell scale and a method of making large bells.[4]

The method of bell-making has changed very little over the centuries. This is confirmed by Diderot's great *Dictionnaire*, which was published in the mid-eighteenth century and provides details and illustrations of the design, facture and tuning of large bells.[5] In England, however, cast-iron moulding cases have been used for at least the last 200 years.[6]

Fig. 1. Sand-casting mould and core for a small bell. From Biringuccio 1540, VIII, 120v.

There are no large Italian bells in the collection of the period.[7] Both the small bells and mortars appear to have been cast by the lost-wax method, with many of them showing signs of the turning of the clay core on their interior, together with the joins in the applied wax decoration.[8] Every part of the process demanded skill and extreme care. The techniques described below are derived from the texts of Theophilus and Biringuccio.

Making bells

The moulds for bells could be prepared horizontally (fig. 2) or vertically (fig. 4, p. 26), as the illustrations show. Theophilus only described the former. Biringuccio, while stressing his preference for this method, outlined the upright approach as used for larger bells and by masters who did not understand how to use the horizontal trestle. Whichever method was used, the mould consisted of three parts: the core (representing the space inside the bell); the false bell (an exact replica of the bell itself in shape and dimensions); and the cope (outer mould or investment). The false bell could be made of wax, clay, or clay with wax applied to the surface.

If the bell was to be cast horizontally, as the smaller bells often were, a wooden framework was constructed, reminiscent of a spit, consisting of a central, tapered oak spindle, which would be supported on a box or trestle. The spindle, which was at least partially rounded, was longer than the required height of the bell and formed the axis around which the form of the core and the false bell would be constructed.

A special clay mix (forming the core) was then applied to the spindle (fig. 2). Theophilus dictated that this should be added in small amounts ('two fingers thick at first') and needed to be thoroughly dried before the next layer was applied. Biringuccio, on the other hand, stated that a pyramidal mass should be applied first, about one-third of the thickness of the core, known as the 'core support', and then subsequent layers of wash ashes thickened with ordinary moulding

Fig. 2. A bell core on a horizontal spindle, with scale drawing in the background. From Biringuccio 1540, VI, 98.

clay were added, each dried out with fire. This process was continued until the cylinder nearly matched the interior diameter of the bell. If not already in place, the spindle was fitted onto the trestle and a handle attached to the end. The final layer of clay was applied and the spindle turned, while the clay was smoothed with wet cloths or appropriate tools.

These wooden tools – variously called 'strickles', 'hooks' or 'sweepboards'[9] – were based on drawings of the outer and inner profiles of the bell. The profile of the bell is known as the 'rib' (fig. 3). Drawings of the bell design were the starting point for the foundrymen, according to Biringuccio, who recommended dry, well-seasoned nut wood for the strickles. The inner profile provided the template for the core, while (when used) the strickle of the outer profile made the false bell or mortar. In the case of bells, the profile was calculated from a scale that related the width of the mouth (or the 'sound bow') to the height and therefore the weight of the bell, which in turn related to the tone required. The thickness of the rib fluctuates to create the necessary reverberation for the desired tone (see p. 31). The sound bow is thicker than the rest of the bell to allow for the impact of the clapper.[10]

Once the core was finely finished, it was covered in ash, and the wax or clay of the false bell could then be applied. Following Theophilus's instructions, wax was kneaded and rolled out into strips of the same thickness desired for the bell. Two boards were, therefore, cut to

the required depth and placed parallel to each other to provide a guide for rolling the wax. These guide boards were placed on a smooth surface, moistened to prevent the wax from sticking.[11] The soft wax was then rolled and the strips were quickly applied to the core of the bell and a hot iron used to join the seams. Additional wax was attached where greater thickness was required

Fig. 3. Diagram showing parts of a bell.

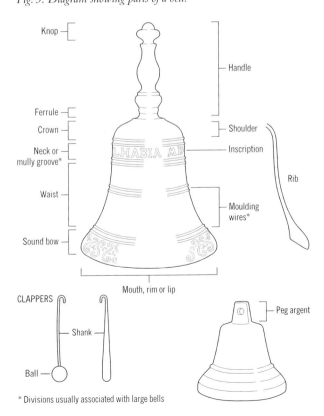

Knop

Handle

Ferrule

Crown

Shoulder

Neck or mully groove*

Inscription

Rib

Waist

Moulding wires*

Sound bow

Mouth, rim or lip

CLAPPERS

Peg argent

Shank

Ball

* Divisions usually associated with large bells

4a

4b

4c

4d

4e

4f

4g

4h

4i

4j

4k

4l

Fig. 4 (left). Making a mortar (or bell) using the vertical method:
a. the spindle
b. spindle with strickle (or sweepboard) attached, showing the profile of the core, and the design of the outer profile of the mortar
c. the clay core is applied and outlined with the strickle
d. core with strickle, showing the profile (or rib) of the mortar
e. the wax is applied and shaped using the strickle
f. the undecorated model for the mortar
g–j. applying decorative wax reliefs
k. projecting handles are added in the wax to be cast-in
l. a section showing the pouring cup attached at the top (under the base of the mortar), and the outer clay mould (or cope). In the case of a bell, which does not have a foot to restrict it, the cope could be lifted off from the core after the wax had been melted out during firing. A gap would be left at the rim to allow the wax to escape prior to pouring the molten metal, and a vent or riser attached to allow the air and gases to escape. From Lise and Bearzi 1975

Fig. 5 (top right). Making wax reliefs from moulds. Colbacchini foundry, Padua. From Lise and Bearzi 1975

Fig. 6 (right). Refining details of the applied wax decoration on a bell. Colbacchini foundry, Padua. From Lise and Bearzi 1975

(around the sound bow), and once cold and hard the wax could be sharpened up and perhaps inscribed. Theophilus referred to decoration being inscribed into the tallow. This would, however, produce inset decoration, which is not evident on any of the European bells examined. Biringuccio specifically states that the decoration must be added to the exterior of the bell, so as not to impair the sound. This included the 'moulding wires', which articulated the changes of shape of the bell or provided guidelines for inscriptions.

Wax decoration could be applied as individual motifs or in strips. These were later created either from plaster casts, usually made from wooden models with the pattern carved in relief, or by incising the decoration into the wooden panels themselves (figs 5 and 6). It has also been suggested that metal moulds may have been used in light of the sharp decoration on some bells and utensils.[12] The molten wax was brushed onto the dampened (negative) mould to the required thickness and, when firm but still flexible, it was pulled off and applied.

Neither Theophilus nor Biringuccio mentions such moulds, but their use is clearly evident from the bells, as well as from surviving fragments of moulds themselves.[13] This method is still practised in Italy, as the examples from the Colbacchini foundry in Padua attest, while in England the decoration is punched into the interior of the dried cope after it is lifted (see below), a technique that was also used by earlier practitioners.[14]

Some foliate and animal decoration was clearly cast from nature. The well-known description of life-casting by Cennino Cennini states that it is possible to cast 'a bird, a beast, and any sort of animal, fish and other such things. But they have to be dead…'[15] Using this method, moulds could be used to make reproductions. However, it was also possible to cast in bronze directly from the animal carcass, which was burnt out in the process.[16] The leaf or animal was attached to the surface of the bell (or mortar) with wax, alongside the inscriptions and other applied motifs (see cat. no. 15 and p. 48).

Clay was used as an alternative to wax or tallow to form the false bell (or 'case' in Biringuccio's terminology). The strickle attached to the framework again moulded the rib of the bell in clay. A thin layer of wax was added and wax decoration applied to the surface. A mixture of fine liquid clay, iron filings and the ashes of young rams' horns was brushed or rubbed onto the finished surface of the wax in successive layers, which were each allowed to dry outdoors. This formed the cope.

The mould was tightly bound with iron wire and the spindle was struck, releasing it, together with the attached 'core support', from the interior of the mould. For larger casts, a fire was placed in the hollow thus created and the mould heated right through, the thin layer of wax disappearing in the process. The cope could then be lifted or winched off the core, and the false clay bell/mortar removed. Any necessary repairs were made and the final touches put to the core and cope, including decoration where desired.

An iron loop to support the clapper had to be inserted into the core, projecting into the space left by the false bell, where the bronze for the bell would be run. With large bells it was important to orientate this appropriately in relation to the handles (or 'canons'), the mould for which would be separately cast and secured into the cope at the crown.[17] For hand bells, the handles were usually cast separately and attached through what would have been the pour-hole (see, for example, cat. no. 50). Finally, the gate that fed the metal to the mould, and the vents for the air to escape, had to be attached to the crown.[18] Vents were attached to either side of the canons of larger bells to ensure that the metal ran smoothly throughout.

These attachments were affixed with clay, the joins carefully smoothed over, and the core and cope were then thoroughly heated. They were both again covered in ashes and reassembled, the core being placed on a star or cross of iron or wood, and the bound cope lowered and fixed so as to prevent the core from moving inside it. Marks were made on the cope and core to ensure exact relocation, as any misalignment would alter the profile of the bell and the work would be ruined.[19]

The lost-wax method, described earlier, varied from the clay technique in that the false bell (including the clapper hook, attached where the spindle was removed, plus the wax canons, gate and vents) was covered in layers of clay forming an investment. This was bound and left to dry before the centre of the core of larger bells was hollowed out. The mould was placed in a pit, and a furnace constructed with a fire in the core cavity, so that it could be thoroughly baked. The firing had the dual effect of hardening the outer casing of the mould and allowing the wax to burn out through specially made holes in the rim of the mould, leaving an empty space in the profile of the bell. All the wax had to be removed, since it could react with the hot metal as it was poured, preventing a successful casting, or release moisture and gases that might cause the mould to explode.[20] The mould was then sealed with clay, and the firing continued to remove any remaining moisture, again to avoid any steam and excessive gases from fracturing the mould during casting. The metal was melted in pots over fire, or in a furnace.[21] When the mould was sufficiently baked, the fire would be removed from around it and the pit filled with earth in order to prevent the mould splitting under the weight of the molten metal as it was poured in, which took place while the moulds were still hot. Hand bells were obviously much simpler to make and required less elaborate binding.

Once the metal had solidified, the mould was dug out enough to allow it to cool fairly quickly. The investment and core were removed and the bell cleaned up. Theophilus suggested that it was placed on a spindle, similar to that used in the making, but with the necessary additional support inside the mouth of the bell. It was then smoothed using a sandstone.

Making mortars

Mortars could most easily be made using the lost-wax method, being cast with the foot uppermost (fig. 4a–h). This is confirmed by the physical evidence of the majority of mortars in the collection. A circular, shallow pit on the base, for example, indicates where the pouring sprue was attached. This pitting was probably caused by shrinkage due to the differential between the thickness of the pouring rod and the mortar itself (evident on numerous examples in the collection).[22] In some cases these hollows may indicate that the metal did not sufficiently fill the mould. Mortars could, however, be made in the horizontal position.[23] It is obvious that if a 'false mortar' of clay were made, the foot would prevent the cope from being removed in one piece. This necessitated a different approach, which is not precisely outlined in the primary sources. Following the tract on manufacturing bells, Biringuccio merely states: 'In the same way are made mortars, basins, and all other vessels that need to have a hollow in the middle, if they are round in shape.'[24] It is possible that the body of bell-shaped mortars was prepared in wax, as described, and then a wax foot attached prior to investment. This possibly explains the smearing and cracking on some mortars where the bulk of the wax foot may have been added.

An alternative means of facture was to grease the core before the false mortar of clay was applied, thereby allowing the cope and false mortar to be removed together. Another approach may have been to make the cope in two parts, although metal flashing would presumably have seeped into the join during casting, which would then have required removal when cold.[25] There is also evidence of hardwood moulds made in two halves being used for sand-cast mortars. These were, however, only employed at a later date and their use was apparently confined largely to north of the Alps.[26]

Clays

As with the alloy, there was a variety of recipes for the clay to be used in moulding. It played a significant role in the outcome of the casting. Before electric power allowed for flashing to be removed comparatively easily, it was essential that the casts came out of the mould as cleanly as possible, so that only minor after-working was necessary, particularly when dealing with bell-metal, which cannot easily be chased. Great care was therefore taken in preparing the mould, which was both time-consuming and skilful. According to the Colbacchini foundry in Padua, even today 'dozens of specialists [are employed] for at least forty days' in the preparation of the 'false bell' alone.[27]

Theophilus does not provide details about clay, but Gauricus's recipe is to mix clay thoroughly with equal proportions of animal hair and horse dung, adding ashes and brick powder from time to time.[28] This mixture was dried, scraped and sieved before remixing it to a paste. Vasari also recommends finely beaten earth with horse dung and hair for both cores and moulds.[29] Cellini and Biringuccio go into more detail.[30] Cellini, for example, provides his own 'trade secret' for the preparation of core material in the context of casting bronze sculptures, whereby dry, sifted clay and an equal quantity of cloth frayings are beaten with an iron rod and left to decompose for 'at least four months or more'. He also advises on the sources of suitable clay found near rivers in soil that was not too sandy, or in hills and grottoes. Rome and Florence are mentioned, but it is the clay from the grottoes in Paris that he considered the finest. The loam used for bell-casting today still contains horse manure and is chosen and prepared to reduce shrinkage and cracking.[31]

Preparing the metal

Guidelines for the relationships between the weight of clay, bronze, beech wood, wax and copper, tin, silver, lead, gold, and *aes album* and *orichalcum* (or *aurichalcum* – that is, brass) are given by Gauricus to assist in preparing the correct amount of alloy.[32] Vasari quotes ten parts of wax to every one part of bronze;[33] Biringuccio 7–8 lbs (3–3.5 kg.) of metal for every 1 lb. (450 g.) of clay used in preparing the false bell. Such guidelines were useless unless you were an experienced foundryman, as it was difficult to calculate the exact alloy content or amount lost due to evaporation, particularly of tin. Biringuccio specifically states that this should be accounted for, depending on whether the metal was 'old or new, coppery or fine in tin'.[34] The potential problems are dramatically illustrated by Cellini's famous and oft-quoted account of how, in order to save the cast of the *Perseus*, he had to throw in a 'thick pig of fine pewter', followed by his own pewter dishes, until the metal would run freely enough to fill the mould.[35] The tonal quality required for bells added to this complication, and depended on various factors, including the precise shape and evenness of the casting (see p. 25).

Theophilus paints a picture of frantic activity, which required that the workmen should not be 'indolent…but quick, keen ones for fear the mould be broken by carelessness of any kind, or some one gets in the way of, or hurts, another or makes him lose his temper, which is to be guarded against at all costs'.[36] This was partly to do with the need for accurate timing and care, with various activities taking place concurrently: dismantling the mould furnace and ramming the earth around the mould, as well as preparing the alloy in one or a number of crucibles. A furnace of stones and clay was built around the clay-lined iron crucibles, fanned by bellows.

The timing for melting the alloy was crucial and related to the readiness of the mould. When it was red-hot inside the mould furnace, the copper and some coals were added to the crucibles. 'When you see a green flame rise, the copper is beginning to melt.'[37] The mould furnace was dismantled, the copper was stirred

with a charred stick and, if fully melted, the tin was added. The stirring of the metal, or 'poling', is an essential element, still carried out today using a willow branch.[38] This releases salicylic acid, which acts as a flux, aiding the alloying of the metal.[39] Numerous fluxes are mentioned in the texts to assist in making the metal run. These include saltpetre, borax and sal ammoniac, and Biringuccio advised that it was best to 'make use of them all according to the kinds of metal, as the indications of the operation will make clear to you'.[40] The required preparation also differed for old and unrefined metal.[41] During the process noxious gases were produced,[42] and dross had to be scraped off the surface of the molten metal. When ready, the molten metal was poured. A particularly dangerous part of the process was carrying the hot crucibles to the mould, although the metal could be fed via a channel running from the fire to the mould.

Crucibles are still used for small castings, but the development of the reverberatory furnace had a significant effect on bronze production.[43] Instead of a direct flame under the crucible, the metal was melted by hot air reverberated from an adjacent chamber in the furnace. This method appears to have been developed in the fifteenth century in response to the demand for larger cannon and more efficient casting.[44] It allowed larger quantities of metal to be cast at one time, and a number of furnaces could also be linked to cope with casts of exceptional size. Leonardo planned such a scheme for the monumental equestrian bronze of Francesco Sforza, which was never executed. Biringuccio refers to Leonardo's proposal to use three furnaces at one time, and quotes a story of a Flemish bell-founder who used two furnaces to cast a bell.[45] Each bell had to be cast in one pour, so reverberatory furnaces facilitated casting larger bells with greater ease.[46]

Patination and gilding

Bronzes patinate naturally in time, or patination can be created by applying oils and resins to the surface. There is evidence that some of the bells and mortars have been treated, probably using oils brushed onto the surface, which was then heated.[47]

There is just one Italian mortar in the Museum that retains traces of gilding (cat. no. 5), although examples survive in other collections.[48] A hand bell, acquired as Italian in 1858, but now identified as German (Appendix 3, no. 1), is also mercury- or fire-gilded.[49] This results in the gold fusing with the metal to which it has been applied, and it is therefore quite resistant to wear. However, bronzes with a substantial lead or zinc content can prove difficult to gild using this technique,[50] and it is also possible to apply gold leaf using an adhesive, usually oil, size, bole or gesso (often referred to as 'mordant gilding').[51] This method was less durable, as is evident on the relief of the *Virgin and Child with angels*, known as the 'Chellini Madonna', by Donatello (V&A, inv. no. A.1–1976), where the pseudo-kufic lettering (apparently applied with animal glue – probably rabbit – over gesso around the rim) has rubbed off in places.[52] In contrast, the mercury-gilding on the statuette of *Meleager* by the Mantuan court sculptor Antico (V&A, inv. no. A.27-1960) is still apparently as fresh as the day it was applied.[53] A similar comparison can be made between cat. no. 5 and the bell cited above.

Tones and tuning

Theophilus sets out a table for producing a set of musical bells from proportionally related amounts of wax. These produced the basic tone, which could be adjusted by filing the bottom of the rim, or by reducing the depth of the sound bow with a special 'clipping hammer', to make a higher tone; reduction on the outside of the rim made it lower.[54] Apart from rejecting lead as giving a poor tone, Biringuccio recommends that the metal should not be too hot when poured. However, he stresses that different practices abound, including the addition of antimony brought to Venice from Germany 'in cakes for the use of those masters who make bells, because they find that by mixing a certain part of it with the metal the sound is greatly increased'.[55] A handful of silver or gold was said to improve the tone, and analysis does sometimes show traces of these precious metals.[56]

According to Biringuccio, the tone of the bell improved continually during the first year, as the cast-

ing was consolidated by the clapper blows.[57] True carillon bells should not only be in tune with each other but in tune with themselves, in an elaborate system of related tones. Today, in addition to the tuning fork, the ear of the tuner is aided by an electronic device, and metal is removed from different areas of the bell until it is completely in tune.[58]

Clappers

The final part of making a bell was attaching the clapper. Clappers, which are often made of iron, take different forms in the examples that survive in the present collection.[59] Like handles (see p. 28), they are a separate part of the bell and it is often difficult to know whether they are original.

Those clappers made in one piece (for example, cat. no. 46) are usually tapered to ensure that they strike the sound bow, which, as has been seen, is thicker than the main body. They are made in proportion to the bells, as shown in Biringuccio's drawing of a bell with a clapper beside it,[60] and when fixed project beyond it. As a result, bell ringers lay their hand bells on their side on the table in front of them. Bells with a shorter or two-part clapper, which tend to have a round ball at the end (such as cat. no. 40), can stand upright as the clapper either fits or folds inside the body of the bell. However, in contemporary illustrations hand bells are shown placed upright (fig. 8, p. 36), which most likely could have resulted in damage to the brittle rims (cat. nos 40 and 46).

The Renaissance foundry

The role of the foundryman was often integral to the production of bronze sculpture throughout the Renaissance period, as it is today. Artillery, bells and mortars were largely produced by such specialists, and despite Biringuccio's assertion that bell-founders rarely became recognized artillery makers, many foundries seem to have produced a variety of works, as exemplified by the Alberghetti (see pp. 96–8), de Levis (see cat. nos 49–51) and Cavadini (cat. no. 67).[61] The diversity of production is also evident in the well-known woodcut of 1525 illustrating a foundry by the Sienese artist,

Fig. 7. Domenico Beccafumi, Founding of bells and canons.
Woodcut, c.1525.

Domenico Beccafumi (*c.*1486–1551) (fig. 7). Beccafumi
was one of the many sculptors who were also capable of
casting his own works. The relevant experience of
working with metals was obviously essential and was
usually gained by the sculptor having initially trained as
a goldsmith or by assisting on large casting projects, such
as the Baptistery doors in Florence. Bronze production
therefore varied according to the apprenticeship and
facilities of the sculptors, and sometimes depending on
the region in which they worked.[62]

Two important sculptors who are also known to have
cast bells are Michelozzo di Bartolomeo (1396–1472)
and Andrea del Verrocchio (1434/7–88). Michelozzo,
who worked with Ghiberti on the bronze doors for the
Baptistery and was at one time in partnership with
Donatello (*c.*1386–1466), was an experienced founder

and bell-maker. In 1448 he and his brother, Maso,
melted down an old bell to cast a large bell, weighing
1,000 or 1,100 lbs (about 4.5 tons; or 450–500 kg.) for
the clock of the Palazzo Vecchio. Further documents
detail a commission he received in July 1450 with the
goldsmith Bartolomeo Fruosino for a bell for the nuns
of San Giovanni Cavalierie (now S. Giovanni dalla
Calza). By October, it had not been completed, the failure of the first casting being attributed to the absence
of Michelozzo, who was described as *chosi buono maestro
dj fare champane* ('such a good bell maker').[63] Despite his
skill, the second casting was also a disaster, as the
investment had not sufficiently dried, causing the
mould to break when the metal was poured. In 1445
Michelozzo made a bell for Cosimo de' Medici for the
Medici Chapel in Santa Croce. Cosimo also paid for
another important bell, known as 'La Piagnona' (San
Marco, Florence), attributed to Verrocchio on stylistic
grounds, and made in the early 1460s.[64] Verrocchio is
also known to have cast a bell for the Vallombrosan
house at Montescalari in 1474 (now lost).

Even in Florence, where many others had the
relevant training and experience, sculptors often
collaborated with foundries, among them Donatello,
Giambologna (1529–1608) and even Cellini, who was,
however, critical of the founder's usefulness and
made claims to instructing them in his methods. The
problems with casting the *Perseus* were laid at the door
of inept foundrymen, as when Cellini stated that
'Ofttimes we figure casters call in the help of ordnance
founders to aid us, but the most terrible misfortunes
not infrequently occur owing to their insufficient experience and want of care, and all our labour is lost.' He
did, however, acknowledge the abilities of the Parisian
founders – a view that was shared by Vasari, who
praised their technical capabilities, stating that their
works apparently emerged from the cast so perfectly
that they required little after-work.[65]

Biringuccio gives a vivid impression of the lowly but
underestimated founders – 'despised as fools' for working in such unsavoury conditions of heat, fumes, dirt
and sweat with such uncertain results.[66] Nevertheless,
in his view, they were akin to the sculptor in that they

needed skill in drawing and an understanding of the sculptor's art in order to produce their works. From his comments, it appears that Biringuccio (perhaps for obvious reasons) believed that the foundryman should hold a higher status, closer to that of the sculptor, which by that time had risen considerably from humble artisan to artist, with the concomitant intellectual associations. This was reflected in the social relationships enjoyed by the leading artists, exemplified by close associations with their patrons, by land-owning, a role as emissaries, and so on, which were not the lot of the founder. Maintenance of property and status, however, could have a direct bearing on the founder's livelihood, and was on occasion an issue of some importance. This is evident from the rivalry between the Alberghetti and di Conti workshops over allocation of the Venetian foundries.[67] While certain foundries became established, many founders still travelled. Biringuccio cites 'certain Savoyard and French masters' who were itinerant bell-casters,[68] and important founders often produced works for and in different centres. In the sixteenth century, the Venetian di Conti family also ran the artillery foundry at Brescia (which supplied armaments for various centres in the region), to which Giulio Alberghetti was sent for an inspection in 1561. Giovanni di Giulio Alberghetti moved from Venice to Florence, where he collaborated with Giambologna in the casting of the equestrian monument to Cosimo I de' Medici (of c.1587–93), in the Piazza della Signoria.[69]

The guild to which founders belonged often governed or restricted practices, most particularly because of the dangers of working with furnaces and hot metals. In Venice, for example, the public foundries were initially based at Canareggio in an area known as the ghetto (from *gettare*, the Italian for 'to cast'), but moved to the Arsenal in about 1390. However, casting sculptures in the Arsenal was prohibited. Instead they were produced in the private foundries based predominantly outside, unless special permission was obtained from the Council.[70] Venetian bell-founders were required by the guild statutes to mark their bells, and many guilds took a role in ensuring that quality was maintained. In Florence in 1174, an area near the Ponte Vecchio on the Oltrarno was sold for use as a bell-foundry, and later in 1286 the blacksmiths and locksmiths petitioned the consuls of the guilds not to permit the operation of forges or furnaces, nor the manufacture of objects in metal and related works in the city or *contado*, unless the smiths were members of one of the relevant guilds. Bell-founders in Florence would have belonged to the *Arte de' Fabbri* (blacksmiths' guild). This was ranked tenth in the hierarchy of the powerful Florentine guilds from 1236 until 1415, when it rose one place, replacing the shoemakers. This gives some idea of the status of its members. Specialist bell-founders did not have their own guild in Verona, but were apparently part of the *Arte de' Fabbri e Calderai*.[71]

Membership of the trade guilds could be based on a relationship to an existing guild member, or restricted to those who were born within a certain parish. The regulations varied from city to city, with some being primarily concerned with the way the trades operated, ensuring that their members' livelihoods were protected from cheap imports or unfair competition. These restrictions perhaps also account for the considerable number of bell-founding dynasties of the period, such as the Bonaventurini and de Levis of Verona, and the De Maria of Vicenza.[72] A mortar dated 1440 is signed by Crescimbeni of Perugia (see p. 38), and in 1535 a bell was similarly inscribed, indicating that the Crescimbeni were also a family firm.[73] In Venice, for example, the offer of tax benefits encouraged the employment of members of one's own family.[74] This doubtless contributed to the number of workshops that followed this practice, including those of the painters Bellini and Vivarini, and, of course, the great rival foundries of the Alberghetti and di Conti dynasties, which dominated the Venetian bronze industry from the sixteenth century.[75]

Bells: History and Uses

Bells can be divided into two basic types. The closed, or crotal, bell is associated with Morris dancers and is often seen adorning the saddlery of horses. It usually takes the form of an oval or circular hollow ball of metal, either with a slit or claw-shaped opening, inside of which is a metal 'pea'. Large crotal bells hang from the saddlery on the monumental wooden group of *St George and the Dragon* (1486?–9) by Bernt Notke (*c.*1440–1509) in the Storkyrka at Stockholm.[1] The open or cup bell is the more traditional bell shape; the examples in this catalogue are all small bells of this type.

The origins of the hand bell can be traced back at least to the third millennium BC in China, when the emperor, Huan T'i, commissioned a set of pitch standards in the form of twelve small bells. These did not have handles, but looked like grain scoops, which would presumably have been tucked into the palm of the hand. The earliest examples with handles are, again, Chinese and date from about 1600 BC, but it was not until the early Middle Ages that bronze bells of a large scale were first produced in Europe. The evidence for exact dating of their development is inconclusive, but it has been suggested that it was as early as the fifth or sixth century AD that the Benedictines in Italy first cast them. Dated Italian examples survive from the eighth or ninth century, such as the small liturgical bells from Canino,[2] and the former bell tower of St Peter's in Rome was erected in 745, housing three large bells.[3]

Open bells can take various forms, from the low, 'beehive' shape common in the eighth and ninth centuries, found particularly in Germany, to the taller, conical, 'sugar-loaf' form typical of Italian examples at least from the twelfth century.[4] Due to the difficulty of transporting large bells, foundries were often established at the site for which the bells were being cast. Bell-founders were therefore itinerant, which meant that forms were transmitted throughout Europe. The more open 'krater' shape was established by the fourteenth century and was gradually developed, with the flattening of the crown of the bell, until the nineteenth century. Since then bell shapes have become fairly standardized.

Small bells could either be rung by hand or suspended by 'canons' to a beam and struck with a hammer. Nowadays there is a clear distinction between 'hand bells', which are musical and made of bell-metal, and 'handle bells', which are more functional and need to be quite robust.

Secular and liturgical contexts

The use of small hanging or hand bells is widespread through a variety of cultures, usually as part of a religious or magical ritual. China also produced the earliest form of musical bell sets, the *pien-chung*, which consisted of between nine and sixteen bells fitted to a frame and struck by hammers. It was played as part of the ceremonies associated with Confucianism in the fifth century BC. Other eastern religions, such as Hinduism and Buddhism, incorporated the use of hand bells, which were themselves often directly venerated, or were a symbol of potency for the bearer. Such bells attracted mystical associations, and their manufacture might involve elaborate ritual. Similarly, in the Christian context, hand bells were commonly decorated with the name or image of a saint (for example, cat. no. 61), and were venerated in their own right.

From the Middle Ages onwards, bells played a significant role in everyday life and their importance was emphasized by the practice of naming them. They signalled the times of day, announcements or events; regulated activities; and called the population to prayer or celebration. In Renaissance Venice, for example, the *Marangona* summoned workers to the Arsenal, and the *Trottiera* called members of the Great Council to the chamber.[5] Similarly, several cities had a bell named the *Rengo*, so named because it called the members of the council (or 'Arengo') to meetings. That in Verona was documented as being first cast for the ruling Scaliger family in 1311. Chronicles date its smaller partner in the

Torre Civico, another *Marangona*, even earlier. Large bells were frequently repaired or recast by successive founders, the Veronese *Rengo* being a case in point.[6]

In Florence the bell that announced the start and finish of the working day was originally that in the campanile of the church of S. Maria Ughi, near the Strozzi Palace. This role was later transferred to the Duomo's large bell by Grand Duke Cosimo I. Another bell was donated by a wealthy member of the bankers' guild, which was rung at the opening and closing of the money market each day. Bells therefore gained a particular relevance to the population, sometimes epitomizing the community and the citizens' pride in it. Their capture was seen as a triumphal achievement, due both to the value of the bells and as a symbol of military and psychological victory. In 1436, for example, the papal legate Giovanni Vitelleschi carried off the cathedral bell of Palestrina, following his successful campaign against the Colonna stronghold.[7] Similarly, the Palazzo Vecchio's imposing tower housed the bell named *La Montanara*, named after the town (Montanera) from which it was taken in 1302. This bell served to announce an evening curfew under Cosimo, but was destroyed by Alessandro de' Medici on his succession to the duchy in 1532, 'lest its sound should awaken echoes of lost freedom'.[8]

Catholic canon law prescribes that every church should have at least one bell. The bells undergo a ceremony of benediction following their casting.[9] Except when warning of danger, church bells were supposed to be used exclusively for liturgical purposes, although, as we have seen, there could be exceptions to the rule. Chimes denote times of worship or remembrance on a daily and weekly basis, as well as on special occasions. The tolling of the morning and evening Angelus to announce the repetition of the Ave Maria was of particular importance in encouraging devotion. The Dominicans were instrumental in establishing this due to their close association with the cult of the Virgin, and in the fifteenth century in Italy a midday Angelus was added.[10] In the monastic setting, bells were used to signal the times of services: vespers, compline, terce, and so on.

Hand bells also served various functions, although sometimes the boundaries between their liturgical and secular use were blurred. The earliest hand bells in the West were made at and for monasteries, where they replaced the sounding-board or *semantron*. Theophilus, himself a monk, as well as an experienced bell-caster, provides a description and defines the relationship between the different tones in a set of musical bells. Several illustrations of these sets survive in manuscript illuminations.[11] Small hand bells were also carried by itinerant orders, the hospitallers and other missionaries, who rang them to attract alms.

The sanctus or altar bell probably originates in the twelfth century, when the elevation of the host was introduced to the Mass; its use was established by the thirteenth century. Ringing the bell signalled to the worshippers (who may not have been able to see the priest) the celebration of the presence of Christ, symbolized by the raising of the consecrated host. Altar bells, often made of precious metal, were regularly given by members of the laity or clergy.[12] Inscriptions can assist in identifying them, such as the bell dated 1580, decorated with the Virgin and Child and saints, and inscribed with the name of Federico Bettini, the parish priest of Telvi, who undoubtedly commissioned it for use on an altar.[13] The bell from Teglio (cat. no. 60) is said to have served as an altar bell, on the basis of its provenance and religious imagery. The appearance of the tau (if the T is intended as such), however, may indicate that it was made for the Order of Hospitallers of St Anthony, who suspended bells from their tau crosses. A series of bells were sometimes attached to a wheel, and slightly larger bells were hung outside the chapel or sacristy, suspended from a frame fixed to the wall and rung by pulling a cord.[14] An example can be seen in Albrecht Dürer's *Melancholia* print of 1514.[15]

Similarly, small bells of this type would have been used as domestic doorbells, fixed outside the main entrance to the house.[16] Hand bells also served a variety of secular functions, being used to summon servants (such as cat. nos 40 and 41) and call committees to order. A fine example of the latter was made for the Veronese College of Judges (Bargello, Florence).[17]

Although no direct evidence has come to light, it is possible that confraternities commissioned such bells not only for their committee meetings, but also for use on the altars that they maintained in the church of their patron saint.[18]

Raphael's famous painting of *Pope Leo X with two cardinals* of about 1517 (Uffizi, Florence) and Domenichino's *Gregory XV and Cardinal Ludovico Ludovisi* (1621–3; Musée des Beaux-Arts, Béziers) show the pontiffs with a hand bell nearby. In addition, the hand bell appears in a number of portraits of cardinals, almost in the manner of an attribute. Among these are Francesco Trevisani's *Portrait of Pietro Ottoboni* of the 1690s (Bowes Museum, Barnard Castle), *A Cardinal and Secretary* (SMB-PK, Gemäldegalerie, Berlin), the portrait of *Cardinal Marcello Cervini degli Spannocchi* (Galleria Borghese, Rome), and two versions of a *Portrait of Cardinal Bernardo Cles*, attributed to Barthel Bruyn (Galleria Nazionale, Rome and Gemäldegalerie,

Kunsthistorisches Museum, Vienna).[19] Many of the bells appear to have been made of precious metals and bear the arms of the owner, with the cardinal's hat as decoration. In some instances, they were probably commissioned shortly after the cardinal's appointment. A bronze example, possibly made for Cardinal Badia of Mutina, survives in the Kunstgewerbemuseum, Berlin.[20]

The post-mortem inventory of Cardinal Francesco Gonzaga (d. 1483) lists a silver bell, apparently received as a gift from Cardinal Mella in 1462.[21] This was probably kept in his studio, in a similar context to that shown in Lorenzo Lotto's drawing of *An Ecclesiastic in his Study* (British Museum, London).[22] Probably the most well known of all such examples is the canvas from

Carpaccio's cycle in the Scuola di San Giorgio degli Schiavoni in Venice (about 1505) of *St Jerome in his study* (fig. 8). His surroundings reflect a contemporary humanist *studiolo*, with some of the apparatus associated with it, including small bronzes on the shelf to the left and the hand bell beside him. The hand bell could, therefore, signify the piety of its owner, as well as power and status.

In its variety of contexts, the sound of the bell can be seen to have carried numerous resonances from protection to warning, civic pride and personal status, and the organization of daily routine or events.

ʡ

Mortars: History and Uses

The word 'mortar' comes from the Latin *mortarium*, itself said to be based on the root word *mordeo*, meaning 'to bite'. It is possible that this in turn derives from the Sanskrit for 'to grind or pound' – *mrdi* – which also refers to the vessel used for this purpose.

The origins of the mortar can be traced back to the flat, ribbed stones of the Neolithic period, but a form of mortar may have been developed at an earlier date. Evidence of early grinding equipment has survived from Persia and the Middle East, including Egypt and Iraq, where large, shallow stone dishes were used for pulverizing grain, with a smooth, hand-held stone performing the function of a pestle. The largest of these 'saddle querns' were over a metre in diameter – half a metre was quite common – making it possible for the women of the community to gather round and work together. The early ribbed type evolved into a hollowed form, an example of which from Jericho (*c.*7000 BC) is in the British Museum.[1]

The exact origins of the grinding bowl are unclear, but there are examples from Palestine as early as 9000 BC (British Museum).[2] The form was firmly established by the first millennium BC in Anatolia, Syria, Cyprus and the Aegean, and also in Greece. The bowl varied in shape, as did the pestle, at least one example taking the form of a human lower leg and foot.[3] Boat-shaped mortars have also continued to be used in various cultures, and the Romans are known to have used another form of quern or metal mortar, with a lid fitting around the pestle. The lid was presumably designed to prevent any of the ground material from flying out of the vessel, a common occurrence when using hard ingredients in a broad, rimmed bowl.

The majority of surviving early mortars were made of stone: sandstone, marble, basalt and other stones, largely depending on what was available locally. Examples do survive in various other materials, however, such as marble, bronze and terracotta. The Romans made mortaria for export to Rome and Gaul,[4] and a signed terracotta example was found in London.[5] These bowl-shaped vessels, used mainly for mixing dry and wet ingredients, which could then be poured from the lip, seem to have been based on a Greek spouted form that dates back to at least the fifth century BC. This form became popular once again for the ceramic mortars developed by Josiah Wedgwood in eighteenth-century England. Otherwise, spouted mortars, such as the two examples in this collection (cat. nos 10 and 11), are rare.

Although the history of the bronze mortar stretches back into antiquity, increasing numbers were produced in Europe from the medieval period, with important survivals from the late thirteenth century onwards.[6] The earliest dated English example (York Museum) bears the legend above the foot: + FR. WILLS DE

TOVTHORP ME FECIT AD. MCCCVIII – Brother William of Towthorp made me, AD1308.[7] The legend around the rim indicates that it was dedicated to St John the Evangelist and belonged to the Infirmary of the Blessed Mary of York: + MORTARIV. SCI. IOHIS EWANGEL. DE IFIRMARIA BE MARIE EBOR. The earliest known dated bronze mortar of Italian origin appears to be that signed by Crescimbene da Perugia in 1440,[8] but the earliest signed Italian mortar is believed to be that bearing the legend IOANES dE GIBERTIS ME FECIT FIERI A MAGISTER FRANCISCO PISANO, given on the basis of form and style to the late trecento or early quattrocento.[9]

Medieval mortars were usually quite squat, becoming more elegantly proportioned as time progressed. The diameter of the rim was generally greater than that of the height for the Italian mortars in the period covered here, but shapes and decoration varied according to where they were made, and could be as diverse as octagonal, cup-, bowl-, vase- or bucket-shaped. Only rarely is there difficulty in establishing the country of origin, as the forms tend to follow distinctive patterns, even if the decorative motifs are similar.[10] Middeldorf provides an analysis of the different forms, concentrating primarily on those produced in Italy, which he divides into ten groups.[11] He indicates a broad development from the 'Archaic' (low and squat) and two 'Early' types (more articulation with the foot and lip) through various 'Renaissance' types (including those with flared, conical shapes and richly decorated, bell-shaped bodies) to the 'Baroque' and 'Neoclassic'. The categories are useful in themselves, but it is important to remember that they do not suggest a neat progression by date, as Middeldorf himself acknowledged. Examination of the surviving examples confirms that it is difficult to date mortars by profile alone. However, eighteenth- and nineteenth-century mortars are more easily recognized by both shape and the nature of their casting.

The use of bronze mortars declined from the end of the seventeenth century, partly due to the development of grinding machinery, but also in final recognition of the dangers of using copper-based materials to prepare food or medicine for digestion. Concerns had been raised at least as early as the mid-sixteenth century, when William Bullein (d. 1576) advised that 'stynking brass' should be avoided, and many later writers noted the problems of absorption of verdigris or copper contamination.[12] This advice was ignored for some time, however, perhaps because of the efficacy of the metal mortar. In the late 1770s the ceramic manufacturer Josiah Wedgwood produced a suitable alternative in response to the needs of his friend, the chemist Joseph Priestley.

As with bells, mortars played an integral part in everyday life. Wherever there was a need to grind a substance, there would be a mortar and pestle. The most obvious application is in the context of medicine and pharmacy, but they were also essential pieces of equipment in the household, where they were used not just to prepare food but also simple medicines and cosmetics. Similarly, they would be found in the studios of artists and craftsmen, as well as the laboratory of the alchemist, whose art was so closely bound up with medicine. Evidence for the use of mortars is widespread, including examples of civic mortars, and mortars used to prepare gunpowder. They even had a liturgical use, in preparing incense.[13]

Pharmaceutical mortars: context and practice

Mortars have been used to symbolize the art of pharmacy since about the thirteenth century,[14] and bronze (or bell-metal) examples are still cast for pharmaceutical societies as presentation pieces for members.[15]

The exact origin of the pharmaceutical mortar is unclear, but its use (or that of a similar utensil) is implicit in descriptions in early Egyptian pictorial scripts, such as the Ebers Papyrus (1536 BC), which provides hundreds of formulas for preparing pills and potions.[16] Pharmacy is, of course, intimately linked to the study of medicine and both, in the medieval and early modern period, were still bound up with other philosophical approaches to the material world, including alchemy and the beliefs regarding the nature of matter. The ancient Greeks used a humoral system of diagnosis, based on blood, phlegm, yellow and black

Fig. 9. Title-page from The Florentine Book of Prescriptions, *showing a mortar with two pestles. 1670 edition (first published 1498).*

bile, and medicine continued to be largely based on this principle throughout the Middle Ages and the Renaissance, despite the advances in medical knowledge that took place within the period, including those in anatomy. Prescriptions illustrate the complicated interrelationship between practice and belief, regarding the nature of man and his surroundings and the universe. Bestiaries, herbals and pharmacopoeiae were available, containing information on the ingredients and how to treat them.

In addition to the numerous herbal remedies, those from animal sources (including humans) were also advocated. It seems that there was no part of the animal – indeed no product of its function – that could not be utilized, including sparrows' brains, frogs' hearts and the excrement of virtually every beast. Their use was recommended in *The Florentine Book of Prescriptions*, the title-page of which (fig. 9) shows a large mortar with leaf decoration, reminiscent of the arrangement on those bearing the signature of Giuliano Mariotto

*Per Veleni per Flati e mile mali
La Triaca ghà el primo in sti Canali*

de' Navi of Florence (cat. nos 10–11).[17] Mythological beasts fell into the category of the animal kingdom. Unicorn horn (actually narwhal or rhinoceros) was particularly valued for its effectiveness against poisons, although its very existence was debated throughout the Renaissance, while at the same time it was collected and treasured as a valuable and potent asset.[18] Francesco Calzolari (1522–1609), 'the apothecary of the Golden Bell' of Verona, and Ferrante Imperato (1550–1625) of Naples were both important pharmacists who opened up their collections of naturalia to the public, densely displayed alongside small sculptures, containers and other equipment.[19]

One important cure-all was theriac, which consisted of a large variety of vegetal substances and viper's flesh. A colourful ceremony took place in Venice during May, illustrated here (fig. 10), when the pharmacy assistants ground the ingredients in large bronze mortars. Theriac from Venice was considered to be of particularly high quality, but other cities also carried out such ceremonies, supervised by the authorities, in order to ensure that the correct ingredients were used.[20]

Similarly, the minerals and metals themselves were valued for their recuperative powers. Pliny speaks of the 'astringent and cooling properties' of antimony. It was used in 'beauty-washes' for women's eyebrows as it magnified the eyes. It also provided a cure for ulceration of the eyes by combining it with 'powdered frankincense and an admixture of gum'. A complicated mixture was produced, which was 'pounded in mortars'.[21] From the fifteenth century on, mercury (or quicksilver) was particularly marketable, being an apparently successful cure for syphilis, although secondary symptoms appeared later.

Unless distillation was required, the primary means of preparing these diverse ingredients involved grinding, and many potions needed a combination of various techniques. Trituration (crushing or bruising) was identified as having three purposes: to allow substances to be mixed together, to enable them to perform in a new way, or in order to overcome any harmful properties.[22] Although the chemical function of a substance was of primary importance, the particle size was often considered to have a bearing on the type of treatment required, as discussed in a variety of seventeenth- and early eighteenth-century texts. For example:

> Those [drugs] that consist of a meane substance, as many odoriferous simples, must be bruised moderately, lest their more subtill and odoriferous parts should exhale, and be dissipated, yet they must be beaten very small, when they go to the confection of any electuary, and when we would have them to search and penetrate to the remotest parts, then must they be beaten very fine, when we would have them stay long in the body, then they must be coarser, provided they be not imbued with any maligne quality; some must be beaten very fine and small, that they may sooner performe their operation, and manifest their power.[23]

The relevant mortar would have been chosen depending on the required function, although there are comparatively few specific references. One is the recommendation of Robert Recorde (c.1510–58) that:

> … corall, ought not to be beaten in a brazen mortar, but pearls and corall ought to be beaten in a mortar of white marble;… Also purgations or electuaries, pills or powders mingled with syrups ought not to be dissolved in brazen morters, but in morters of glasse, of stone, or of some fine wood… Also some ointments ought to be made in morters of lead.[24]

The dangers of lead were already known in Pliny's day, although it was still used as a cosmetic to whiten women's faces, and clearly there was still no fear of a lead mortar contaminating a potion for external use.

Marble mortars were suitable for powdery and dry materials, while bronze mortars were particularly appropriate for hard substances, such as resins, barks and spices.[25] However, in the mid-seventeenth century Moyse Charas (c.1619–98) recommended the 'great brass mortar' for the preparation of widely varying quantities of ingredients where trituration was involved. In contrast, one mid-nineteenth-century source singled out small mortars for trituration, where a circular motion was required with the pestle, rather than the up-and-down pounding motion (or contusion) required to break up hard materials, for which only metal mortars were considered suitable.[26] The choice of size of bronze mortar was therefore only partly connected with the quantity of material needed, and had as much to do with the nature of the material to be broken down.

Charas also specifically recommended bronze mortars for the preparation of drugs containing ingredients that required heating. He identified various examples, including gum arabic and talc; the drying and crushing of saffron and tobacco and melting gum resins.[27] There are no conclusive signs that any of the mortars in the collection were used in this way. Crucibles probably doubled as mortars when heating was required, as is apparent from the de Levis example (cat. no. 51), which was presumably designed for this very purpose. This versatility would, theoretically, have been useful for potions that involved a combination of several processes, often carried out over a period of days. Numerous examples are provided by the Swiss physician and alchemist Paracelsus (c.1493–1541) in his writings on hermetic medicine, although the use of mortars is usually implicit rather than specifically mentioned. In a preparation of magnet and clax of eggs for wounds and ulcers, for example, he instructed:

> Set in layers in a crucible. Place in a fire of reverberation a day and a night. Extract, and it will be prepared. Otherwise, if not prepared by pounding, it misses its true extractive efficacy. But if previously prepared, then pounded and mixed, the oppoldeltoch has an excellent effect.[28]

Sizes ranged from those that were not much more than the size of a thimble to those of considerable diameter (cat. no. 16).[29] It is difficult to see how the really tiny mortars had any practical purpose; they were possibly used as advertisements. Some formed part of collections of curiosities, such as one in the Kunstschrank sold by Philipp Hainhofer of Augsburg (1578–1647) to Gustavus Adolphus of Sweden (1611– 32) and now in the Gustavianum Museum at Uppsala. The usefulness of this miniature gilt mortar and pestle is debatable, and it may in this instance have been solely symbolic, as it was shown alongside some of the natural substances that would have been ground in such an instrument.[30]

At the other end of the scale, some mortars were so large that the pestle had to be supported from a bar suspended from the wall or from the ceiling, as it was too heavy to be handled (fig. 11, p. 45).[31] This probably also gave greater power to the blow and reduced the effort needed. Large mortars were supported on pedestals of either stone or wood at the correct height for working; sometimes the pedestals even took sculptural form.[32] The support also absorbed the blows of the pestle, thereby increasing efficiency. Smaller ones could stand on the kitchen or pharmacist's counter. These two groups are precisely categorized by Matthews. The first included the large bell-metal mortars, 'weighing from 50 to 100 kg. or more', mounted with the supported pestle. The second group comprised the 'counter mortars of brass, copper, bell metal, glass, iron, marble or stone', which varied in height from '4 to 6 inch [10–16 cm.]'.[33] Sometimes they were hung up by an iron ring through the handle (e.g. cat. no. 1),[34] which would have necessitated storing the pestle separately on a shelf.

Drug trade and practitioners: apothecaries, doctors and the household

During antiquity doctors prepared and dispensed their own remedies, but this process began to be ceded to what eventually became the pharmacist, a practice that was severely criticized by Pliny, who believed that doctors should be knowledgeable in this way.[35] He had a scathing opinion of apothecaries, whom he accused of being charlatans, only out to make money. This view was repeated in the twelfth century by Bernardo Provenzale, and in the sixteenth by the Flemish anatomist Andreas Vesalius (1514–64). Vesalius regretted that apothecaries were taking over the preparation of medicines, linking it to the influx of foreign drugs and herbs: 'Thus the apothecaries arose, and as long as there are apothecaries and mortars, there is no art in medicine other than child's play, confusion, and drunken revelry.'[36] This view was shared by Paracelsus, himself a physician, and there were therefore doctors who continued to practise this function.[37]

The monasteries and hospitallers played a significant role in preparing and administering medicine, and their infirmaries – as well as their kitchens – would have included mortars and pestles. In fact, with the founding of the Abbey of Montecassino in 529 by St Benedict of Norcia, the study of pharmacy was established, largely based on Hippocrates and Galen. During the 1130s the practice of pharmacy was greatly criticized and the monks were prohibited by the Pope from pursuing it. Nevertheless, it continued. Among the most important of the early hospitals were San Sepolocro and San Giovanni in Pisa (1113), together with those of the priory of the Order of the Knights of St John of Jerusalem, the latter being instrumental in establishing many hospitals in Italy. The Knights' early statutes show that their doctors were 'accustomed to make the necessary syrups' for the sick.[38] At their headquarters in Malta they minted their own coin, and it is likely that they also cast their own mortars for use in the hospital.[39]

Rules began to emerge regarding pharmaceutical practice during the Middle Ages, notably in the Statutes of Arles (1162–1202) and the Ordinance of

Frederick II at Naples (1240). The Capitulary of the Venetian doctors and chemists of 1258 outlined clearly the different roles. A fourteenth-century miniature by Nicolao di Giacomo da Bologna in the *Statuto dell'Arte de' Speziali di Bologna* (statute of the pharmacists' guild of Bologna) shows shields bearing mortars and two pestles.[40] The mortars have stubby side-handles and zigzag decoration, perhaps indicating a form similar to cat. no. 68. Where there was no specific guild, pharmacists belonged to existing ones alongside merchants and other professionals. In Mantua they were included with the cheesemongers (*formaggiai*) until 1700, and in Verona they did not become independent until 1549.[41] Like all such members, they had to abide by the rules of the guild, and these could often be quite stringent, although practices varied.[42]

Pharmacy became more firmly established as a governed profession in the fifteenth century through the authority of the papacy in Rome. At that time apothecaries also made sweets and cakes, and quite often sold books and other goods.[43] Papal pharmacists (*farmacisti palatini*) enjoyed a comparatively high status; they were placed between doctors and surgeons in the hierarchy of the papal court; they were given a living; and they participated in the distribution of gold and silver medals.[44] They were even included in the conclave of cardinals during the election of a new Pope.[45] The large and impressive mortar dated 1642 (cat. no. 15) is known from the legend to have been made for the papal pharmacy by one of the leading bronze founders of the time.

As exploration opened up far-flung territories, so new spices and drugs were imported from the East and the New World to the whole of Europe, predominantly through Italy, which basically held a monopoly on the drug trade in Europe from the fourteenth century. The Ferrarese Antonio Musa Brasavola (1500–55), who was physician to the Este court but also taught at the university, stressed the importance for both apothecary and doctor of an awareness of plants and other ingredients available locally. He spotted rhubarb for the first time in the aptly named (in this context) Campana pharmacy in Venice.[46] Venice was at the heart of the drug

trade and consequently supported numerous pharmacists in its empire. Not surprisingly, the majority of the mortars in this volume are from that area.

As we have already seen, the mortar was an essential and fundamental piece of equipment for the pharmacist. The French physician Philbert Guibert is quite specific in his 1625 manual, stating that it is:

> necessary to furnish an Apothecary [with] … a great Morter of Brasse weighing fifty or sixty pound or more, with a pestle of iron. A little Morter weighing five or six pound with a pestle of the same matter. A middle sized Morter of Marble, and a pestle of wood, and a stone morter with the same pestle.[47]

Not surprisingly, this range of mortar types is referred to not just in other writings, but also in inventories that confirm the materials at the practitioner's disposal. An extensive pharmacy inventory from Gubbio in 1432, for example, includes: *Mortaioli tre* (34 *libbre*) and *Uno mortaio* (100 *libbre*).[48] The material from which these mortars was made was not identified and there was no reference to pestles, but a distinction was clearly made between the three small mortars and one large. The listing of the Benedictine convent of Santa Giustina in Padua, dated 1689, is more specific. It includes three bronze mortars (large, medium and small) with their *mazze* (pestles) of iron; three stone mortars (two of Istrian stone, one of Veronese) with their pestles; a porphyry mortar with its pestle of porphyry and a cover of Greek marble; a lead mortar and pestle; and five tufa mortars. In addition there were six pedestals for mortars, five of stone and one of wood.[49] Among the ingredients and preparations were listed antimony, cardamom, coral, *mumia* (or mummy, being the dried skin of dead bodies), three different forms of deer's horn, *oglio di scorpion del Mattioli* (Mattioli's preparation for scorpion oil)[50] and *pilole del Paracelso* (a pill recipe from Paracelsus). There are many similarities between the 1432 Gubbio inventory and the contents of the Paduan pharmacy nearly 250 years later.[51]

According to Guibert, in addition to the functional mortars, there was an elaborate one for show, which was also often utilized. The name or sign of the pharmacy was frequently included on the mortar to denote ownership, and the pharmacist may have specified his requirements when placing his order with the foundry. The papal pharmacist's mortar already cited (cat. no. 15) may be one such example, as might the impressive mortar made for one of Napoleon's pharmacists in 1802.[52]

The study of pharmacy interested a wide range of people during the Renaissance. Perhaps not surprisingly, Leonardo da Vinci refers to the writings of Avicenna and Hippocrates; the latter's works were first printed after the artist's death, indicating that he had access to a manuscript.[53] Members of the élite were also often well versed and practised in the preparation of medicines.[54] Medical texts were frequently found in libraries, such as those of the fifteenth-century Cardinal Bessarion (which became the foundation of the Biblioteca Marciana in Venice) and of Cardinal Francesco Gonzaga (1444–83).[55] The role of the Medici has already been noted, most particularly that of Cosimo I, whose intimate involvement in the manufacture of medicines and alchemical experimentation is well documented. Not only did he own a copy of Mattioli's translation of Dioscorides, but he personally annotated it. Cosimo also commissioned mortars of serpentine and porphyry, the latter from the leading sculptor specializing in this material, Francesco del Tadda (1497–1585), who carved the porphyry relief of Cosimo now in the Museum (inv. no. 1-1864; signed and dated 1570).[56]

As noted by Peacock, 'nearly all families above the rank of peasantry dispensed drugs and medicines in various forms'.[57] Each important household would, therefore, have possessed several mortars for use in preparing these potions – at least one designated exclusively for grinding poisons – as well as those for culinary use (see p. 46). Many of the grander households had gardens attached, in which they grew plants from which they would make their own remedies for particular ailments. Such planting was recommended by Alberti in his treatise on architecture, *De re aedificatoria*, printed in 1485, but circulating from the mid-fifteenth century.[58] Large gardens were laid out in Padua, Florence and Pisa in 1545. The last two were founded by Cosimo de'

Medici; the latter was attached to Pisa University, a practice followed by other centres of learning to encourage study. As suggested by Nutton, Alfonso d'Este's palace garden, set up in the 1530s, was doubtless established under Brasavola's influence.[59]

Alchemical use[60]

Alchemy incorporated both the desire to transform base metals into gold and the search for the elixir of life. It was, therefore, both an experimental science and a philosophy, which encompassed the relationship between the macrocosm and the microcosm (people to their universe; the 'inner' person and the 'outer') and within this the precepts of astronomy (incorporating the power of the heavens). Many alchemists were also physicians, including such notable men as Paracelsus and Agricola. They would have used mortars of various materials, both in the preparation of medicines and in their laboratories (fig. 11) to grind the 'philosopher's stone' and other powders for use in their transmutation experiments. The 'philosopher's stone' was an ill-defined substance that acted as a catalyst. Examples of mortars in the collection that can be associated with alchemical use have been identified by their decorative imagery (see, for example, cat. nos 21 and 72).

Despite the dismissive comments of some writers – such as Biringuccio, who gives a long discourse on his disbelief of the claims of alchemists[61] – there was an obvious interest in the possible outcome of alchemical experiments. While one cannot disregard Biringuccio's observation that even 'those who have good judgement' can become blinded by their desire for riches, the pursuit of the 'black art' sat happily in some senses beside the Renaissance thirst for knowledge, and understandably attracted men of power. The obvious example is Francesco I de' Medici, who is said to have practised alchemy himself and is famously represented in the grand-ducal laboratory – a mortar and pestle prominently illustrated.[62] The complicated philosophy of the art combined elements of metallurgy and casting with associations of creation and life-giving properties, which would have been appreciated by learned scholars and even artists of the time.[63]

Fig. 11. Philip Galle, An alchemist's laboratory. *Engraving after a painting by Giovanni Stradano in the Palazzo Vecchio, Florence.*

Culinary and cosmetic use

In the household – as well as the monastery – mortars were part of the daily preparation of food, being used to grind herbs and spices, cakes of sugar, grains and other ingredients, virtually all of which were supplied whole until the eighteenth century. Some of these ingredients were difficult to break up, and it was doubtless the job of the women or servants to spend hours in such labours. These commodities were often extremely valuable, especially the exotic imports that were flowing into Genoa and Venice. Among these were coriander seeds from North Africa and mace from the Far East. Like copper, pepper was a secure investment, and its price was often used as a yardstick in trading.[64]

Again, an inscription and/or coat of arms declared ownership of these valuable objects (cat. nos 4–5, for example). However, it is not always possible to tell for which purpose 'household' mortars were used. Not surprisingly, many examples bearing the Medici arms survive, including one at the Philadelphia College of Pharmacy and Science.[65] The magnificent example at the Musée Jacquemart-André at Chaalis bears the Medici papal arms, signifying either Leo X (1513–21) or Clement VII (1523–34), and was therefore possibly made for the papal pharmacy as opposed to the Medici household.[66]

As already noted, mortars played a part in the preparation of cosmetics. Some of the aromatic ingredients were also costly imports, including gum arabic and myrrh. Among the 'secrets' of Antonio de' Medici were several connected with the making of soaps and perfumes. Some of these specify the use of a mortar, notably one recipe for *Pastiglie alla Cipriana*, in which all the ingredients were to be pulverized in a *Mortario di Bronzo*.[67]

The inclusion of mortars in household inventories, and even in wills, gives a further indication of their importance and value. In an English context, Matthews quotes an inventory of 1543 listing a stone mortar with pestle in the kitchen, and another of the same year in which a stone mortar and two pestles plus a spice mortar were numbered among the goods.[68]

The artist's studio

Mortars were part of the essential equipment of an artist's or craftsman's workshop, for such activities as milling gold and grinding colour. Theophilus's design for a mill, referred to above (p. 23), illustrates this, as does that of Giovanni Branca of 1629, which basically consisted of two mortars with mechanized pestles driven by steam. In *The Craftsman's Handbook* Cennini describes how bronze mortars should be used in the preparation of red (from hematite: 'pound this stone in a bronze mortar at first, because if you broke it up on your porphyry slab you might crack it'), yellow (giallorino) and ultramarine pigments, although in most instances he does not specify the fabric of the mortar.[69] The porphyry slab was particularly recommended for grinding colours, with a stone of the same material, flat underneath and rounded on the top, in a similar arrangement to the early querns. The process could be extremely tedious, as indicated by Cennini's comments on the efficacy of lengthy grinding. If vermilion, for example, was ground 'every day for twenty years, it would still be better and more perfect'.[70]

Metal mortars were also utilized in some contexts. Cellini described how to prepare enamel by grinding it in a 'little round mortar of well-hardened steel, and about the size of your palm & then you pound it up with very clean water and with a little steel pestle specially made for the purpose of the necessary size'. These mortars, which were 'made in Milan', in his view surpassed the porphyry or serpentine stone that they replaced.[71] In England, too, the use of metal mortars is evidenced by the inventory of King Henry III of England, which contained two parcel-gilt silver mortars, with two pestles and stones, used for grinding colours.[72]

Pestles

Pestles varied in design from the simple to the more sophisticated, and could be either single- or double-ended.[73] The optimum diameter of the grinding head was approximately one-third the diameter of the interior bowl of the mortar.[74] While there is no doubt that the vast majority of metal mortars have lost their accompanying pestles, these were not necessarily of bronze, but frequently of iron. This is clear from the inventories quoted above, and from the will of, for example, Margaret Legatt of Wootton, who bequeathed to Thomas Lord Berkeley a brass mortar with an iron pestle.[75]

Numerous examples of an uneven number of pestles and mortars suggest that the pestle was sometimes used independently.[76] It is therefore perhaps not so surprising that there are only two pestles in this catalogue (cat. nos 8 and 59). This poor survival rate reflects the sentiments of the oft-quoted Italian rhyme:

> *Il mortaio e raro e bello*
> *Ma villan ov'e il pestello?*
> (The mortar is rare and beautiful
> But where, [o] peasant, is the pestle?)[77]

Decoration of Bells and Mortars

The application of motifs and inscriptions served not just to decorate, but also to declare ownership or authorship, and, on occasion, to impart symbolic meaning appropriate to the object itself, or to the person commissioning it. Naturally, however, founders took advantage of the availability of moulds to reuse patterns on a variety of related utensils, so bells and mortars often have the same imagery, particularly during the Renaissance when their decoration was part of a broader language of ornament. The smaller objects were portable and the founders were often itinerant, so patterns could easily be transmitted from one workshop or centre to another. In the absence of a signature or mark, therefore, it is often difficult to assign an object to a particular foundry, unless it bears a combination of designs that can confidently be attributed. Even then, precise dating can be a problem, as moulds were reused by successive generations.[1]

During the late medieval and early Renaissance period the decoration of Italian bronze mortars was confined to varying forms of projecting ribs (cat. nos 1 and 68) attached to the rather squat, conical mortars. Similar ribs, usually with a serrated or undulating edge, can be seen on other European mortars, particularly those of France and Spain. As the fifteenth century progressed, the plain ribs became refined (cat. no. 70) and 'gothic'-style architectural ornament can be found on some pieces (cat. nos 4–7). The new 'Renaissance' style happily coexisted with the traditional, as tastes did not necessarily change. There was, at the same time, an increasing use of classical ornamental motifs and subjects, evident in the majority of the pieces in the collection.

Architectural decoration, such as egg and dart, acanthus leaf, bead and reel, and palmette and anthemion lent themselves to application to objects of circular form. Foliate and fruit swags, cornucopiae, trophies, putti, grotesques and bucrania were also borrowed from the classical repertory. In addition, figural groups were applied, showing religious and secular subjects. Such images may have been purely decorative, but sometimes also carried symbolic meaning.

A fascinating letter written by the sculptor and bronzist, Vincenzo de' Grandi, then in Padua, to Cardinal Madruzzo in Trento describes a large inkstand that he had made for the cardinal. He attached significant meaning to the decorative elements. The inclusion of an eagle, symbol of St John the Evangelist and *impresa* of the cardinal, was highlighted in an effusive manner, relating Madruzzo's use of the inkstand to the saint's writings in the name of Christ. The bucrania were associated with the effort from which comes glory and immortal fame; the festoons demonstrating the triumph of virtue and the honour of glory.[2] Bucrania and festoons feature prominently in Renaissance ornament (see cat. no. 47, for example), and this passage raises the possibility that other decorative elements may, on occasion, have been read on different levels.

Hercules, for instance, was one of the most popular subjects in the late fifteenth and early sixteenth centuries, being widely depicted in painting, architectural reliefs, sculpture and numerous decorated objects. The son of Jupiter and Alcmena, a mortal woman, he was both god and hero, the personification of strength and the representative of good overcoming evil. The most common depictions are scenes of combat, including the labours of Hercules and the infant Hercules strangling the snakes (see cat. nos 17, 18 and 22), and in many contexts he was an exemplar of virtue.

This imagery was particularly suitable for men of power, notably Ercole d'Este (1471–1505), Duke of Ferrara, who wanted to declare associations with the qualities of his namesake. The combination of motifs on a hand bell signed by Giovanni Alberghetti, now in the National Gallery of Art, Washington, including figures of Hercules, suggests that it may have been made for the Este court, possibly on the occasion of the marriage in 1491 of Ercole's daughter Beatrice (1475–97) to Ludovico Sforza, 'il Moro' (1451–1508), whose profile portrait also appears (see cat. no. 17).[3]

Hercules' first labour was to kill the Nemean lion, after which he wore the lion's skin, making him invincible. Hercules and the Nemean lion served as a symbol of Strength or Fortitude (one of the four 'cardinal virtues') in the tarot (or *tarocchi*), here indicating both physical and spiritual strength.[4] There were also parallels with Christian iconography, most particularly Samson, another symbol of strength, who slew a lion. For the alchemists, possibly due to a combination of Christian and mystical beliefs, Hercules represented immortality.[5] Additional connections were made between his various trials and the signs of the zodiac. Herculean iconography was therefore replete with meaning.[6] Hercules's presence on mortars may refer to his perceived ability to conquer all adversaries, including the plague (cat. no. 22).

The cockerel was another motif that carried both Christian and classical associations, through St Peter's denial and a link with Asclepius, the god of medicine.[7] It was believed to have curative qualities, and can therefore be recognized as appropriate for mortars, on which it regularly appears (cat. no. 25). One exceptional example is a mortar inscribed with a dedication from Marco Pollastro to Pope Julius II on 5 August 1510, decorated with cockerels holding ears of corn.[8] The use of the cockerel in this instance was also a rebus (*pollastro* being Italian for cockerel), and the specific motif may be an *impresa*. The lizard, an attribute of Logic, was also common,[9] often shown with foliage in its mouth.[10] In the Museum's example (cat. no. 15) both the reptile and sage leaf are cast from nature (see p. 28). A series of impressive bells and mortars by Wenzel Jamnitzer (master 1534, died 1585) of Nuremberg, an expert in nature casting, demonstrates the technique most vividly. Notable among them is the so-called Cellini bell (previously attributed to that master) in the Waddesdon Bequest at the British Museum, and a mortar in the Victoria and Albert Museum.[11] Another animated nature-cast of a lizard forms the handle of an Italian mortar in the Fitzwilliam Museum, Cambridge.[12]

Representations of fabulous animals or beings are common, including griffins (cat. no. 24), sphinxes, unicorns (cat. no. 25) and dragons (cat. no. 71). All of these have symbolic associations; and in the context of mortars, the dragon – with its alchemical and hermetic connections – was an especially appropriate symbol.[13] The unicorn was doubtless chosen because so-called unicorn horn (actually narwhal or rhinoceros) was used in medicine, but also had other associations.[14] The decoration may, on occasion, have indicated that the mortar was used to grind the horn. Without textual references, however, it is not possible to state conclusively that this form of marking was practised, although identifying the use of a mortar by its decoration could have been desirable, particularly when grinding poisons.[15] Pharmaceutical ceramics were often clearly labelled with their contents, but were similarly decorated with classical ornament and figural representations.

Appropriate motifs were applied to mortars made for religious settings, such as cat. no. 16, which bears the IHS monogram in the form adopted by the Jesuit Order.[16] Christ was represented as a pharmacist in paintings, prints and other settings, sometimes with the patron saints of medicine, Cosmas and Damian, and surrounded by various instruments of the trade; occasionally a mortar is among them.[17] The figure of Christ is even found on mortars themselves.[18]

A suitable choice of decoration for hand bells was Orpheus playing to the animals. Several variant compositions survive. One design, known in plaquette form, is attributed by Pechstein to the 'Meister der *Blattfries*', referring to the row of leaves that appears on some of the plaquettes in this group.[19] These are variously attributed to sixteenth-century Germany, or to Italy in about 1550. The motif was apparently taken up in Italy from the north, and appears in Italian manuscript illumination and enamels.[20] The plaquette shows the naked Orpheus, seated and playing a viol, surrounded by animals and birds. Designs from closely related dies appear on several bells, including one in the National Gallery of Art, Washington, and another, dated 1544, in the Rijksmuseum, Amsterdam.[21] Inscriptions on two examples in the present collection (inv. nos M.175-1929 and M.70-1953) confirm their Flemish origin. However, the figure of Orpheus and various animals based on this model are also found on a bell in the Museo Correr, Venice, which appears to be Italian in shape and overall design.[22]

An earlier depiction of the subject, showing a distinctive figure of Orpheus in classical armour, is found on bells signed OPVS PETRI, identified by Radcliffe as the signature of the Paduan founder, Pietro di Gaspare Campanario (active 1479–96).[23] However, as noted by Radcliffe, this image also appears on a bowl associated with the Grandi workshop in Trento. An animal motif (usually described as a dog, but difficult accurately to identify) applied to one of the bowls in this group also decorates a pastiglia box in the Österreichisches Museum für Angewandte Kunst, Vienna.[24] Other motifs are shared by pastiglia boxes and bronzes, notably bells and mortars associated with the Alberghetti

workshop (see cat. no. 19). Similar designs have been recognized on wafering irons, used for making both secular cakes and holy wafers.

The pastiglia workshops appear to have been largely based in north Italy, including Ferrara and the Veneto. The wafering irons are primarily attributed to Umbria, as the wafers, or *cialdoni*, were believed to be a particularly Umbrian speciality; signed wafering irons were produced in and near Perugia.[25] Some were made for families based elsewhere and many contain Venetian armorials. They were therefore either exported or, as seems probable, produced in other Italian centres, as they were also in Germany.[26] One Italian example dated 1481 shows a mortar with two pestles on one iron, and a coat of arms with a three-towered castle on its pair.[27] Apothecaries were given the right to sell a number of products besides potions and medicinal goods, including cakes (see p. 43). Blacksmiths, goldsmiths and masters of the mint are known to have produced wafering irons. Bronze foundries could, therefore, have used the dies or made their own moulds from them. The engraving skills required to make the irons themselves may also have been available in the foundry.[28] There is, therefore, evidence of an interchange of decoration between different artisans and workshops, although the detail of how this occurred remains to be discovered.[29] The diversity of tasks assigned to court artists, for example, indicates that there was considerably more overlap between the different trades than has been suggested.[30]

Casts were made from antique and modern intaglios, and the designs disseminated in three-dimensional form through plaster casts or bronze plaquettes, as well as by prints. These were then utilized by the bronze foundries, either directly from casts of gems, or via plaquette copies (see cat. nos 53 and 55).[31] The casting and reuse of these images is suggested in Biringuccio's description of moulding reliefs.[32] A Venetian footed bowl in the Bargello, Florence (associated with the Alberghetti), displays a composition showing *Apollo, Marsyas and Olympus* after the antique, known also in a related image seen on small plaquettes.[33] Designs taken from Renaissance plaquettes also appear, such as the

Virgin and Child after Donatello on a large bell by Giulio and Ludovico Bonaventurini in the Museo di Castelvecchio in Verona, of 1590.[34] The appearance of a Ferrarese plaquette showing the *Virgin and Child with Angels* on another example in the Castello del Buonconsiglio at Trento, dated 1486, is apparently the earliest securely dated representation of this plaquette, usually assigned more broadly to the last quarter of the fifteenth century.[35]

In addition to the subtle messages imparted by the decoration of bells and mortars, inscriptions, foundry marks and heraldic devices were intended to acknowledge the makers and owners. These specific identifiers are often invaluable in building a picture of the contexts in which the objects were used (cat. nos 9 and 10). They demonstrate the importance of the cult of personality or family position (cat. nos 46 and 47), or advertise the commercial or charitable organization for which they were made (cat. nos 1 and 15). On occasion they commemorated an event, such as a marriage,[36] and some were doubtless produced just for show or ceremonial use. Embellishment with costly gilding may indicate such a use, or emphasize the wealth and status of the owner.[37] One fascinating example is the hand bell of Emperor Rudolf II (dated *c*.1575–1600), which is said to be cast from an alloy containing each of the so-called 'seven metals of antiquity'. The metals were each allied with celestial elements: gold – sun; silver – moon; iron – Mars; copper – Venus; lead – Jupiter; tin – Saturn; mercury (quicksilver) – Mercury. The bell is decorated with the associated planetary gods and the signs of the zodiac that they rule.[38]

Today the significance of the decoration has often been lost. Specific dates become meaningless or difficult to decipher if the context is unknown (cat. no. 9), and without the benefit of tincture, it is often impossible to identify coats of arms securely (e.g. cat. no. 33). Similarly, foundry marks are no longer recognized (e.g. cat. no. 40) unless they can firmly be associated with a particular workshop, such as the de Levis (cat. no. 49) and Bonaventurini (see cat. no. 46). The use of clear foundry marks or signatures apparently increased, however, from the seventeenth century

onwards. These objects continued to sport much of the same decoration, although generally it was applied more sparsely and cast more crisply. Even today, bell-founders continue to use the moulds of their predecessors.

In addition to the applied decoration, handles are frequently formed by figural or foliated forms. Handles on bells are, however, often missing or replaced, and it is therefore particularly interesting when a handle is clearly original, such as the imposing figure of a judge on Giuseppe de Levis's bell for the Veronese College of Judges.[39] Particularly relevant is the figure surmounting a bell in Cologne, which holds one finger over its mouth, as though calling for silence at the commencement of the meeting (fig. 12).

Fig. 12. Hand bell. Possibly workshop of Gaspare di Girolamo Macri, Brescia. Museum für Angewandte Kunst, Cologne, inv. no. H.457.

However, because of their sometimes suspect status in connection with an individual bell, it is dangerous to rely solely on these figure handles to identify the origin of the bell itself. A notable example of the problem can be seen on another bell attributed to Giuseppe de Levis, where the handle takes the form of a small version of a *Tobias* from the workshop of Severo da Ravenna.[40] On the other hand, there are two identical figures on bells signed OPUS CASTELLI, which bear similar applied decoration.[41] Further difficulties are presented when it is not possible to determine whether a handle is original or a replacement, and this could lead to a mistaken attribution.

A group of stylistically related figures, which are close to those found on Venetian firedogs, include *David with the head of Goliath* and *Venus with a dolphin*, which are effectively based on the same composition.[42] However, they appear to form two different groups, the David appearing on bells of one style, with the Venus appearing on bells of another.

The same distinctive figure of a female appears on the handle of a bell in the Bargello, Florence,[43] as on the bell in Padua signed 'Opus Petri', but the applied decoration is quite different from known examples from the same workshop.[44] However, a connection can perhaps be made between the other examples of variants of these two groups (also in Padua), the handles of which are formed by similar putti.[45] Similar firedog-style figures were reproduced on bells in the nineteenth century by, for instance, Giuseppe Michieli, and some surviving examples may therefore have come from such foundries.[46]

Alloy Analysis

As an integral part of this catalogue, the alloy compositions were studied. There are few published results on compositional analysis of these types of object. The findings of the present programme will provide a database for future reference and expansion. Similar examination will be carried out in connection with the further study of the Italian bronzes in the collection.

Due to the nature of bells and mortars, it was not possible to remove material for analysis without disfiguring the objects. A non-invasive method of analysis was therefore essential. By using Energy Dispersive X-Ray Fluorescence spectrometry (EDXRF)[1] it is possible to analyse the elemental composition of the surface of the object, without removal of material and (in the case of this study) without intervention to the surface finish. X-ray beams directed at the object excite the elements from which the metal is com- posed.[2] These excited elements emit an X-ray that can be measured with the aid of computer software, pro- ducing a quantitative analysis of the composition of the metal. In order to obtain the most accurate results, a 'standard' alloy is chosen, against which the parameters for computation are set. A standard that is similar to the alloy being examined provides the best results. A repre- sentative sample (cat. nos 2 and 49) was selected and analysed in order to identify the most appropriate stan- dard prior to proceeding with the programme. As anticipated, the sample indicated a predominantly high-tin alloy and standards were chosen accordingly.

The EDXRF spectrometer used in this study was a modified Spectrace 6000 unit produced by Spectrace Instruments, Inc., USA. The equipment was modified to obtain a variable angle (with an air path) between the excitation source from which the beam was emitted and the X-ray detector. The geometry and air path changes gave a considerable advantage in that almost any size of object could be analysed with ease. The disadvantage of this particular arrangement was the potentially lower analytical precision due to variable geometry (notably the difficulty of dealing with curved surfaces onto which the X-ray beam had to be focused). Surface changes that may have occurred, and the lower sensitivity of the lighter elements due to air absorption of the fluorescent X-rays on the return path, also caused analytical error.

The use of this technique facilitates the examination of different areas and different components of the same object – without any intrusion or damage to the object. However, the results are limited to the readings obtained from the surface, with all the drawbacks and pitfalls of surface analysis. Any process that may alter the composition of the surface, such as patination, abrasive cleaning or corrosion, is likely to affect the analysis results. The individual concentration of the elements in the alloy has an additional effect on the overall signal strength for each elemental component. For example, the X-ray emission obtained from one element may be absorbed by an atom of another element, resulting in a misleading reading. This is known as the matrix effect.

The results confirmed that the majority of the bells are bell-metal, but a wide variety of alloys was used to produce the mortars and related utensils.[3] Ideally, therefore, a broader range of standards would have been used for calibration. A summary of the individual results appears in each catalogue entry and the normalized analysis is set out in Appendix 1.

Graham Martin

Summary of the results of analysis

Analysis has revealed that the objects in this volume vary considerably in alloy composition.[4] While the majority of bells and a number of the mortars are bell-metal, as described in the treatises, there are numerous exceptions to the rule. Many of the bells have a particularly high tin content, making them especially brittle (cat. no. 40). Those that are not bell-metal may, at first sight, appear to be questionable in terms of authenticity. However, the decoration on one of the brass bells (cat. no. 47) confirms that, as today, household bells were also made of less expensive and more durable alloy.

Conclusions concerning the mortar analysis are uncertain. In some cases, objects that appear similar in facture and decoration also have related alloy analysis (for example, cat. nos 21–3). This may strengthen the argument for production within the same workshop, but it is difficult to identify any real pattern, particularly when comparing the alloy analysis for the Fabriano group (cat. nos 4–7) and the Mariotto group (cat. nos 8–11). The inscriptions indicate production within the same workshop of each group, but the analysis is not particularly closely related. While the metal might be taken to provide some insight into whether a mortar was made by a specialist bell-founder, or an artillery maker, our current knowledge of foundry practices, and the demands of those ordering these utensils, does not allow for firm conclusions to be drawn. As has been seen (pp. 31–2), many foundries produced a variety of objects, and potentially utilized a range of alloys. The situation is further complicated by the reuse of metals, making the alloy mixes less standardized than they are today (see p. 23). It is clear, however, that mortars are not necessarily bell-metal, nor is it possible to date Italian mortars on the basis of their alloy content as suggested by Peal for English mortars.[5]

Notes and Summary Bibliographies

Collecting and Collectors

1. For the Museum's history, see Somers Cocks 1980; Baltimore 1997; and Burton 1999.

2. Reproduced in the Inventory 1863, pp. iii–iv. This clause of the Minute probably reflects a concern at the extensive sculpture holdings that had been built up primarily by John Charles Robinson (see below), although recent research has shown that Henry Cole also played a significant role (see Wainwright 1999).

3. The report of the Committee of Re-Arrangement (adopted on 29 July 1908) suggested that 'heavy foundry work, such as fire-backs, fire-dogs, bells and ordnance (Eastern and European)' were displayed in the West Entrance Corridor of the Museum.

4. Williamson 1996, p. 10; see also pp. 8–24 for the history of the Sculpture Department.

5. Inv. no. 629-1865 was allocated to Sculpture (see Rosenheim 1995, no. RO 106, p. 301), 630-1865 to Metalwork. A smaller version was also given to Metalwork (628-1865). See also London 1999, pp. 108–9, no. 37.

6. Much weeding was done by overenthusiastic auditors of the archive from the Department of Education and Science, notably in 1935, when a vast amount of information disappeared. The process ceased in 1968. I am grateful to Maureen Mulvanny of the V&A Archive and Registry for this information. In some cases, however, the acquisition is noted in the Précis of the Board Minutes of the Science and Art Department, which was then responsible for the Museum.

7. For Webb, see Somers Cocks 1980, p. 65; Wainwright 1989, pp. 45–6, 292–3; Williamson 1996, pp. 11–12; Baltimore 1997, esp. pp. 161–2.

8. For Piot, see Edmond Bonnaffé in Hotel Drouot (Piot) 1890, pp. 7–30; TDA 1996, 24, pp. 837–8; *Les donateurs du Louvre*, Paris, 1989, pp. 293–4.

9. National Art Library, Robinson papers, 14 April 1864.

10. National Art Library, Robinson papers, 20 May 1864.

11. Inv. no. 475-1864; see Baltimore 1997, pp. 178–9, no. 55, citing earlier literature.

12. In this instance, it is possible that Robinson colluded in the Piot purchases in the hope of winning over the Board at a later date, which he eventually succeeded in doing.

13. These include one with the arms of the Moro family, now in Washington (see cat. no. 55) and another from a group by the founder signing 'Opus Petri' (see Radcliffe 1992, p. 23).

14. For Soulages, see Robinson 1856; Wainwright 1988, pp. 266–7; idem, 1989, pp. 292–3; London 1990, p. 207, cat. 218.

15. For example, two 'Renaissance lamps' from the Soulages Collection (inv. nos 563 and 565-1865; Robinson 1856, p. 113, nos 349 and 350) are made up of a combination of elements from lamps and candlesticks – some genuine casts from the workshop of Severo Calzetta da Ravenna (*c*.1496–before 1538); others apparently nineteenth-century casts or after-casts. For discussion of furniture of questionable date from the Soulages Collection, see Clive Wainwright in London 1990, loc. cit. at n. 14 above.

16. Robinson 1856, p. iv.

17. Hotel Drouot, Paris, 9–10 May 1870.

18. Inv. no. 314-1878; Pope-Hennessy 1964, pp. 335–7, no. 364; Baltimore 1997, pp.180–1, no. 57.

19. Nobili 1922, p. 147. I am grateful to Jemma Street for this reference.

20. For Castellani and his family, see TDA 1996, 6, pp. 19–21 and bibliography.

21. See Carl Brandon Strehlke, Exhibition Review of *Florence in the 1470s*, London, in *The Burlington Magazine*, CXLII (January 2000), pp. 47 and 48, nn. 6 and 7, including reference to G. C. Munn, *Castellani and Giuliano, revivalist jewellers of the 19th century*, New York, n.d., *c*.1984, for discussion of Castellani's activities as a faker of ancient jewellery.

22. Castellani nominal file (Museum Archive), letter from Naples, 2 November 1870.

23. Castellani nominal file (Museum Archive), 19 December 1883.

24. Inv. no. 702-1884; Williamson 1996, p. 40.

25. See Helbing 1913; Stefania Moronato in Venice 1988, pp. 205–12.

26. An example of which was formerly in a private collection in Brighton (sold at Sotheby's, Billingshurst, between 1994 and 1999, but the records have not been located).

27. Not all the documentation has survived on the Museum's Guggenheim file. Earlier purchases are noted in the Précis 1872, p. 224 (11 February 1869), which refers to 'Silver angels and specimens of porcelain' purchased from 'Mr Gügenheim' by Henry Cole in Italy, for £16, during the same trip that he acquired the two mortars from Baslini (cat. nos 5 and 14).

28. For Bardini, see TDA 1996, 3, p. 228 and bibliography; also Humphrey Ward, 'Bardini's at Florence' in *Art Journal*, 1893, pp. 10–15, including an interesting discussion on Bardini's relationship with South Kensington. I am grateful to Diane Bilbey for this reference.

29. Letter to Thomas Armstrong (1833–1911), Director (1881–98), dated 30 October 1889 in Bardini nominal file (Museum

Archive). Bode was Director of the Berlin Gemäldegalerie from 1890, and Director General of the Berlin Museums from 1905 (Burton 1999, p. 160; Henning Bock, Arne Effenberger and Janni Müller-Hauck (eds), *Wilhelm von Bode, Museumsdirektor und Mäzen*, Berlin, 1995).

30. See Pope-Hennessy and Radcliffe 1970.

31. Probably disposed of in 1958. The relevant file (Department of Education and Science) appears to have been destroyed.

32. See TDA 1996, 27, pp. 641–2 with bibliography; Coppel 1996; Warren 1996, pp. 125–6; Peta Motture '"…none but the finest things": George Salting as a Collector of Bronzes', *Sculpture Journal*, V (forthcoming 2001).

33. DNB Concise II, 1982, p. 112; *Who Was Who…1916–28*, London, 1929, p. 174.

34. For the staff, see Margaret H. Longhurst, *Catalogue of Carvings in Ivory*, II, 1929, pp. 59–60, and P. B. Cott, *Siculo-Arabic Ivories*, Princeton, 1939, cat. no. 176, pl. 65. For Durlacher, see TDA 1996, 9, pp. 451–2. Durlacher himself gave two sculptures to the Museum: a Paduan terracotta *Virgin and Child* (inv. no. A.43-1934; Pope-Hennessy 1964, I, no. 361) and an English ivory *Trinity*, *c.*1330 (inv. no. A.49-1937; see Jonathan Alexander and Paul Binski (eds), *Age of Chivalry. Art in Plantagenet England 1200–1400* (exh. cat., Royal Academy of Arts), London, 1987, pp. 424–5, no. 519).

35. A wood group of *Hercules, Achelous and Deianeira*, attributed on acquisition to the 'School of Giovanni da Bologna', later reclassified by Pope-Hennessy as German, late sixteenth- or early seventeenth-century: inv. no. 939-1901; Pope-Hennessy 1964, II, p. 699.

36. The gift and bequest were both given in the name of the Alfred Williams Hearn Gift.

37. See Anthony North et al., *Pewter at the Victoria & Albert Museum*, London, 1999.

38. Information from Hearn nominal files (Museum Archive). See also Review 1923, pp. 1–2, 53–4 (for Metalwork); Review 1931, see p. xiii for index.

39. Described and illustrated in *The Chemist and Druggist*, 9 January 1932, p. 25; apparently acquired for the collection of a Cambridge professor – possibly Hemming.

40. TDA 1996, 14, p. 525.

41. *Pharmaceutical Journal*, 26 March 1938, p. 329.

42. Museum records.

43. See Inventory 1907 (1901, Jermyn Street Collection) for the full listing.

44. See Peter Laverack (ed.), *Daniel Katz Ltd. 1968–1993. A Catalogue Celebrating Twenty-Five Years of Dealing in European Sculpture and Works of Art*, London, 1993; Johannes Auersperg, *Daniel Katz. European Sculpture* (exh. cats, New York and London), London, 1996 and 1998.

45. See Appendix 3, nos 3 and 4, to which this mortar is related. It is omitted from Appendix 3 as it was not acquired as Italian.

46. Bode 1910, I, p. 1.

47. Ibid.

48. Ibid.

49. *Abundance*, inv. no. A.14-1961 (Christie's (Bardini) 1902, pl. 1, fig. 4; Bode 1910, I, no. 89, p. 25, pl. LVII); *Inkstand with the Martyrdom of St Lawrence*, inv. no. A.3-1963 (see Bode 1910, II, no. 158; John Pope-Hennessy, *Essays on Italian Sculpture*, London and New York, 1968, pp. 197, 229, n. 135, fig. 245).

50. A few are in the Pierpont Morgan Library in New York. For those in the Frick, New York, see Pope-Hennessy and Radcliffe 1970; for the Frick, Pittsburgh, see Avery 1993. Due to the dispersal of the Morgan Collection bronzes, the whereabouts of many of them are now unknown.

51. The German private collection housing a variety of mortars, including two signed Mariotti examples (see nos vii and viii under cat. no. 8), is owned by a pharmacist.

The Materials

1. However, some modern 'bronzes' do not contain tin, but are still referred to as bronzes (e.g. phosphorus bronze). I am grateful to Sophia Strang Steel for this information.

2. The term *aes* is used by Pliny, see Pliny/Rackham 1961, IX, pp. 126–7. Although this term embraced brass, this copper-zinc alloy was also identified with *aurichalcum*: see below (n. 14) for a further discussion of brass; see also ibid., pp. 128–9, and Theophilus/Hawthorne and Smith 1979, pp. 143–4, n. 1, for use of the terms *aes* and *aurichalcum*.

3. References in the treatises to copper extraction include Theophilus/Dodwell 1986, pp. 120–1; Theophilus/Hawthorne and Smith 1979, pp. 139–40 (and n. 1); Biringuccio/Smith and Gnudi 1990, pp. 52–4 (Biringuccio 1540, I, 12–13).

4. TDA 1996, 4, p. 849; ibid., 7, p. 812; copper can also be quite fluid when liquefied, and was successfully used for the production of sculpture at various periods in different regions of the world.

5. Aitchison 1960, pp. 61–2.

6. Copper-tin alloys had the same benefits as copper-arsenic alloys with fewer of the disadvantages. The drawbacks to copper-arsenic included difficulties in controlling the quality and the toxic effects of arsenic fumes; see TDA 1996, 4, p. 849.

7. See Biringuccio/Smith and Gnudi 1990, p. 210: 'it is called by skilled workmen metal of more or less fineness as it contains more or less tin' (Biringuccio 1540, V, 74); see also p. 23 and n. 51 below.

8. Technically lead does not alloy with other metals, but sits as globules in the mix, but a copper-tin-lead mix is usually referred to as a ternary alloy, and a copper-tin-zinc-lead mix as a quaternary alloy (see p. 66 for terminology).

9. Although it was known in classical antiquity, being deposited in furnaces during smelting; see Theophilus/Hawthorne and Smith 1979, p. 141, n. 1, with details of the properties of

zinc. It is mentioned by Swiss physician and alchemist, Paracelsus (see below) as 'not commonly known…of peculiar nature and origin'; but, surprisingly, among its properties he states that it 'stands alone', and indicates that it cannot be alloyed with other metals (Paracelsus/Waite 1992, p. 254).

10. Bewer 1996, pp. 29–30, with further references to David Scott, *Metallography and microstructure of ancient and historic metals*, Los Angeles, 1991; see also n. 14 below.

11. See Blackmore 1976, p. 408.

12. It is possible that Fanelli used brass for the bronzes he cast in England as the preferred alloy. Further analysis is required to determine the pattern of production.

13. Pliny/Rackham 1961, pp. 128, 129.

14. Biringuccio/Smith and Gnudi 1990, p. 70 (Biringuccio 1540, I, 19v); and for notes on the history of brass, and attribution of the discovery to alchemy; 'it seems to me impossible to deny that [brass] is one of the works of alchemy, since copper is red by nature and this redness is taken from it by art and converted into yellowness' (Biringuccio/Smith and Gnudi 1990, p. 75; Biringuccio 1540, I, 21). See also Theophilus/Dodwell 1986, p. 121. See Aitchison 1960, pp. 154–5, for a detailed description of brass production, and Craddock 1990 for the history of brass.

15. Pliny/Rackham 1961, p. 127.

16. Pliny/Rackham 1961, p. 133. He also describes that the 'addition of lead to Cyprus copper produces the purple colour seen in the bordered robes of statues' (p. 200).

17. Gauricus/Chastel and Klein 1969, p. 218; see below for statuary bronze recipe.

18. See Avery 1981, p. 198 and idem 1988, pp. 169–72 and 208–9, cat. no. 14. The horse is described as 'Brasse' in the contract, but the alloy has not yet been analysed.

19. See Boström 1995, pp. 814, 818, Doc. 3.

20. Biringuccio/Smith and Gnudi 1990, p. 210; Biringuccio 1540, V, 74.

21. See particularly Boström 1995, pp. 814–15 and further literature, with a detailed discussion of rosette copper; p. 815, n. 29 for Fugger references; and Jardine 1997, pp. 39, 96–8 (including Fuggers as arms suppliers), 286–7.

22. Biringuccio/Smith and Gnudi 1990, p. 49 (Biringuccio 1540, I, 10v).

23. Biringuccio/Smith and Gnudi 1990, p. 49 (Biringuccio 1540, I, 11).

24. Biringuccio/Smith and Gnudi 1990, p. 48 (Biringuccio 1540, I, 10-10v). By 'Venice', Biringuccio presumably meant the mountainous area to the north of Venice. Following various journeys around Germany (Innsbruck, Halle, and so on) and Italy, he concluded that the purest silver was found in the region of Vicenza.

25. Biringuccio/Smith and Gnudi 1990, pp. 222–3, note on gunfounding, for brief history and bibliography; see also Diderot *Planches* 1767, 'Fonderies des Canons'; Gush 1978, pp. 17–19; Guilmartin 1980, pp. 284–91; Parker 1988, p. 128 (I am grateful to Neil Carleton for the last three references); and Jardine 1997, pp. 42–4, for the importance of cannon technology.

26. Jardine 1997, pp. 286–7.

27. See Welch 1997, p. 49; Wackernagel 1981, p. 30, n. 19.

28. Biringuccio/Smith and Gnudi 1990, p. 297 (Biringuccio 1540, VI, 108).

29. One mine (Blue Hills Tin Streams) is currently (February 2000) still surface-mining for jewellery making.

30. Biringuccio/Smith and Gnudi 1990, p. 211 (Biringuccio 1540, V, 74v). He describes the alloying of tin with lead, of which he disapproved, as well as its use as a solder for working with copper.

31. Biringuccio/Smith and Gnudi 1990, p. 60 (Biringuccio 1540, I, 15v).

32. Biringuccio/Smith and Gnudi 1990, pp. 55, 56 (Biringuccio 1540, I, 13 and 13v). See Theophilus/Hawthorne and Smith 1979, p. 139, n.1 for a description of this process, believed to have originated in the fifteenth century (but possibly known much earlier), and practised until the nineteenth century.

33. Alloy calculations are complicated by the unclear use of terminology, notably with regard to brass, which being an alloy itself has no set copper-zinc ratio (see p. 19). Another difficulty is highlighted by the results of analysis, which indicate a wide variety of alloys used. This was partly due to differing foundry experience and practice (see esp. pp. 30, 31–3). Ratio calculations have therefore been limited to those that can most accurately be assessed.

34. The German physician and alchemist, Georg Bauer, known as Georgius Agricola (1495–1555), also published several works on a variety of subjects concerned with the natural world, including his famous *De Re Metallica* (1556), another important source on the subject. See also Aitchison 1960, esp. pp. 292–4.

35. Pliny/Rackham 1961, p. 199; he goes on to describe the blend used for making moulds (p. 201); see also p. 27 re the use of metal moulds.

36. For all Gauricus's recipes quoted here, see Gauricus/Chastel and Klein 1969, pp. 218–19; n. 12 for reference to Pliny (Cyprian copper presumably refers to copper that came from Cyprus). The use of the terms 'black' lead and 'argentarium' distinguishes between lead and tin – tin at the time being taken to be a silver-coloured lead.

37. Gauricus also identified a specific mix for plaquettes, being 10 lbs (4.54 kg.) of tin in 100 (45.36 kg.) of copper (*c.*91/9 per cent).

38. Vasari/Maclehose 1960, p. 163. This assertion suggests a much lower zinc content.

39. For example, Verrocchio's *Christ and St Thomas* included some lead (2.15 per cent); see New York 1993, p. 90.

40. Vasari/Maclehose 1960, p. 164.

41. See Boström 1995, esp. pp. 814–15.

42. See Blackmore 1976 for further recipes for artillery, including the Italian Alessandro Capo Bianco (*Artiglieria*, 1598) as copper-tin-latten 100/20/5 (equivalent to approximately copper-tin-zinc 103.5/20/1.5 – i.e. *c.* 82.8/16/1.2 per cent).

43. Leonardo/Richter 1970, p. 24. See Bewer 2002 for further discussion of cannon founding, notably in the northern context, with further references. I am grateful to Dr Bewer for allowing access to her research prior to publication.

44. Blackmore 1976, p. 408, quoting Sieur de Praissac, *Les discours militaires*, 1625. See, for example, Engels and Sanderson-Engels 1996, p. 48 (I am grateful to Jean-Marie Welter for this reference), citing a Viking bell with a copper-tin-lead ratio of 75/19/6. They give modern bell alloy as containing a minimum of 20 per cent tin; stating that 2 per cent of impurities are tolerated, including no more than 1 per cent lead; see also nn. 48 and 49 below, and Jennings 1988, p. 12, re. impurities.

45. Biringuccio/Smith and Gnudi 1990, p. 268 (Biringuccio 1540, VI, 97).

46. Theophilus/Dodwell 1986, p. 121; Theophilus/Hawthorne and Smith 1979, p. 140.

47. Gauricus/Chastel and Klein 1969, p. 218.

48. Biringuccio/Smith and Gnudi 1990, p. 210 (Biringuccio 1540, V, 74). See p. 31 re. tuning bells, and for the addition of antimony, silver and gold to improve the tone.

49. *Ciga Hotels Magazine*, XXI, 107, 28 July 1993, pp. 38 and 41, gives the proportions used by the Colbacchini foundry near Padua as 78/22. The two remaining English bell-foundries use the other proportions quoted; Jennings 1988, p. 12. See also n. 44 above.

50. Theophilus/Dodwell 1986, p. 25 (Theophilus/Hawthorne and Smith 1979, p. 34); although this alloy is still basically bell-metal, it differs from Theophilus's recipe for bells (80/20).

51. Biringuccio/Smith and Gnudi 1990, p. 300 (Biringuccio 1540, VII, 109v).

52. See p. 22 and n. 48 above.

53. See nn. 51 and 7 above.

54. For a full discussion, see Biringuccio/Smith and Gnudi 1990, p. 300 (1540, VII, 109–109v). The addition of tin does not, in fact, counteract the negative properties of the copper, see p. 38.

55. Peal 1974, p. 827.

56. Gauricus/Chastel and Klein 1969, pp. 220, 221, n. 18. See p. 30 for further comments on foundry experience and practice.

57. Leonardo/Richter 1970, II, pp. 23–4; Richter 740.

58. See also Blackmore 1976, quoting George Smith, *Universal Military Dictionary*, 1779, where he states that the alloy for cannon was often kept secret and that each founder used his own proportions. See also Bewer 2002, with further references.

59. See pp. 31–3; also Launert 1990, pp. 27–8.

60. See p. 32 for bells; see Blackmore 1976 for cannon, some of which had a comparatively short life.

61. See de Tolnay 1969, p. 38; Scalini 1988, p. 68.

62. John Evelyn, *A discourse of Medals, Ancient and Modern*, London, 1697, p. 70. I am grateful to Philip Attwood for bringing this reference to my attention; he advises that these were actually ancient coins, rather than medals.

63. At least 3,200 mortars were destroyed in 1936 to cast the bell (now lost) for the Principe di Piemonte hospital in Addis Ababa, Ethiopia, then an Italian colony under the fascist regime. The mortars were displayed in an exhibition before the majority were melted down; those considered to be the best were conserved in the Nobile Collegio Chimico Farmaceutico in Rome (Sbarigia 1985 illustrates mortars from the collection). The bell was cast in the papal foundry at Agnone, but although it arrived in Addis Ababa, it was not put in place at the hospital because of the war and passed eventually to a church of St George. However, it was never rung, either due to damage or poor conservation. I am grateful to Dott. Patrizia Catellani, who recounted the story in a letter of 31 August 1997.

    A list of regions in Italy, with numbers alongside, published under the title 'Mortai alla Patria!' in *Il Farmacista*, 1936, Ser II, XIV, IV, n. 1, pp. 148–9, presumably indicates some of those donated.

64. Launert 1990, p. 5.

Summary Bibliography
Primary sources: Pliny; Theophilus; Gauricus; Leonardo; Biringuccio; Cellini; Vasari.

Secondary sources: Fortnum 1876; Rich 1947, pp. i–ccx; Aitchison 1960, with additional references; Craddock 1990; Launert 1990; Penny 1993; Roberts 1994; Francesca Bewer in Berlin 1995, pp. 82–91; Boström 1995, esp. pp. 814–15; Bewer 1996; Butters 1996, with additional references; Paul Craddock in TDA 1996, 4, pp. 848–52, 855.

Facture and Foundries

1. Theophilus/Dodwell 1986, pp. 150–8; Theophilus/Hawthorne and Smith 1979, pp. 167–79.

2. Biringuccio/Smith and Gnudi 1990, p. 72 (hammering brass; Biringuccio 1540, I, 20) and p. 73 (casting brass; Biringuccio 1540, I, 20); pp. 260–77 (Biringuccio 1540, VI, 94–100v); pp. 327–8 (sand-casting; Biringuccio 1540, VIII, 120v); pp. 329–32 (reliefs, including plaquettes; Biringuccio 1540, VIII, 121–2v). See also Cellini/Ashbee 1967, pp. 62–3 re. sand-casting silver seals.

3. For a clear description, see Jennings 1989, pp. 14–21.

4. Schilling 1988, pp. 55–8, and figs 84–8; also included is a chronological list of sources.

5. Diderot, III, 1753, pp. 539–43; Diderot *Planches* 1767, 'Fonte de Cloches' pls I–VIII, with an explanation of the method.

6. See Jennings 1987, pp. 1–4; Jennings 1988, pp. 9–16 for a well-illustrated description of this method.

7. A church bell inscribed RESTORO ME FECIT MCCLXXIII (Restoro ordered me [to be made] 1273) falls outside the scope of this catalogue (inv. no. M.127-1929; Metalwork Department).

8. Evidence of facture is highlighted in the catalogue entries.

9. Jennings 1988, p. 9, distinguishes between 'iron strickle, crook or wooden sweepboard', but in the primary texts only wooden tools are mentioned.

10. For a detailed description, see Biringuccio/Smith and Gnudi 1990, pp. 261–2 (Biringuccio 1540, VI, 94–100); see p. 31 for further discussion of the bell-scale.

11. See Drescher 1992, p. 407, fig. 3, for a reconstruction of Theophilus's description.

12. Hildburgh 1946, p. 132; Montagu 1989, p. 50, refers to the use of lead dies, also described by Biringuccio in connection with casting reliefs (Biringuccio/Smith and Gnudi 1990, p. 330; Biringuccio 1540, VIII, 121). The use of copper moulds is illustrated in Diderot *Planches* 1767, loc. cit. at n. 5, pl. III, figs 8 and 9. A brass mould for a small figure of the *Virgin and Child* is in the Collection (M.97-1929; Metalwork Department). See also The Materials, n. 5.

13. See Blagg 1974, notably for a detailed study of production. Schilling 1988 illustrates numerous models for wax inscriptions and decoration.

14. Verona 1979, p. 123; the Jacopo bell from S. Zeno was incised into the inner surface of the cope (Thomas Blagg, lecture for the British Archaeological Association, 3 March 1993).

15. Cennini/Thompson 1960, p. 129.

16. For life-casting in bronze and ceramic, see Ernst Kris, 'Der Stil "Rustique". Die Verwendung des Naturabgusses bei Wenzel Jamnitzer und Bernard Palissy' in *Jahrbuch der Kunsthistorischen Sammlungen in Wien*, 18, 1926, pp. 137–208; Montagu 1989, pp. 52–5, for the so-called 'lost-lizard' process; Leonard N. Amico, *Bernard Palissy. In search of earthly paradise*, Paris and New York, 1996, pp. 86–107, for a detailed description of the casting from moulds of animals used by a sixteenth-century goldsmith and by the Palissy workshop.

17. Biringuccio gives examples: a lost-wax mould was made from either modelled or moulded wax, or the canons were modelled in clay from which a two-part mould was taken, which could be reassembled for insertion into the cope (Biringuccio/Smith and Gnudi 1990, p. 266; Biringuccio 1540, VI, 96).

18. Modern sand-cast bells are gated at the rim.

19. The method of location of the core varies according to the different foundry practices.

20. In relation to casting bronze figures, Vasari emphasizes the importance of removing all the wax from the mould, and the skill involved, as 'if any of the wax be left, it would ruin the whole cast, especially that part where the wax remains'. Vasari/Maclehose 1960, pp. 162–3. See also Cellini/Ashbee 1967, p. 118, where he stressed the need to remove the wax by gentle firing and added, 'When the wax is all out give the mould yet another but very moderate firing, in order to get rid of any moisture that may be left in the mould'. See also Biringuccio/Smith and Gnudi 1990, pp. 249–55 (Biringuccio 1540, VI, 89v–91v) on moulds in general, including the importance of baking thoroughly. This applies to all casting.

21. For furnaces, see p. 30; nn. 43 and 46 below.

22. See Bewer 1996, pp. 73–4, re. shrinkage.

23. See Launert 1990, illus. on p. 32.

24. Biringuccio/Smith and Gnudi 1990, p. 268 (Biringuccio 1540, VI, 97).

25. Biringuccio also talks of slitting the bell cope at one side with an iron cutting tool, although it is unclear how this is then repaired; Biringuccio/Smith and Gnudi 1990, p. 265 (Biringuccio 1540, VI, 95v–96).

26. See Lothian 1958, pp. 706–8, for descriptions and wooden moulds.

27. Publicity leaflet of the Colbacchini foundry, *c.*1996, kindly provided by Giovanni Colbacchini.

28. Gauricus/Chastel and Klein 1969, p. 216.

29. Vasari/Maclehose 1960, pp. 159, 161.

30. Cellini/Ashbee 1967, p. 113; Biringuccio discusses clays for cores and moulds in various contexts; see Biringuccio/Smith and Gnudi 1990, pp. 218–21, for general bronze casting (Biringuccio 1540, VI, 76v–78v); and pp. 228–9 for statues (Biringuccio 1540, VI, 81). See also Blagg 1974.

31. See Jennings 1988, p. 9, for a modern recipe.

32. Gauricus/Chastel and Klein 1969, p. 222.

33. Vasari/Maclehose 1960, p. 163.

34. Biringuccio/Smith and Gnudi 1990, p. 266 (Biringuccio 1540, VI, 96). He recommends these calculations in case there are any discrepancies in the bell-scale; his calculation for metal loss varies between 5 and 10 per cent. Jennings 1988, p. 12, suggests an allowance of 5 per cent loss through evaporation.

35. Cellini/Ashbee 1967, p. 124, where he outlines the various tasks required to remedy the problem of the cake of metal that had formed in the cast, including adding oak to the furnace as opposed to the usual softwoods required for bronze furnaces, to provide greater heat; Cellini/Bull 1956 (1979), p. 347, where he gives more detail. The reason for the problem was apparently due to Cellini lending new metal and receiving metal with less tin in the replacement batch (Bewer 1996, p. 16). See also Cole 1999 for the *Perseus*. Biringuccio also mentions a variety of woods used for furnaces: Biringuccio/Smith and Gnudi 1990, p. 295 (Biringuccio 1540, VII, 107).

36. Theophilus/Dodwell 1986, p. 155.

37. Ibid., p. 154.

38. Biringuccio mentions chestnut: Biringuccio/Smith and Gnudi 1990, p. 296 (Biringuccio 1540, VII, 107v).

39. Jennings 1988, p. 12.

40. Biringuccio/Smith and Gnudi 1990, p. 333 (Biringuccio 1540, VIII, 122v).

41. Biringuccio contains many references to the preparation of alloys, and Baxandall 1966 also provides recipes (especially p. 130).

42. Largely consisting of cupric and stannic gases (from the copper and tin).

43. For reverberatory furnaces, see Blagg 1974, pp. 137–8, with additional references, including Biringuccio 1540, VII, 101v–104 (Biringuccio/Smith and Gnudi 1990, pp. 281–8, with diagrams).

44. See Biringuccio/Smith and Gnudi 1990, note on pp. 222–3 on the development of gun founding, with additional references.

45. Biringuccio/Smith and Gnudi 1990, p. 285 (Biringuccio 1540, VII, 103); for Leonardo, see Bewer 1985; Cole Ahl 1995.

46. For means of melting metals, including furnace construction, see Biringuccio/Smith and Gnudi 1990, pp. 281–300 (Biringuccio 1540, VII, 101v–109v); see also Cellini/Ashbee 1967, p. 81 for casting precious metals in a 'mortar', p. 82 re. 'bake-oven' interior furnace; pp. 118–21 (re. *Perseus*), pp. 127–33 re. furnace construction. See also n. 43 above re. reverberatory furnaces.

47. Patination will be dealt with in greater detail in subsequent volumes. See Vasari/Maclehose 1960, pp. 165–6; Richard Stone, Raymond White and N. Indictor, 'The Surface Composition of Some Italian Renaissance Bronzes' in *ICOM Committee for Conservation, Proceedings from the 9th Meeting*, Dresden, 1990, II, pp. 568–73.

48. For instance, the mortar attributed to the Alberghetti foundry in the Louvre (see cat. no. 8, no. xii), which has (probably modern) parcel gilding.

49. See Glossary, p. 223. Gilding will be dealt with in more detail in subsequent volumes. For mercury-gilding, see in particular Pliny/Rackham 1961, IX, pp. 50, 51; Baxandall 1965; Cellini/Ashbee 1967, pp. 96–7; Oddy et al. 1979, pp. 182–6; Bennett and Wilkins 1984, p. 121. Experimentation has also been carried out by Killian Anheuser of the Courtauld Institute of Art, University of London.

50. For Theophilus on fire-gilding, see Theophilus/Dodwell 1986, pp. 88–92 and 126–7 re. gilding brass (Theophilus/ Hawthorne and Smith 1979, pp. 113–15, 145–6). See also Oddy et al. 1979, pp. 182, 184 for the *à l'hache* method of applying gold foil to the roughened metal surface, then hammering and burnishing. See also Penny 1993, p. 301, plus additional pages as indexed.

51. See, for example, Vasari/Maclehose 1960, pp. 248–50.

52. See Anthony Radcliffe and Charles Avery, 'The Chellini Madonna by Donatello' in *The Burlington Magazine*, CXVIII (June 1976), pp. 377–87. The medium has not been analysed, but the suggestion that animal glue was used is based on a visual examination by Jonathan Ashley-Smith in the 1970s.

53. See Baltimore 1997, pp. 183–5, no. 59, with earlier literature.

54. Theophilus/Dodwell 1986, pp. 158–9 (Theophilus/ Hawthorne and Smith, pp. 176–9); Jennings 1988, pp. 17–19 (with clipping hammer illus.).

55. Biringuccio/Smith and Gnudi 1990, p. 92 (Biringuccio 1540, II, 28) re. antimony; pp. 269, 270 (Biringuccio 1540, VI, 97, 97v–8) re. temperature of metal, shape, etc.

56. *Ciga Hotels Magazine*, XXI, 107, 28 July 1993, pp. 38 and 41. The presence of precious metal may be due to addition for such reasons, or due to reuse of metal.

57. Biringuccio/Smith and Gnudi 1990, pp. 270–1 (Biringuccio 1540, VI, 98); a form of rust was also said to form from rainwater, closing any porosity in the casting.

58. For the acoustics of bells, see Schad and Warlimont 1972; Rossing 1984; Schilling 1988, p. 54 ff.; Fletcher and Rossing, 1991.

59. See Jennings 1989, pp. 21–5, for hand bell clappers; he refers to early ones having 'shanks of iron or brass with a percussive ball of hardwood or metal' (p. 23).

60. Biringuccio/Smith and Gnudi 1990, p. 275, fig. 36 (Biringuccio 1540, VI, 100), and detail in Schilling 1988, p. 60, fig. 92. See also Diderot, III, 1753, p. 543, inc. examples of clapper/bell relationships.

61. Some hand bells and mortars may have been cast for general sale (see, for example, cat. no. 48). The time, effort and cost involved in casting, however, probably meant that the majority were made to order. A number of models (probably a little more expensive) were altered in the wax to incorporate the owner's arms (e.g. cat. no. 47), while in many cases the arms were attached subsequent to casting, but were probably still cast to order. Andrea di Scolare, for example, a founder in Mantua, recast two mortars for the ducal pharmacy in 1581. In the case of mortars, this is doubtless true in view of the requirements of the apothecary and the quantity of metal required. A few may have been made, along with other utensils, in the foundry's 'downtime', or perhaps allowance was made for some smaller pieces to be prepared when casting a commissioned work.

62. For further discussion of foundry production, see Motture 1997 and Motture 2002 (forthcoming). See p. 34 for earlier production of bells.

63. Fabriczy 1904, p. 99; see also Caplow 1977, pp. 438–40, esp. n. 39 with additional references; Blagg 1978, p. 431.

64. Rosenauer 1992, inc. figs 55, 58–61; Butterfield 1997, pp. 11–15; p. 202, cat. 2; pls 11 and 12.

65. See Cellini/Ashbee 1967, p. 122; Geneviève Bresc-Bautier in South Brisbane 1988, pp. 15–19, re. the Parisian foundries.

66. Biringuccio/Smith and Gnudi 1990, p. 214 (Biringuccio 1540, VI, 75v).

67. See V. Avery 2002.

68. Biringuccio/Smith and Gnudi 1990, p. 289 (Biringuccio 1540, VII, 104v). See also n. 72 below.

69. See A. Fappani, *Enciclopedia Bresciana*, IV, Brescia, 1981, p. 225, 'Fonderie' re. Brescia; and V. Avery 2001 re. Giambologna. See cat. nos 53–5 for bells probably produced in Brescia.

70. See V. Avery 2002. I am grateful to Dr Avery for allowing me access to her text prior to publication.

71. Staley 1906, pp. 307–8, for Florence; Verona 1979, pp. 63–4: there was no mention of bell-founders in the Veronese statutes of 1536, but they are included as a subdivision in 1756. For the various functions of guilds in general in different centres, see Goldthwaite 1980, pp. 242–86; and see n. 75 below.

72. See Blagg 1974, p. 134, re. itinerant founders; see cat. nos 46–8 for Bonaventurini; 49–51 for de Levis and 62 for De Maria.

73. See Blagg 1974, p. 234, for the dated Crescimbene bell in the church of Civitella Benazzone. See also a mortar signed CRESCENBENE ME FECIT; Buenos Aires 1967, no. 64.

74. See, for example, Welch 1997, pp. 91–3, for 'family firms' and other collaborative workshop practices.

75. For guilds in Venice, see Mackenney 1987; Maria Santini Anzalone et al., *Le Insegne delle Arti Veneziane al Museo Correr*, Venice, 1980; Fortini Brown 1997, pp. 41–8, provides a useful summary on the Venetian guilds.

Bells: History and Uses

1. See Gerhard Eimer, *Bernt Notke. Das Wirken eines niederdeutschen Künstlers im Ostseeraum*, Cologne, 1985, esp. fig. 15.12 and pl. XIV. There are several crotal bells in the Museum's Metalwork collection.

2. Enc. Ital., VIII, pl. CXVIII.

3. See Engels and Sanderson-Engels 1996, p. 48 (giving the origins as being in the fifth century); TDA 1996, 3, p. 627 (as sixth century); Blagg 1978, p. 424 (as probably seventh or eighth century for large bell casting); see also Diderot, III, 1753, p. 539b, for different legends regarding the origin of bells, including that based on Quintillian, that bells were first cast at Nola in Campania, hence their name *campanae*.

4. Enc. Ital., VIII, pls CXVIII and CXIV.

5. Mackenney 1987, p. 17.

6. Verona 1979, pp. 10, 55–6, 59–60, 129, for *Rengo* and *Marangona*; Motture 1997, p. 102. See p. 23 for destruction and reuse of bell-metal; Biringuccio/Smith and Gnudi 1990, pp. 275–7 (Biringuccio 1540, VI, 100–100v) for repairing large bells (with diagram).

7. Hay and Law 1989 (1991), p. 208.

8. Quoted from Staley 1906, p. 74; see also pp. 73, 179 for the Florentine bells, their naming and functions.

9. Padua 1986, pl. opposite p. 34 for a fourteenth-century miniature showing a bishop blessing a bell, and illus. on pp. 225, 227 and 229 for recent blessing ceremonies of bells; p. 228, no. 11, re. the benediction of bell-metal before the bell is cast.

10. Hay 1989, pp. 129 and 139–40; see also Gerhard Podhradsky, *New Dictionary of the Liturgy*, London, 1967; Motture 1997, p. 107, n. 4, for further references. See also Padua 1986, pp. 67–77, for the bells of the Arena Chapel and their function.

11. Padua 1986, pl. opposite p. 40.

12. See, for example, Major Alfred Heales, *The Archaeology of the Christian Altar in Western Europe with its Adjuncts, Furniture and Ornaments*, London, 1881, pp. 79–81.

13. Trento 1993, p. 387, no. 131.

14. See Padua 1986; Montevecchi and Vasco Rocca 1988, pp. 284–6; and Barbolini Ferrari and Boccolari 1996, pp. 86–7, for a variety of examples.

15. Giulia Bartrum, *German Renaissance Prints 1490–1550* (exh. cat.; British Museum), London, 1995, pp. 46–8, no. 33. The print had medical and alchemical associations.

16. For example, Barbolini Ferrari and Boccolari 1996, p. 86.

17. Avery 1981 (1972), pp. 45, 50–1, figs 1 and 13.

18. See Motture 1997, p. 104 and n. 29, for references.

19. Motture 1997, p. 100 and pl. 6.1 for Ottoboni, p. 107, nn. 4–7 for further references; Jaynie Anderson (ed.), Giovanni Morelli, *Della Pittura Italiana, Studii Storico-Critici Le Gallerie Borghese e Doria-Pamphili in Rome*, Milan, 1991, pp. 138, 139 fig. 22 for Cervini; *Bernardo Cles e l'Arte del Rinascimento nel Trentino* (exh. cat.), Trento, 1985, p. 29 (pl. 13) and p. 34 (pl. 19) for Cles portraits.

20. Pechstein 1968, no. 98.

21. D. S. Chambers, *A Renaissance Cardinal and his Worldly Goods: The Will and Inventory of Francesco Gonzaga (1444–1483)*, London, 1992, pp. 37, 105, 147 (no. I 96). See also several references to hand or 'table' bells in the correspondence between Philipp Hainhofer and Gustavus Adolphus of Sweden; for example, Hainhofer/Gobiet 1984, p. 293, no. 488; p. 296, no. 495; p. 631, no. 1204, and so on.

22. See Motture 1997, p. 107, n. 6; Thornton 1997, p. 38, fig. 24 (Lotto) and figs 27 and 28, pp. 42, 43 (Carpaccio), also p. 36 for cardinals' bells, pp. 128, 144 for bells in the scholar's studio.

Summary Bibliography

Enc. Ital. VIII, pp. 56–6, 570–1; Diderot, III, 1753, pp. 539–43; Ellacombe 1872; Blagg 1974; Blagg 1978; Verona 1979; Avery 1981 (1972); Percival Price, 'Handbells from Earliest Times' (1973) in Rossing 1984, pp. 12–27; Schilling 1985; Padua 1986; Schilling 1988; Jennings 1988; Jennings 1989; TDA 1996, 3, pp. 625–8; Engels and Sanderson-Engels 1996; Motture 1997.

Mortars: History and Uses

1. Launert 1990, illus. p. 7.

2. Ibid., illus. p. 9.

3. Ibid., fig. 42: Asia Minor or Cyprus, first century BC, Schweizerisches Pharmazie-Historisches Museum, Basel.

4. Lawall and Lawall 1934, p. 571, no substantiating reference provided.

5. Launert 1990, fig. 46; first century AD, Manchester Museum, Manchester, 'Albinus F[ecit] LUGUDU[NI]'.

6. A variety of interesting mortars are included in Lawall and Lawall 1934, including, for example, a bronze mortar from Palestine, inscribed and dated 1226 (fig. 12), a Syrian coffee mortar of the fourteenth century (fig. 5) and an ornamental anthracite coal mortar (fig. 14). Examples of mortars made of a variety of materials, including ivory, alabaster and wood, are also included. See also, especially, Launert 1990.

7. H. 22.8; diam. 29. Frequently cited, but see Lothian 1958, p. 705; Launert 1990, p. 102, no. 58.

8. Formerly Camillo Castiglioni Collection; h. 28.5, diam. 37.0. Muller (Castiglioni) 1925, no. 98; Lise and Bearzi 1975, pp. 30–2, fig. 25.

9. Archaeological Museum, Istanbul; h. about 42, diam. 38. Lise and Bearzi 1975, pp. 29–30, fig. 22; Launert 1990, p. 69.

10. Evident in the studies on English mortars, and in Launert 1990, where the illustrations are arranged by country of origin. See pp. 47–51 for the decoration of bells and mortars.

11. Middeldorf 1981, pp. 10–12.

12. See Crellin and Hutton 1973, pp. 268–9, and references, including a quote from William Bullein, *Bulwarke of Defence…*, London, 1562, under 'Apothecaries Rules'. Bullein was a physician who travelled and studied in Europe, and wrote extensively on health and cures (see DNB, III, pp. 244–6).

13. Montevecchi and Vasco Rocca 1988, p. 266.

14. *Pharmaceutical Journal*, 1955, p. 354; note, however, that according to Crellin and Hutton 1973, p. 266, n. 2, the mortar 'did not achieve the same popularity [in England] as a symbol as it did on the Continent'.

15. The Whitechapel foundry in London still makes them, for example.

16. Paul Ghalioungui, *The Ebers Papyrus. A New English Translation, Commentaries and Glossaries*, Cairo, 1987. The Ebers Papyrus is so called because it was first translated by Georg Moritz Ebers (1875): there are many references to grinding (e.g. p. 189: 741), but the word 'mortar' is not indexed. Lawall and Lawall are, therefore, apparently correct in their assertion that there is no specific reference to the use of mortars in early pictorial scripts, such as the Ebers Papyrus (Lawall and Lawall 1934, p. 570). This is directly contradicted by Matthews, who cites the Ebers Papyrus as a documented source for the use of mortars for pulverizing acacia gum (Matthews 1971, p. 29).

17. 'One takes the whole, the parts, and the excrements of animals… All animals may be used, such as earth-worms, scorpions, hedgehogs and swallows…' (p. 3), the whole passage quoted by Olmi in Zanca 1987, p. 178. The book was the official pharmacopoeia of the Medici Grand Dukes.

18. Several examples are cited in Impey and MacGregor 1985; see Hainhofer Gobiet 1984, p. 858. For unicorn horn and its various associations, see Lisa Gotfriedsen (trans. Anne Born), *The Unicorn*, London, 1999.

19. See Giuseppe Olmi, 'Science-Honour-Metaphor: Italian cabinets of the sixteenth and seventeenth centuries' in Impey and MacGregor 1985, pp. 5–16 and figs 1 and 4; Olmi in Zanca 1987, pp. 176–7 re. Calzolari. For the Bolognese doctor and philosopher, Ulisse Aldrovandi (1522–1605), his museum and writings, see Olmi, op. cit. 1985, and idem in Zanca 1987, pp. 162–70.

20. See, for example, ibid., pp. 178–9; the exact ingredients were much debated, and its use was gradually banned by the different authorities. See Origo 1992, pp. 286, 376, n. 1; theriac was recommended by some doctors to be taken before leaving the house each day in order to guard against the plague.

21. Pliny/Rackham 1961, XXXIV, p. 79; the type of mortar is not specified.

22. See R. Tomlinson, *Renodaeus his Dispensatory*, London, 1657, p. 60, quoted in Crellin and Hutton 1973, pp. 266–7.

23. Tomlinson 1657, op. cit. at n. 22, p. 61, quoted from Crellin and Hutton 1973, p. 267.

24. Quoted from *The Urinal of Physick*, London, 1651, pp. 160–1, in Crellin and Hutton 1973, p. 268; and unreferenced in Lawall and Lawall 1934, p. 371. Recorde was born in Wales, studied medicine at Cambridge and became the royal doctor. (DNB, XVI, 1917, pp. 810–12.)

25. I am grateful to Jo Castle for her practical advice. She also advised the avoidance of acidic ingredients, such as citrus or vinegar, in bronze mortars.

26. See Crellin and Hutton 1973, p. 268, quoting Moyse Charas, *The Royal Pharmacopoeia*, London, 1678, pp. 187, 131–3, for reference to sizes; p. 271 referring to T. Redwood in 1845, for the link between choice of mortar material and type of grinding action. Charas studied pharmacy at Montpellier and Blois and became pharmacist to the Duke of Orleans, and to Charles II. He wrote on natural history, theriac, as well as the *Pharmacopée royale galénique et chimique*, 1676 (see *Dictionnaire de Biographie Française*, Paris, 1959, p. 464).

27. Crellin and Hutton 1973, p. 268 and references.

28. Paracelsus/Waite 1992, p. 216. According to Hoblyn, the term 'opodeldoc' was an obscure term introduced by Paracelsus, meaning a solution of soap in alcohol with the addition of camphor and volatile oils (Richard D. Hoblyn (rev. John A. P. Price), *A Dictionary of terms used in Medicine…*, London, 1892, p. 508); here it could be interpreted as the

'mixture'. Paracelsus's full name was Auroleus Phillipus Theostratus Bombastus von Hohenheim.

29. Several examples of the small mortars survive in the Science Museum, London.

30. See Hans-Olaf Boström, 'Philipp Hainhofer and Gustavus Adolphus's *Kunstschrank* in Uppsala' in Impey and MacGregor 1985, pp. 90–101, for a discussion, including different views on the usefulness of *Kunstkammer* objects. This particular mortar is of a larger scale than some of the miniature examples. The variety of objects included plant, animal and mineral medicinal ingredients, and small bronzes and silver objects, including life-casts of small mammals and insects. See also Hainhofer/Gobiet 1984, pp. 820, 858, for references to mortars and pestles, alongside other contents of the *Kunstkammern*. I am grateful to Norbert Jopek for this reference.

31. See Origo 1992, p. 293. Horace Wright of Edgware described his memory of using mortars in this way in a letter to *The Chemist and Druggist*, 2 January 1954, p. 9: 'I have always been attracted by mortars, even when I had to use one with its pestle attached to a ratchet on the ceiling, to grind down aloes or resin, or to mix black antimony, sulphur, grains of paradise, and ginger into condition powder for horses, finishing with a very black face and streaming eyes and nose. But that was fifty years ago.'

32. See also Launert 1990, illus. on p. 41 and fig. 156 showing a variety of stands in an illustration of an apothecary's shop, German 1798; Cowen and Helfand 1990, p. 87: 'Large mortars stood on pedestals in the form of feet or claws or even a sculpture of a whole animal.'

33. Matthews 1971, p. 31.

34. Cazala 1953, p. 70. Lawall and Lawall 1934, p. 573, suggests that the ring handle frequently found on Arabic and Moorish mortars facilitated attaching the mortar to caravans for transport; see p. 575, fig. 11b.

35. The terms 'apothecary' and 'pharmacist' have been used interchangeably, although technically 'apothecary' was used until the late seventeenth century and 'pharmacist' thereafter. I am grateful to Jo Castle for this observation.

36. Pagel 1986, p. 322. Vesalius spent much of his time in Italy.

37. Although from at least the fifteenth century commercial liaison between doctors and apothecaries was forbidden in Rome and elsewhere, associations continued in some centres, where joint practices were set up; see particularly Cowen and Helfand 1990, p. 70.

38. Willis 1989, p. 32 (from E. J. King, *The Early Statutes of the Knights Hospitaller*, London, 1932).

39. I am grateful to Pamela Willis for this suggestion.

40. Guilds were established at Padua (1260), Florence (1349), Siena (1346), Bologna (1377), Cremona (1388), Milan (1389); Corvi 1997, pp. 134–5, 138.

41. Pedrazzini 1934, p. 28. Note also that several bell-founders were described as *formaggi* (see Motture 1997).

42. See, for example, A. Corradi, *Gli Antichi Statuti degli Speziali*, Milan, 1886; Bernardo Bernardi, 'Gli Statuti degli Speziali' in Corvi 1997, pp. 131–51; Menichetti 1974, p. 35 for Gubbio. For interrelationships between the guild and doctors' training, see Origo 1992, pp. 298–9; and p. 377, n. 20, re. guild membership in Florence.

43. For the variety, see for example Origo 1992, p. 293.

44. For an interesting discussion on the different views on the interrelationship and comparative status of physicians and surgeons, see Pagel 1986, pp. 320–1.

45. See Pedrazzini 1934, p. 273.

46. Nutton 1997, esp. pp. 15–16.

47. From *Le Médecin charitable*, quoted from Cowen and Helfand 1990, pp. 86–7.

48. Menichetti 1974, p. 53.

49. Maggioni 1952, pp. 492–3.

50. The choice of treatment was often based on a system known as *similia similibus*, whereby a 'like' substance was used to heal the ailment; scorpion bite was therefore treated with the oil of scorpion. Pier Andrea Mattioli (1501–77) was a Sienese doctor who provided an important commentary on Dioscorides (1544), based on his observations of the natural world. His translation and text were of practical use for doctors and apothecaries (see, for example, Giuseppe Olmi, 'The Renaissance of Pharmaceutical Studies', in Zanca 1987, pp. 151–62). Mattioli's emphasis on the need to understand the nature of the substances used, and therefore how they worked, echoed the importance laid on experience and knowledge outlined by Biringuccio and others when they discussed the work of the founder. See below, p. 44, re Cosimo I and Mattioli.

51. For Padua: Maggioni 1952, pp. 493–4; for Gubbio: Menichetti 1974, pp. 45–53, including, among others, antimony, cardamom, mummy, scorpion oil and theriac.

52. See Lawall and Lawall 1934, pp. 580–1, figs 33 and 34.

53. See, for example, Leonardo/Richter 1970, pp. 429, 447 (Richter 1421, 1482, 1483) on Avicenna; p. 449 (Richter 1491) on Hippocrates. There were no fewer than sixty Latin editions of Avicenna's *Canon* printed between 1500 and 1674, together with new commentaries; see Nancy G. Siraisi, *Avicenna in Renaissance Italy. The Canon and Medical Teaching in Italian Universities after 1500*, Princeton, 1987, p. 3. See also Nutton 1993 for the use of Greek texts, including Hippocrates.

54. For example, Pedrazzini 1934, p. 28.

55. Bessarion, a Greek by birth, was a humanist, author, collector and translator of manuscripts. He bequeathed his collection to the Republic of Venice. For Gonzaga, see Chambers 1992, pp. 66, 109, inventory nos. I 822, 829, 876, 895 for medical and surgical texts.

56. See Butters 1996, pp. 245–8, with references. For the relief, Pope-Hennessy 1964, II, no. 479, III, fig. 474; Butters 1996, pl. 1; figs 103–4; 105–7, pp. 311–12, 313, 313 nn., 317.

57. Peacock 1900.

58. Quoted from Olmi in Zanca 1987, p. 175. The various parts of the plants – e.g. leaf, flower, root – were known as simples.

59. See Butters 1996, esp. pp. 220, 246, re. Cosimo with additional references; Nutton 1997, p. 15, for further discussion and references.

60. For alchemy see, for example, H. Stanley Redgrove, 'Alchemy: Ancient and Modern', London, 1911; Thorndike 1923–58; Aitchison 1960; Roberts 1994; Butters 1996; Abraham 1998; additional references are given in the relevant catalogue entries.

61. Biringuccio/Smith and Gnudi 1990, pp. 35–44. Biringuccio discusses alchemy in its fullest sense, including a fascinating passage, in the light of current developments in genetic engineering, in which he dismisses the concept of the creation of animal life outside the mother's body and of plants without the seeds. He concludes with the comment, 'And likewise I can make no answer to those who say that they transmute but do not create, and that they transmute one species into another, for this cannot be done without the total destruction of the thing you wish to transmute'; p. 43 (Biringuccio 1540, I, 8; for the full passage see ibid., 5–8v). He also claimed that copper was the basis for 'all the works of the fraudulent alchemists, indeed it is the very body of their anatomy, as mercury is to the philosophic alchemists', Biringuccio/Smith and Gnudi 1990, p. 54 (Biringuccio 1540, I, 13). Nevertheless, a section of his treatise is devoted to describing the processes (see Biringuccio/Smith and Gnudi 1990, pp. 336 ff.; Biringuccio 1540, IX, 123 ff). See also Gauricus/Chastel and Klein 1969, pp. 214, 216, 224, 225.

62. See Butters 1996, II, pl. 77.

63. Abraham 1998, p. 131, for example, defines a mould and adds, 'The separation of unformed matter and its casting into a mould is a process which originated in the laboratory of the alchemist.' The act of founding was therefore associated with alchemy. Cole 1999 provides a fascinating and detailed insight into these associations, by examining the meaning of the casting of Cellini's *Perseus*, and the alchemical and philosophical associations of Medusa's blood, particularly in relation to the Greek theory of metals being derived from watery substances under the earth. See also Cole 2002.

64. See for example Jardine 1997, pp. 53–4.

65. Lawall and Lawall 1934, pp. 579–80, fig. 30.

66. Inv. no. 118, h. 31, diam. 46 (rim), 32 (base).

67. From MS 485 in the Wellcome Institute Library, dated 1598. Information kindly supplied by Jo Castle, who generously shared her research. See Zanca 1987, p. 186, regarding books of secrets.

68. Matthews 1971, p. 30.

69. Cennini/Thompson 1967, pp. 25, 28, 37.

70. Ibid., p. 24.

71. Cellini/Ashbee 1967, p. 17; see also Butters 1996, p. 198.

72. Quoted from Matthews 1971, p. 33, with the reference MS 1 Ed VI (1546–7) Ants. Gustavus Brander, Book A, fol. 165b.

73. See Middeldorf 1981, p. 19, for examples.

74. I am grateful to Jo Castle for this information.

75. Peck 1932, p. 26.

76. Compare, for example, the listing of the trecento inventory, with the mortars and their pestles identified together, and another of 1631 with them listed as separate items. Marcella Marghelli, 'L'Arredo di una Spezieria Ferrarese del Trecento' in *Atti e Memorie dell'Accademica di Storia della Farmacia*, IV/1, 1997, pp. 25–8: *Item unum mortale de cupro magnum a piperata; Item unum pistonum magnum ad pistandum piperatam; Item unum mortale parvum de cupro et unum pistonum parvum de fero*; and Loredano Pessa, 'Contributo alla Storia della Ceramica. La Farmacia Ligure nel XVII secolo: l'Inventorio della Bottega del Sole' in ibid., pp. 17–24: *no. uno mortaro di pietra; no. 2 mortari di bronzo; no. 3 pestelli di bronzo; no. uno pestello di ferro; no uno mortaro di piombo; no. 3 pestelli di legno.*

77. Pedrazzini 1934, p. 153; Cazala 1953, p. 69. The source of the rhyme is unknown, but it may have had other connotations; see also, for example, Enrico Bianchi, Carlo Salinari and Natalino Sapegno (eds), *Giovanni Boccaccio, Decameron*, Milan and Naples, 1952, pp. 531–7, esp. p. 537. I am grateful to Marta Ajmar for drawing this to my attention, and for refining the translation.

Summary Bibliography

Peacock 1900; Davison 1906; Maskew 1926; Peck 1932; Conci 1934; Lawall and Lawall 1934; Pedrazzini 1934; Cazala 1953; Aitchison 1960; Matthews 1971; Crellin and Hutton 1973; Middledorf 1981; Boussel, Bonnemain and Bové 1983; Pagel 1986; Zanca 1987; Launert 1990; Cowen and Helfand 1990; Paracelsus/Waite 1992; Nutton 1993; Butters 1996; Corvi 1997; Nutton 1997; Abraham 1998.

Further Reading

Numerous articles on the specific regions in Italy are included in *Il Farmacista* (and *Il Farmacista Italiano*), notably 1936, 1948, 1950, 1951, 1952, and *Atti e Memorie dell'Accademia di Storia della Farmacia*; Lloyd 1934; E. Saville Peck, 'Bell Mortars' in *The Chemist and Druggist*, 1952; E. Saville Peck, 'Bell-Metal Mortars' in *Alchemist*, 1952; Alcide Garosi, *Siena nella Storia della Medicina (1240–1555)*, Florence, 1958; Prof. Wolf-Dieter Müller-Jahncke, 'Naturwissenschaften, Naturphilosophie und Alchemie bei Paracelsus', in *Atti del Convegno Internazionale su Paracelso*, Rome, 1994, pp. 69 ff.; and Dr Charles Webster, 'Paracelsus on Natural and Popular Magic' in ibid., pp. 89 ff.

Decoration of Bells and Mortars

1. For further discussion, see Motture 1997 and Motture forthcoming. The problematic question of dating on the basis of emblematic decoration was addressed in connection with English mortars in Peal 1974.

2. Quoted in Benedetti 1923; inkstands are discussed in detail in Thornton 1997, pp. 142–67.

3. Pope-Hennessy 1965, p. 125, no. 462, fig. 550; further discussed in Motture forthcoming.

4. See Gertrude Moakley, *The Tarot Cards Painted by Bonifacio Bembo for the Visconti-Sforza Family. An Iconographic and Historical Study*, New York, 1966, pp. 78–9; Michael Dummett, *The Visconti-Sforza Tarot Cards*, New York, 1986, pp. 118–19 (examples from the set survive in the Pierpont Morgan Library, New York, and the Accademia Carrara, Bergamo). For the Museum's collection, see Jean Hamilton, *Playing Cards in the Victoria and Albert Museum*, London, 1988.

5. The apples of the Hesperides (obtained by Hercules in one of his labours) were seen as precursors to the apple of the Tree of Knowledge, itself a symbol of the Fall and thus of the role of the Redeemer in granting everlasting life. Both the tarot and alchemy had links with Cabalism.

6. See Alison Wright, 'Piero de' Medici and the Pollaiuolo' in Andreas Beyer and Bruce Boucher, *Piero de' Medici "il Gottoso" (1416–1469)*, Berlin, 1993, pp. 129–49, with additional reference; Cirlot/Sage 1977, pp. 144–5; Hall 1974, pp. 147–53.

7. See Cirlot/Sage, p. 51, re. Asclepius and healing associations.

8. See Middeldorf 1981, pp. 46–53, no. 12; *The Burlington Magazine*, CXVII, February 1975, illus p. xli (Albrecht Neuhaus advertisement for the sale of the mortar from the collection of Johannes Jantzen).

9. Ripa 1618 (1986), II, p. 21, refers to a snake not a lizard.

10. See also Pedrazzini 1934, p. 155, for an eighteenth-century mortar, similarly decorated with the lizard and sage and the IHS monogram with sage.

11. Inv. no. M.16-1939 (Metalwork Department); see Pechstein 1968, no. 8, for a related mortar, and a listing of other versions. See Tait 1988, pp. 96–105, no. 11, for the 'Cellini bell'. Several examples are shown in Schilling 1988.

12. Inv. no. M.18-1979.

13. Cirlot/Sage 1971, pp. 85–9; see also cat. no. 71.

14. One example is in the Bargello, Florence; inv. no. 707; acquired in 1913 from F. Pedulli; h. 14.2, diam. 16.2 (rim), 10.2 (base). See also p. 40.

15. English nineteenth-century poison bottles were both marked with ridges and coloured blue. I am grateful to Jemma Street and Reino Leifkes for bringing this to my attention.

16. See Pedrazzini 1934, p. 159, for a stone mortar, dated 1605.

17. See, for example, Pedrazzini 1934, p. 239, for a seventeenth-century flyleaf showing a mortar and pestle in the foreground.

18. For example, a seventeenth-century example from the pharmacy of the Ospedale S. Giacomo in Rome; Pedrazzini 1934, illus. p. 156.

19. Pechstein 1968, no. 185; V&A inv. no. 76-1904 without the frieze (Maclagan 1924, p. 61, pl. VII); and inv. no. 7378-1861 for *The true son refusing to shoot his father* with the frieze (ibid., p. 59, as *A prince receiving a prisoner*) the subject independently identified by Jennifer Montagu and Louis Waldman.

20. I am grateful to Douglas Lewis for this information.

21. Pope-Hennessy 1965, p. 152, no. 560, fig. 583; ter Kuile 1986, p. 237, no. 2280.

22. Inv. no. 1311, h. 7.8 (9.7 with ferrule), diam. 8.9.

23. Radcliffe 1994, pp. 20–3, no. 2; Motture forthcoming.

24. For pastiglia, see Hildburgh 1946, de Winter 1984, Manni 1986 and Pommeranz 1995 (p. 192, no. 244, for Vienna casket; p. 282, figs 76–7, for a version of this motif on a mortar in Berlin); Manni 1993, pp. 11–25, for Carlo di Monlione (from Brittany), active in France in the 1450s (see also Manni 1986, op. cit. pp. 29, 30, 68n and 72; TDA 1996, 24, pp. 248–9; also Franceschini 1995 (index).

25. See Hildburgh 1915.

26. See W. L. Hildburgh, in the *Proceedings* of the Society of Antiquaries for 1913–14, vol. xxvi, 144, for German wafering irons; Fritz Arens, 'Die ursprüngliche Verwendung gotischer Stein und Tonmodel...' in *Mainzer Zeitschrift*, 66, 1971, pp. 106–31, for moulds for marzipan cakes that also appear on German bells and mortars, also discussed in Jopek 2002, (forthcoming).

27. Hildburgh 1915, p. 23, no. 8, fig. 3.

28. Modern bell-foundries (such as the Whitechapel) carry out some ironwork, such as repairing clappers. Cellini also described how to make steel dies for stamping coins (Cellini/Ashbee 1967, pp. 67–71).

29. For a more detailed discussion, see Motture forthcoming.

30. For an interesting exemplar, see Luke Syson, 'Ercole de' Roberti: the making of a court artist' in 'Ercole de' Roberti The Renaissance in Ferrara', supplement in *The Burlington Magazine*, CXLI, April 1999, pp. iv–xiv. James Shaw has advised that his researches indicate an overlap of practices in Venice, despite guild restrictions which were often brought into play as required. This is more clearly evident in some professions than others (cf. apothecaries and doctors/surgeons). I am grateful to Dr Shaw for discussing his views.

31. See, for example, Motture 1997, pp. 105–6.

32. Biringuccio/Smith and Gnudi 1990, pp. 329–32 (Biringuccio 1540, VIII, 121–2v).

33. The variations of this design and their interrelationships are explored in detail in Cagliotti and Gasparotto 1997; see also Rome 1982, pp. 41–4, nos 9 and 10. See Francesco Rossi, 'Le Gemme Antiche e le Origini della Placchetta' (pp. 55–70) and Nicole Dacos, 'Le rôle des plaquettes dans la diffusion des gemmes antiques: Le case de la collection Médicis' (pp.

71–92) in Luchs 1989, for the gem/plaquettes relationship, and Schofield 1992 for plaquettes as a source for architectural decoration (also discussed by Cannata in Rome 1982, loc. cit.; see also Radcliffe in Luchs 1989, pp. 93–103).

34. Verona 1979, p. 10 and fig. 23. A *Virgin and Child* by Moderno also appears on a mortar formerly in the Bardini Collection (Christie's (Bardini) 1902, lot 484, pl. 6, no. 101); for the plaquette, see Rome 1982, pp. 51–2, no. 29, showing also the relationship with two paintings by Giampietrino in the Galleria Borghese, Rome.

35. I am grateful to Jeremy Warren, who made this discovery, for bringing it to my attention. For the plaquette, see V&A inv. no. A.40-1921; Maclagan 1924, p. 43 (as Paduan, *c.*1500–25; another mounted as a pax, inv. no. 4408-1857); Toderi and Toderi 1996, p. 132, nos 238 and 239.

36. See above regarding the Sforza bell in Washington, and a south German mortar (private collection, Washington (February 2000); see sale catalogue of the Collection of Miss Sylvia Adams, *Important Renaissance and Baroque Bronzes*, Bonhams, London, 23 May 1996, lot 80), decorated with clasped hands and initials, possibly indicating a marriage.

37. See pp. 30–1 for gilding and patination.

38. Kunsthistorisches Museum, Vienna, Kunstkammer inv. no. 5969, see *Rudolf II and Prague: the Court and the City* (exh. cat.), London 1997, p. 514, no. II.210.

39. See Avery 1981 (1972), pp. 45, 50–1, figs 1 and 13; Petit (Kann) 1910, lot 338, h. 12, as Paduan, sixteenth-century.

40. Avery 1981 (1977), p. 76, fig. 10; an example of the larger version of this model is in the collection, inv. no. A.22-1960.

41. Bargello, Florence, inv. no. 762, h. 14.8, 7.3 (without handle), diam. 8.2; Sotheby Parke Bernet, Inc., New York, 3 and 4 December 1982, lot 114, h. 15.2 (as figure of Juno).

42. See, for example: 'David' bells: Banzato and Pellegrini 1989, pp. 102–3, no. 79; Museo Correr, Venice, inv. nos. 248: h. 16.1, 7.3 (without handle), diam. 9.1; 436: h. 15, 6.5 (without handle), diam. 8.5; and for Venus: Bargello, Florence, inv. no. 748, h. 18, 7.5 (without handle), diam. 8.6; Trento, Castello del Buonconsiglio, inv. no. 3207, h. 18.6, diam. 8.6. The David figures could also be interpreted as Mercury when the head of Goliath is not defined (see cat. no. 52).

43. Inv. no 756; h. 16.5, 7.5 (without handle), diam. 7.9.

44. Banzato and Pellegrini 1989, pp. 69–71, no. 45; see n. 23 above.

45. Ibid., p. 71, nos 46–7.

46. Evident in pl. XVI of a copy of a catalogue of objects made by the Michieli foundry in the Sculpture Department, (kindly provided by Michael Micheli, a descendant of Giuseppe Michieli); an original version has not been located, cf. for example the figure of Mars on Bargello, inv. no. 775.

Alloy Analysis

1. T. Hackens, H. McKerrell and M. Hours (eds), 'X-ray microfluorescence analysis applied to archeology' in *PACT*, 1, Strasbourg, 1977; N. W. Madden, G. H. Hanepen and B. C. Clark, 'A low power high resolution thermo-electrically cooled Si(Li) spectrometer', *Institute of Electrical and Electronics Engineers, Transactions on Nuclear Science*, 33, 1986, pp. 303–5.

2. For a description of the standard system, see J. Lutz and E. Pernicka, 'Energy dispersive X-ray fluorescence analysis of ancient copper alloys: empirical values for precision and accuracy', in *Archeometry*, 38, 1996, 2, pp. 313–23.

3. See also p. 23.

Summary of the Results of Analysis

4. Many of the readings contained iron, probably due to surface contamination or treatment.

5. See p. 23 and Peal 1974, p. 827.

Select Bibliography of Literature containing Alloy Analysis
Blagg, 1974; H. Blackmore, 'Chemical Analysis of Bronze Cannon in the Tower of London', Appendix III in Blackmore 1976, pp. 407–9; Guilmartin 1980, pp. 284–91; Josef Riederer, 'Metallanalysen Nürnberger Statuetten aus der Zeit der Labenwolf Werkstaff' in *Berliner Beiträge zur Archäometrie*, 1982, 7, pp. 175–202; R. Brownsword and E. E. H. Pitt, 'Alloy composition of some cast latten objects of the 15th/16th centuries', in *Journal of the Historical Metallurgy Society*, 1983, 17, pp. 44–9; Josef Riederer, 'Metallanalysen an Erzeugnissen der Vischer Werkstatt' in *Berliner Beiträge zur Archäometrie*, 1983, 8, pp. 89–99; idem, 'Metallanalysen an Erzeugnissen der middelalterlichen und frühneuzeitlichen Bronzegiessereien' in *Der Anschnitt*, 1984, pp. 153–8; Eugene Farrell, 'Non-Destructive Instrumental Analysis of Metals' in J. Graham Pollard (ed.), *Italian Medals, Studies in the History of Art*, 21, Washington, 1987, pp. 35–43; Josef Riederer, 'Metallanalysen Augsburger Bronze- und Messingskulpturen des 16. Jahrhunderts' in *Berliner Beiträge zur Archäometrie*, 1988, 10, pp. 85–95; D. R. Hook, 'Scientific Analysis of the Copper-Based Medals', Appendix, pp. 305–12, in Mark Jones, *A Catalogue of the French Medals in the British Museum, Volume Two, 1600–1672*, London, 1988; Florence 1988; South Brisbane 1988; J. Graham Pollard, 'The Plaquette Collections in the British Museum', Appendix A, pp. 234–5, in Luchs 1989; Bewer 1993; Florence and New York 1993; Bewer 1996; Marco Ferreti, Lucia Miazzo and Pietro Moioli, 'The Application of a non-destructive XRF method to identify different alloys in the bronze statue of the Capitoline Horse' in *Studies in Conservation*, 42, 1997, pp. 241–6; Francesca Bewer, '"Kunststück von gegossenem Metall". Adriaen de Vries's bronze technique' in Amsterdam 1998, pp. 64–77; Giusti and Matteini 1998.

CATALOGUE ENTRIES

❧

CATALOGUE KEY

Dating and variants

In view of the reuse of motifs over a long period of time, coupled with the enduring use of mortar shapes (see p. 38), precise dating can be difficult. The dating of many of the bells and mortars is, therefore, intended as a guide, but is not prescriptive. The catalogue is organized by region and broadly in date order, but a strict chronology has not been followed; like or related objects have instead been grouped together, and therefore objects of the same date are sometimes separated. The nature of the technique of bronze casting, particularly for the types of object considered here, can add to the difficulties of dating. Some casts have been identified as nineteenth-century, while others are open to doubt. The latter have generally been placed in the catalogue alongside the objects to which they relate stylistically. Known variants are also included where appropriate, but doubtless other versions exist that have not been located.

Definitions of alloy

In order to classify the objects more clearly, the following terminology has generally been adopted when defining the alloy in the Metal Analysis section of each entry:

- *Brass:* copper-zinc alloy with little or no tin.
- *Bronze:* copper-tin alloy; this sometimes includes low levels of other elements.
- *Bell-metal:* copper-tin alloy with tin above 15 per cent.* Additional elements are specified when they appear.
- *High-tin bronze:* copper-tin alloy with tin between 12 and 15 per cent with additional elements.
- *Leaded bronze:* copper-tin-lead alloy with conspicuous lead content (above *c.*4 per cent).
- *Bronze (quaternary alloy):* copper-tin alloy with conspicuous zinc (above *c.*4 per cent) and lead in whatever proportional relationship.

Percentages refer to the proportions by weight.

Plates

The first photograph of each catalogue entry represents the main view; subsequent plates are numbered a, b, etc.

*Biringuccio/Smith and Gnudi, 1990, p. 500: Biringuccio gives bell-metal as between 12 and 25 per cent tin. This is a lower reading than the generally accepted definition of bell-metal as between about 20 and 23 per cent tin and contradicts Biringuccio's own definition elsewhere. The majority of objects defined as bell-metal contain a minimum of 20 per cent, but all high-tin bronzes over 15 per cent are defined as bell-metal.

Weights and measures/inventory numbers

All dimensions are in centimetres.

Weights have been presented as taken, so as to provide the most information. In most instances, for the individual entries, weights under 10,000 grammes are in grammes (g.), and those above are in kilogrammes (kg.). They are followed in each entry by the V&A's inventory number.

In the introductory essays, weights are presented as referred to in the sources, together with a conversion to g. or kg., as appropriate to the context.

Condition and description of facture

Notes on facture appear in the Condition section where appropriate, but further comment on facture can also be found immediately after the description of the object or integrated in the text, as appropriate.

Inscriptions/legends

Full stops are used to represent stops of whatever shape (including lozenges, triangles, and so on); crosses represent all cruciform stops. The term 'inscription', when used in the general sense, refers either to a raised or inscribed legend. When used specifically, the precise term is applied.

Bibliography

Most of the literature referred to is included in the Bibliography (pp. 226–35), which is divided into two sections: books, articles, collection and sales catalogues, etc. (with primary sources indicated by an asterisk), in alphabetical order by author; and exhibition catalogues in date order (abbreviated by location). References that are specific to a particular entry or essay are included only in a note. Other specialist literature can also be found, where appropriate, in the summary bibliographies to individual essays. The Bibliography also includes relevant literature that is not specifically referenced in the text.

Abbreviations

Few abbreviations are used, other than those in the Bibliography. Where unspecified, the use of loc. cit. in the notes of the catalogue entries refers to the relevant references cited in the Bibliography, Provenance or Exhibition details for that entry.

FF = French francs

SMB-PK = Staatliche Museen zu Berlin, Preussischer Kulturbesitz. The Skulturensammlung, SMB-PK, is referred to simply as Skulpturensammlung, Berlin in the main text.

CENTRAL ITALIAN

1. Mortar with rope handle and iron ring

Probably central Italian (Umbria?); *c.*1430–60
Leaded bronze
h. 8.1; diam. 11.1 (rim), 6.8 (base); w. 12.4; wt 1755.2 g.
M.21-1938

Provenance: Collection of Dr W. L. Hildburgh, FSA, London;
on loan to the Victoria and Albert Museum from 14 August
1934 (no. 4838); given by Hildburgh in 1938.

Condition: Rough surface; sandy-grey deposit in interstices; casting flaw and damage to the rim; slight evidence
of turning around the rim; possible repair by the handle,
and signs of cracking to either side of the applied ribs,
running through the projecting rim in places.
Interior: worn.

Base: pitted, with evidence of shrinkage where the pouring sprue was attached.
Dark brown patina with green spotting.
Metal analysis: a leaded bronze with low zinc and high
antimony content; high iron reading. Iron ring.

Conical mortar with plain projecting rim, corded handle
and an iron ring, punched with circular marks on one
side. On the body, four projecting, tapered ribs terminating in a trefoil, and opposite the handle an unidentified
coat of arms (a fess, in chief three vine scrolls); shallow,
recessed foot.

(*a*)

The cracking adjacent to the ribs may indicate that they were applied on panels cut into the main body, which has a slightly uneven surface treatment. Despite the apparent evidence of turning near the rim, the mortar may, therefore, have been modelled in wax and largely smoothed by hand. The handle was cast separately and attached. This type of mortar was designed to hang from a bench or wall hook. When the mortar was hanging, the pestle could not be placed inside, as so often illustrated, but instead a variety of pestles would probably have been stored nearby and a suitable selection made for the job in hand.[1]

The basic form is close to that of a much larger mortar in the Castello Sforzesco, Milan, catalogued by Lise as fifteenth-century Lombard, which also bears a heraldic shield.[2] The Milan mortar was categorized by Middeldorf as 'early type, second group', but it has an archaic high recessed foot which varies from the present mortar.[3] The present piece was presumably developed from an earlier model with plain ribs, numerous examples of which survive.[4] Similar trefoil ribs are seen on a large, more elaborate mortar from the Castiglioni Collection, signed by Crescimbene of Perugia and dated 1440.[5] Though different in type and overall style, this indicates a possible earlier date for the present piece, which was also given to early quattrocento Perugia on acquisition, later broadened to Umbria and dated slightly later.[6] The early dating is

supported by the evidence of facture. A more advanced expression of the same type is provided by cat. no. 70.

Ribs are so common, on early mortars in particular, that it is not possible to assign a place of origin on the basis of that feature alone. However, two mortars from the Castelli Collection, Siena, which have similar trefoil ribs and broadly the same form, have also been given to central Italy.[7] Although the evidence is inconclusive, it is probable that this small mortar is of central Italian origin, from the early to mid-fifteenth century.[8]

Notes

1. See p. 42.
2. Alberici 1976, pp. 28–9, fig. 21; Lise 1983, p. 249, no. 2; h. 17, diam. 18.8.
3. Middeldorf 1981, pp. 42–3.
4. See, for example, Middeldorf 1981, pp. 30–1, no. 4, citing related versions; Lise 1983, p. 248, no. 1, h. 14, diam. 16.5.
5. Present whereabouts unknown. Muller (Castiglione) 1925, lot 98; Lise and Bearzi 1975, p. 31, no. 25, h. 28.5, diam. 37.
6. Museum records.
7. Lise and Bearzi 1975, pp. 55, 56, no. 68 (as central Italian, end of the fifteenth century, h. 12.5, diam. 9.5) and 57, no. 69 (as Umbrian, mid-fifteenth-century, h. 13, diam. 9.5).
8. The metal analysis, showing a quaternary alloy (with low zinc) and high antimony, compares to alloys used in Venice for firedog figures produced in the sixteenth and early seventeenth centuries. The iron content may indicate contamination.

2. Mortar with IHS symbol

Central Italian (Perugia?); *c*.1460–1500
Bell-metal
h. 10.5; diam. 14 (rim), 9.1 (base); w. 14.5; wt 3105.4 g.
M.26-1938

Provenance: Collection of Dr W. L. Hildburgh, FSA, London; on loan to the Victoria and Albert Museum from 14 August 1934 (no. 4839); given by Hildburgh in 1938.

Condition: Traces of a cast-in 'label' on base below the IHS symbol; some pitting; squashy, waxy cast; evidence of flux around the handle.
Interior: scratched in the bowl, revealing lighter metal, and green deposit/corrosion; central pit; white metal near the upper rim.
Base: smooth; evidence of shrinkage around the pour-hole; pitting.
Dark brown patina.

Metal analysis: bell-metal with some zinc and lead; antimony noted in the main body. The base shows a much lower tin reading; the handle has significantly more lead. The iron content may be due to surface contamination or treatment. The white metal on the inner surface of the upper rim proved to be high-tin bronze with zinc and a higher quantity of lead than the body.

Conical mortar with spreading rim, recessed inside, and small, reeded, semicircular handle. The rim encircled by cable pattern. On the body, six pilasters decorated with candelabra or stylized vases and flowers, the panels designed to fit the body between the rim and an astragal delineating the foot; opposite the handle, the sacred monogram of Christ, IHS, encircled with flames. Slightly concave foot with scotia at the bottom.

The indication of flux around the handle suggests that it was cast separately and joined, as expected. The possibility

that the white metal around the rim may be some form of solder fixing a separate rim in place was considered during analysis. This would be surprising, and in fact the analysis indicated a different alloy content from that expected from visual examination. This analysis was possibly affected by the focus, and the mortar appears to be of a consistent alloy.

Acquired with cat. no. 1, this mortar was described on entering the collection as being 'from Perugia', possibly indicating its recent provenance. Both mortars are decorated with applied panels, but in a different arrangement. More closely related panels are found on a group of mortars associated with Melfi (see cat. no. 69). However, these are common decorative features and not sufficient in themselves to identify the place of origin.

　Two virtually identical mortars – one of which was in the Corsi Collection (Florence) and the other on the New York art market in 1981 – vary only by the addition of a decorative frieze around the foot.[1] The shape falls into Middeldorf's 'early Renaissance' category.[2] The form of the IHS symbol is that associated with S. Bernardino of Siena (1380–1444), a Franciscan friar renowned for his preaching.[3] In his youth he assisted in helping the victims of an outbreak of plague in Siena, and his association with a mortar used for preparing medicines is therefore appropriate. However, mortars were also used to grind incense, and an example with the sacred monogram is illustrated by Montevecchi and Vasco Rocca in this connection.[4] At one time believed to be an after-cast,[5] there is no direct evidence to support this assertion, and on the basis of its form and decoration, the mortar probably dates to the second half of the fifteenth century.

Notes

1. See Middeldorf 1981, pp. 54–7, no. 13; h. 10.8, diam. 14, w. 14.2; Sotheby Parke Bernet, Inc., *European Works of Art, Furniture and Tapestries*, New York, 29 and 30 May 1981, lot 204, h. 10, as Italian, sixteenth-century (with pestle, not illus.).
2. Middeldorf 1981, p. 11.
3. LCI 1990, V, pp. 390–2.
4. Montevecchi and Vasco Rocca 1988, p. 266.
5. Museum records.

(*a*)

3. Mortar decorated with lions and hares

Central Italian (Perugia?); *c.*1480–1520
Leaded bronze
h. 9.4; diam. 12.5 (rim), 8.9 (base); w. 13.6;
wt 1972.7 g.
M.24-1938

Provenance: Collection of Dr W. L. Hildburgh, FSA,
London; on loan to the Victoria and Albert Museum from
14 August 1934 (no. 4840); given by Hildburgh in 1938.

Condition: Worn, undefined decoration; greenish-grey
deposit with green corrosion product; casting flaws and
chips around the rim but with smooth edges. Handle cast
separately and soldered into place.
Interior: scratched, possible recess at centre and deposit.
Base: smooth with some pitting.
Dark brown patina.
Metal analysis: consistent leaded bronze for the body and
handle; fairly high tin content, with significant lead and
some zinc.

Conical mortar with projecting rim, recessed lip and
semicircular ribbed loop handle. The body is decorated
with symmetrically disposed panels containing a lion
flanked by two hares (affronted), and two birds with foliate scroll; two separate panels with a vase of flowers on
either side. The four outer panels fill the height of the
body and rest on an astragal that delineates the plain foot.

On acquisition, the mortar was described as Italian (from
Perugia), fifteenth-century. This probably indicated the
presumed area of origin, rather than the place of acquisition by Hildburgh, which is noted in some instances.
Although ill-defined and with no evidence of a pouring
sprue attachment under the base, there is nothing to indicate that the mortar is a later after-cast. It was presumably
a poor casting that has suffered considerable wear. The
mortar is of a similar type to one in the Castello Sforzesco
in Milan, dated 1507, and also ascribed to central Italy by
Lise.[1] A comparable but more elaborately moulded mortar
was in the Berna Collection, Milan.[2] The use of decorative
panels is also seen on cat. no. 69, associated with Melfi,
but is quite common and therefore cannot provide a
secure place of origin.

(*a*)

Notes
1. Inv. no. 93; h. 13.5, diam. 16; see Lise and Bearzi 1975,
   pl. XXIII; Lise 1983, pp. 254–5, no. 6.
2. Lise and Bearzi 1975, p. 52, fig. 64 at right, h. 11.

4. Mortar

Attributed to the workshop of Guidoccio di Francesco da Fabriano (active 1460s)
Central Italian (Fabriano, March of Ancona); dated 16 August 1465
Leaded bronze
h. 10.1; diam. 12.9 (rim), 9 (base); w. 14; wt 3030.8 g.
M.684-1910

Provenance: Collection of Sir Thomas Gibson Carmichael, London, until 1902 (Christie's (Gibson Carmichael) 1902, lot 50);[1] collection of George Salting, London; on loan to the Victoria and Albert Museum from 15 March 1907; bequeathed by Salting in 1910 (Salting Bequest, no. 2525).

Condition: Areas of the decoration are worn (notably the warrior head medallions, see below).
Interior: smooth.
Base: evidence of shrinkage where the pouring sprue was attached; a label marked '42'.
Dark brown patina.
Metal analysis: leaded bronze, with antimony present in the bowl and base, the latter also including nickel.

Cylindrical mortar with recessed lip and foliate handle terminating in a pine cone. Around the rim, in relief, the legend: + IO . DE . PANCIONIBVS . L . CAR . DE . VRSINIS . AGRI . PICENI . LEGATI . PHISICVS . M . CCCC . LXV (Giovanni de Pancioni, physician of Cardinal Orsini, legate of the lands of Piceno, 1465).

On the body, six crocketed, trefoil ogee arches springing from the mouths of confronted dog-like beast heads (or snakes), which form the capitals of projecting spiral columns, themselves actually the intertwined (hairy) necks of the beasts emanating from the bases of the columns; beneath three arches are coats of arms (a fess between three roses), alternating with two flowering plants, the sixth arch framing and cut by the handle; within the spandrels are medallions containing alternately the same shield of arms, simplified and with an illegible inscription around it, and the profile head of a warrior. The central plume of the arches and the medallions overlap the lower mouldings of the projecting rim. Around the foot, in relief, the legend: + INFABRIANO . DIE . XVI . MENSIS . AVGVSTI . IVXIT . FIERI (ordered [this] to be [made] in Fabriano on 16 August).

The inscription around the rim and base announce that the mortar was made (or commissioned) in Fabriano on 16 August 1465 by Giovanni de Pancioni, whose arms are doubtless those on the mortar.[2] According to the inscription, Pancioni was the physician of Cardinal Orsini, the papal legate to the region around Piceno. He is perhaps identifiable with the Giovanni Battista Pancio (or Panzi) of Ferrara, who taught at the University of Ferrara in 1508–9, by which time he would have been elderly.[3] Latino Orsini (1416–77) was appointed cardinal on 20 December 1448 by Pope Nicholas V (Tommaso Parentucelli; b. 1397, Pope 6 March 1447–24 March 1455) with the title of Sts John and Paul.[4] He administered various posts prior to being made legate of the March of Ancona on 1 October 1464 by Paul II (Pietro Barbo; b. 1417, Pope 30 August 1464–26 July 1471),[5] and sustained an illustrious career until his death in 1477.[6] Precise dating of a mortar is unusual, and may therefore have been significant.

The close relationship between this mortar and those signed by Guidoccio di Francesco da Fabriano in London, Berlin and New York leaves no doubt that it was produced in the same workshop.[7] It is closest to the slightly larger Berlin example, having the same flowering plant, basic decoration and style of inscription, but a simpler treatment of the crocket decoration. The additional medallions with arms and profile warrior heads are too worn to decipher accurately.

(a)   *See also illustration on half-title.*

Notes

1. The mortar was bought at the Gibson Carmichael sale for £200 by Durlacher, who apparently immediately sold it to Salting for £210; Christie's (Gibson Carmichael) 1902, loc. cit. annotated catalogue; Salting notebook, GSVII, p. 63 indicates that it cost £210 in 1902, and notes the 'name of artist being Gendreino Francesci in Fabriano'. This was presumably based on the association with cat. no. 5 noted in the Gibson Carmichael sale catalogue (loc. cit.).

2. Incorrectly noted as from 'Sabrieno' by Wittop Koning, loc. cit. The legend is applied in individual letters. I am grateful to David Rundle for his assistance in translation.

3. Giovanni Battista Pancio of Ferrara (fl. 1507–8) appears in Juliana Hill Cotton, *Name-list from a Medical Register of the Italian Renaissance, 1350–1550*, Oxford, 1976, p. 89. Doubtless the same doctor is listed as a doctor of medicine and philosophy (1508) in Francesco Raspadori, *I Maestri di medicina ed arti dell'Università di Ferrara 1391–1950*, Florence, 1991, pp. 22 and 258 (noting his written works). This Giovanni Battista may, however, have been a relative of the Giovanni to whom the mortar belonged; two other doctors by the name of Panzi appear in Raspadori's listing during the sixteenth century. No other Pancio or Pancioni has yet been identified; a Georgius de Pancottis from the March of Ancona received a doctoral diploma at Ferrara in March 1460, but was presumably not from the same family (see Giuseppe Pardi, *Titoli Dottorali Conferiti dallo Studio di Ferrara nei sec. XV e XVI*, Bologna, 1901, p. 36).

4. See Conrad Eubel, *Hierarchi Catholica Medii Aevi sive Summorum Pontificum S R E Cardinalium Ecclesiarum Antistitum*, vol. 2: *Series AB Anno 1431 usque ad annum 1503 Perducta e documentis tabularii praesertim Vaticani*, Regensberg, 1914, p. 34, no. 254. For a biography of Latino Orsini, see Litta III 1833, pl. XXIX. I am grateful to Paul Williamson, Norbert Jopek and Mark Evans for their helpful suggestions.

5. Eubel 1914, op. cit. at n. 4, p. 34, no. 253.

6. Ibid; p. 10, n. 1, and Litta, loc. cit. at n. 4, for death date of 11 August 1477.

7. See cat. no. 6 for discussion of the other examples.

Bibliography

Wittop Koning 1975, pp. 22–3 (illus.).

5. Mortar with arms of the Manassei

**By Guidoccio di Francesco da Fabriano
(active 1460s)
Central Italian (Fabriano, March of Ancona);
signed and dated 1468**
Bronze
h. 11.1; diam. 14.9 (rim), 10.2 (base); w. 15.9;
wt 4727.3 g.
11-1869

Provenance: Collection of Sig. Tordelli of Spoleto until
1868(?); bought from Giuseppe Baslini, Milan, in
December 1868 for £24.[1]

Condition: The lower legend is poorly cast in places.
Interior: smooth.
Base: smooth, but with faint evidence of shrinkage
where the pouring sprue was attached.
Dark brown patina with traces of gilding; silver-grey
in bowl but dark brown elsewhere inside and brassy on
the base.
Metal analysis: bronze with lead and zinc content. The
spectrum for the motif shows a higher lead and tin content, together with iron, possibly due to the inadvertent
targeting of particles. There is an unusually high arsenic
content, which may suggest an alloy component or surface treatment.

Cylindrical mortar with recessed rim and a foliate handle,
with an acorn (?) at the base. Around the rim, in relief
and between plain mouldings, the legend: + DOMINI .
LIBEROCTI . DEMANASSEIS . LEVW . DOCTOR .
INTERANENSIS . GENERALIS . MARCHIE . ANCONI-
TANE . LOCVMTENENTIS . ([This belongs to] Lord
Liberotto de' Manassei of Terni, Doctor of Civil Law,
Lieutenant General (*Luogotenente Generale*) of the March of
Ancona). On the body, six crocketed, trefoil ogee arches
springing from the mouths of confronted dog-like beast
heads (or snakes),[2] which form the capitals of projecting
spiral columns, themselves actually the intertwined
(hairy) necks of the beasts emanating from the bases of the
columns; five of the arches frame coats of arms; the sixth
arch frames and is cut by the handle. Around the recessed
foot, in relief, the legend: . + . ETFECIT . GVIDVCIVS .
FRANCISCI . DEFABRIANO . M . CCCCLXVIII (and

Guidoccio di Francesco da Fabriano made it, 1468).

The legend is applied as individual letters, the W of
LEVW presumably being an M applied upside-down, providing the reading LE[g]VM.[3]

The mortar was not (surprisingly) associated with the
Marches on acquisition, nor specifically by Fortnum, who
designated it purely as 'Italian'.[4] At a later date the inscription was partially translated and the arms (party per fess
1. A lion passant holding in the dexter paw a fleur-de-lis
and charged with a baton, and with a label of four points
with three fleur-de-lis between the points; 2. Barry wavy)
identified as those of the Manassei of Terni.[5]

A mortar by the same founder dated 1466 is cited by
Lise and Bearzi.[6] Another of similar design and bearing
the same signature and date is in the Skulturensammlung,
Berlin.[7] The legend on the Berlin mortar indicates that it
once belonged to the goldsmith Alexander of Padua and
bears what are presumably his arms and monogram surmounted by a Maltese cross. The dating of another, larger,
signed example (private collection, New York) is applied
as MVXXXII and therefore erroneous and difficult to
interpret.[8] If meant to read MDXXXII (1532), this may
be an example of a foundry continuing to use a former

(a)

master's name at a much later date.[9] Three other related mortars survive in the Museum, one of which is undoubtedly from Guidoccio's workshop (cat. no. 4), and the other two (one dated 1507) can also be confidently attributed to the same orbit (cat. nos 6 and 7). Another example formerly in Berlin, decorated with an identical distinctive foliate form as cat. no. 4, also forms part of the group.[10] No information has yet come to light on the founder, Guidoccio di Francesco of Fabriano.

As the inscription suggests, the present mortar must have been made for Liberotto de' Manassei of Terni, about whom no additional details have been found.[11] The quality of the cast, together with the apparent remains of gilding and the lengthy inscription advertising its ownership, underline that the mortar was a prized possession. The Guidoccio mortars are beautifully designed, with their intertwined beasts, elaborate trefoil arches and elegant handles. The beasts themselves, particularly if taken as snakes, probably have some significance, especially in relation to the Berlin mortar, which was the property of a goldsmith. The snake had associations with both medicine and alchemy; it represented rebirth, the meaning possibly enhanced by the foliage emanating from the beast's mouth. The decoration relates to fourteenth-century architectural forms found also in metalwork, ivories, altarpiece frames and other media. While initially appearing retardataire in style, these mortars are among the most sophisticated survivals of the period (compare, for example, cat. nos 1 and 70). While the present mortar was made for a local lord,[12] the Berlin example indicates that Guidoccio's workshop perhaps received commissions from major centres such as Padua, where there was a well-established bronze industry. However, the lack of documentary evidence for a goldsmith named Alexander, active in Padua in the 1460s, indicates that he may have left his native city and settled in Fabriano.[13]

Notes

1. See cat. no. 14 for details of purchase by Henry Cole.
2. See Bode, loc. cit. at n. 7 below.
3. See Fortnum, loc. cit.
4. Inventory and Fortnum, locc. citt.
5. Label text in Museum records (undated). See Spreti 4, 1931, pp. 288–9 for the Manassei of Terni, the arms on the mortar depicted slightly differently. Liberotto is not mentioned, but other members of the family had held office in Florence, Recanati in Ancona, and elsewhere in the late fourteenth and early fifteenth centuries.
6. Lise and Bearzi 1975, p. 30, as bearing the legend 1466 FECIT GUIDICIUS FRANCISCI DE FABRIANO and belonging to the Castellani Collection (source not located).
7. Inv. no. 7184, h. 10.4, diam. 15.5 (rim), 10.6 (base). The legend applied in relief: + GVIDVCIVS . FRANCISCI . DEFABRIANO . M.CCCCLXVIII . + . ALEXANDRI . SVM . AVRIFICIS . PADVANI . FECIT (Guidoccio Francesco da Fabriano made [this] for Alexander, chief goldsmith of Padua, 1468); Bode 1930, p. 56, no. 268. The mortar is slightly larger than the present example, and of better quality. This mortar is smooth inside, but indented at the bottom, indicating use. It bears the unidentified arms: four lozenges conjoined in bend cotized between two mullets of six points (the arms could be variously blazoned depending on the tincture). The listing in Wittop Koning 1975, p. 30, and Launert 1990, p. 70, of a mortar signed by 'Guiducius Francisci de Fabriano (1468)' could refer either to the London or Berlin mortar.
8. h. 23, diam. 17.8 (rim), 11.5 (base), max. w. 17.8. Legend applied in relief: MASTRO GUIDUCIO DA FABRIHANO MVXXXII AEV MA M OERALDO DE BENEDETO FRANCISCO, with unidentified arms. I am grateful to the owner for kindly supplying details of the mortar, which I have not examined.
9. See, for example, cat. no. 61.
10. Formerly SMB-PK, Berlin (now lost), inv. no. 5054, h. 10.5, diam 14.3; see Bode 1930, p.56, no. 269.
11. See n. 5 above.
12. As *Luogotenente Generale*, Manassei would have been responsible for the armed forces in the region.
13. Alexander has not been identified; see Antonio Sartori, *Documenti per la Storia dell'Arte a Padova*, Vicenza, 1976, 4, p. 246, for goldsmiths by that name documented in Padua, none of whom was documented as being active in the 1460s.

Bibliography

Inventory 1870, p. 2; Fortnum 1876, pp. 175–6; Christie's (Gibson Carmichael) 1902, p. 19 under lot 50.

6. Mortar with putti frieze around the base

Attributed to a successor to Guidoccio di Francesco da Fabriano (active 1460s)
Central Italian (Fabriano, March of Ancona);
dated 1507
Leaded bronze
h. 11; diam. 14.4 (rim), 9.5 (base); w. 14.5; wt 3431.4 g.
M.29-1938

Provenance: Collection of Dr W. L. Hildburgh, FSA, London; on loan to the Victoria and Albert Museum from 14 August 1934 (no. 4968); given by Hildburgh in 1938.

Condition: Worn decoration; legend poorly cast; large crack near the handle.
Interior: indented from use; green corrosion in the bowl.
Base: smooth.
Mottled brown patina, with flecks of shiny black material, notably around the obliterated legend on the rim; brassy underneath.
Metal analysis: leaded bronze with some zinc.

A cylindrical mortar with recessed rim and a single semicircular handle with reeding and cable pattern. The projecting rim bearing the legend: ANO D. MCCC-CCVII… (the remainder illegible). On the body, five crocketed, trefoil ogee arches springing from a plant. A recessed base with a frieze of cavorting, naked putti.

The putti frieze is applied as eight identical panels of three putti, with one additional putto filling the gap in the frieze below the handle. Unlike the other related mortars (see below), the arcading here does not frame the handle.

The mortar bears an obvious relationship to those produced in the workshop of Guidoccio di Francesco da Fabriano in the 1460s, and was probably produced by his successors in the workshop, or at another workshop in the city.[1] Here the arches are supported by a similar plant to that which appears between the arcading on earlier examples. This gothic-style arcading was already out of date at that time, and its appearance in 1507, when this mortar was made, highlights the traditional approach to the decoration of these objects. The arcading is, however, coupled

with dancing putti, which are ultimately derived from classical *erotes* or *amoretti* (winged boys), such as those that inspired Donatello's cherubic figures on the external pulpit at Prato Cathedral and those of both Donatello and Luca della Robbia for the *cantorie* made for the Duomo in Florence (now in the Museo dell'Opera del Duomo).[2] Comparable figures can be seen in a bronze relief of the *Triumph of Silenus* attributed to Bertoldo di Giovanni (*c.*1440–91), dated to around the 1470s.[3] The left-hand and central putti are particularly close to figures in the frieze. However, by the date of the mortar, such putti had become a common decorative feature and the same group of putti can be seen on cat. no. 38. It is possible that the blank arcading was intended to be filled by coats of arms or other separately cast decoration. The arms appear to have been integrally cast on cat. nos 5 and 6.

Notes
1. See cat. no. 5 for a full discussion; plus cat. nos 4 and 7 for additional examples.
2. See, for example, Pope-Hennessy 1993, pp. 97–114, with relevant illustrations including Luca's *'Drummers'* panel; Bober and Rubinstein 1986, pp. 90–1, nos 52 and 53. The della Robbia dancing children do not have wings, while the Donatello examples retain the wings seen on classical *erotes*.
3. Draper 1992, pp. 107–12, no. 7, for a detailed discussion; Toderi and Toderi 1996, p. 54, no. 89.

7. Mortar with foliate arcading and lion masks

Attributed to the workshop of Guidoccio di Francesco da Fabriano (active 1460s) or a successor Central Italian (Fabriano, March of Ancona);
c.1460–1510
Bronze
h. 12.5; diam. 16.5 (rim), 11.6 (base); w. 16.5; wt 5132.5 g.
344-1889

Provenance: Bought from Michelangelo Guggenheim, Venice, in 1889 (with 335 to 354-1889, £300).

Condition: Surface scratched; minor dents and casting flaws around the rim, with possible cast-in repairs; faint evidence of turning; green corrosion around the decorative motifs.
Interior: pitted.
Base: apparent cast-in repair, but smoothed over and chipped; evidence of shrinkage during cooling near the rim on one side.
Dark brown patina; mottled on the interior.
Metal analysis: a bronze with some lead and minimal zinc content. The analysis of the applied motif indicates a higher tin and lead content, possibly due to inadvertent targeting of a lead/tin density.

Cylindrical mortar with recessed rim and single semi-circular handle of cable pattern, and a moulded rim. Decorated on the body with six crocketed, trefoil ogee arches springing from 'plumed' lion heads, framing five inverted heads surmounted by plumes (giving the appearance of grotesque masks), with lion heads in the spandrels. The handle fits neatly into the central beaded arch, with a plumed, inverted head below. The central crocket of the arches overlaps the lower moulding of the projecting lip. Recessed foot, with projecting moulded base.

The inset under the base was possibly caused by excessive shrinkage during cooling where the pouring sprue was attached. This would have necessitated repair and thickening to allow for use.

Acquired as sixteenth-century Italian, the mortar was subsequently identified as originating from the Marches, and dated to about 1500.[1] The mortar relates to those signed by Guidoccio di Francesco da Fabriano in the 1460s (see, for example, cat. no. 5), and another, unsigned example, dated 1507 (cat. no. 6), bearing similar arcading. In scale, it falls between smaller examples in Berlin and London, and a larger mortar in New York.[2]

Notes
1. Inventory, loc. cit., and Museum records.
2. See cat. no. 5 for details of related examples, including Skulpturensammlung, SMB-PK, Berlin, inv. no. 7184 (Bode 1930, p. 56, no. 268) at n. 7, and private collection, New York, at n. 8.

Bibliography
Inventory 1890, p. 36.

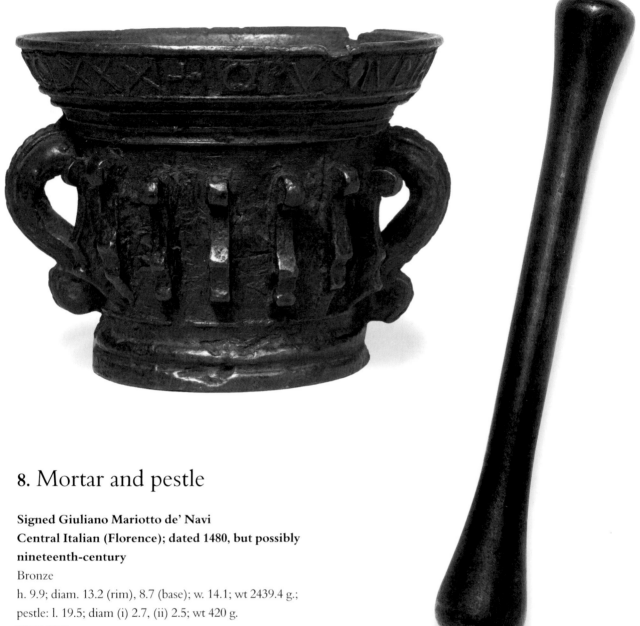

8. Mortar and pestle

Signed Giuliano Mariotto de' Navi
Central Italian (Florence); dated 1480, but possibly
nineteenth-century
Bronze
h. 9.9; diam. 13.2 (rim), 8.7 (base); w. 14.1; wt 2439.4 g.;
pestle: l. 19.5; diam (i) 2.7, (ii) 2.5; wt 420 g.
7847-1861

Provenance: Bought for £2 8s. (£2.40) in 1861
(provenance unknown).

Condition: Roughly cast with waxy treatment and evidence
of turning; grainy/porous appearance; chipped/casting
flaws around the rim; base unevenly cast.
Interior: smooth.
Base: pitted.
Dark brown patina, worn to golden brown inside the bowl.
Metal analysis: bronze, with variable alloy readings; much
higher tin and lead in the rim; pestle: leaded bronze with
traces of antimony and silver.

Conical mortar with two scroll handles with cable pattern.
On the projecting rim, in relief, the legend: + OPVS .
IVLIANI . DENAVI . FLORENTINI . MCCCCLXXX
(work [of] Giuliano de' Navi of Florence, 1480). On the
body, beneath a band of fillet mouldings, 14 projecting
ribs, bracket-like in form. Moulded foot.

The letters of the legend were applied individually, and
the ribs are coarse and uneven. The metal analysis readings suggest the presence of solder on the body itself, and
X-ray indicates that the ribs were added after casting.

It is interesting to note that, despite its poor quality, the mortar has been signed. The signature of Giuliano de' Navi also appears on a larger mortar with different rib decoration, signed with what appears to be his full name and dated 1490 (cat. no. 9), and on two mortars dated 1515 also in this collection (cat. nos 10 and 11), as well as several other extant examples (listed below). It is unusual for so many signed mortars from the same foundry to have survived, particularly of this early period, with two (and possibly two others) carrying the same dates. No other example of ribs with the same profile has been identified, and their apparent application after casting is not the standard method of facture for mortars. This observation, coupled with the apparent lack of use of the mortar, raises questions about the authenticity of this piece, which must be considered as possibly nineteenth-century.[1]

Other related variants

No other version with the same rib pattern has been found. See cat. no. 9 for the more common design, and following entries for further discussion.

Mortars associated with the Mariotto workshop

i. 1480: Ohio private collection; BARTOLOMEO . DAVERRAZAON . MCCCC—XX; h. 11.9, diam. 17; Cleveland 1975, no. 5.

ii. 1480: present mortar; + OPVS . IVLIANI . DENAVI. FLORENTINI . MCCCCLXXX; h. 9.9, diam. 13.2 (rim), 8.7 (base); w. 14.1.[2]

iii. 1490: cat. no. 9; + . OPVS . IVLIANI . MARIOCTI . DENAVI . MCCCCLXXXX; h. 15.2; diam. 19.7 (rim), 14.4 (base); w. 20.1.

iv. 1490: Museo Nazionale del Bargello, Florence, inv. no. 482; + OPVS . IVLIANI . DENAVI . FLORENTINI . MCCCCLXXXX; h. 13.3; diam. 17.1 (rim), 12.4 (base); w. c.17.3; acquired in 1883; Lise and Bearzi 1975, p. 64, fig. 79; Rome 1982, p. 46, no. 16.

v. 1494: Museo Nazionale del Bargello, Florence, inv. no. 473; + OPVS . IVLIANI . DENAVI . FLORENTINI . MCCCCLXXXXIIII; h. 11; diam. 14.4 (rim), 10 (base); w. 15.5; acquired in 1883; Lise and Bearzi 1975, pl. XXX.

vi. 1500: private collection, Germany; OPVS . IVLIANI . MARIOCTI . FLORENTINI . MCCCCC; h. 8, diam. 12; Christie's, London, 30 November 1983, lot 171.

vii. 1502: private collection, Germany; OPVS . IVLIANI . MARIOCTI . FLORENTINI . MCCCCCII; h. 8.2; Sotheby's, London, 22 April 1993, lot 205.[3]

viii. 1504: private collection, London; + OPVS . IVLIANI . MARIOCII [MARIOCTI] . FLO[R]ENTINI . MCCCCIIII; h. 8.5, diam. 12; Sotheby Parke Bernet, New York, *Fine European Works of Art, Tapestries and Furniture*, 29–30 May 1981, lot 205.

ix. 1505: Museo Nazionale del Bargello, Florence, inv. no. 709; OPVS . IVLIANI . MARIOCTI . FLORENTINI . MCCCCCV; h. 10.5; diam. 15.1 (rim), 9.5 (base); w. 15.8; acquired from F. Pedulli in 1913; Lise and Bearzi 1975, p. 11, fig. 3.

x. 1515: cat. no. 10; + OPVS . IVLIANI . MARIOCTI . FLORENTINI . MCCCCCXV; h. 10.6; diam. 15.3 (rim), 10.3 (base); w. 15.8.

xi. 1515: cat. no. 11; + OPVS . IVLIANI . MARIOCTI . FLORENTINI . MCCCCCXV; h. 10.6; diam. 15.3 (rim), 10.4 (base); w. 17.

xii. 1557: Musée du Louvre, Paris; OPVS . IVLIANI . MARIOCTI . FLORENTINI . MCCCCCLVII; h. 14, diam. 18.7 (rim), 12.7 (base). Given by Davillier; Migeon 1904, pp. 160–1, no. 159.

Undated

xiii. Corsi Collection, Florence; no inscription (h. 9, diam. 12.5); Middeldorf 1981, pp. 70–1, no. 16.

xiv. Private collection, Florence; no inscription (h. 7, diam. 12); Lise and Bearzi 1975, pp. 74–5, fig. 84.

xv. Museo Nazionale del Bargello, Florence, inv. no. 716 (no details available); acquired from C. Angeli in 1914. A ribbed mortar of similar form and with scrolled rope handles.

Cited by Middeldorf (unlocated)

xvi. Tolentino Sale, American Art Association, New York, 25 April 1920, no. 239; h. 9.5; Grassi Sale (idem, 20 January 1927, no. 23).

Notes

1. The status of this group is discussed in more detail in cat. no. 9.
2. The mortar is listed in Wittop Koning and Launert, locc. citt. as Julianus Mariogti [*sic*] de Navi, Florence 1480.
3. See Buzinkay 1996, fig. 46 for vii, and loc. cit. below; the captions have been transposed, giving an incorrect date of 1502 for the present mortar.

Bibliography

Inventory 1868, p. 26; Fortnum 1876, p. 177; Wittop Koning 1975, p. 30; Launert 1990, pp. 70–1, 195, no. 215; Buzinkay 1996, p. 50, fig. 47.

9. Mortar with ribs

**By Giuliano Mariotto de' Navi (active *c*.1480–1515)
(Florence); signed and dated 1490**

Bronze
h. 15.2; diam. 19.7 (rim), 14.4 (base); w. 20.1;
wt 6633.5 g.
M.21-1923

Provenance: Collection of Mrs Ellen Hearn, Menton,
France, from 1907;[1] given by Mrs Hearn in 1923 as part of
the first instalment of the Alfred Williams Hearn Gift in
memory of her late husband.

Condition: Some pitting; cracks around the ribs; scratches
and extraneous metal; chipped around the rim; rusted
repair to side where misshapen.
Interior: pitted, with grey deposit in bowl.
Base: smoothed; convex, apparently where worn through
use.
Dark brown patina.
Metal analysis: bronze with variable alloy readings.

Conical mortar with two corded scroll handles and a
moulded foot. On the projecting rim, in gothic script,
the legend: + . OPVS . IVLIANI . MARIOCTI . DENAVI .
MCCCCLXXXX (work [of] Giuliano Mariotto de' Navi,
1490). On the body beneath two fillets, 12 projecting ribs
of triangular section.

As with the previous mortar (cat. no. 8), the legend was
applied as individual letters, the ribs are coarse and
uneven, and the handles were cast separately and then
attached. On acquisition, the inscription was noted as
MCCCCIXXXX – and read as 1439 – but examination
confirms the later date, the L being poorly formed. The
lettering differs from that on the other mortars in the
group in the use of gothic script, and – in showing the full
name of the founder – it links the ribbed mortars with
those decorated with a band of acanthus from the same
workshop (see cat. nos 10 and 11).

Mortars with some form of rib decoration were clearly
popular, and were doubtless made in various regions; it is
therefore difficult to attribute those that are unsigned.
However, there are several examples that are closely
related, one of which is in a private collection in Ohio,

bearing the legend BARTOLOMEO . DAVERRAZAON .
MCCCC..XX. The name has been taken as that of the
founder, to whom the model was credited by Wixom in
view of the apparent early dating of 1420.[2] Middeldorf,
on the other hand, believed that the inscription referred
to the owner, as the Daverrazzo were an important
Florentine family. He also points out the problems with
the date, suggesting various possible pairs of Roman
numerals to fill the lacuna.[3] In comparison with the
present example, a date of 1480 (LX missing) appears the
most likely, together with an attribution to the founder
signing himself Ivliano Mariocto.

In his discussion of the facture of a similar mortar,
Bearzi confirms that the ribs were added in the wax, but
that, as an experienced craftsman would not voluntarily
allow the evident distortion in their positioning, this
movement must have occurred during the investment of
the wax model.[4] Similar misalignment of the ribs is evident in all the other versions, which leads one to question
– following Bearzi's assumption that the founder was
experienced – why this was not rectified. Slippage is a
common feature of the works that can confidently be
assigned to this workshop, and numerous mortars of poor
quality have survived alongside those that are clearly more
competent. The most obvious conclusion seems to be that
these were primarily practical objects, and that provided
they fulfilled their purpose it was not worthwhile recasting them.

The issue of their authenticity has, however, been considered further in light of the unusual survival rate from
the workshop, taken with other factors. Few have
significant signs of use, although this does not necessarily
have any bearing on date. It has not been possible to
confirm an early date through the documented history
of any of the mortars in the group.[5] The reproduction
of similar objects in foundries in the nineteenth and
early twentieth centuries suggests that mortars were also
probably made at that time.[6] The nature of genuine
nineteenth-century mortars is quite distinct from that of
the Mariotti group, however. It is also difficult to draw
conclusions from the unusual alloy analysis. Apart from
the present version, which has a different script – unusual
for this date[7] – there are three other mortars in the group
that are distinctive: cat. no. 8, which has unusual ribs,
apparently cast separately; the large Bargello mortar,
which has figural decoration; and the Louvre mortar,

which is not only much later in date, but bears a different style of decoration with some of the lettering applied in reverse.[8] The image of an Amazon on the Bargello mortar is based on a plaquette, which also appears on the portal of Palazzo Stanga in Cremona (now in the Louvre), giving a *terminus ante quem* of the late fifteenth century, fitting appropriately with the dating of 1490 on the mortar.[9]

There are sufficient questions regarding the facture and survival of these pieces, therefore, to warrant raising the possibility that some of this extended group are forgeries, possibly based on a surviving original. The nature of the inscriptions and the variable combinations of signature of the group, however, suggest a faker who was astute enough to provide credible Latin inscriptions, but was not very skilled in casting.[10] In addition, unless high prices could be commanded for the fakes, their production would not be worthwhile.[11] In the absence of conclusive evidence, therefore, the inscriptions cannot be dismissed, although the unusual facture of cat. no. 8 allows the suggestion that it may be a later cast. On balance, the present mortar can be accepted as late fifteenth-century.

Other related variants

i. Private collection, Germany, dated 1502; see cat. no. 8, no. vii.
ii. Collection of Dr Giorgio Corsi, Milan; see cat. no. 8, no. xiii.
iii. R. Tolentino sale (New York, American Art Association, 25 April 1920, no. 239, h. 9.5), cited by Middeldorf; see cat. no. 8, xvi.

Notes

1. Bought by or for Mrs Hearn in August/September 1907 for [equivalent of] FF312.50 at Eastbourne (presumably referring to her agent, Thomas Sutton's premises there).
2. Cleveland 1975, no. 5; h. 11.9, diam. 17.
3. Middeldorf 1981, pp. 70–1, no. 16.
4. Lise and Bearzi 1975, pp. 74, 75, fig. 84; mortar in private collection, Florence, h. 7, diam. 12.
5. None has a known provenance earlier than the nineteenth century, including the Bargello mortars (inv. no. 473, acquired 30 January 1883; inv. no. 482, acquired 19 October 1883; inv. no. 709, acquired 30 December 1913 from F. Pedulli; see cat. no. 8 listing for further details). However, this is not in itself unusual.
6. The Michieli foundry in Venice, for example, reproduced bells, door knockers, candlesticks and other utensils.
7. See Blagg 1974, pp. 122–3; although gothic script was still used – see, for example, a bell signed by Maestro Orlando and dated 1494 in Verona 1979, fig. 7.
8. See cat. no. 8, nos iii and xii, for details of the Bargello and Louvre mortars.
9. See Rome 1982, p. 46, no. 16.
10. An alternative (but less likely) conclusion would be that Mariotto was not a founder by trade, but possibly a doctor or alchemist who had the facility to make mortars for his own use. Several doctors called Mariotto (though none called Mariotto de' Navi) appear in Juliana Hill Cotton, *Name-list from a Medical Register of the Italian Renaissance, 1350–1550*, Oxford, 1976, p. 78, around the 1470s.
11. See Lockner 1976b for sand-cast fakes, which were comparatively easy to produce.

Bibliography

Launert 1990, p. 71.

10. Mortar with projecting lip

By Giuliano Mariotto de' Navi (active *c.*1480–1515)
Central Italian (Florence); signed and dated 1515
Leaded bronze
h. 10.6; diam. 15.3 (rim), 10.3 (base); w. 15.8;
wt 3867.8 g.
7848-1861

Provenance: Bought in 1861 for £3 (provenance unknown).

Condition: Waxy treatment; large dent in the foot; one head filed off; other damage and cracking, and extraneous metal. Repairs to the spout and handle to its right; handles cast separately.
Interior: evenly encrusted with green and grey deposit; the bowl reddish in colour.
Base: unevenly filed down and pitted.
Dark brown patina.
Metal analysis: a fairly consistent bronze alloy with lead content. Iron content probably due to surface contamination.

Conical mortar with two cabled scroll handles and projecting rim with recessed lip. On the rim, a spout with acanthus decoration and the legend: + OPVS . IVLIANI . MARIOCTI . FLORENTINI . MCCCCCXV (work [of] Giuliano Mariotto of Florence, 1515); below, a band of 18 classical female heads. On the body, beneath a fillet moulding, 10 acanthus leaves. Moulded foot.

This mortar is virtually identical to cat. no. 11, bearing the same poorly cast legend, the letters individually moulded with the exception of the last two letters of the date; on the other version these were cast from one mould. The frieze on the other mortar consists of 10 heads on each side, relating to the five leaves below, while here one head has been filed off to accommodate the handle to the right of the spout, and another (adjacent to the other handle) was never cast. The placement of the spout also varies, the present version being centred on the rim, while that on the other is centred on one of the heads and therefore at an angle to the rim, making it less practical for use. Close examination of the two mortars together, therefore, indicates that, while cat. no. 11 bears some similar but less crisp damage, neither is an after-cast of the other.[1]

(a)

The form and condition of the present object indicate its probable use. The reddish colour in the bowl points to copper enrichment at the surface (or some form of contamination), and as there is no evidence that the mortar has been heated externally, this suggests that the contents (possibly a gum or resin) caused this effect.

There are several other mortars apparently from the same foundry, varying in date from 1480 to 1515, and this survival rate is rare. None of them is of fine quality and, despite the practical rather than artistic nature of the objects, this raises some questions, which are discussed under cat. no. 9. Two similar signed mortars, without a spout or the frieze of heads, dated 1500 and 1504, survive in private collections (see cat. no. 8, nos vi and viii). There are also two mortars in the Bargello that are closely related to the present example and another in this collection (cat. no. 11), in both decoration and scale (see cat. no. 8, nos v and ix). The detail of the decorative arrangement and shape of the mortars differ; one (inv. no. 473, no. v under cat. no. 8) is decorated with an additional row of fleurs-de-lis below the legend, and is therefore slightly larger.[2] Although at first considered a possible forgery, the inscription and evidence of wear cannot be dismissed, and the mortar must, therefore, be accepted as a rare survival of the early sixteenth century.

Notes
1. For further discussion of authenticity, see cat. no. 11.
2. For full dimensions, see listing in cat. no. 8.

Bibliography
Inventory 1868 (objects acquired in the year 1861), p. 26; Fortnum 1876, p. 177; Launert 1990, p. 71.

11. Mortar with projecting spout

By Giuliano Mariotto de' Navi
(active *c*.1480–1515)
(Florence); signed and dated 1515
Leaded bronze
h. 10.6; diam. 15.3 (rim), 10.4 (base); w. 17; wt 3573.8 g.
M.685-1910

Provenance: Stefano Bardini, Florence (Christie's (Bardini) 1899, lot 403); collection of Sir Thomas Gibson Carmichael until 1902 (Christie's (Gibson Carmichael) 1902, lot 46);[1] collection of George Salting; on loan to the Victoria and Albert Museum from 15 March 1907; bequeathed by Salting in 1910 (Salting Bequest, no. 2524).

Condition: Waxy treatment; large pit by handle to right of spout, together with other areas of damage and repair, and extraneous metal; handle to left of spout crooked and overlapping one of the heads.

Interior: evidence of green corrosion around rim and inside bowl, together with signs of abrasion and pitting.
Base: unevenly filed down with cuts to the edge; smooth underneath, bearing label marked '43' in blue ink.

(a)

Dark brown patina.

Metal analysis: a bronze alloy with substantial lead content; the reading taken from the lip showing much higher proportions of lead and tin (see below).

Conical mortar with two cabled scroll handles and moulded foot. Projecting rim with recessed lip, decorated with – on the rim – a spout with acanthus leaf decoration and the legend: + OPVS . IVLIANI . MARIOCTI . FLO-RENTINI . MCCCCCXV (work [of] Giuliano Mariotto of Florence, 1515); below, a band of 20 classical female heads. On the body, beneath a fillet moulding, 10 acanthus leaves.

The mortar is discussed in comparison with the other virtually identical example, cat. no. 10. The handle to the left of the spout is crooked and overlaps one of the heads. There is evidence of repair, and the placement of the handles on both these mortars indicates that they were cast separately and then attached. The alloy of the present example contains much higher levels of lead than cat. no. 10 and the presence of zinc is also evident. Solder is apparently present around the rim, indicating that the rim may be an attachment. This would be unusual, and it is possible that a spill of solder was picked up in the testing.

This piece passed from Bardini through two important collections during the late nineteenth and early twentieth centuries, before which its provenance is unknown.[2] The inscription was never doubted, but in light of the close relationship with the Museum's other mortar (acquired in 1861) (cat. no. 10), the possibility of its being an after-cast

was considered. Taking a cast from an existing bronze reproduces the original, but usually with less definition and smaller dimensions in view of shrinkage of the cooling metal.[3] The present example has areas of greater wear (especially around the heads) and a similar unevenness on the base, but does not reproduce the same areas of damage. Examination at first suggested that the earlier acquisition might have been based on the present mortar, in view of the modification to the frieze of heads. However, close examination of the facture confirms that neither is an after-cast, both being made by the standard method for producing mortars. They have identical dimensions other than the width, the variation in which is caused by the addition of the handles.

These two mortars are the only bronze examples seen by the author that incorporate a lip for pouring, although such lips exist on ceramic mortars both from antiquity and following the development of modern ceramic mortars by Wedgwood in the eighteenth century (see p. 37). In view of the unusual quantity of surviving examples of comparatively poor quality, the issue of whether some of the group may be fakes has been considered, and the apparent unusual facture of cat. no. 8 supports this possibility.[4] However, the combination of the inscription and the evidence of wear indicates that the present example must be accepted, along with cat. no. 10, as an early sixteenth-century cast.

Notes

1. Both the Bardini and Gibson Carmichael sale catalogues list the mortar as signed by MARIOCITI.
2. It was bought at the Bardini sale by Durlacher in 1899 for £105, and from Gibson Carmichael by Stettiner for £90.
3. A system for identifying after-casts from bronze statuettes was proposed in Allison and Pond 1983, pp. 32–46. The question of variable dimensions in after-casts requires further research, however, as it may be affected by a number of factors (see p. 222).
4. For a further discussion of authenticity of the group as a whole, see cat. no. 9; for a listing of related types, see cat. no. 8.

12. Hand bell with handle in the form of a dancing putto

Central Italian (Florence?); 1500–50
Bronze
h. 17.1, 7.5 (without handle); diam. 8.9; wt 603.5 g.
M.671-1910

Provenance: Strozzi Collection, Florence (date unknown);[1] collection of George Salting, London; on loan to the Victoria and Albert Museum from 4 August 1903; bequeathed by Salting in 1910 (Salting Bequest, no. 2334).

Condition: Minor surface irregularities, and possible working of seam lines or flashing; evidence of turning. The tambourine is bent and there are indentations and scratches to the back.
Interior: iron clapper; strike marks that do not tally with the sound bow, indicating that the clapper is a replacement and not striking correctly. Possible evidence of turning; rough area under the crown.
Dark brown patination (worn), brassy inside.
Metal analysis: bronze of consistent alloy, with minimal lead.

Hand bell with a handle in the form of a naked dancing putto, with a cloth draped over the left shoulder and playing a tambourine. Decorated around the crown with swags and pendants suspended from 'buttons' or *paterae* with fluttering ribbons. On the neck, a band of tied foliate scrolls. On the waist, seven draped dancing putti, two of which support a blank shield and grasp the surmounting helm. Undulating sound bow consisting of an upper section decorated with fleshy, downward-facing acanthus, and plain below.

Three other examples of this bell are known: inferior casts in the Bargello, Florence,[2] and the Metropolitan Museum of Art, New York[3] and a sharply chased, gilt version in the Museum für Kunst und Gewerbe, Hamburg.[4]
The New York version is virtually identical, but bears an unidentified coat of arms (a Maltese cross in chief, three lions salient), also surmounted by a helm and mantling. The coat of arms on the Bargello and Hamburg bells is that of the Medici family surmounted by a crown.

The putto handle on the Hamburg version is fixed onto the bell in a different position, as is the hand playing the tambourine. The putto's left foot is provided with a support, and a cord winds around the back of the figure with a tassel (screwed into the groin) covering the genitals. Although not the smoothest cast, the present putto is perhaps the most charming, with the more clearly defined details accentuating the chubby features, particularly in the dimples and rolls of flesh on the thighs. The chasing on the face and hair adds a liveliness that only the Hamburg version comes close to. The Hamburg bell is smaller than the other versions (which are comparable in scale to one another), and is the crispest cast. It also has the most refined surface treatment, with evidence of chasing, suggesting that the alloy is not bell-metal.

(b)

(a)

The bell was said to be formerly in the Strozzi Collection, together with two statuettes also acquired by Salting, who had noted an attribution to the Florentine sculptor, Andrea del Verrocchio, who also cast large bells (see p. 32).[5] Bode designated it as after Donatello.[6] On acquisition, however, it was identified simply as Florentine, late fifteenth- or early sixteenth-century, doubtless based on comparison with the Bargello version, which was noted.[7] Schottmüller, on the other hand, gave the Hamburg Medici bell to central Italy, about 1600.[8] The Medici coat of arms consisting of one 'hurt' (charged with the fleur-de-lis) and five torteaux, as seen in both the Hamburg and Florence bells, was first used when Lorenzo de' Medici effectively governed Florence (1469–92). The inclusion of the crown, however, suggests that the bell was made for a Medici duke.[9] The putti arguably hold the crown more convincingly than the helm, having perhaps been originally designed to do so, with subsequent versions having been adjusted to accommodate a helm. The absence of a coat of arms in this instance is, therefore, surprising as a heraldic helm of this type usually represents a king, duke or prince,[10] although there is no surmounting coronet by which to make a distinction.

The handle putto was apparently developed from Donatello's *Putto with a Tambourine* of 1429 from the Siena Baptistery font (now in the Skulpturensammlung, Berlin), which in turn evolved from antique prototypes.[11] The differences in style are marked, and the putto was probably not based directly on the Donatello, but is more likely a later variant. Dancing putti were basically adapted from classical prototypes showing cavorting *erotes*. The design of the present bell is well balanced and delicately cast, with the putti alternating with winged counterparts. The obvious sources for these figures are those that appear in the work of the Florentine sculptors Donatello, Luca della Robbia and Bertoldo. The fluid handling of the movement of the figures is accentuated by the flying draperies.

The survival of four such closely related bells is unusual and, taken with the use of bronze rather than bell-metal, the possibility that some are later casts cannot be ruled out. However, bronze is more robust than bell-metal, and therefore appropriate for a household bell (see also cat. no. 47). The present example is probably Florentine from the first half of the sixteenth century.

Notes

1. See n. 5 below, and cat. no. 39, n.4, for Strozzi.
2. Inv. no. 743, h. 17.2, *c*.7.2 (without handle), diam. 8.9; exhibited Palazzo Vecchio, *Commitenza e collezionismo*, Florence, 1980, cat. 715.
3. Inv. no. 41.190.53, h. 17.2, George Blumenthal Bequest 1941. Stella Rubinstein-Bloch, *George and Florence Blumenthal Collection*, Paris, 1926, II, pl. XXXLVIII, as Donatello, Paduan school, early sixteenth-century.
4. Inv. no. 1878,195, h. *c*.16.9 (?), *c*.7.5 (without handle; figure *c*.9.4), diam. 8.4; Schottmüller 1921, p. 122, fig. 94.
5. The statuettes of *Hercules Pomarius* (A.76-1910) and a *Dancing Boy* (A.109-1910), together with the bell, are mentioned in a letter from Salting to Wilhelm Bode, 12 May 1882 (SMB-PK, Zentralarchiv, Bode Nachlaß, Salting 4197), in which he states, 'Pinti told me they all three came from Casa Strozzi & this he gave on authority of Bardini'; I am grateful to Jeremy Warren for drawing Salting's letters to my attention, and for the transcription. This provenance is also noted in Salting's Notebooks. The bell was valued at £200, rising to '250 or 300' according to Salting's earlier notebook (GSIV, late 1880s to early 1890s?). Later it was amended from 300 to '600 or more' and finally to 800 (GSVII, p. 62, unknown date).
6. Bode and Bode/Draper, locc. citt.
7. Museum records.
8. Loc. cit. at n. 4.
9. Cosimo I de' Medici was made Duke of Tuscany in 1537. The crown takes the form identified as the Venetian, rather than the Tuscan, ducal crown (see Coronelli 1702, in the introductory material on blazons, crowns and helms, no page numbers), but the precise form of the heraldic coronets varies according to different sources. There were, however, other Medici dukes (see Langedijk 1981, I, pp. 10–11, and TDA 1996, 21, pp. 8–9, for the Medici family tree).
10. See, for example, Coronelli, loc. cit. at n. 9 above.
11. Pope-Hennessy 1993, p. 87, fig. 75; Berlin 1995, pp. 130–1, no. 1.

Bibliography

Bode 1907, p. 11, pl. 6;
Bode/Draper 1980, p. 5, no. 6.

(*c*)

13. Mortar
inscribed 'MARIO LILLA'

Central Italian (?); 1500–50
Bronze
h. 9.4; diam. 13.7 (rim), 10 (base); wt 2291.7 g.
M.996-1926

Provenance: Collection of Lt Col G. B. Croft-Lyons, London, by 1915; on loan to the Victoria and Albert Museum from 5 November 1915; bequeathed by Croft-Lyons in 1926.

Condition: Waxy casting; worn surface; chipped around the rim.
Interior: patina worn inside the rim; evidence of turning, and use; slight indentation in the base and deposit. Printed label marked 827 inside.
Base: smooth, slightly convex.
Dark brown patina.
Metal analysis: bronze of a consistent quaternary alloy.

Conical mortar with projecting lip bearing the legend: + . N . MARIO . LILLA . with seven additional lozenges, decorated with geometrically arranged ornament. The rim separated from the body by a cavetto between two torus mouldings. The body decorated with six panels containing standing, draped female figures depicted as three pairs in mirror image, between which alternate female heads in profile, facing left, with large medallions of a horseman with billowing cloak attacked by a lion. The projecting foot formed by an ogee moulding.

The decoration and the letters and symbols of the legend are all applied in separate panels. The poor quality may be due in part to the use of ill-defined moulds, but is probably largely due to wear.

The mortar was registered on acquisition as fifteenth-century, but with an unknown Italian origin, although according to the Museum records, the mortar was acquired at Rome by Lt Col Croft-Lyons. Examples with similar shape and decoration can be seen in the Alda Bergna Collection, Milan,[1] and in the Columbia Museum of Art, Columbia (SC), which also has profile busts between applied panels, but rather different in style.[2] The design also recalls a mortar from Palermo, dated 1510, although the decoration varies considerably in style and that mortar is on a larger scale.[3] The prototype for the horseman medallion has not yet been identified.

Accurate dating is problematic as the bronze combines a comparatively early profile with portraits and elongated figures that are stylistically later in date. It most probably dates to the first half of the sixteenth century. The legend presumably refers to the owner.

Notes
1. Lise and Bearzi 1975, p. 52 (h. 11).
2. Inv. no. CMA 1963.41, see Pope-Hennessy 1965, no. 565, fig. 593; h. 11.1, diam. 15.4 (rim), 10.2 (base), wt 3969.2 g.
3. Middeldorf 1981, pp. 46–53. Some similarities can also be seen with Middeldorf's 'Renaissance types' and also with French seventeenth-century mortars of the 'later Renaissance and Baroque types' (ibid. pp. 88 ff. and 186 ff. respectively). This is due to the general variations on the conical form, which were common throughout Europe over a long period.

(a)

14. Mortar with the arms of Caterina Cibo

**Central Italian (March of Ancona); probably
1520–7**
Leaded bronze
h. 7.8; diam.10.5 (rim), 6.9 (base); wt 1016.9 g.
10-1869

Provenance: Collection of Sig. Tordelli of Spoleto until
1868(?); bought from Giuseppe Baslini, Milan, in
December 1868 for £16.[1]

Condition: Poorly cast and heavily worn; extensive chipping and casting flaws around the rim; green corrosion.
Interior: green corrosion; colour differential in bowl,
which is worn.
Base: evidence of shrinkage at pour-hole visible under the
(lopsided) base, together with pitting.
Dark brown patina.
Metal analysis: a high-tin leaded bronze, with some zinc.
The coat of arms showed an exceptionally high tin reading, with some iron contamination. However, the mortar
appears to be cast in one.

A small vase-shaped mortar with recessed rim, decorated
with two identical groups of four cavorting figures
(described below), alternating with two coats of arms (see
below) on tournament shields, a crown filling the area at
the top of the shield, with smaller heater-shaped shields to
either side.

The mortar was originally described as Italian, sixteenth-
century.[2] Fortnum was not so sure of the dating, indicating
that it could equally be fifteenth-century, but he described
the arms as impaled, vair-en-point on the dexter side, with
the sinister quartering the Medici arms with another, now
obliterated.[3] The main arms were subsequently identified
as those of Caterina Cibo (married 1520, d. 1557), wife
of Giovanni Maria Varano, Duke of Camerino (d. 1527),
and the mortar identified as Marchigian, doubtless due to
the association with Camerino in the March of Ancona.[4]
Although the arms are partially obliterated, this interpretation appears to be correct, and they can, therefore,
be blazoned as vair impaling quarterly 1 and 4, a bend
checky in three rows a chief charged with a cross, 2 and 3
six torteaux (or Medici *palle*).[5] The dexter side of the

shield and the two smaller coats of arms are those of
Varano. Caterina's arms (on the sinister side of the shield)
reflect her lineage, her father being Francesco Cibo
(*c.*1449–1519), the natural son of Pope Innocent VIII
(Giovanni Battista Cibo, b. 1432, Pope 29 August 1484–
25 July 1492), and her mother Maddalena de' Medici
(1473–1519), daughter of Lorenzo the Magnificent.

The figures were recognized by Fortnum as those that
decorate a number of small pedestals, at that time attributed to Donatello.[6] A fine example of a four-sided pedestal
survives in the Museum, each side decorated with a different figure, doubtless adapted from plaquettes on which
they also appear.[7] Many examples of the pedestals are triangular, illustrating the same three figures as seen on the
mortar.[8] The figure to the left of the shield can be identified
as the same as that on a (probably Venetian) bell in the
Castello Sforzesco in Milan,[9] which belongs to an extended
group of similar bells (see cat. no. 55). There it forms part
of a triumphal scene, alongside trophies and a bull and
horse pulling a chariot. The figure holds a thyrsus, or
wand, with a pine-cone at the tip, a symbol of fertility
and attribute of Bacchus and his followers, the satyrs. The
handling of snakes (the figure holds one in his left hand)
was also part of Bacchanalian ritual.[10] This figure is not the
usual representation of Bacchus himself, but has been
identified as such, and the accompanying Maenads or
Bacchantes, dancing and variously playing pipes or tam-
bourines, support this view.[11] A figure from the fourth

related plaquette (identified by Molinier as Fortune) is missing, and the dancing Maenad is repeated. The Maenad and flautist are among the images similarly adapted from plaquette sources that appear on the doorway of the Palazzo Stanga from Cremona (now in the Louvre), providing a *terminus ante quem* of about 1490–1500 for the design, and a north Italian context for their use.[12] Although the mortar could be north Italian in origin, it is more likely that it was made locally in the Marches.

The plaquettes in this context probably represent a generic decorative motif, particularly as they were reproduced in different contexts. However, the decoration has some relevance to mortars, with its imagery of snake handling. Snakes had various associations, including that with Bacchus (as shown here), as well as Asclepius, the Greek god of medicine.[13] Two other slightly larger mortars that bear some relationship are decorated with snakes. One, formerly in the Emil Weinberger Collection, is of a variant form but has a similar (obliterated) shield, here flanked by snakes and with a foliate frieze above and below.[14] The other, in the Musée des Arts Décoratifs, Paris, apparently carries an identical coat of arms to the present mortar, but is flanked by the same snakes that appear on the Weinberger mortar.[15] The imagery could, therefore, have been interpreted in different ways. Giovanni Maria Varano died of the plague at the age of 46 in 1527. The mortar may have been made at the time of his marriage to Caterina in 1520, the poor quality of the mortar being in part due to facture and also potentially to wear. In any event, it was most likely made while Giovanni Maria was still alive, because of the inclusion of the two smaller Varano shields, and can therefore be dated between 1520 and 1527.

Notes

1. The purchase of this mortar and cat. no. 5 for £40 is mentioned in the *Précis of the Board Minutes*, 1872, p. 224, among a number of purchases under the heading 'By Mr Cole in Italy' (see p. 15).
2. Inventory, loc. cit.
3. Fortnum, loc. cit.
4. Museum records.
5. For Caterina Cibo, see DBI 25, 1982 (?), pp. 237–41. The Cibo arms vary (see, for example, Crollalanza 1965, I, p. 291). Those of Caterina combine the same arms as used by Giovanni Battista Cibo, Pope Innocent VIII (see Jacques Martin, *Heraldry in the Vatican*, Gerrard's Cross, 1987, p. 65), with those of the

(a)

Medici. Similarly those of Varano di Camerino take various forms (see Crollalanza 1965, III, pp. 69–70), but see Litta III, 1835, pl. III. I am grateful to Fiona Leslie for her assistance, and to John Meriton for his comments on the arrangement and blazon of the various Cibo arms, his confirmation of the identification and probable dating.

6. Fortnum, loc. cit.
7. Inv. no. 568-1865; Fortnum 1876, p. 179. A medallion containing a bust of Apollo is set under the base. See Molinier 1889, I, pp. 13–15, nos 25–8; Toderi and Toderi 1996, pp. 133–5, nos 242–4 for the plaquettes.
8. See Rome 1982, pp. 46–7, no. 18.
9. Inv. no. Br.113, h. 17, 9.5 (without handle), diam. 8.8; Alberici 1976, fig. 20, as Venetian, sixteenth-century.
10. The snake is not identified in the cited literature, but was perhaps believed to be the tail of the lion's skin.
11. See Toderi and Toderi, loc. cit. at n. 7.
12. See p. 103; Rome 1982, loc. cit. at n. 8.
13. For example, in a paper entitled, 'Country Medicine in the Urban Piazza: snake handlers and other itinerants' at the Wellcome Symposium for the History of Medicine, 26 March 1999, Professor Katharine Park, Harvard University, discussed the snakebite healers known as the Paoliani. These men claimed to be descendants of St Paul, who had inherited an immunity to snakebite, and travelled around performing shows of snake handling that often served to frighten city folk into buying their curing powder (sometimes called Maltese or St Paul's earth), which they presumably ground in mortars. St Paul was in Malta when he was bitten by the snake that he shook off into a fire, remaining unharmed, leading the islanders to take him to be a god. The snake handler is sometimes shown as a naked man.
14. Weinberger 1929, lot 161, as north Italian, sixteenth-century; h. 10.8, diam. 15.
15. Metman and Vaudoyer 1910, pl. IX, p. 3, no. 106; inv. Pe394; h. 7.8, diam. 14, as Italian, sixteenth-century.

Bibliography

Inventory 1870, p. 2; Fortnum 1876, p. 176.

15. Mortar with coat of arms and lizard

Cast by Ambrogio Lucenti (1586–1656)
Central Italian (Rome); dated 1642
Bell-metal
h. 33.5; diam. 43 (rim), 25.4 (base); wt 76 kg.
A.2-1974

Provenance: Bought with assistance from the Bequest of Captain H. B. Murray from Arthur Davidson Ltd, Jermyn Street, London SW1, for £3,000.

Exhibited: *Objects*, Victoria and Albert Museum, 31 May–13 August 1978.

Condition: The surface abraded and dented in places. Green deposit around the decoration.
Interior: greenish-white deposit; indentation in centre of bowl, plus elsewhere.

Base: smooth with imprint of what appears to be material; vague evidence of pour-hole with cracking; minor pitting; green corrosion spots. Marks: ⚹⚹ and ✳✳.
Dark brown patina.
Metal analysis: bell-metal with some lead and zinc. The iron content on the handle is doubtless due to contamination.

Bell-shaped mortar with projecting rim and recessed lip, and two elaborate scroll-formed handles, each decorated with a lion's head and projecting beads, terminating in a grotesque mask. On the rim, two astragals, and between two torus mouldings is the legend applied in relief: SIMANDIVS . DE . TOTIS . VRBEVETANVS . CIVIS . ROMANVS . ANNO . D . M . D . CXLII . FECIT + (Simandio de Toti (or Tozzi) of Orvieto, citizen of Rome. Made 1642). On the body, two parallel torus mouldings

(a)

into which the lion heads of the handles are fitted. Decorated on one side is a coat of arms (a rampant lion, a bend) with a helm and cresting. On the other side is a lizard with a skeletal leaf in its mouth and a copper disc with a profile portrait of Pope Urban VIII (see below). Beneath this decoration, another set of two parallel torus mouldings, flanked by astragals, between which (below the lizard) is the stamped inscription: . AMBROSII LVCENTIS ROMANI . F . C . A . OPVS . (Work [of] Ambrogio Lucenti F. C. A. of Rome). Plain bowl and moulded foot.

The mortar is of an exceptionally well-balanced design. The handles, which appear to have been cast separately and attached, fit neatly into the mouldings, the lion heads imitating a herm-like support for the projecting rim. It is apparent from some of the letters around the rim that they were applied in the wax on small panels, in the usual manner, but the panels have mostly been smoothed out prior to casting. The lizard and leaf are cast from nature (see p. 28). The indentation at the centre of the mortar suggests the use of a pestle suspended from a rod projecting from the wall (see fig. 11), or alternatively a wooden lid with a hole at the centre to guide the pestle and prevent material from flying out during grinding. The mortar was reported to have been used as a flower pot prior to acquisition, and the white deposit inside was probably caused by water.

The coat of arms is presumably that of the owner, Simandio de Toti or Tozzi of Orvieto, whose name appears around the rim. According to the applied legend, he originated from Orvieto, but was a Roman citizen in 1642 and, because of the inclusion of the image of the Pope, may have worked in the papal pharmacy.[1] Urban VIII (Maffeo Barberini, b. 1568, Pope 6 August 1623–29 July 1644) is noted for his architectural embellishment of Rome, notably his patronage of the leading sculptor and architect, Gianlorenzo Bernini (1598–1680), which included the commissioning of the bronze *Baldacchino* marking the high altar and burial place of St Peter in the Cathedral at Rome (executed 1624–7).[2] Much of the bronze for casting the *Baldacchino* was supplied by stripping the portico of the Pantheon, a source that Urban also used to equip the improved fortifications of Castel Sant'Angelo with cannon.[3]

The roundel inserted into the mortar is based on the obverse of a medal by Gaspare Mola (c.1580–1640), a prolific artist who served numerous princely patrons. In addition to being a medallist, he was a gem and die-cutter, as well as a silver- and goldsmith, gun-maker and art dealer. The surface of the medal is worn, preventing firm identification of the original model, but it appears closest to the image on the commemorative medal cast for the unveiling of Bernini's revised crowning canopy of the *Baldacchino* on the Feast of St Peter, 29 June 1633.[4] This

(b)

would be particularly relevant as Ambrogio Lucenti, who cast the present mortar, was one of the specialist founders employed in the casting of the *Baldacchino*, which (like the mortar) features nature-casts. Ambrogio was a member of a family of bronze founders, the best known probably being his son, Girolamo, who was a pupil of Bernini's rival, Alessandro Algardi (1598–1654). Ambrogio was also employed to cast sculpture after models by Algardi. In 1640, he supplied the metal and cast a bust of Gregory XV for S. Maria in Vallicella, and in 1650 he cast the bronzes of the Trinità dei Pellegrini memorial to Pope Innocent X. He was not involved in the chasing and finishing of the sculptures, and appears to have been primarily a foundry-man, specializing particularly in bells and ordnance.[5] The abbreviation F. C. A. after Ambrogio's name may possibly be translated as Fusorem [Reverenda] Camera Apostolica, the title borne by other founders, such as Giovanni Giardino (1646–1722), whose tomb inscription describes him as 'FVSOREM R . C . A . ET ARGENTARIUM S . PAL . AP.'[6]

A closely related mortar on the London art market, dated 1653, can safely be assigned to the same foundry.[7] The basic form of this mortar developed considerably earlier, as is evidenced by examples in the Metropolitan Museum of Art, New York, and the J. Paul Getty Museum, Los Angeles, which can be dated to the mid-sixteenth century.[8] The Metropolitan mortar bears the date of 1544, and the Getty mortar has been similarly dated on the basis of its relationship to the former, in conjunction with analysis of the decorative motifs. These two mortars and the 1653 mortar attributed to Lucenti are all decorated around the bowl with an acanthus frieze. On the Lucenti mortar, however, the leaves are treated more lushly and with a windswept appearance.

Notes

1. Luca Tozzi (1638–1717), possibly a relative, was a celebrated physician who was called to Rome by Innocent XII to become professor at the Sapienza (University) and principal papal doctor (Enc. Ital., 34, p. 127). Simandio de Tozzi, and the coat of arms on the mortar, have not yet been firmly identified.

2. Rudolf Wittkower, *Gian Lorenzo Bernini. The Sculptor of the Roman Baroque*, Oxford, 1981, pp. 189–90, no. 21; Montagu 1989, pp. 55–6; Avery 1997, pp. 95–100.

3. Kelly 1986, pp. 280–1.

4. For Mola, see Ivan Mirnik, 'Medals by Mola and Morone Mola in Zagreb' in *The Medal*, no. 22, 1993, pp. 27–33. For the 1633 medal, see Nathan T. Whitman, *Roma Resurgens. Papal Medals from the Age of the Baroque* (exh. cat., Michigan Museum of Art, 1981), Michigan, 1983, pp. 67–8, no. 50; Aidan Weston-Lewis (ed.), *Effigies & Ecstasies. Roman Baroque Sculpture and Design in the Age of Bernini* (exh. cat., National Gallery of Scotland), Edinburgh, 1998, p. 106, cat. nos 61 and 62, and pp. 104–5, cat. nos 58–60, for the *Baldacchino*.

5. Details of Ambrogio's documented works kindly provided by Jennifer Montagu from notes she had taken in the Archivio di Stato di Roma. See also Montagu 1985, I, p. 184, II, p. 427, no. 150, pp. 430–1, no. 155, and further references; Thieme-Becker 1992, 23, pp. 435–6.

6. See Vincenzo Forcella, *Iscrizioni delle chiese e d'altri edifici di Roma dal secolo XI ai giorni nostri*, (14 vols), Rome, 1869–84, X, p. 269, no. 426; for Giardino, see Thieme-Becker 1992, 13/14, p. 590 (under Giardini). I am grateful to Jennifer Montagu for identifying this possibility, and for advising me of the reference. She has also found a reference to Orazio Censore (active 1569–d. 1622) as *fonditore della Camera*, but it has not been possible to establish what form any official title took at this date. I am also grateful to Dr Rundle for his initial identification, and to Dr Montagu for her assistance in trying to identify Tozzi.

7. With Daniel Katz Limited (January 2000); Sotheby's *European Sculpture and Works of Art*, London, 16 December 1998, lot 75A, as north Italian; Agnew's, London, November–December 1989, no. 70, as north Italian.

8. Metropolitan Museum, inv. no. 10.37.1, h. 37.5, diam. 48.3, with the legend: MANNVS . CROCVLVS . AMERINVS . FIERI . FECIT . ANNO . MDXLIV (Mannus Croculus of Amelia [?] had it made in 1544). Getty Museum, inv. no. 85.SB.179, h. 48.9, diam. 59.7, see Peter Fusco, *Summary Catalogue of European Sculpture in the J. Paul Getty Museum*, Los Angeles, 1997, p. 68, as probably Venice, possibly Padua, *c.*1550. I am grateful to Dr Fusco for showing me his draft entry for the forthcoming *Catalogue of Sculpture in the J. Paul Getty Museum*. Another mortar of similar form and with closely related acanthus around the bowl appears in Corvi 1997, p. 92 (Farmacia A. Corvi, Piacenza, h. 36, diam. 43), noted as bearing the legend: PETRUS FECIT ANNO MDCCXLI (1741); a partial legend is visible in the illustration, which reads 'PIETRO ANTONIO'. Assuming the dating on these mortars is correct, it is evident that the form and style continued in use over an extended period.

Bibliography

Montagu 1989, pp. 52 and 54, fig. 59; Avery 1997, p. 100, fig. 116.

16. Mortar of the Jesuit College in Rome

Central Italian (Rome); dated 1647
Bronze
h. 46.3; diam. 58.3 (rim), 34.7 (base); wt 248 kg
M.2681-1931

Provenance: Collection of Mrs Ellen Hearn, Menton, France, from August 1906; given by Mrs Hearn in 1931 as part of the second instalment of the Alfred Williams Hearn Gift in memory of her late husband.[1]

Condition: Chipped around the rim.
Interior: indented surface with worn hollow in base.
Base: mottled; cracks filled with material of different colours, possibly including some lead. Remains of filler. Very dark brown patina.
Metal analysis: the analysis gave variable results from the different spectra. The base analysed as a bronze with low lead content, the rim and breast of the applied figure leaded low-tin bronze, and the shield a bronze with an exceptionally high lead content.

Large bell-shaped mortar with projecting, moulded rim and recessed lip, and two handles in the form of winged female demi-figures. Around the rim, between a large fillet raised and torus mouldings, is the legend, applied in relief: + AD . LAVDEM . DEI . ET . B . V . M . ET . SS . IGNIATII . ET . FRANCISCI . COL . ROM . SOCI . IESV . AN . DO . M . DC . XLVII (To the Glory of God and the Blessed Virgin Mary and Sts Ignatius and Francis. Roman College of the Society of Jesus, AD 1647).

Below, two parallel astragal and torus mouldings. Each side of the main body decorated with an elaborate cartouche, one filled with the monogram IHS with cross and anchor, the other with the figure of St Ignatius of Loyola. Moulded foot.

The significantly different lead content of the coat of arms may indicate that it was cast separately and soldered on, although this is not immediately evident from visual examination. The hollow inside indicates where the pestle, probably supported from above, had pounded the substances (see fig. 11).

This spectacular vessel was listed by Mrs Hearn as 'Renaissance mortar, large (dated 1647)'.[2] It was on the list of objects offered to the Museum in 1923, when Mrs Hearn gave the original gift in the name of her late husband, who had died in 1904. At that time the mortar was situated outside the library at her villa in Menton, France.

St Ignatius of Loyola (c.1491–1556; canonized in 1622) founded the Society of Jesus (the Jesuits), the setting up of which was sanctioned by Pope Paul III in 1540. Ignatius, who was born at Loyola in northern Spain, remained in Rome directing the Society until his sudden death in 1556. In addition to taking vows of obedience to the Pope and an anti-Protestant stance, the Jesuit Order had a powerful charitable mission, including education of the young. One cartouche represents the badge of the Jesuits, with the sacred monogram 'IHS' (the abbreviation of the name of Jesus in Greek), which they had adopted as their device.

The legend indicates that the mortar was made for the Jesuit College at Rome, the Collegio Romano, situated close to the church of St Ignatius.[3] The saint is represented without a halo, but holding a book (one of his attributes), symbolic of his role as teacher appropriate to the college. He is usually portrayed as balding, with a short dark beard, but here appears youthful and clean-shaven. There would presumably have been an infirmary at the college where potions would have been ground to make drugs, and the large scale of the mortar indicates that this was its likely use. Alternatively the mortar could

(b)

have been used in the kitchens, where there would have been a need for grinding large quantities of material in the preparation of meals for members of the college.

Stylistically, the mortar is related to that made by Ambrogio Lucenti in 1642 (cat. no. 15). It is therefore possible that this mortar emanates from the same workshop. The metal composition is, however, different from that of the Lucenti mortar, which is primarily bell-metal as opposed to leaded bronze (see Appendix 1). The handles are clearly of a standard type. Their appearance on a mortar produced for the Jesuit College seems inappropriate, but the combination of decoration based on the antique with contemporary religious devices was common.

(a)

Notes

1. It was either bought for or valued at FF1,950 in 1906, and when finally acquired after her death it was given the lower value of FF1,500 for probate (details from Museum registered files). The donation is discussed in *Review* 1931, p. 63.

2. Mrs Hearn's notebook in Museum registered file, p. 10. A reference to Eastbourne as the apparent place of purchase presumably refers to the offices of her agent, Thomas Sutton, who was based there.

3. See Brizzi, Marini and Pombeni 1988, p. 219, for the opening of a public school in the Jesuit College, near to the church of S. Lucia in 1551; p. 221 for various other significant events in the Jesuit College between 1635 and 1645. See also Ravanelli Guidotti 1994 for the Jesuit pharmacy, Novellara. The Museum acquired objects from the Museum of the Collegio Romano in 1859; three Italian bronzes were among them, inv. nos 4699 to 4702-1859.

NORTH ITALIAN

༺༃༒

The Alberghetti Family

The Alberghetti were a family of bronze-casters who originated in the Massa Fiscaglia (Ferrara) and were active primarily at Ferrara, Florence and Venice. They were based at the Venice Arsenal from the late fifteenth until the nineteenth century. The founder of the dynasty, Alberghetto I, was active in Ferrara by 1483 and documented in the service of Lorenzo de' Medici in Florence in 1485. By 1487 he was working for the Este court at Ferrara, before moving to Venice in 1498. Among Alberghetto's sons were Sigismondo, who was active from 1487 and became Director of one of the Arsenal foundries in Venice, and Giovanni (Zanin). The latter was also working for the Ferrarese court in 1484. Subsequently he cast sculptures for the Zen Chapel in S. Marco, Venice, in collaboration with Antonio Lombardo and Paolo Savin in 1505–8, and worked as a cannon-founder for the Gonzaga in Mantua in 1509. Two hand bells signed by him survive (see cat. no. 17), the decoration of that in Washington indicating that it was produced in Ferrara in the early to mid-1490s.

Later members of the family include Giulio (b. 1536, foundry Director 1551–72). In 1554 he received the contract for casting the bronze statue of Tommaso Rangone after a model by Jacopo Sansovino, but after several failed attempts to cast the statue, the task was carried out by Tommaso dalle Sagome and Giacomo di Conti. Giulio's surviving works include a mortar in the Museo Nazionale del Bargello, Florence (fig. 13). Alfonso was active in the 1560s–70s, and his attributed

works include one of the large bronze well-heads in the courtyard of the Palazzo Ducale in Venice of 1559 (the other signed by his rival Nicolo di Conti in 1556), and he signed a footed bowl, dated 1572 (Museo Artistico Industriale, Rome; fig. 14). A number of cannon are recorded as having been made by members of the family and examples survive in the Museo Storico Navale, Venice, and the Museo Storico Nazionale dell' Artiglieri, Turin.

Fig. 13. Signed mortar. Giulio Alberghetti, Venice, c.1555–70. Museo Nazionale del Bargello, Florence, inv. no. 715.

Fig. 14. Signed footed bowl. Alfonso Alberghetti, Venice, 1572.
Museo Artistico Industriale, Rome.

Many of the numerous works associated with the Alberghetti foundry depend on a relationship with the signed works cited above, together with two bowls in the Louvre that are widely accepted as the product of the workshop (fig. 15; see cat. no. 19). While generally convincing, the attribution is based on the appearance of various decorative elements on the bowls, which can be linked to the signed works. As already noted, such motifs were frequently used by other foundries, and some caution must therefore be attached to extending the attribution to associated works. Similarly, the signature on the Bargello mortar is inscribed within a *tabula ansata* rather than being cast-in, as with the works signed by Giovanni and Alfonso. There is no reason seriously to doubt the authorship of the mortar, and it therefore seems reasonable to assign related mortars to the workshop. However, the complicated interrelationships of the various groups of north Italian bells and mortars are noted in the relevant entries and should be borne in mind.

The following entries (cat. nos 17–32) can be associated with the Alberghetti foundry. Commencing with a hand bell signed by Giovanni I Alberghetti, they include an after-cast of one of the Louvre bowls, some attributed works, several more tentatively related pieces (which cannot securely be given to the foundry) and others that bear a stylistic relationship but are probably later casts.

Summary bibliography

Cicogna, 1, 1824, pp. 141–2; 2, 1827, p. 431; Angelo Angelucci, *Documenti Inediti per la Storia delle Armi da Fuoco Italiane,* I, part 1, Turin, 1869, pp. 277–311; Quarenghi 1870, esp. pp. 14–17, p. 16 for Alberghetti family tree; Angelo Angelucci, 'I Cannoni Veneti di Famagosta. L'Armeria dell'Arsenale ed il Museo Civico di Venezia. Lettera al chiarissimo Signore Giambattista Cav. di Sardagna' in *Archivio Veneto,* VIII, 1874, pp. 5–24; de Champeaux 1886, p. 10; DBI, I, 1960, pp. 628–33; Pope-Hennessy 1965, p. 124; Jestaz 1986 (references indexed); Scalini 1988, pp. 68, 69 and figs 264, 266, 269, 278 and 279; Boucher 1991, 2, pp. 338–9; Radcliffe 1992, pp. 222–9, nos 37 and 38; Thieme-Becker 1992, 1, p. 182; Franceschini 1995, docs 455b and n, re. Giovanni at Ferrara; Motture forthcoming; V. Avery 2002, including updated family tree.

Fig. 15. Footed bowl. Alberghetti foundry, Venice, 1500–50.
Musée du Louvre, Paris, inv. no. 1719.

17. Hand bell with peacocks and vases

Signed by Giovanni Alberghetti
(documented 1484–1509)
North Italian (Ferrara); *c.*1491–6
Bell-metal
h. 11.4, 8 (without handle); diam. 9.2; wt 482.7 g.
335-1886

Provenance: Bought from Cav. Attilio Simonetti, Rome, in 1886 for £12.

Condition: Handle replaced and loose; several chips around the rim.
Interior: iron pendulum-shaped clapper.
Green-grey patina with applied brown wax and oil (?), worn in places.
Metal analysis: the analysis has produced an odd result with a high iron content for the bell itself, and proportionately lower copper; possibly caused by contamination. The handle is brass.

A hand bell with replacement handle, decorated in six bands. On the crown, (i) a row of water leaves superimposed by a row of acanthus in the interstices. On the neck, (ii) the legend: OPVSZANINIALBERGETI (work [of] Giovanni Alberghetti). On the waist, (iii) fleshy foliage (possibly lotus flowers), palmettes and shells (four); below, (iv) three vases or urns containing fruit and flanked at the base by void cornucopiae (?), supported by peacocks; the tail of each peacock intertwined with a flower and the tail of the bird behind. On the sound bow, (v) egg and dart bordered by rows of beads; below, (vi) water leaf and acanthus, as above. Rows of bead and reel separate the third and fourth, and the fifth and sixth, bands of decoration.

The legend identifies the founder as Giovanni Alberghetti, a member of the family of bronze-founders who originated from Ferrara, but operated in Venice from the late fifteenth to the early nineteenth centuries.[1] Giovanni's father, Alberghetto, went into the service of Ercole d'Este, Duke of Ferrara, in 1487 before working in Faenza (date unknown) and finally settling in Venice in 1498. Giovanni was also active in Ferrara and presumably moved to Venice with his father. It is unclear when he became a master in his own right, but his documented work at the Este court includes a bell and two mortars.[2] Another bell signed by Giovanni survives in the National Gallery of Art, Washington (Kress Collection), and bears much of the same decoration, including the shell and foliage motif, the

egg and dart, and the vases, flanked by different, smaller birds.[3] A third related bell of equally high quality in the Kunstgewerbemuseum, Berlin, is doubtless from the same workshop.[4] Its decorative elements include a disc with a crab (or lobster) and the initials I and A. It has not been possible to identify whether the motif represents a coat of arms or device of someone with those initials or whether (perhaps less likely) the I and A are the initials of Giovanni Alberghetti himself.

The Washington bell displays two profile portraits of Ludovico Sforza, 'Il Moro' (1451–1508), (Duke of Bari, 1479; Duke of Milan, 1494–9 and again in 1500), below which appear two of his personal *imprese*. One has the *scoppetta* (brush) and the other a cloth held by two hands, a device that Ludovico assigned both to his nephew Gian Galeazzo Maria (d. 1494), then Duke of Milan, and to his wife, Beatrice d'Este (1475–97), daughter of Ercole, whom he married in 1491.[5] A possible reference to the Ferrarese duke also appears on the bell in the form of his namesake, shown here as the *Young Hercules strangling the snakes* and as *Hercules resting at the end of his Labours*.[6]

Another bust of Ludovico Sforza can be seen on a bell in the Museum of Fine Arts, Richmond, Virginia.[7] As well as being of similar shape, the Richmond example displays other motifs associated with the Alberghetti workshop, such as the egg and dart, guilloche, and garlands with suspended foliage. The latter two motifs are found on utensils ascribed to later members of the family, but their use was widespread.

The imagery of the Washington bell, notably the *imprese*, strongly suggests that it was made in the early to mid-1490s, possibly in connection with the marriage of Ludovico and Beatrice, as argued elsewhere.[8] It could have been commissioned by a close associate of Ludovico, or by the Duke himself,[9] perhaps as a gift to Ercole d'Este. The mould of the portrait would then have been available for reuse by the workshop, as seen on the Richmond bell.[10] Reproductions of such profile portrait busts may have come into vogue later, as purely decorative examples of *uomini famosi* (famous men). The present bell is of exceptional quality, with its waxy and luscious treatment of the foliage and shell motif, the crisp and clear inscription and the lively birds. The close relationship in style and form to the Washington bell suggests that this example was also made while Giovanni Alberghetti was still in Ferrara, dating it most probably to the 1490s.

Notes

1. Zanin is the Venetian dialect form of Giovanni; Zanino, Zanini and Zuanne also appear in north-eastern Italy.
2. See Franceschini 1995, pp. 313, 314, docs 455b and n, for his work there in 1484, including '*dui mortali per la Illustra nostra Madama*' (two mortars for our illustrious Lady); see also Motture (forthcoming).
3. Inv. no. 1957.14.110 (A.263.107C), h. 15.1, *c*.8 (without handle), diam. 9.9; Pope-Hennessy 1965, p. 125, no. 462, fig. 550; Washington 1994, p. 20; for a full discussion of this bell, see Motture forthcoming.
4. Inv. no. 91,215, h. 15.2, *c*.8.2 (without handle), diam. 10.4; Pechstein 1968, no. 62, as Paduan, end of the fifteenth century. The handle, which is in the form of a putto, may be a replacement. The fitting for the iron clapper appears to be so.
5. Welch 1995, pp. 236 and 243 (*scoppetta*) and p. 198 (cloth). I am grateful to Evelyn Welch and Luke Syson for helpful discussions.
6. See also cat. no. 18.
7. Inv. no. 37-11-20, h. 13.8, diam. 9.8. Gift of Mrs John Kerr Branch in memory of her husband, April 1937. I have not examined this bell.
8. Motture forthcoming.
9. See Wilson 1983, p. 123.
10. However, the possibility that the Richmond bell is the product of another workshop cannot be entirely ruled out.

Bibliography
Inventory 1887, p. 40;
Pope-Hennessy 1965,
p. 125, no. 462;
Radcliffe 1992, p. 225;
Motture forthcoming.

(*a*)

18. Footed bowl decorated with images of Hercules and Apollo

Alberghetti foundry
North Italian (Venice); probably 1550–1600
Bronze
h. 22.3; diam. 25.5 (rim), 14.8 (base); wt 3152.6 g.
736-1893

Provenance: Bought from Murray Marks, London, in 1893 for £70.

Condition: Crisp casting, but with worn areas, particularly on the bowl decoration. Diagonal crack on bowl (from the rim to above Hercules resting, see below), and casting flaw (?). Evidence of turning.
Interior: undulating surface. Crack repaired with solder. Extraneous metal in some areas where the upright side joins the bowl. Small pits visible in the bowl, possibly due to porosity in the cast.

Foot: cracks around the rim of the base, repaired with solder. The foot appears to be soldered to the bowl. Small chips or casting flaws to the projecting mouldings.
Brassy patina throughout.
Metal analysis: the body, base and waist are bronze with varying, low amounts of lead. The white solder appears to be a lead-tin mix.

Circular footed bowl or wine cooler with a moulded lip and decorated with, on the bowl, (i) fleshy acanthus on a cyma recta moulding; (ii) fruit and foliage swags with bell-shaped ends emanating from busts of females (?), which project into the acanthus border and from which are suspended horns of fruit with flying foliage; above the swags, shells containing a bust of a man with a bow on his back (probably Apollo) on cornucopiae bound with ribbon; two gadrooned, boat-shaped vases with fruit and foliate horns flanked by sea monsters with human heads and spiked headdresses emanating from foliage forming fantastic fish, alternated with two gadrooned vases flanked by flowers and griffins; these motifs separated by smaller figures flanked by foliage showing: (a) Apollo playing a *lira da braccio*, (b) a naked man (Apollo?) leaning against a tree, (c) Hercules slaying the Hydra, and (d) Hercules resting; (iii) acanthus on a shallow moulding; (iv) gadrooning. On the foot, (i) foliage and fruit swags with similar pendants suspended from a fine moulding; below, flowers with figures between them showing: (a) Hercules slaying the Nemean lion, (b) Hercules and Antaeus, (c) Apollo leaning against a tree (?) (as above), (d) Hercules slaying the Hydra (as above), (e) the young Hercules with the snakes, and (f) Apollo playing a stringed instrument (as above); (ii) acanthus on a cyma reversa moulding; (iii) plain moulding; (iv) guilloche.

(*a*)

The bowl was described as Florentine, late fifteenth-century, on acquisition.[1] It is closely related in decoration to another version in the Columbia Museum of Art, Columbia (SC) (formerly Kress Collection), attributed to the workshop of Giovanni Alberghetti by Pope-Hennessy on the basis of 'close affinities' to the bronze bells signed by the founder. In fact, the images of the *Hercules strangling the snakes* and the *Hercules resting* are identical to those appearing on the bell signed by Giovanni in the National Gallery of Art, Washington (Kress Collection).[2] Another closely related bowl in the Museo Nazionale del Bargello, Florence, includes many of the same motifs and appears to be of similar facture.[3] The distinctive foliate and fruit festoons and acanthus border can also be seen on another footed bowl in the Bargello, which has itself been related by Radcliffe to a bowl in the Louvre, Paris, bearing similar stiff leaf decoration on the foot.[4] This Bargello bowl has been associated with Alfonso Alberghetti by comparison with a vase in the Museo Artistico Industriale, Rome, signed by the founder and dated 1572 (see fig. 14). Motifs from the signed vase also appear on shallow bowls in the Kunstgewerbemuseum, Berlin, the National Gallery of Art in Washington (Kress Collection) and the Museo Correr, Venice.[5]

The complicated interrelationships of these vessels is discussed in detail by Radcliffe, who concludes that they were probably produced by the Alberghetti workshop in the third quarter of the sixteenth century.[6] It is difficult, however, to establish the date of the present bowl and related pieces with certainty. The motifs and handling of the signed vessel have closer affinities with the shallow bowls in Berlin and Washington than with the crisper and rather more sophisticated treatment of the large Louvre bowl. The latter has a pendant with figurative decoration, including similar but not identical Hercules motifs to the present bowl. The appearance of two of these on the Kress bell by Giovanni, which can be safely dated to the 1490s, confirms that they are early Alberghetti motifs.

The images are drawn largely from the legends of Apollo and Hercules, but in some cases they cannot be firmly identified. The 'man with a bow' is probably Apollo, as is the naked man leaning against a tree, although the serpent Python does not appear, as would normally be expected. The projecting heads may have been based on a plaquette representing Diva Faustina, but may be intended to show the somewhat androgynous

(b) *Detail showing Hercules and Antaeus.*

Apollo in this instance. A version of the Faustina plaquette survives from the Este Collection in Modena,[7] and the Alberghetti are known to have worked for the Este court in Ferrara. The busts of the sea monsters are based on the heads above. The form of the bowl, together with elements of the decoration – including the projecting heads – is also closely related to a footed bowl in the Musée Jacquemart-André, Paris.[8]

Not only is the overall decorative style of the bowl seen in Lombard architectural sculpture of the late fifteenth and early sixteenth century, but specific motifs can also be identified. Both the Apollo playing the *lira* and the Apollo leaning against the tree appear on the door jamb from the Palazzo Stanga at Cremona (now in the Louvre), dated to the late fifteenth century.[9] The centaur carrying off a woman, which appears on the Louvre figurated bowl, also appears on the doorway.[10] In relation to the Louvre bowl, Migeon recognized the source of this motif as a plaquette by Caradosso Foppa (1452–1527), who was active in Milan between 1475 and 1505.[11] The Cremona doorway incorporates Hercules iconography and is a prime example, along with the Colleoni Chapel at Bergamo and the Porta della Rana at Como, of the use of plaquettes, medals and other small-scale sources for architectural decorative motifs.[12] The same Apollo with *lira* can be seen on a pastiglia casket, alongside reduced but similar forms of dolphins flanking forms distinctly reminiscent of the decorative motifs appearing on the bowl signed by Alfonso and the related pieces.[13] In the pastiglia relief these take the form of scrolling foliage emanating from bucrania, while on the bowl they appear as fountain-like structures with sprouting cornucopiae and wings. The vegetal forms on the pastiglia boxes and on a number of bronze utensils, including this footed bowl, bear some resemblance to the decoration employed by the sculptor Amadeo (*c.*1447–1522) on the upper part of the Colleoni Chapel at Bergamo *c.*1470–5.[14]

The Hercules and Antaeus, however, is more closely related to the bronze statuette by Antonio Pollaiuolo (Museo Nazionale del Bargello, Florence) – notably in the pose of Antaeus – than to those found in Lombard architectural decoration, and the design perhaps combines elements from different sources.[15] The attenuated forms are most closely related to plaquettes by the Master IO. F. F., but this is possibly coincidental.[16]

The use of sources known in Lombard architecture, coupled with a similar arrangement and iconographical relationship, therefore suggest that the decorative motifs date from the end of the fifteenth or beginning of the sixteenth century. The appearance of images from a signed bell of the 1490s further supports the likelihood that the model was produced when the foundry was still based in Ferrara. The nature of the casting itself, however, being thin and light and soldered at the foot, raises some questions as to the date of production of this particular example. The closely related Bargello bowl bears an inscription inside, which provides a *terminus ante quem* for its facture of 1793.[17] These bowls are less likely to be the products of the seventeenth or eighteenth century, and are therefore probably sixteenth-century casts.

Other related works

See cat. no. 22 and related pieces.

Notes

1. Inventory, loc. cit.
2. Inv. no. CMA 1963.49, h. 18.7, diam. 25.5 (rim), 12.3 (foot); wt 3345.1 g; see Pope-Hennessy 1965, p. 125, no. 463 for the bowl (foot replaced); p. 125, no. 462 for the signed bell; Washington 1994, p. 20, for the bell. See also cat. no. 17.
3. Inv. no. 250C (Carrand Collection, given in 1889); h. 22.8, diam. 25.1 (rim), 14.3 (base).
4. See Radcliffe 1992, pp. 226–9, no. 38, for a full discussion.
5. Pechstein 1968, no. 89 (as workshop of Alfonso Alberghetti), with references to other related pieces; Pope-Hennessy 1965, p. 144, no. 526, as Padua or Venice late fifteenth/early sixteenth century. Pope-Hennessy does not make the connection with the signed bowl, but compares it instead to cat. no. 57. The (thinly cast) bowl in the Correr, inv. no. 105, bears simple armorials, possibly identifiable with a branch of the Ferri of Venice (bendy azure and or; see Coronelli 1694, p. 16; Crollalanza 1965, I, p. 404).
6. Radcliffe loc. cit. at n. 4 above.
7. See Rossi 1974, p. 53, no. 68, listing other versions, including those from the Este Collection and one in the V&A (inv. no. A.405-1910; see Maclagan 1924, p. 15).
8. Inv. no. 109, formerly Salting Collection, *Catalogue Itinéraire* 1948, p. 71; see Bode/Draper 1980, p. 47 and pl. CXXI as unlocated, probably Venetian, early sixteenth-century.
9. See de Jouy-Guitton 1876, p. 315.
10. Ibid., pp. 40, 329–30.
11. Migeon 1904, p. 104.
12. See, for example, Schofield 1992 for a discussion of small-scale and other antique sources.
13. See Hildburgh 1946, p. 137 and pl. XXIII b; and p. 39 above. Pastiglia workshops were active in Ferrara and the Veneto, where the Alberghetti also had their foundries.
14. Schofield 1992, p. 37, fig. 6.
15. See Alison Wright, 'Dimensional tension in the work of Antonio Pollaiuolo' in Currie and Motture 1997, pp. 65–86, esp. pls 4.1–4.3, showing the bronze and related painting; Leopold D. Ettlinger, *Antonio and Piero Pollaiuolo*, Oxford, 1978, p. 147, no. 18, figs 78–82 for the bronze, and fig. 22 for an engraving by Cristofano Robetta, showing the composition of the painting (illus. at fig. 92). Plaquettes by Moderno and Caradosso provide designs for other subjects; for Moderno's *Hercules and Antaeus*, see Douglas Lewis, 'The Plaquettes of "Moderno" and His Followers' in Luchs 1989, pp. 105–41, p. 118, fig. 8. See de Jouy-Guitton 1876, p. 314, for the composition of this subject on the Stanga doorway.
16. See, for example, Christopher B. Fulton, 'The Master IO. F. F. and the Function of Plaquettes' in Luchs 1989, pp. 143–62.
17. The inscription reads: TRIBVTO DELLA FAMILIA CARONNI MONZESE AL MUSEO VITZAI 1793. See DBI, 20. 1977, pp. 542–6 for the antiquarian and the numismatist Felice Caronni of Monza, including his relationship with Count Michele di Wiczai.

Bibliography

Inventory 1895, pp. 102–3; Pope-Hennessy 1965, p. 125, no. 463; Radcliffe 1992, p. 228.

19. Footed bowl with foliate motifs

After an original attributed to the Alberghetti foundry (1500–50)
French (probably Paris); 1800–50
Brass
h. 37; diam. 43.1 (rim), 24.2 (base); wt 14 kg.
1581-1855

Provenance: Bought in 1855 for £25 (provenance unknown).

Condition: Damage and repair to the rim. Thinly cast in places, with flaws. Underneath there is a clear join in the foot, which was cast separately in two halves; a staple is also visible, together with solder, pins and inserts. There is no base to the bowl. The foot is attached from the inside by modern screws.
Interior: shadow of basic shape of external decoration. Remains of greyish deposit inside.
Very dark brown patina
Metal analysis: brass with varying zinc content and some lead.

The bowl is decorated around the rim with a foliage motif, moulding and acanthus. On the shoulder of the bowl a foliate arcaded relief, egg and dart, and bead. On the upper part of the body, below a moulding, a frieze of paired cornucopiae flanking winged vases from which emerge caducei, linked by foliate scrolls to the foliage motifs with which they alternate. On the lower part of the body, a row of bead, and a moulding from which are suspended foliate and fruit pendants and swags, with cherub heads above. Below (emanating from the base of the bowl) is acanthus, alternating with and overlapping stiff leaf, from which flowers emerge. On the foot, downward-facing stiff leaf. Around the rim of the foot, beneath an indented moulding, is a scrolled foliate pattern with alternating motifs of a chalice with an emerging crucifix and vases flanked by half-figures, bordered by rope decoration.

Acquired as a sixteenth-century bronze from an unknown source in 1855, the bowl was dated to the first half of the sixteenth century by Fortnum, who considered it 'A fine vase, the foot of which, if not a modern restoration, has been detached and repaired'.[1] It was identified by Radcliffe as an after-cast of one of the two large *tazze* in the Louvre attributed to the Alberghetti foundry (see also fig. 15).[2] The various attributions of the Louvre bowls, together with the circumstances under which copies were probably made, have been fully discussed by Radcliffe in connection with another, differently cast version in the Thyssen-Bornemisza Collection.

The originals have long been accepted as a product of the Alberghetti foundry, but have been variously associated with Giovanni I Alberghetti,[3] giving a date in the late fifteenth or early sixteenth century, and Alfonso Alberghetti, who was responsible for a footed bowl dated 1572 in the Museo Artistico Industriale, Rome (fig. 14).[4] The assignment of the Louvre bowls to the mid-sixteenth century is supported by Radcliffe on the basis of the close relationship between the frieze on Alfonso's footed bowl and those in the Louvre, coupled with the appearance of the same stiff-leaf decoration on the foot of a bowl in the Bargello, Florence, also apparently cast by the foundry.[5] As argued elsewhere (see cat. no. 18), it is difficult accurately to determine the date of production of these objects based on the use of motifs alone, in view of the reuse of moulds over a long period, and therefore an earlier date cannot be ruled out.

The nature of the casting of this bowl, described above, together with the metal analysis, confirm its status as an after-cast of the Louvre original. It lacks the legend around the interior of the rim, which appears both on the original and the Thyssen copy, and it has a ghosting of the gadrooning on the interior.[6] The present example differs markedly in facture from the bowl in the Thyssen Collection, and was doubtless produced by a different foundry. Copies were presumably made while the original was in the Musée des Monuments français, and the bowl was therefore probably made in Paris.[7]

Notes
1. Fortnum, loc. cit.
2. Migeon 1904, pp. 100–3, no. 70; Radcliffe 1992, loc. cit. and pp. 228–9. See pp. 96–7 above for comment on the attribution.
3. Pope-Hennessy 1965, p. 125, no. 463.
4. Pechstein 1968, no. 89.
5. Radcliffe 1992, p. 229, fig. 3.
6. The legend suggests that it was designed as a baptismal font (see Radcliffe 1992, p. 228).
7. A. Lenoir, *Musée des Monumens français* [*sic*], IV, Paris, 1805, pp. 143–4, illus pl. 155, no. 136 (ascribed to Benvenuto Cellini). I am grateful to Anthony Radcliffe for his comments on the relationship with the Thyssen bowl, which I have not seen, and the likely origin of these copies.

Bibliography
Inventory 1868 (objects acquired in the year 1855), p. 109; Fortnum 1876, p. 208; Radcliffe 1992, pp. 226–7.

20. Mortar with handles in the form of fantastic fish

Alberghetti foundry (?)
North Italian (Ferrara or Venice?); 1480–1520
Bronze
h. 12.5; diam.14.9 (rim), 10.5 (base); wt 3189.5 g.
350-1889

Provenance: Bought from Michelangelo Guggenheim, Venice, in 1889 (with 335 to 354-1889, £300).

Condition: One handle broken; decoration uneven and squashy in places; worn, with some cracks and pitting; one coat of arms obliterated, the other indistinct.
Interior: dark red around the bottom with green corrosion and rust-coloured deposits.

Base: incised concentric rings with infill (cast-in repair?) and evidence of shrinkage around pouring cup.
Mid-brown patina, brassy where worn.
Metal analysis: high-tin bronze with low lead content; handles bell-metal with higher lead content; the infill on the base is bell-metal with some zinc.

Conical mortar with two handles in the shape of fantastic fish with large dorsal fins and flanking foliage. A projecting rim decorated with an overlapping acanthus and rope motif. On each side of the body, two foliate swags tied at the centre with cherub heads above; between the swags a female (?) bust emerging from foliage, below which is a coat of arms (two bendlets at the base of a chief a closet on

a chief [an unidentified object]) flanked by foliage and supported by naked boys with haloes, each holding a branch, with a peacock to either side; above the left-hand peacock, a vase with handles in the form of fish. On the foot (separated by an ovolo moulding), bands of bead and reel and dentil reversed (?) between two bands of rope (cable).

There are signs of wear inside the mortar and corrosion suggests that it may have been used to grind salt or other chemical substances. The bowl has been discoloured or the copper has been drawn to the surface, a phenomenon sometimes caused by heat, or perhaps in this instance by a chemical reaction. Similar reddening occurs when using certain gums or resins.[1] The infill in the base could be either a contemporary repair to a casting flaw or a later repair necessitated by wear.

(*a*) *base*

The mortar was acquired as Italian, sixteenth-century; it was re-dated by Launert to the end of the fifteenth century, but without refining the region of origin.[2] The putti flanking shields are closely related to those on the base of cat. no. 27 and a footed bowl in the Musée Jacquemart-André, Paris, which bears decorative features associated with the Alberghetti foundry.[3] These putti are variations on a basic model; on both the London and Paris bowls they support overlapping shields and form mirror images with the putto's free hand lowered. The Paris figures hold a different type of foliage from the present example and

show no trace of any haloes. In contrast to the present example, the boys form exact mirror images. Similarly, and unusually for this type of decoration, the design of each side is asymmetrical. Putti were popular decorative motifs, appearing in a variety of forms and styles, and frequently as shield supporters.[4]

Other motifs provide links with a coherent group of mortars, discussed in detail under cat. no. 24. Both the Washington and Paris mortars from the group bear a relief of a fantastic fish similar to those forming the handles of the present mortar; the former also has the same style of shield. The arms were tentatively identified in the Museum's records as being those of the Millini, although their indistinct nature makes firm identification impossible.[5] While it is not possible to assign the mortar securely to the Alberghetti, its decoration – notably the form of the handles and shield, coupled with the provenance – suggests a Venetian origin.[6] The shape of the mortar matches Middeldorf's 'Renaissance type', which he relates to Venetian well-heads.[7] The decoration is, however, more elaborate and the lip less prominent than any of his examples. The mortar probably dates from the late fifteenth or the early sixteenth century; a question as to its authenticity springs from the ill-defined coats of arms (although this may have been accentuated by wear), which would doubtless have been a disappointment to any commissioning owner.

Notes

1. I am grateful to Jo Castle for this information.
2. Inventory and Launert, locc. citt.
3. *Catalogue Itinéraire* 1948, p. 71, no. 910, as Paduan, end of the fifteenth century. See also cat. no. 18.
4. See, for example, Middeldorf 1981, p. 113, for other examples, plus cat. no. 75.
5. Crollalanza 1965, II, p. 141 including Millini di Romagna (*Bandato d'azzurro e d'oro, col capo del primo sostenuto di rosso, e caricato di un M antica d'oro*); also Millini of Rome in Rietstap 1887, II, p. 227; Rietstap/Rolland 1912, IV, pl. CCXIII: blazoned by John Meriton as bendy of six azure and or at the base of a chief azure charged with an antique [gothic] M or a closet gules.
6. Paired fish are frequently found as handles, particularly on cannon.
7. See Middeldorf 1981, pp. 11 and 86–99, nos 21–6.

Bibliography

Inventory 1890, p. 36; Launert 1990, pp. 70 and 196, no. 216.

21. Mortar with dancing figures

Alberghetti foundry (?)
North Italian (Ferrara or Venice); *c*.1480–1550
Bronze
h. 9.7; diam. 13.1 (rim), 8.7 (base); w. 14.5; wt 1995.6 g.
M.22-1923

Provenance: Collection of Mrs Ellen Hearn, Menton, France; given by Mrs Hearn in 1923 as part of the first instalment of the Alfred Williams Hearn Gift in memory of her husband.

Condition: Poor cast, with signs of porosity;[1] uneven areas of wear. Handles probably cast-in.
Interior: rough with porous appearance; green deposit or corrosion.
Base: shadow of shrinkage where the pouring sprue was attached; a few pits; otherwise smooth but with tiny air bubbles, possibly indicating porosity.
Dark brown patina worn to reveal a brassy colour; brown/black patina inside; mottled dark brown underneath.
Metal analysis: a consistent, fairly high tin-bronze, with some lead content. Antimony is present in the body and slightly more lead in the handle.

A conical mortar with two plain projecting handles. Decorated around the rim with guilloche between plain mouldings and, below, overlapping acanthus on a cyma recta moulding. On the body, a frieze of flying birds facing and alternating with exhaling cherub heads with two sets of wings, to either side of which is a *tazza*, vase or fountain (?) flanked by rosettes and dancing, naked figures. Moulded foot.

The decorative friezes around the rim appear each to have been applied in two halves, although the joins are worn. Much of the decoration is heavily rubbed, but it is more clearly defined in the protected areas. The mortar is comparatively light, presumably due to the porosity of the cast.

Close examination of the decoration suggests associations with alchemical imagery, as all the elements appear in illustrations to texts on the subject.[2] The figures facing right on the present mortar are possibly female, and appear to have longish hair, flopping over their foreheads. Those facing left appear to be crowned and bearded. They possibly represent the chemical wedding, a crucial ritual in the preparation of the philosopher's stone and the creation process, based on classical and pre-Christian tradition. The imagery would be appropriate for mortars used for grinding the philosopher's stone or in a similar context.[3] In an engraving of 1617, the image of creation consists of the physical world placed at the centre of a series of concentric circles representing the liberal arts and different elements. The three outermost rings show Paradise with two bands of small gesticulating figures, some of which are putti and others crowned figures reminiscent of those on the present mortar. The final ring of the celestial plane shows winged cherub heads.[4] Exhalation also features strongly in alchemical philosophy, and diverse exhaling figures, including similar cherub heads (usually representing the Winds), can be seen in hermetic literature.[5]

Although the unusual arrangement of the decoration on this mortar allows consideration of a specific use, some of the motifs appear on other mortars. The same *tazza* (vase or fountain?), for example, can be seen on a mortar in Washington, described by Pope-Hennessy as Italian, fifteenth- or early sixteenth-century.[6] Another mortar in Rotterdam bearing this motif belongs to a group of related pieces, including cat. no. 30. A link between the Washington mortar and cat. no. 25 is provided by the appearance of the same horn-blowing putti. The stiffness and unwieldy poses of the figures are also reminiscent of other related utensils, such as a hand bell in the Kunstgewerbemuseum, Berlin.[7] All can be associated with north Italy, and have links with pieces produced by the Alberghetti foundry.[8]

The form of the mortar and the nature of its decoration can be compared with that of another example from the Hearn Collection, cat. no. 22, which also displays patterns associated with the Alberghetti foundry. The indistinct casting of both has raised the question of whether they could be after-casts. However, in both instances the designs appear to have been individually applied in the wax, and there are signs of use. The closeness of the two in style, including the alloy content, suggests that they may have been produced by the same foundry. The dating of the present piece, acquired as an Italian fifteenth-century mortar, was later refined to the last part of the century.[9] The type was categorized as 'Classical Renaissance' by Middeldorf, and assigned to Padua or Venice in the first half of the sixteenth century.[10] Precise dating is, however, problematic due to the use of the form over a long period.

Notes

1. Porosity implies that small air bubbles are trapped in the metal, but does not indicate that the mortar was not waterproof.

2. Some of these illustrations are later in date than the mortar (see below).

3. The marriage represented the moment when the chemical combination of opposites was achieved: for example, sulphur and mercury, spirit and body, hot and cold. It was perceived in a variety of ways, including the union of king and queen. For illustrations of the chemical wedding see, for example, Roberts 1994, illus. on p. 85, from Johann David Mylius, *Anatomia auri*, Frankfurt 1628; numerous images from alchemical literature are reproduced in Calvesi 1986. I am grateful to Jemma Street for her suggestions regarding the imagery of this mortar.

4. See, for example, Jocelyn Goodwin, *Robert Fludd: Hermetic Philosopher and Surveyor of Two Worlds*, London, 1979, p. 23. Fludd was an English physician who practised medicine and published his theories on alchemy.

5. See, for example, a diagram showing the Zodiac and the Winds representing the creation of the world and the separation of the sky from the earth in D'espagnet 1972, p. 43; several examples from Fludd in Goodwin, op. cit., at n. 4 above, such as p. 57, fig. 63 (*The Four Archangels and the Twelve Winds*) and p. 58, no. 64 (*The Qualities of the Winds*). For issues surrounding exhalation and the philosophy of metals, see Cole 2002 (forthcoming).

6. Inv. no. 1975.14.99 (A.252.96C), h. 13.3, diam. 17.6 (rim), 11.5 (base); wt 4643.4 g; Pope-Hennessy 1965, p. 155, no. 569; Washington 1994, p. 115. Pitting inside and signs of use; evidence of shrinkage where the pouring sprue was attached; waxy cast with some wear; dark brown patina.

7. Inv. no. 75,89; Pechstein 1968, no. 53 as north Italian, end fifteenth-/early sixteenth-century.

8. See cat. nos 25 and 30 for details.

9. Museum records.

10. Middeldorf 1981, p. 11.

22. Mortar with Hercules and Antaeus

Attributed to the Alberghetti foundry
North Italian (Venice); 1500–50
Bronze
h. 11.9; diam.16.2 (rim), 11.1 (base); w. 19.6;
wt 5574.2 g.
Circ. 382-1923

Provenance: Collection of Mrs Ellen Hearn, Menton, France; given by Mrs Hearn in 1923 as part of the first instalment of the Alfred Williams Hearn Gift in memory of her late husband.

Condition: Surface worn and pitted in places. Some extraneous bronze on the surface. Indentations to rim and cracking around the foot moulding.
Interior: indented at the surface, pitted and with a hairline crack adjacent to the exterior crack on the foot.
Base: smooth.
Brassy patina with dark mottling.
Metal analysis: bronze of consistent alloy between the body, base and handle.

Bell-shaped mortar with recessed lip and two plain projecting handles. Decorated around the rim with guilloche with plain mouldings, and acanthus on a cyma recta moulding. On the body, swags with suspensions of similar foliage, stamps of *Hercules and Antaeus* and a naked male leaning against a tree (Apollo?), a cockerel and a goose (beneath the handles), each motif flanked by curling foliage. Plain moulded foot.

The guilloche pattern is joined above one handle and was apparently cut down in the wax. There is no evidence of a pour-hole underneath the mortar. The handles are possibly cast in. The cracking is probably due to use, perhaps precipitated by a weakness in the casting.

The mortar was dated to about 1500 when acquired, but not specifically localized.[1] The nature of its facture together with its heavily worn surface subsequently led to the suspicion that it was an after-cast or fake.[2] However, the ornamentation has retained its crispness in the protected areas, and there appears to be no reason to doubt the mortar's authenticity.

Both figural stamps are identical to those on a footed bowl in the present collection (cat. no. 18), although extremely worn. They form part of a series of such images, two of which appear on a bell in the National Gallery of Art, Washington (Kress Collection), signed by Giovanni Alberghetti and datable to the early 1490s.[3] Similar swags can be seen on a bell in the Museo Nazionale del Bargello, Florence,[4] which also displays male busts with spiked hair identical to those on the footed bowl signed and dated (1572) by Alfonso Alberghetti in the Museo Artistico Industriale, Rome (fig. 14).

In view of the combination of elements associated with the products of both early and later members of the Alberghetti family, it is difficult to date the mortar accurately. Its shape falls into the category of the 'Classical Renaissance type…usually attributed to Venetian and Paduan foundries of the first half of the 16th century', according to Middeldorf.[5] Radcliffe agrees that this style of mortar developed later than the conical ones, which Middeldorf classified as 'Early Renaissance' and 'Renaissance' types.[6] It differs in both profile and decoration from the Bargello mortar signed by Giulio Alberghetti (1536–72); it may represent a variant of the same period, but was more likely produced earlier in the sixteenth century.

Other related examples

i. Musée Jacquemart-André, Paris; inv. no. 467, h. 12.5, diam. 15.3 (rim), 10.4 (base); *Catalogue Itinéraire* 1948, p. 40, as Paduan, end of the fifteenth century. There are no signs of use, but the motifs are worn, similar to the present example.

ii. Formerly London art market; London 1988, no. 8. Identical in shape and bearing much of the same decoration, it also displays vases flanked by griffins similar to those found on cat. no. 18.

iii. Private collection, Buenos Aires; h. 14, diam. 17 (rim), 10.5 (base); see *Bronces del Renacimiento Italiano* (exh. cat.), Museo Nacional de Arte Decorativo, Buenos Aires, 1967, cat. no. 70, as Florence *c.*1550. Similar form and style of decoration, but with different motifs (including griffins, *tazze*, cornucopiae, masks, swags and pendants), applied more densely.

Notes

1. Museum records.
2. Verbal advice from Anthony Radcliffe.
3. See cat. no. 17.
4. Inv. no. 751 (Girard Gift, 1920). The bell bears the Mula arms and is inscribed AM (see also cat. no. 26, n. 5). This is apparently the same bell as appeared in the sale of the Guggenheim Collection, Venice, 1913, lot. 124, but with the damaged handle covered or replaced by a tassel.
5. Middeldorf 1981, p. 11.
6. Ibid., and Radcliffe 1992, p. 225.

(*a*)

23. Mortar decorated with stags and lions

Attributed to the Alberghetti foundry
North Italian (Venice); 1500–50
Bronze
h. 11; diam. 12.9 (rim), 8.1 (base); wt 1892.4 g.
M.25-1938

Provenance: Collection of Dr W. L. Hildburgh, FSA, London; on loan to the Victoria and Albert Museum from 14 August 1934; given by Hildburgh in 1938.

Condition: Pitted cast (appearing pockmarked), with ill-defined decoration; area of cracking and staining around one of the stags; casting flaws and chips around the rim. Faint evidence of turning. Sandy material in the interstices.
Interior: pit at the centre of the base.
Base: pitted; centre hole and other pits filled with sandy material.
Brassy patina; dark interior with scratchy surface.
Metal analysis: bronze with consistent alloy throughout, but with unusually high iron content, notably on the base (probably caused by surface contamination).

A conical mortar, decorated around the rim with two plain mouldings, and stiff leaf on a cyma recta moulding. On the body, foliate swags, below which appear two lions passant and two stags statant between trees. Moulded, concave foot.

Acquired as 'from Venice' and dated to the fifteenth century, the mortar was later re-defined as sixteenth-century and of uncertain Italian provenance in the Museum records. It appears to belong to an extensive group of works associated with the Alberghetti workshop, including cat. no. 24. It displays the same stag as on the mortar in the Museo Nazionale del Bargello, Florence, signed by Giulio Alberghetti (foundry director 1551–72) (fig. 13), but otherwise bears little direct relationship to the latter.[1] The closest variant is in the Kunstgewerbemuseum, Cologne, which appears to be virtually identical, apart from the shape of the foot, the dimensions and weight.[2] Another related example is in the Kunsthistorisches Museum, Vienna, which includes the stag and identical tree.[3] Radcliffe has suggested that the conical shape of the

present mortar 'represents an earlier phase of practice in the foundry than the bell-shaped',[4] such as the signed example in the Bargello or cat. no. 24.

The decoration of the present mortar is ill-defined, and there is no clear evidence of turning or application of wax motifs. These factors, taken with the 'pockmarked' appearance of the cast, could suggest that it is a sand-cast. However, the existence of a pin-hole at the centre (both inside the bowl and on the base) indicates the use of a spindle. Its general appearance varies from the sand-cast forgeries identified by Lockner,[5] and the pitted surface is perhaps due to porosity.[6]

Notes
1. Museo Nazionale del Bargello, Florence, inv. no. 715, see cat. no. 24, n. 2, for details.
2. Inv. no. H4, h. 12.2, diam. 15 (rim), 10 (base), wt 3700 g; Launert 1990, p. 199, fig. 220, as Italian, sixteenth-century. Details and description kindly provided by Gerhard Dietrich.
3. Planiscig 1924, p. 79, no. 144.
4. Radcliffe, loc. cit.
5. See Lockner 1976b.
6. Radcliffe (loc. cit.) saw no reason to doubt its authenticity.

Bibliography
Radcliffe 1992, p. 225.

24. Mortar with fish handle

Attributed to the Alberghetti foundry
North Italian (Venice); 1550–80
Bronze
h. 13.2; diam. 16 (rim), 9.9 (base);
wt 3100.2 g.
345-1889

Provenance: Bought from Michelangelo Guggenheim,
Venice, in 1889 (with 335 to 354-1889, £300).

Condition: Cracking and thinning along one side, one handle missing and remaining rough patches of metal where it was attached. Misalignment in the wax on the gadrooning near the handle, with further cracking and damage. The motifs applied to the main body are worn.
Interior: irregular surface to the bowl with pitting.
Base: smooth, no evidence of pouring cup attachment.
Brassy patina; mottled and patchy inside and mottled on the base.
Metal analysis: bronze of similar composition throughout.

A bell-shaped mortar, with one remaining handle in the form of a fish. Decorated around the rim with arabesque ornament flanked by rope, with a plain moulding; upright stiff leaf on a cyma recta moulding delineated by plain mouldings. On the body, garlands with foliage pendants suspended from a narrow plain moulding, a star or flower (?) above each swag; below, fruit trees flanked by two kinds of flowers (or thistles) and eagles, with a griffin, a lion passant, a walking stag and a scratching hind. Below, a recessed moulding (misaligned) and gadrooned bowl. Moulded foot.

The mortar was acquired as part of the Guggenheim purchase, with an uncertain Italian provenance and dated to the sixteenth century.[1] The stag and scratching hind appear on a mortar in the Museo Nazionale del Bargello, Florence, the only known example signed by Giulio Alberghetti who directed one of the family foundries in Venice from 1551 to 1572.[2] The signature on this is inscribed into the cold metal on a *tabula ansata*, in contrast to the cast-in legend of the two surviving bells signed by Giulio's great-uncle, Giovanni Alberghetti (see cat. no. 17). This and other related mortars are discussed in detail by Radcliffe, who has convincingly suggested that they are the products of the Alberghetti workshop during the sixteenth century, in view of the appearance of 'Alberghetti' motifs and the close relationship of the decorative style of the group.[3] This attribution had already been suggested by Kris for another mortar once in the Emil Weinberger Collection, Vienna.[4]

The stag and the scratching hind are frequently combined with other animal motifs, including the lion and griffin. Eagles similar to those on the present piece also appear on a mortar in the National Gallery of Art,

Washington (Kress Collection).⁵ The remaining decoration of the Kress mortar (and the others of the same group) bears some relationship to works associated with the Alberghetti in style and content, but the profile of the mortar is distinct. When it is compared with the signed Bargello mortar there are no direct links. However, it seems likely that the workshop produced mortars that varied substantially in profile and decorative design. Examples are known of bell-shaped and conical mortars displaying 'Alberghetti' motifs (see, for example, cat. no. 23). As suggested by Radcliffe, these may reflect the production of different periods of the workshop, with the bell-shaped mortars probably being later.⁶ However, Radcliffe's assertion that motifs pressed from the same moulds must indicate production in the same workshop requires qualification, as some motifs were used by other foundries, although the exact method of transfer is not always clear. Notable are 'Alberghetti' motifs that appear also on works associated with the Grandi and Pietro Campanario workshops.⁷ In addition, the arabesque ornament on the present mortar is identical to that on a hand bell probably produced by the Brescian foundry of Gaspare di Girolamo Macri (cat. no. 53). This bell bears other decorative motifs usually associated with the Alberghetti. Many factors can affect the transfer of wax casts to the finished bronze, and it is therefore difficult to be certain whether the same moulds were indeed employed. Nor can we preclude the re-cutting or re-moulding of these templates within the same workshop.

Nevertheless, the weight of evidence indicates that the Alberghetti foundry probably cast the present mortar, although the possibility that it is the product of another north Italian foundry utilizing the same motifs cannot be dismissed.

Related variants
i. National Gallery of Art, Washington (Kress Collection), inv. no. 1957.14.97 (A.250.94C), h. 15, diam. 17.1 (rim), 12.7 (base), w. c.18.5; Pope-Hennessy 1965, p. 154, no. 566; Washington 1994, p. 230, as probably Venetian, sixteenth-century. A heavy mortar, with very dark patina and signs of wear inside.
ii. National Gallery of Art, Washington (Kress Collection), inv. no. 1957.14.97 (A.251.95C), h. 12.8, diam. 14.4 (rim), 9.5 (base), w. c.15.8, wt 3934.2 g.; Pope-Hennessy 1965, pp. 154–5, no. 567; Washington 1994, p. 115, as Italian, sixteenth-century. Considerably worn decoration; dark brown patina and no clear evidence of use.
iii. National Gallery of Art, Washington (Kress Collection), inv. no. 1957.14.103 (A.256.100C), h. 13.3, diam. 16.1 (rim), 10.2 (base), w. c.16.5, wt 4519.9 g.; Pope-Hennessy 1965, p. 155, no. 568; Washington 1994, p. 230, as probably Venetian, sixteenth-century. Mid-brown patina and smooth interior.
iv. Kunstgewerbemuseum, Berlin, inv. no. 88,327, h. 15.3, diam. 18 (rim), 12.5 (base); also acquired from Guggenheim, Venice, in 1888; Pechstein 1968, no. 65; Launert 1990, p. 198, no. 218.
v. Skulpturensammlung, Berlin, inv. no. 2580; h. 15.1, diam. 17.6 (rim), 12.1 (base); Bode 1930, p. 60, no. 291. The two coats of arms (bendy of six) have not been securely identified. Worn; coppery patina and pitted inside, presumably due to use.
vi. Kunsthistoriches Museum, Vienna, inv. no. 5945, h. 12, diam. 15.6; Planiscig 1924, p. 79, no. 144.
vii. Museum für Kunst und Gewerbe, Hamburg, inv. no. 1909.266, h. 14.7, diam. 17 (rim), 12.2 (base). Smooth interior, with dark/mid-brown patina.
viii. Musée Jacquemart-André, Paris, inv. no. 1089, h. 13.7, diam. 19.5 (rim), 11 (base); *Catalogue Itinéraire* 1948, p. 95. Poor cast, with unidentified coats of arms and worn medallions containing profile heads above the festoons.
ix. Musée du Louvre, Paris; h. 21.5, diam. 24; Migeon 1904, p. 50, no. 38, illus. p. 47. Crisply cast foliage decoration around the rim, (modern?) gilding on two foliate heads; clean inside. Previously identified as nineteenth-century by Radcliffe, who now accepts an early dating.
x. Museo Correr, Venice, inv. no. 1325; h. 10, diam. 12 (rim), 7.5 (base). Close in form to the signed Bargello mortar (see n. 2), but with a shallower rim, the mortar is decorated with a scratching hind, tree and walking stag, and a winged figure, truncated at the base (similar to that seen on a mortar in the Columbia

(*a*)

Museum of Art, Columbia (SC), (formerly Kress Collection), Pope-Hennessy 1965, p. 157, no. 581, fig. 605). One missing handle evident from two marks where it has become detached. Some evidence of turning. Smooth interior; concentric rings evident on the base, and some shrinkage. Bronzy patina.

Nineteenth-century casts, with identical patterns, as identified by Radcliffe

a. Thyssen-Bornemisza Collection; Radcliffe 1992, pp. 222–5, no. 37.

b. Metropolitan Museum of Art, New York; Jack and Belle Linsky Collection, inv. no. 1982.60.111.

c. Metropolitan Museum of Art, New York; Lehman Collection, inv. no. 1975.1.1367.

d. See ix above.

e. *European Works of Art, Sculpture and Metalwork*, Sotheby's, London, 9 July 1987, lot 71.

Notes

1. Inventory, loc. cit.
2. Museo Nazionale del Bargello, Florence, inv. no. 715 (see fig. 13), h. 15.6, diam. 17.7 (rim), 10.9 (base), w. *c*.21.8; acquired in 1914 from G. Salvadori. See Lise and Bearzi 1975, pp. 78–9. The mortar is heavy, with a smooth base and interior (with some spots), but a worn exterior. See pp. 96–8 for Alberghetti.
3. Radcliffe 1992, pp. 222–5, no. 37.
4. Kris (Weinberger) 1929, lot 187 (and illus.); formerly in the Bardini Collection (Christie's (Bardini) 1902, lot 77, pl. 2, no. 18, as Florentine, late fifteenth-century).
5. Pope-Hennessy 1965, p. 155, no. 570. See cat. no. 25, no. ii.
6. See Radcliffe 1992, p. 225.
7. See cat. no. 28 and Motture forthcoming.

Bibliography

Inventory 1890, p. 36; Radcliffe 1992, p. 224.

25. Mortar with rope handle

Possibly Alberghetti foundry
North Italian; 1520–50
Leaded bronze
h. 15.2; diam. 15.8 (rim), 11.6 (base); w. 17; wt 5016.6 g.
342-1889

Provenance: Bought from Michelangelo Guggenheim, Venice, in 1889 (with 335 to 354-1889, £300).

Condition: Casting flaws on the rim above the handle; cracking near one of the coats of arms (per fess; see below); some details failed, ill-defined or rough from poor casting. Scratchy and porous appearance to the surface, notably around the foot. Areas of wear, notably the frieze around the rim, the lion supporter and adjacent leaping lion.
Interior: faint evidence of turning; generally smooth.
Base: smooth with indentations, apparently caused by shrinkage around the pouring sprue during cooling.
Brassy patina on both exterior and interior.
Metal analysis: leaded bronze. The higher lead content towards the rim indicates that the mortar was cast upside-down, as expected.

A conical mortar with projecting recessed lip and rope handle. Decorated around the rim with a low relief frieze of a hunting scene, consisting of a repeating pattern of a dog pursuing a boar towards another dog (confronting), set above a row of fine bead; below the rim are imbricated scales. On the body are animals, birds, putti and foliate decoration ranged around a coat of arms on each face, both on a *scuodo sagomato* (a type of 'Tuscan' shield). The handle is flanked by unicorns pursued by putti, and (above each) a bird displayed, with an additional small bird in flight inserted at the right; below the handle is a floral device surmounted by a bird. On one face (pl. 25b) is a coat of arms (party per fess) with griffin and lion supporters, and (above) a floral and foliate device on which perch two birds; flanked by seated putti blowing horns, and (above) two birds in flight, further flanked by pairs of birds and cupids. On the opposite face (pl. 25) the arms (on a bend a double-headed eagle displayed) are supported by putti with (above) a device of leaves, corn and flowers, surmounted by a bird and flanked by cockerels. To the right of this group, another foliate device with (above) two birds and a griffin. Opposite the handle (pl. 25a), a tree with (above) another scrolled foliate device

surmounted by three birds and flanked with (at the base) two swans(?) and (above each) a bird displayed; below the bird at the right is a small bifurcate siren. Around the base between these devices is a frieze of running animals: starting at the handle (from right to left), a hound, lion, hound, boar, rabbit, fox, hound and stag. High moulded and waisted base.

The hunting scene around the rim is applied in four strips showing the repeated group, plus an additional partial insert. The imbricated scales are similarly applied in four larger strips and one small infill.

The mortar was acquired with no stated place of origin and dated to the sixteenth century, subsequently refined to

the first half of the century.[1] It is one of a number of utensils (listed below) with similar decoration, including several mortars of identical form. Among these works is a bell in the Kunstgewerbemuseum, Berlin (see b below), bearing the distinctive, seated horn-blowing putti that appear on the present mortar. The Berlin bell shares several decorative features, as well as the overall quality and handling, with two bells signed by Giovanni Alberghetti (active *c*.1484–1510) and can therefore confidently be attributed to his workshop (see cat. no. 17). A mortar in Washington, which forms part of the group (see ii below), includes the scratching hind, which is also found on mortars generally associated with the Alberghetti foundry (see cat. no. 24).

(a)

(b)

These associations, therefore, suggest an attribution for the related group of bells and mortars to the Alberghetti. Evidence of transmission of images from one workshop to another, however, leaves room for doubt, particularly as some of the same images seen on the mortars in this group are found on *secchielli* (or buckets) attributed to the Grandi family, who were active in Padua and Trento (see c below).[2] In addition to individual motifs, such as the unicorn and other animals, the use of fine, low-relief decoration around the rim is similar to that used by the Grandi. The manner in which the elements are spaced over the surface is reminiscent of a footed bowl and a bell, both formerly in the Kress Collection,[3] although the more flattened style of their decoration suggests that they were made by a different workshop from the present group.

While possibly a product of the Alberghetti, the present mortar may well have been produced by another north Italian foundry that was utilizing some of the same motifs.

Neither coat of arms has been firmly identified. One of them (party per fess) is too common to assign with certainty without the benefit of tincture,[4] and the other more distinctive *stemma* (on a bend a double-headed eagle displayed) remains to be identified. The two different arms, however, may represent those of a husband and wife, as evidenced by a mortar in a private collection in Washington bearing two separate coats of arms combined with imagery that has been associated with a marriage.[5] When compared with dated examples, the form of the mortar indicates production around 1530–50.[6]

Main related variants

i. Musée Jacquemart-André, Paris, inv. no. 916, h. 15.5, diam. 16.6 (rim), 10.2 (base), w. *c*.17.8 (*Catalogue Itinéraire* 1948, p. 72, as Paduan, end of the fifteenth century). The mortar is of lower quality but has much of the same decoration, including the cupid, several of the birds, and the lions. A dolphin frieze around the rim.

ii. National Gallery of Art, Washington (Kress Collection), inv. no. 1957.14.100.a and b (A.253.97C), h. 15.2, diam. 17 (rim), 10.2 (base), w. *c*.17.5, wt 3951.9 g. (pestle 378.3 g.); Pope-Hennessy 1965, p. 155, no. 570; Washington 1994, p. 118. The proportions of this mortar differ from the present example, and it weighs considerably less. It is linked by the shape, style and type of decoration, but none of the animals appears to be the same. The mortar can also be linked to cat. no. 24 due to the appearance of the same eagle and the scratching hind; and more tenuously to cat. no. 21, which has similar birds.

iii. Formerly Bardini and Figdor Collections, h. 14.9, diam. 16; Christie's (Bardini) 1899, lot 402 (no. 34, pl. 2; bought by Miller); Planiscig (Figdor) 1930, no. 418. Less elaborately decorated, but of the same form, decorated with similar putti, shields and birds.

iv. Location unknown (formerly with Alfred Spero, London (?)), h. *c*.20.3, diam. *c*.21. This example, known only from a photograph in the Sculpture Department archive, is closely related, but with two projecting rope handles. Much of the imagery is shared with the present example and that in Paris; the swags and displayed owls are closely related to the Washington mortar (ii above) and cat. no. 21. It displays what appears to be a pharmacy sign (illegible).

v. National Gallery of Art, Washington (Kress Collection), inv. no. 1957.14.99 (A.252.96C), h. 13, diam. 17.6 (rim), 11.5 (base), wt 4643.4 g.; Pope-Hennessy 1965, p. 155, no. 569; Washington 1994, p. 115. A mortar of different form, which displays the seated horn-blowing putti, seen also on the present mortar, as well as two bells (a and b below). It shares other similarities in the griffin supporters and the *tazza*, vase or fountain (?) decoration (see also cat. no. 21).

vi. Musée des Arts Décoratifs, Paris, inv. no. 14667. Identical in type; the bowl is unevenly cast; the decoration is worn, but includes several similar images and the same low-relief frieze of dolphins around the rim as i above.

vii. Formerly Kunsthaus Lempertz, Cologne (*c*.1990), h. 14, diam. 17; Launert 1990, p. 199, no. 219, as Paduan about 1500. Mortar with two projecting moulded handles, but of similar form to the present example and including the two putti 'supporters'; it bears similar decorative features to those related to the Alberghetti foundry.

viii. Kunstgewerbemuseum, Berlin, inv. no. 87,600, h. 14.1, diam. 16.4 (rim), 11 (base); Pechstein 1968, no. 56, as north Italian, beginning of the sixteenth century. Similar form, but with elegant dolphin handles. Crisp decoration, with similar patina to the present example, and including unicorns and the unidentified beast, usually described as a dog, also seen on the Grandi buckets, possibly also identifiable with an unusual animal on mortar no. i above (see also p. 49).

Other utensils with related decoration

a. Musée Jacquemart-André, Paris, inv. no. 1117, h. 7.8, diam. 7.8; *Catalogue Itinéraire* 1948, p. 97. Bell, decorated with unicorns, the horn-blowing putti, small birds and other images dotted across the surface.

b. Kunstgewerbemuseum, Berlin, inv. no. 91,215; Pechstein 1968, no. 62 (see cat. no. 17, n. 4, for details). Including the horn-blowing putti and several features that appear on bells signed by Giovanni Alberghetti.

c. Kunstgewerbemuseum, Berlin, inv. no. 91,18; Pechstein 1968, no. 88, as Trento, mid-sixteenth-century. A bucket, including the same birds, griffins, unicorn and unidentified animal found among those on the mortars. Other related buckets are in the Kunst und Gewerbe Museum, Hamburg (inv. no. 1957.75), Museo Nazionale del Bargello, Florence (inv. no. 738), and the Museo del Buonconsiglio, Trento (inv. nos 3452 and 3451); see Trento 1999, pp. 196–9, nos 6 and 7, for further literature, identified as by Vincenzo and Gian Girolamo Grandi, *c*.1532–9.

Notes

1. Inventory loc. cit. and Museum records.
2. See also p. 49; no. vi above and, for a full discussion, Motture forthcoming.
3. The footed bowl is now in the University of California, Los Angeles; the bell in the National Gallery of Art, Washington; see Pope-Hennessy 1965, p. 154, no. 564 and p. 148, no. 542, fig. 537 respectively (see also cat. no. 28, n. 18, for the bowl and cat no. 55 for the bell); the arms on neither of these objects have been identified.
4. See cat. no. 28, n. 2, for examples.
5. The mortar was formerly in the collection of Sylvia Adams, London (Bonhams, *The Adams Collection, Part V, Important Renaissance and Baroque Bronzes*, London, 23 May 1996, lot 80); and see p. 50.
6. The mortar combines the conical form with a more elaborate moulded foot (cf. mortar dated 1540, Appendix 2).

Bibliography

Inventory 1890, p. 36.

26. Vase with anthemion and palmette decoration

Possibly Alberghetti foundry
North Italian (Venice?); 1520–60 or possibly
nineteenth-century
Bronze
h. 31.6; diam. 18.2 (body), 11.2 (top), 11.5 (base);
w. 23.3; wt 6542.2 g.
35-1865

Provenance: Collection of Eugène Piot, Paris,
until 1864 (Hotel Drouot (Piot) 1864, lot 41); bought
from John Webb, London, in 1865 for £206.[1]

Condition: Some minor surface pitting. Evidence of
turning. Handles soldered on.
Interior: smooth. Bowl recessed to follow the contour
of the basic exterior form, but does not reflect the
gadroons.
Base: hollow. Evidence of turning
under the foot, but with rough
surface in the recess. The
recess under the foot has
been filled with a hard
brown substance
(possibly wax),
obscuring the metal.
Two casting flaws.
Dark brown patina,
slightly worn in places.
Metal analysis: low tin bronze;
handles of a quaternary alloy.

A vase with handles in the form of
acanthus, decorated on the neck
with acanthus on a cyma recta
moulding; palmette with foliage and
flowers; cornucopiae and alternating
suspended bucrania and flowers.
On the body, anthemion and palmette
with interwoven foliage and flowers.
Gadrooned bowl. Plain moulded foot.

The vase was ascribed 'with probability' by Bode, together with a table fountain and footed bowl now in the Victoria and Albert Museum (cat. no. 27), to the workshop of Alessandro Leopardi by comparison with various works, including the decoration of the Colleoni monument and the standard base in the Piazza San Marco in Venice. The attribution was revised by Draper to 'Venetian, about 1520–30'.[2] This high-quality cast in fact shares decorative elements with objects associated with the Alberghetti workshop in Venice, notably the friezes around the neck of the vase, which also appear on a mortar in the Kunstgewerbemuseum, Berlin, similarly related to Leopardi by Pechstein, but attributed to the Alberghetti by Radcliffe.[3] The footed bowl cited above bears a slightly smaller but otherwise identical frieze.

A number of objects with Alberghetti associations are linked through their decoration. Another smaller vase of similar shape, in a private collection, sports related festoons suspended from bucranes, large acanthus leaves (like the present handles but applied to the body of the vessel), and a gadrooned bowl.[4] The remaining foliate decoration on this related vase can be compared to that on a bell in the Museo Nazionale del Bargello, Florence.[5] The bell is also decorated with distinctive heads with spiked hair identical to those that appear on a footed bowl in the Museo Artistico Industriale, Rome, signed by Alfonso Alberghetti in 1572.[6] The acanthus that decorates Alfonso's bowl is very close in style to that on a mortar in the Wallace Collection, London.[7] The Wallace mortar bears a pacing horse, frequently associated with the founder Pietro Campanario, who has been identified by Radcliffe as the Paduan founder active between 1479 and 1496.[8] However, this same motif can also be seen on Alfonso Alberghetti's footed bowl, and was clearly a design shared by different foundries.[9] These interconnections stress, once again, the ubiquitous nature of much of the decoration of this type of object. Only when truly distinctive motifs appear is it possible to identify a workshop on the basis of decorative motifs alone. The same festoon around the neck of the present vase, for example, is also found on bells that can safely be associated with Brescia (see cat. no. 53). Over the years, many objects formerly attributed to Leopardi have been re-assigned, but there is no reason to suspect that his foundry did not produce such objects. Unfortunately, the decorative motifs found on his known works are too generic in nature to allow

firm attribution of related pieces. The vase can therefore be assigned to Venice, with a possible attribution to the Alberghetti foundry, but production by another foundry cannot be ruled out. The dating of the cast is more problematic, due to the rarity of its form and lack of comparable dated pieces. A design for a vase of about 1515, possibly by Giovanni Antonio da Brescia, is similar in form, and a large maiolica vase in the collection is also related.[10] The position of the handles, however, differs from the maiolica piece, being less practical on the present vase. The facture also bears some comparison with the Museum's vase from the Cavadini foundry, which is datable to the 1820s or 1830s (cat. no. 67), and it is, therefore, possible that it is a nineteenth-century cast.[11]

Notes

1. See p. 14 for details of the purchase of this vase.
2. Bode/Draper, loc. cit. and caption to pl. CXXIV, no. 2.
3. Radcliffe 1992, pp. 222–5, cat. 37; see Pechstein 1968, no. 65 (iv under cat. no. 24); the frieze of festoons on the Berlin mortar has only suspended bucranes.
4. Frankfurt 1985, p. 528, no. 250, as Workshop of Alessandro Leopardi, Venice, end of the fifteenth/beginning sixteenth century; h. 13.5. See also cat. no. 30.
5. Inv. no. 751, h. 16.8 (with tassel), 7.3 (bell only), diam. 9.8; Girard Gift, 1920. Decorated with a coat of arms, possibly identifiable with the Mula of Venice (quarterly of six, argent and azure; Coronelli 1694, p. 331).
6. See p. 97, fig. 14 and Radcliffe 1992, p. 229, fig. 4.
7. Mann 1931 (1981), p. 27, no. S64.
8. See Radcliffe 1994, pp. 20–3, no. 2.
9. See cat. no. 28 for further discussion and references.
10. See Miller 1999, p. 228, cat. no. 65, and pp. 229–54, and Lynda Fairburn, *The North Italian Album. Designs by a Renaissance Artisan*, London, 1998, frontispiece, for the album in Sir John Soane's Museum, London, for other vase and ewer designs. See also, for example, Allison 1994, pp. 87–95, cat. no. 7 (the Gonzaga Urn or Vase by Antico), datable to about 1481–3, for a different example of vase design. For the maiolica vase (inv. no. C.2106-1910), see Bernard Rackham, with emendations and additional bibliography by J. V. G. Mallet, *Victoria and Albert Museum. Catalogue of Italian Maiolica* (2 vols), London, 1977, pp. 66–7, cat. no. 208, pl. 35, c.1500–10 (see also p. 46, cat. no. 157, pl. 28).
11. The Alberghetti foundry continued to operate into the nineteenth century.

Bibliography

Bode 1908, p. 13, pl. CXXIV; Bode/Draper 1980, p. 47, pl. CXXIV.

27. Footed bowl decorated with anthemion and palmette

Alberghetti foundry (?)
North Italian (Venice?); 1520–60 or possibly
nineteenth-century
Leaded bronze
h. 28.2; diam. 30 (rim), 18.6 (foot); wt 6459.8 g.
M.690-1910

Provenance: Massimo Collection;[1] collection of Eugène
Piot, Paris, until 1890 (Hotel Drouot (Piot) 1864, lot 42
(Vases); Hotel Drouot (Piot) 1890, lot 21;[2] collection of
George Salting, London, from 1890;[3] bequeathed by
Salting in 1910 (Salting Bequest, no. 2891).

Condition: The head of one putto obliterated, probably in
the wax before casting, and a casting flaw in the gadrooning apparently filled with wax.
Interior: scratchy surface. An indentation appears where
the upper frieze of acanthus was apparently joined to the
bowl in the wax, and the gadrooning appears in negative
inside. There is a raised circle at the centre on which there
is an old paper label inscribed in pen '*aux armes de la famille
Contarini*', the last word corrected to Venier. The casting
flaw filled with brown wax. A patch of corrosion.
Foot: cast separately and soldered (?) onto the bowl, but
there is a large square nut attached to an apparently

machine-made screw underneath,[4] a fixing that is not evident on the inside. Two paper labels underneath bear the numbers 2326 (obliterated in pencil) and 2891.[5]

Dark brown patination.

Metal analysis: leaded bronze, the foot showing a higher level of lead.

Footed bowl or wine cooler decorated with, around the bowl, broad acanthus and, below, anthemion and palmette and foliage and flowers with three identical coats of arms (barry of six) superimposed. Gadrooned bowl below heavy moulding. On the foot, pairs of naked putti supporting two oval shields bearing the same arms as above, placed over an oval shield showing poles terminating in crescents, with fluttering ribbons behind, and two vases.

It is part of a group of similar objects usually designated as wine coolers and considered by Bode under a section on the work of 'Paduan and other artists of the Quattrocento', but reassigned as north Italian, sixteenth-century, by Draper. On acquisition it was described as Venetian and dated to the early sixteenth century. Bode grouped the bowl with a table fountain and a vase (cat. no. 26), and identified the armorials and decoration as pointing to a Venetian origin at the beginning of the sixteenth century. He saw a relationship with the decoration on the base of the Colleoni monument, the mast stems in the Piazza S. Marco and the altar plinth of the Zen Chapel at St Mark's in Venice, and therefore suggested they could be ascribed to Alessandro Leopardi.[6] The decoration bears only a general relationship to the works by Leopardi. The arms have been variously identified as Venier and Contarini, but do not in fact match either, being identical (without tincture) to those of the Venetian patrician family of Diedo (barry of six or and azure).[7] Armorials with the same flanking putti can be seen on a footed bowl in the Musée Jacquemart-André, Paris, which has closer affinities to cat. no. 18.[8]

The main decorative frieze is identical in design (but smaller and in lower relief) to that on the vase in the present collection (cat. no. 26), which was also previously in the Piot Collection. The overall treatment can be related to similar vessels in the Museo del Castello Sforzesco, Milan, and the Museo Nazionale del Bargello, Florence, but it may be distinguished by the facture.[9] The interior contour follows the shape of the gadrooning, as seen on cat. no. 19, which is an after-cast of one of the Alberghetti bowls in the Louvre.[10] The bowl has abutting gadroons apparently added in the wax to the outside of the bowl. Despite the treatment of the gadrooning, the quality and nature of the casting give no indication that the present bowl is an after-cast. While the bowl is stylistically related to products of the Alberghetti foundry of the late fifteenth and early sixteenth centuries, the comparatively thin casting and 'ghosting' of the gadroons indicate that it is probably a later cast, and may even be a product of the nineteenth century.

Notes

1. Note in Museum records, based on information from an A. Bremont (identity unknown). For the Massimo family, see TDA, 20, pp. 587–8.
2. The bowl reached a bid of FF3,050 in the 1864 Piot sale but was withdrawn; Hotel Drouot (Piot) 1890, loc. cit., annotated copy.
3. George Salting paid £2,100 for it, but valued it as £2,500 'at least'; Salting notebooks, GSIV; GSVII, p. 57, both note the value as £2,500: a substantial sum at the time.
4. Only a hint of the screw is visible, indicating that it is of narrow diameter, commensurate with a modern screw, but it is not possible to identify the gauge without dismantling the object.
5. The former number was apparently allocated when the bowl came into the Museum for photography in 1903.
6. Bode and Bode/Draper, locc. citt.
7. Coronelli 1694, p. 14; Crollalanza 1965, I, p. 360.
8. See cat. no. 18, n. 8.
9. Bode/Draper 1980, p. 47 and pls CXX no. 1, CXXI no. 1 and CXXII. The examples in the Bargello, inv. nos 249C and 248C (Carrand Collection, given 1889; ibid. CXXII and CXXI, no. 1 respectively) have more substantial mouldings and the feet are attached by visible fixings through the bowl (see also Caglioti and Gasparotto 1997, fig. 38, re. inv. no. 248C).
10. A relationship to the two Louvre bowls, now attributed to the Alberghetti foundry, was acknowledged in the 1890 Piot sale catalogue.

Bibliography

Bode 1908, p. 13, pl. CXX, no. 2; Bode/Draper 1980, pl. CXX, no. 2.

28. Mortar with hunting scene

Alberghetti foundry (?)
North Italian (Venice?); 1500–50
Bronze
h. 13; diam. 14.2 (rim), 10.2 (base); w. 18.4; wt 3311.3 g.
M.702-1910

Provenance: Stefano Bardini, Florence (Christie's (Bardini) 1902, lot 81); collection of George Salting, London, from 1902; on loan to the Victoria and Albert Museum from 15 March 1907; bequeathed by Salting in 1910 (Salting Bequest, no. 2523).

Condition: Squashy, waxy cast; casting flaw on the rim of the base. The decorative ovals show signs of removal of material after casting. Yellowish deposit in the interstices. The handles cast separately and soldered unevenly into place.

Interior: green deposit in the centre; the bowl apparently recessed through wear.
Base: dented. An outer rim is visible, into which the centre appears inset. Irregular cast-on repair.
Dark brown patina worn to reveal bronze colour.
Metal analysis: low-tin bronze of consistent alloy. High iron reading on the body, with a small amount of zinc.

A vase-shaped mortar with recessed lip and handles in the form of foliate scrolls. Decorated around the rim with overlapping acanthus above a plain moulding; acanthus on a cyma recta moulding below. On the body, a hunting scene, punctuated with stylized trees, tufts of grass and flying birds, and showing on one side (from left to right): (a) a pacing huntsman with a stick and antler suspended over his left shoulder, (b) a running hound, (c) a hunter stooping to pick up an object, and (d) a hunter blowing a horn and carrying a spear in his left hand; on the other side: (e) a running stag, (f) a leaping hound emerging from bushes, (g) a hound attacking a stag. On the bowl, a foliate design incorporating an oval shield with a trace of horizontal division.[1] On the foot, downward-facing acanthus, with a plain base.

The mortar was related to the school of Pisanello (*c*.1395–1455) and dated to the late fifteenth century in the Bardini sale catalogue.[2] Salting described it as north Italian, fifteenth-century.[3] The mortar was mentioned by Pechstein as a variant of one in the Kunstgewerbemuseum, Berlin, which relates in form.[4] However, the decoration of the Berlin mortar is actually more closely related to cat. no. 29. Launert notes the present mortar simply as Italian, sixteenth-century.[5] Radcliffe cited both this one and a related piece in the Metropolitan Museum of Art, New York, as good examples of a class of Venetian bell-shaped mortar apparently of the mid-sixteenth century. He suggested that motifs were derived from this type for use on a mortar in the Thyssen-Bornemisza Collection, which he considered a modern forgery.[6] The latter is of a different form and otherwise bears little resemblance. According to Hackenbroch, a mortar (actually a footed bowl or wine cooler) signed by Alfonso Alberghetti and dated 1572 (Museo Artistico Industriale, Rome) bears a close resemblance to the Metropolitan mortar cited above.[7] The flying bird and running dog that appear on the stem of the Alberghetti bowl are also found on the present mortar. However, these motifs alone are not sufficient to identify a foundry with certainty.

On Alfonso's signed bowl, the bird appears with a pacing horse, and both motifs are found on hand-bells signed 'OPVS PETRI', as well as on utensils associated with the Grandi workshop of Trento. The identity of the founder 'Petrus' was discussed by Radcliffe, who concluded that of two documented bell-founders bearing that name, he was more likely to be the Paduan Pietro di Gaspare dalla Campane (Campanario) da Treviso (documented active in Padua 1479–96). This proposal was based on the appearance of several of the 'Opus Petri' motifs, including the flying bird and pacing horse, on bell-metal buckets from the workshop of Vincenzo and Gian Girolamo Grandi, combined with motifs devised by the Grandi themselves.[8] Radcliffe suggested that Pietro's workshop may have

passed to the Grandi when they moved to Padua from Trento in 1507. The association of the motif with Padua supported the identification of Pietro di Gaspare as the relevant founder.[9] However, as Radcliffe noted, the Campanario family originated in Vicenza, like the Grandi, leaving the possibility that these were motifs common to Vicentine foundries.

Planiscig proposed that the Venetian founder Pietro di Giovanni dalle Campane was the author of the 'Opus Petri' bell formerly in the Figdor Collection.[10] Born in about 1462, he was active in Venice until his death in 1542 and worked alongside Giovanni Alberghetti in casting bronzes for the Zen Chapel at San Marco in 1505–21.[11] The appearance of the same motif on a later Alberghetti utensil therefore raises possible further questions about the identity of the 'Opus Petri' founder, and the interrelationship of the whole group. Clearly these motifs were used by at least three foundries, which is hardly surprising when one considers the portability of the moulds, the itinerant nature of the founders, the likely use of pattern books and the possibility of casting from existing objects.

The treatment of the decoration on the related Metropolitan mortar, notably the spiky acanthus overlapping the rim, is reminiscent of another bell-shaped mortar in the Wallace Collection, which itself bears the combined bird and pacing horse motif.[12] This distinctive acanthus leaf does not appear on any known 'Opus Petri' bells, although a plant similar to one of the four individual motifs on the Wallace mortar can be seen on a signed Petrus bell in Berlin.[13] Similar acanthus does appear, however, on a mortar inscribed 'IVLIO ALBERGETI',[14] where it is also applied over a moulding as seen on the Wallace example. The signature of Giulio Alberghetti (director of one of the foundries, 1551–72) provides a date span for this type of decoration, although acanthus – albeit treated distinctively – is too widely used to be firmly categorized and dated.[15] The Wallace mortar, bearing a combination of the pacing horse and spiky acanthus, both of which are associated with the Alberghetti, could, however, be tentatively attributed to the foundry around this date.[16]

While of a larger scale, the figures on the present mortar can be compared to those on a bell in the Kunstgewerbemuseum, Berlin, in their style and layout.[17] Pechstein relates the decoration on the bell to that on a footed bowl in Los Angeles.[18] There is also a general stylistic relationship between these pieces and a large bowl in the Louvre,

(a)

(b)

similarly decorated with hunting scenes, which is attributed to the Alberghetti.[19] This broad relationship can be extended to the group of mortars related to cat. no. 25, with their animal motifs haphazardly dispersed over the surface, but these also share motifs with the Grandi *secchielli* cited earlier. A further link between the diverse groups is provided by a mortar on the London art market, which combines elements from a range of these objects.[20]

The present mortar is similar to the Louvre bowl in arrangement; the standing figure on both fits exactly within the borders of the decorative band, for example. However, the figures on the mortar, though comparatively fine for an object of this type, are noticeably cruder; the trees vary from the distinctive examples on the bowl, and the overall quality is far less refined. There are a number of small bronzes of this type depicting hunting scenes, or animals from the hunt.[21]

It is not possible to conclude that these apparently related objects are the product of one workshop, particularly in the light of the known reuse of motifs by various foundries. The figural decoration is fifteenth-century in style, but the form of the mortar appears to have developed later. Mortars are notoriously retardataire, and figure style is not necessarily a guide to dating. A dated example of this precise form has not been found, but simpler bell-shaped mortars were in production by the early sixteenth century and a more articulated example dated 1535 survives.[22] Several other mortars carry the same type of fleshy foliate decoration but vary slightly in shape.[23] The appearance of two known Alberghetti motifs, together with the general stylistic relationship to the bowl in the Louvre, suggest a possible connection with that foundry, although the exact location and date of production remains an open question.

Notes

1. Possibly a shield of arms, party per fess. See, for example, Dandolo and Querini; Coronelli 1694, pp. 145 and 387 respectively.

2. Christie's (Bardini) 1902, loc. cit. The hunt appears in several of Pisanello's works, and the association was perhaps based on this relationship. Stylistically, the stiff handling of the mortar scene contrasts dramatically with the delicate, but animated studies in Pisanello's drawings, paintings and medals. See, e.g., Pisanello's painting of St Eustace in the National Gallery, London. Several copies of Pisanello's designs are illustrated in *Pisanello Le Peintre aux Sept Vertus* (exh. cat.), Paris (Louvre), 1996, e.g. no. 58, illus. p. 113; nos 181, 181A and 182, illus. pp. 282–3; nos 305 and 206 for examples of the medal of Alfonso V of Aragon, with his motto VENATOR INTREPIDVS on the reverse. See also Dominique Cordellier and Bernadette Py (eds), *Pisanello* (Acts of the Louvre Colloquium, of June 1996), Paris, 1998. I am grateful to Luke Syson for useful discussion; see his paper in ibid., '*Opus pisani pictoris* Les médailles de Pisanello et son atelier', pp. 377–426.

3. Salting noted in 1902 (presumably shortly after purchasing it at the Bardini sale) that it had cost £155, but was worth £200; Salting Notebook GSVII, p. 64.

4. Pechstein, loc. cit.

5. Launert, loc. cit.

6. Radcliffe, loc. cit., for full references to the Metropolitan mortar, inv. no. 64.101.1453, h. 8.7.

7. Hackenbroch 1962, fig. 63, pl. 60 and p. 20. The Rome bowl (see p. 97, fig. 14) is mistakenly dated to 1562; Alfonso's dates are given as 1559–85, but the source is unknown. He took over direction of the foundry in about 1568, and therefore must have been born before 1559.

8. See Cessi 1967, pp. 62–3, 102–3, figs 21–4, and particularly Trento 1999, pp. 56–9, nos 6–7, for examples in Trento (Museo del Buonconsiglio) and Florence (Museo Nazionale del Bargello); Pechstein 1968, no. 88, for Berlin (Kunstgewerbemuseum). Another *secchiello* is in the Museum für Kunst und Gewerbe, Hamburg, no. 1957–75, w. 20.2, 21 (including masks), h. 10.5. All are so closely related that they were undoubtedly produced by the same workshop (see also cat. no. 25).

9. Radcliffe 1994, pp. 20–3, no. 2 with full list of Opus Petri bells known at the time. Another (damaged) example was formerly with Anthony Blumka in New York (1994); Radcliffe, loc. cit., also for references to Grandi, and n. 8 above.

10. Planiscig (Figdor) 1930, p. 272, no. 374; see Radcliffe 1994, loc. cit. at n. 9, for further references.

11. Jestaz 1986, docs 22, 23, 25, 27, 28, 55, 59, 69 for reference to both founders; additional documents for Piero (see Jestaz index). Giovanni Alberghetti is not documented there beyond 1508, but is referred to in a document of 1512 (no. 69).

12. Mann 1931 (1981), p. 27, no. S64, as Italian (Florentine?), last part of the fifteenth century.

13. Pechstein 1968, no. 96; another example with the pacing horse.

14. Museo Nazionale del Bargello, Florence, inv. no. 715, see also cat. no. 24, for example, and fig. 13.

15. See also p. 97 for discussion of this mortar and the inscribed signature.

16. See also a mortar formerly with Cyril Humphris (Sotheby's 1995, II, lot 229). This bears the pacing horse and bird and a monogram (GBT) in the form of a mark, most likely a pharmacy symbol in view of its scale and prominence. This mortar is of a different form from the signed Alberghetti one, but bears a similar, though not identical, foliate and floral frieze.

17. Pechstein 1968, no. 53.

18. University of California (formerly Kress Collection); see Pope-Hennessy 1965, p. 154, no. 564, figs 590–1. This apparently high-quality bronze (unseen by the author) bears a coat of arms and a mark (a monogram of B, I(?) and inverted R), both as yet unidentified. If a foundry mark, it does not appear to be that of the Alberghetti.

19. Migeon 1904, pp. 103–7; see also p. 98, fig. 15, and cat. no. 32; Radcliffe 1992, pp. 226–9, no. 38 summarizes the previous literature.

20. With Daniel Katz Ltd, London, in January 2000, h. 13.6, diam. 14 (rim), 10.1 (base), w. *c.*17.5. The mortar bears the same form as the present example, with identical handles and decoration of the rim and foot. The body has anthemion and palmette decoration with central oak-style leafs, reminiscent of cat. nos 26 and 27, and the bowl is gadrooned in the same style as the mortar signed by Giulio Alberghetti in the Bargello.

21. Another example is a bell in the Museo Nazionale del Bargello, Florence, inv. no. 760 (Girard Gift 1920); h. 13, 7.5 (without handle), diam. 8.4; around the rim: ANTONIV PANTO IS O + . The 'NTO' is inscribed instead of applied in relief, possibly indicating an amendment (perhaps originally ANTONIV PADOVANIS (?), for St Anthony of Padua). See van Marle 1931, p. 252 ff., for representations of the hunt in fifteenth-century art; van Marle 1932, p. 108, fig. 125, for a Venetian woodcut of *c.*1525 with a scene of the *Hunt of Virtue* (a huntsman on foot with his two dogs, Desio and Pensier, pursuing a stag).

22. See cat. no. 36, citing a related example dated 1535. The form of the present mortar falls into Middeldorf's 'Classical Renaissance' type (Middeldorf, pp. 11, 100–27). These are usually given to the mid-sixteenth century and, as noted above, this mortar was cited as a good example of a mid-sixteenth-century Venetian mortar by Radcliffe (loc. cit.).

23. See also cat. nos 29, 30 and 45.

Bibliography

Pechstein 1968, no. 58; Launert 1990, pp. 70 and 203, no. 226 (illus.); Radcliffe 1992, p. 230.

29. Mortar with foliate decoration

North Italian (Veneto); 1520–60
Bronze
h. 12.8; diam. 14.7 (rim), 9.5 (base); w. 18.6; wt 3688.4 g.
M.701-1910

Provenance: Collection of George Salting, London; on loan to the Victoria and Albert Museum from 24 March 1907; bequeathed by Salting in 1910 (Salting Bequest, no. 2522).

Condition: Squashy, waxy appearance, particularly around the join of the foot, but with evidence of turning. White encrustation to the moulded detail. Handles crooked.
Interior: smooth, with spots of corrosion; dull, dark crackled surface in the bowl.
Base: smooth, with some shrinkage where the pouring sprue attached, and pitting. There is a ridge around the foot.
Dark brown patina, on both exterior and interior.
Metal analysis: consistent low-tin bronze alloy.

A vase-shaped mortar with two handles of scroll form. On the lip, an astragal, and below acanthus on a cyma recta moulding. On the body, vine-leaf scrolls emanating from dolphins, a shield (quarterly) superimposed at the centre of each side over a basket of fruit, *tazza* or vase (?);[1] an ovolo below. On the bowl, upright acanthus. On the foot, downward-facing acanthus. The handles obscure, on one side, a large acanthus and, on the other, finer foliage.

The cracking around the foot could be due to differential cooling between the foot and the bowl.

The mortar was designated Italian, sixteenth-century, on acquisition.[2] A virtually identical mortar in the Kunstgewerbemuseum, Berlin, was dated around 1500 by Pechstein, who suggested Padua as the possible place of origin.[3] Bode's previous dating to the quattrocento was revised by Draper to the early sixteenth century and located more broadly to north Italy.[4]

The arms on the present mortar are too common to identify with certainty in the absence of tincture,[5] as are those on the Berlin example (a fess), which appear on the bowl of the mortar. Pechstein identified several variants, among them a small mortar in the Wallace Collection,

London.[6] Although the latter is of the same basic form, the style and nature of the decoration vary. There does not seem to be any reason why the group should be given to Padua specifically, as there is no distinctive feature of the decoration. An origin in the Veneto is the most precise attribution that can be given at present. The form appears to have been developed from bell-shaped mortars, dated examples of which appear at the beginning of the sixteenth century.[7] Comparison with an example dated 1535 suggests a similar date for the evolved shape of the present example, although the date span is potentially quite broad.[8]

Other related variants
i. Formerly Stefano Bardini, Florence, Christie's (Bardini) 1899, lot 401, pl. 2, no. 34, as Italian, late fifteenth-century.
ii. See cat. nos 28 and 30 for further related examples.

Notes
1. Compare the similar motif on cat. no. 21 (see also cat. no. 30).
2. Museum records. This is possibly the small, two-handled mortar with acanthus and dolphins mentioned in Salting's Notebook and valued at £110 (GSVII, p. 61).
3. Inv. no. 94,447, h. 12.7, diam. 14.4 (rim), 10.6 (base); see Pechstein 1968, no. 58, where M.702-1910 (cat. no. 28) was given as a variant; probably a misprint for the present example. See also Launert 1990, p. 202, no. 225, for the Berlin mortar.
4. Bode/Draper 1980, CXXVIII, no. 3.
5. Possibilities include the Bovin and Nordi of Treviso (Morando di Custoza 1985, I, pl. CCLVI and CCLXXXI respectively), and the Ruffi and Ruggieri of Padua (ibid., I, pl. CLXIX); kindly identified by Fiona Leslie.
6. Mann 1931 (1981), p. 27, no. S64, as Italian (Florentine?), last part of the fifteenth century. For a further discussion of the Wallace mortar, see cat. no. 28.
7. A bell-shaped mortar dated 1502 (Sotheby's, London, 8 July 1976, lot 178) is included in Appendix 2.
8. See cat. no. 36 for a related example.

30. Mortar decorated with foliate scrolls

North Italian (probably Venice); 1520–60
Bronze
h. 13; diam. 14.5 (rim), 9.9 (base); w. 17.7; wt 2923.5 g.
348-1889

Provenance: Bought from Michelangelo Guggenheim, Venice, in 1889 (with 335 to 354-1889, £300).

Condition: Waxy cast, worn in places, but the acanthus on the bowl crisply cast; evidence of turning; some green corrosion.
Interior: indent at centre; pitting with white deposit.
Base: smooth with pin-hole at centre, visible as larger indent inside.
Brassy exterior; uneven mottled red-brown colour inside.
Metal analysis: low-tin bronze.

Mortar of a modified bell-shape with handles in the form of S-shaped foliate scrolls. Decorated around the rim with acanthus; on the body, foliate scrolls with suspended grotesque heads and two heraldic shields. The bowl

divided by a torus moulding with (above) a frieze of downward-facing acanthus and (below) elongated acanthus. On the foot, downward-facing acanthus.

The friezes of acanthus appear to have been applied as individual leaves with uneven spacing. The handles were separately cast and soldered on. The discoloration of the interior may have been caused by a chemical reaction with the substances that were ground.

Registered as Italian, fifteenth-century, on acquisition, this mortar belongs to a group that are so similar in form and decoration as to allow attribution to the same workshop, at least for the four most closely related (listed below). The example in Milan (i) has a fleshy plant motif in place of the grotesques and shield, but bears the same characteristics of facture (separate scroll handles, turning and application of individual leaves). The Milan variant is apparently identical in decoration to an example on the French art market in the 1990s, formerly in the collection of Rudolphe Kann, Paris (ii), the latter differing only in the addition of a coat of arms identified as that of the

Badoer family of Venice.[1] The same arms appear on a mortar in the National Gallery of Art, Washington (Kress Collection), catalogued as probably Venetian, fifteenth- or early sixteenth-century, by Pope-Hennessy, alongside motifs also found on a mortar signed by the Venetian founder Giulio Alberghetti (director of one of the foundries, 1551–72) in the Bargello.[2] The Paris mortar was also given to Venice by Laroussilhe (see ii below), but attributed to a workshop close to Alessandro Leopardi (late fifteenth-/early sixteenth-century) by comparison with the mast pedestals in the Piazza San Marco and a vase (private collection) assigned to Leopardi's workshop on the same basis.[3]

The third variant, closest to the Paris example but without handles, survives in the Royal Museum of Scotland, Edinburgh (iii). Here the coat of arms matches one on a hand bell in the Museum's collection (cat. no. 54), and, given a Venetian context, can be identified as that of the Pesaro family (party per pale indented azure and or).[4]

Another potential member of the group is a mortar in the Boijmans Museum (iv), given to Padua, about 1500 in the museum records, but formerly described as School of Andrea Riccio.[5] There is a clear similarity in form and style, but the actual decoration varies. It bears the same *tazze*(?) as a mortar in Washington, which can itself be compared to others probably made in Venice, possibly by the Alberghetti foundry.[6] The seated, trumpeting putti on the Washington mortar can also be associated with the Alberghetti foundry of the early sixteenth century.[7] However, the prominent griffin supporters are similar to those on a bell in Hamburg bearing the mark of Bonaventura Bonaventurini of Verona (c.1490–after 1555).[8]

As usual, these motifs are too common to be used in isolation as evidence of origin. A firm attribution of these particular utensils to Leopardi cannot be sustained for the same reason. Although there are superficial similarities with the mast stem, the treatment of the foliate style is too generalized to be directly related to it. However, the presence of Venetian arms on two of this group, while not conclusive, allows the suggestion that Venice was the centre of production. The mortars that have been examined were apparently made in the same way and, unusually, the three sets of handles (applied after casting) take the form of identical foliate scrolls.[9] The waxy treatment of the fleshy foliage, together with the elegant and unusual form, makes a particularly attractive group, the present example

being of slightly lower quality than the others. The elaborate profile probably developed from bell-shaped mortars, and suggests a later date than that given formerly, probably mid- to late sixteenth century.

Close variants

i. Museo Poldi-Pezzoli, Milan; inv. no. FC 30/68 (Fondazione Crespi); h. 12.9, diam. 13.8 (rim), 9.6 (base), w. *c.*17. An outer ring appears visible on the base, with the middle set in.

ii. Art Market, Paris, 1993 and 1996; h. 13.5, diam. 14. Brimo de Laroussilhe, *Sculptures et Objets d'art précieux du XIIe au XVIe siècle*, Paris, 1993, pp. 68–9, no. 13; colour illus. in an unidentified advertisement dated November 1996 (Sculpture Department archive).

iii. Royal Museum of Scotland, Edinburgh, inv. no. 1877.20.45; h. 13.8; diam. 14.5 (rim), 10 (base); wt 2839.7 g.; formerly in the Shandon Collection, Robinson 1865, p. 69, no. 831 (with pestle), as Italian, sixteenth-century.

iv. Boijmans Van Beuningen Museum, Rotterdam, inv. no. L.23, h. 11.5, diam. 12.4. Decorated with rampant lions, and *tazze* (?) supported by foliate dolphins. The profile differs from the others: the lip is more splayed and the 'waist' where the bowl and foot join is narrower.

Notes

1. See Coronelli 1694, p. 7; Crollalanza 1965, I, pp. 77–8.
2. Washington mortar, inv. no. 1957.14.103 (A.256.100C); see Pope-Hennessy 1965, p. 155, no. 568, fig. 594; Washington 1994, p. 230 (as probably Venetian, sixteenth-century). See p. 96, fig. 13, and cat. no. 24 for a discussion of the Alberghetti mortar.
3. For the vase, see Frankfurt 1985, p. 528, no. 250, and cat. no. 26 in this volume.
4. Coronelli 1694, p. 351. Noted in the Museum records by Anthony Radcliffe as possibly the arms of the Corbizzi; see Marquand 1972, p. 103.
5. Formerly Hollitscher and J. W. Frederiks Collections, given by Dr E. Frederiks; see Bode and Friedländer 1912, p. 5, illus. p. 13; exhibited New York, 1923, no. 10 (no further details); von Falke 1922, pl. 30.
6. Inv. no. 1957.14.99 (A.252.96C); see Pope-Hennessy 1965, p. 155, no. 569, fig. 595; Washington 1994, p. 115 (as Italian, sixteenth-century); cf. cat. no. 21 for the *tazza*.
7. See cat. no. 25 and discussion under cat. no. 17.
8. See cat. no. 46, nn. 13 and 14, for details.
9. A superficial examination of the Paris mortar was carried out; that in Rotterdam has not been seen.

Bibliography

Inventory 1890, p. 36.

31. Mortar with projecting handles

North Italian (Veneto); *c.*1520–60
Bronze
h. 15.2; diam. 19.2 (rim), 13.8 (base);
w. 24.8; wt 9937.1 g.
336-1889

Provenance: Bought from
Michelangelo Guggenheim, Venice,
in 1889 (with 335 to 354-1889, £300).

Condition: Waxy cast, chipped in places.
Interior: pitted, with green and white corrosion; indentation in the bottom.
Base: large area of shrinkage where the pouring sprue was attached; pitted.
Dark brown patina.
Metal analysis: consistent bronze alloy, with unusually high copper content, with minimal tin and about twice as much lead. The iron reading is probably due to surface contamination.

Mortar with recessed lip and two projecting handles in the form of a cable (or rope). The rim formed by a prominent lip, and acanthus on a cyma recta moulding. On the body, four identical motifs (those at the sides cut by the handles), consisting of sprouting cornucopiae supporting and flanking a vase on which a blank label rests, the label itself supporting a foliate decoration flanked by confronting dolphins; between the cornucopiae and the label are displayed birds perched on tendrils and pecking at branches emerging from the horn. On the bowl, downward-facing acanthus on an elongated ogee; a torus moulding, and acanthus on a cyma recta moulding. The foot takes the form of an elongated ogee, decorated with downward-facing acanthus. The void 'label' may originally have housed (or been intended to house) a separately cast insertion.

The mortar was acquired as Italian, sixteenth-century, with an unknown origin.[1] The treatment of the foliate decoration, in a rather flattened style, can be compared to cat. nos 29 and 30.[2] The latter belongs to a coherent group of smaller mortars of similar shape. This form is comparatively rare and not directly comparable with any of Middeldorf's categories of mortar types.[3] It can be assumed to have developed from the bell-shaped mortars, suggesting a date around the middle of the sixteenth century. Although the place of facture cannot be firmly identified, general similarities with decorative motifs produced in known foundries in the Veneto, such as that of the Alberghetti, suggest that the present example was also produced in that area. The alloy is unusual and raises a question regarding the date of facture. The indentation inside, however, suggests that it has been used.

Notes
1 Inventory, loc. cit.
2. See these entries for a full discussion.
3. Middeldorf 1981, pp. 10–12, and p. 38 above.

Bibliography
Inventory 1890, p. 35.

32. Mortar with cornucopiae, putti and a muse(?)

North Italian (Venice?); *c.***1540–60**
Bronze
h. 9.1; diam. 11 (rim), 7.3 (base);
wt 1.56 kg.
354-1889

Provenance: Bought from
Michelangelo Guggenheim, Venice,
in 1889 (with 335 to 354-1889, £300).

Condition: Worn decoration; evidence of turning; minor casting flaws around the rim, one on the foot and another on the body. The bottom of both double acanthus friezes is smeared or cut; grey deposit in the interstices.
Interior: patchy, with reddening around the bowl and slight indentation.
Base: slightly sunken from shrinkage during cooling; smooth at the edge.
Dark brown patination evident in the interstices, and with a coppery appearance where worn; brassy where worn underneath.
Metal analysis: a low-tin bronze with traces of lead and zinc and comparatively high antimony content.

A bell-shaped mortar with projecting recessed rim, decorated with a fillet and a row of overlapping acanthus on a cyma recta moulding. On the body, beneath a bevel moulding, four patterns comprising masks from which emanate cornucopiae surmounted by winged putti, with foliage and a pedestal(?) emerging from the head, surmounted by a female figure playing a lyre; between each of these is a foliate-footed vase with leaves and flowers emerging. The bowl is delineated by a projecting moulding and decorated with a frieze of overlapping acanthus on

a cyma recta moulding. The foot, separated by bead and reel, is decorated with downward-facing acanthus on a cyma reversa moulding.

The mortar was acquired as Italian, sixteenth-century,[1] but no exact parallel has been found for the design. The form of the mortar is both elegant and oddly arranged, with the mouldings appearing heavy for its small scale, giving the impression that the body is compressed. The decorative elements are quite refined, but the detail is worn. The lyre played by the standing figure is most commonly represented as an attribute of Apollo, but it is also that of the personification of Poetry, and of the Muses Erato (lyric poetry) and Terpsichore (dancing and song), one of whom may be represented here. It relates in style to other mortars associated with the Alberghetti and other north Italian workshops (see cat nos 29–31), and its form and decorative style suggest a date around the mid-sixteenth century.

Notes
1. Inventory, loc. cit.

Bibliography
Inventory 1890, p. 37.

33. Mortar with festoons supported by putti

North Italian (Venice); 1450–1500
Bronze
h. 14.8; diam. 17.7 (rim), 10.3 (base); w. 20.4; wt 5397 g.
339-1889

Provenance: Bought from Michelangelo Guggenheim, Venice, in 1889 (with 335 to 354-1889, £300).

Condition: Evidence of turning throughout; some cracking; uneven moulding of foot; some wear.
Interior: dented by one handle and faceted; discoloured patch through to exterior of the rim; some chipping and deposited residue.
Base: shrinkage where the pouring cup was attached; smoothed off.
Dark brown patina over mottled brassy metal.
Metal analysis: a bronze with minimal lead content.

Bucket-shaped, conical mortar with projecting rim and recessed lip with two handles formed by foliate swags. The upper part of the body decorated with foliate swags supported by putti and tied in the centre with fluttering beaded cords; below are two heraldic shields and, applied in panels, hunting scenes set in woodland, each element separated by rope columns. On one side an elaborate coat of arms (see below) flanked by a running stag (to the left) and a pacing hunter; on the other side, a shield with chevron (pl. 33a) flanked by a running hound (to the left) and a running hind, facing backwards; a foundry mark appears above the swag on this side.

The mortar is described in the Museum records as Italian, sixteenth-century, of uncertain origin.[1] There are two other examples of mortars of identical form in the Kunstgewerbemuseum, Berlin, and the Musée

(*a*)

Jacquemart-André, Paris, bearing the same foundry mark and decorative motifs, but arranged differently.[2] A mortar bearing a similar foundry mark, but otherwise bearing little resemblance, survives in the Skulpturensammlung, Berlin.[3] A bell in the Museo Nazionale del Bargello, Florence, has the same distinctive flying cords.[4]

The arms (a bend) on the Berlin example are too common to be identifiable, as is the chevron on the present mortar. However, the complicated armorials on the other side of the mortar appear to represent a stylized version of those of the Venetian noble family of Cappello (party per fess argent and azure a brimless hat counterchanged the cords crossed saltirewise gules).[5] It is possible that the arms are those of a husband and wife. The Paris mortar bears arms with a crowned double eagle, which have been identified as those of the Giustiniani of Venice.[6] A similar charge is also a variant of the Cappelli arms.[7]

These mortars are considered by Pechstein to be Paduan, from the second half of the fifteenth century, after Bode, on the basis of the relationship of the putti to those of Donatello.[8] A provenance from Venice seems most likely if the complicated arms are indeed those of the Cappelli.

Notes

1. Inventory, loc. cit.
2. Kunstgewerbemuseum, Berlin, inv. no. 86,605, h. 14.2, diam. 17.3 (rim), 10.7 (base); Pechstein, loc. cit.; Launert 1990, p. 194, no. 214, as Paduan, second half of the fifteenth century. A squashed casting, with the running hind, and young deer looking behind, dog and huntsman, with two shields of arms. Musée Jacquemart-André, Paris, inv. no. 1080, h. 14.6, diam. 18.7 (rim), 11.5 (base), w. *c*.23; *Catalogue Itinéraire* 1948, p. 94, as Venetian, beginning of the sixteenth century. Decorated on one side: young deer facing behind, arms, running hind; on the other: the huntsman, running hind. The foundry mark is placed in a different position. Squashy and worn decoration, with dark brown patina.
3. Inv. no. 3149, h. 12.5, diam. 15 (rim), 9.9 (base); Bode 1930, p. 60, no. 289.
4. Inv. no. 775; see cat. no. 41, n. 6, for details.
5. Coronelli 1694, pp. 96–7, and showing variations on the arms; Rizzi 1987, p. 55; see also Crollalanza 1965, pp. 222–3, for details of branches of the Cappelli in Venice and Verona.
6. Gules a double-headed eagle crowned and displayed or on its breast an oval escutcheon azure charged with a fess or (Litta, VI, 1840, pl. I). See also Spreti, III, 1930, pp. 495–8, for other branches of the family.
7. Coronelli 1694, loc. cit. at n. 5.
8. Pechstein, loc. cit.; Bode loc. cit. at n. 3, although the putti on this mortar are not directly related.

Bibliography

Inventory 1890, p. 35; Pechstein 1968, no. 64.

(*b*)

34. Mortar with swags and coat of arms

North Italian; 1480–1520
Leaded bronze
h.10.7; diam. 12.8 (rim), 8.5 (base);
wt 2407.1 g.
M.23-1938

Provenance: Collection of Dr W. L. Hildburgh, FSA,
London; on loan to the Victoria and Albert Museum
from 14 August 1934 (no. 4841); given by
Hildburgh in 1938.

Condition: Evidence of turning and surface hammering.
Chipped/casting flaws around the rim; waxy decoration,
heavily worn, and with green deposit in interstices; one
pendant not attached to the swag.
Interior: green deposit/corrosion; some evidence of wear.
Base: large area of shrinkage where the pouring sprue was
attached.
Natural bronze-coloured patina.
Metal analysis: consistent bronze alloy with lead and low
zinc content.

Conical mortar with flared rim decorated with imbricated
scales; on the body, six swags and foliate pendants (irregularly spaced), beneath which are one coat of arms (a bend),
paterae and foliate decoration. Moulded foot.

The imbricated scales are apparently applied in six sections, with one slim infill adjacent to the lacuna in the
decoration on the body. This space may have been left to
allow for the attachment of a handle.

The present mortar was acquired simply as 'Italian, 15th
century', which is consistent with its style and form. A
similar, though more elaborately moulded, example of

this type of mortar is reproduced by Middeldorf as an
'early Renaissance type'. It displays the Sforza-Visconti
arms, suggesting a Milanese origin.[1] It is not possible to
attempt to identify such common arms as the bend without the benefit of tincture, but the *scudo sagomato* (a form
of 'Tuscan' or 'modern' shield) on the present mortar is
frequently found on north Italian bells and mortars,
including those associated with Venice and Brescia.[2]

The basic shape, with some variations in the proportions and moulded detail, is shared by cat. no. 23, the
decoration of which can be associated with the Alberghetti
workshop. Similarly, the form can be likened to that of cat.
no. 33. However, many conical mortars can be seen to
bear some relationship, their forms being a variation on a
theme. It is, therefore, not always useful to make such
comparisons, as origin cannot be securely identified on
the basis of profile alone. The present example dates from
the late fifteenth or the early sixteenth century.

Notes
1. Middeldorf 1981, pp. 64–9, no. 15.
2. Goodall 1958–9, pp. 210–11; Rizzi 1987, fig. 20; see also, for
   example, cat. nos 20 and 25.

35. Mortar with scalloped decoration

Probably North Italian; *c.***1520–50**
Bronze
h. 10.9; diam. 13.2 (rim), 9.3 (base);
wt 3163.7 g.
352-1889

Provenance: Bought from Michelangelo
Guggenheim, Venice, in 1889
(with 335 to 354-1889, £300).

Condition: Chipped around the rim.
Interior: some pitting and fine marks. An apparent indentation at the centre of the bowl.
Base: smooth with spindle hole, casting flaw and some other marks. No. 16935 faintly written and opposite 13 055 (the '13' possibly an 'h' or 'B'). Large '73'.
Speckled black patination, worn and scratched to reveal dark brown bronze.
Metal analysis: bronze, with lead content. Higher lead and tin at the rim.

Bell-shaped mortar with moulded rim formed by a cove. Decorated on the body with scallops and stylized papyrus. Gadrooned projecting bowl. Moulded foot.

The fine hole in the base indicates where the spindle was attached during facture. There is clear evidence of use, with the wear indicating the up-and-down motion associated with contusion, used to break up hard materials. The apparent higher lead content of the rim may be due to separation of the elements during casting. The higher tin content is more puzzling. It does not seem likely that the rim would be a separate casting from a different alloy.

In terms of its shape and type, the mortar is closest to Middeldorf's 'classical Renaissance' or 'degenerate classical Renaissance' types, although there are no directly related examples.[1] A mortar decorated with vine leaf in the collection (cat. no. 59) bears some resemblance in form, as does a mortar in the Museo Nazionale del Bargello, Florence, which is also decorated with scallops and has a gadrooned bowl.[2] The Florence mortar is of much lower quality, and the differences are sufficient to preclude any firm conclusion regarding a potential relationship. No other example of this type of decoration has been found, and it is therefore difficult to assign the mortar accurately to any region or date. On the basis of its provenance and shape, a north Italian origin can be suggested, around the early to mid-sixteenth century.

Notes
1. Middeldorf 1981, pp. 11, 100–33.
2. Inv. no. 717, h. 9.3, diam. 12.3 (rim), 7.8 (base).

Bibliography
Inventory 1890, p. 37.

36. Mortar inscribed 'FRANCESCO ROSSI'

North Italian (probably Veneto); *c*.1535
Bell-metal
h. 14.5; diam. 17.4 (rim), 10.8 (base); w. 21; wt 4659.5 g.
337-1889

Provenance: Bought from Michelangelo Guggenheim, Venice, in 1889 (with 335 to 354-1889, £300).

Condition: Considerable cracking and pitting, including long crack around the bowl; decoration around the top and central band on the side, with lettering crisper than the rest; evidence of working/filing.
Interior: apparently worn; varnish scratched.
Base: rough indentation underneath with some smoothing; thick, dark brown and white deposit.
Green-grey patination, scraped.
Metal analysis: bell-metal with exceptionally high tin content. Analysis indicated the use of a lacquer.

A bell-shaped mortar with projecting rim and two handles in the form of male heads facing downwards.
Decorated around the rim with foliate scrolls.
On the body, swags suspended from rings; a central band of grotesque decoration comprising panels of alternating heads and beads in medallions or scrolls (arranged as bearded male/bead/female/bead/putto, and a truncated section of female/bead/putto); on one side in relief the name FRANCESCO ROSSI; around the bowl, upright veined leaves. Shallow moulded foot.

The smeary working around the foot contrasts with the clear evidence of turning on the body itself, suggesting that it may have been attached as a separate entity in the model, indicating the use of a clay false bell. The band of decoration around the top was applied in five large and two small sections. The worn appearance of the central band of decoration can perhaps be accounted for by the use of old moulds from which the wax impressions were taken.[1]

Recorded as sixteenth-century on acquisition, the mortar is extremely similar to another that appeared at Sotheby's in Florence in 1974, dated 1535. The Florence mortar differed in the decoration around and just below the rim, but was otherwise apparently identical in shape and detail apart from the name it bore, being PINI GUSEPPE.[2] It seems that the legends on both these examples, applied as individual letters, must therefore refer to the different owners.[3]

The distinctive leaf decoration is close to that used by Giuseppe Ruffini (*c*.1721–1801), a bell-founder active in

Trento and Mantua, before working in Verona, where he finally settled in 1776.[4] Leaf of a similar style appears on a bell in a private collection in Verona, and an example of the cast leaf, believed to have been invented by Ruffini, was inherited by the Cavadini foundry there.[5] It can also be seen on a mortar signed by Dominicus Barborini of Parma, dated 1729.[6] It is clear from the date of 1535 on the Florence mortar, however, that this decoration originated at a much earlier date. A closely related leaf is also evident on two mortars in the Civici Musei d'Arte e Storia in Brescia, one of which is clearly from the same foundry as a mortar formerly on the London art market, catalogued as Venetian, fifteenth-century.[7] The latter pair display a cockerel with large flower motifs. They are of similar form to the present mortar, but with additional mouldings and 'turned', projecting handles. There is a vaguer relationship between the leaf decoration on all these examples and the smaller, more refined and detailed leaf on a group of objects attributed to Gaspare di Girolamo Macri of Brescia, who was active in the second half of the sixteenth century (see cat. nos 53–4).

This form of mortar was popular from the sixteenth through to the nineteenth centuries, with dated examples of similar shape throughout the period. Stylistically, the projecting heads are similar to those found on north Italian utensils of the sixteenth century,[8] and it is therefore probable that the mortar was made in the Veneto.

Notes

1. I am grateful to Anthony Radcliffe for this suggestion.
2. Sotheby's of London s.r.l., *Medaglie, Placchette, Bronzi e Scultore*, Florence, 8 April 1974, lot 114. The date is not visible in the illustration, and the inscription should presumably be read as Giuseppe Pini. For the Pini family, see Spreti, V, 1932, pp. 375–6.
3. For the various branches of the Rossi family, see Spreti, V, 1932, pp. 806–24.
4. Verona 1979, pp. 11, 89, 96, 131.
5. Verbal advice from Sig. Luigi Cavadini.
6. Tolentino 1925, lot 240; see cat. no. 44, n. 4, for Barborini.
7. Rizzini 1915, p. 34, nos 166 and 167. No. 166 bears much of the decoration seen on a mortar formerly with Cyril Humphris Ltd, *Twelve European Works of Art*, London, 1–18 June 1967, no. 3.
8. No exact parallel has been identified, but see, for example, Berlin 1995, pp. 306–7, no. 87, for one of a group of door knockers bearing some similarity in the head types.

Bibliography
Inventory 1890, p. 35.

37. Hand bell with swags and masks

North Italian (probably Venice), 1500–50
Bell-metal
h. 13.6, 7.7 (without handle); diam. 9.8; wt 524 g.
M.675-1910

Provenance: Stefano Bardini, Florence (Christie's (Bardini) 1899, lot 416; no. 17, pl. 1); collection of George Salting from 1899; bequeathed by Salting in 1910 (Salting Bequest; no. 2938).

Condition: Some areas of minor wear and blurring around the top and lower mouldings. Evidence of turning. Baluster handle, fitted with a washer.
Interior: iron clapper, fixed into a sleeve in the hole of the bell itself. Marked in red crayon ('14'?). Rough interior, but with evidence of turning.
Greenish-brown patina.
Metal analysis: high-tin bell-metal, with evidence of zinc. The high iron content on the body is probably due to surface contamination or treatment.

A hand bell with turned handle, decorated around the crown and sound bow with downward-facing overlapping acanthus of two different forms. Around the neck, a band of vine leaf between rows of beads. On the waist, swags of fruit and foliage supporting birds (pelicans?), which peck at the fruit, together with similar pendants with fluttering ribbons, suspended from flowers; below the swags are alternating grotesque and female masks.

The vine leaf and bead is applied as a single band, with the join clearly visible.

The bell was bought at the Bardini sale by Durlacher for £21, from whom Salting presumably purchased it.[1] It was classified as Paduan of the early sixteenth century on acquisition, and the relationship was noted with a comparable bell, formerly in the Pierpont Morgan Collection, London (now in the Pierpont Morgan Library, New York).[2] The Morgan bell is more closely related to cat. no. 39, which is also possibly from the same workshop.

Swags and masks are common decorative motifs for the period, but they vary considerably in form and there is not, therefore, necessarily any direct relationship between objects bearing these motifs. However, a similar female mask can be seen on other bronze utensils, including a bucket formerly in the Piet-Lataudrie Collection, Paris, which were possibly produced in the same workshop or centre.[3] The broadly splayed rim, scale and general character of the decoration are not far removed from cat. no. 38, but there is nothing distinct to indicate the place or specific date of manufacture. A similar bell, formerly in the Beit Collection, London, is attributable to the same workshop.[4]

The complicated interrelationships of these bells is again evident when looking at a group with two examples in the National Gallery of Art, Washington (Kress Collection), and one in the Tesoro del Duomo in Padua, which have basically the same shape and treatment of the decoration, but share elements with cat. no. 55, notably the form of festoon with intertwined ribbon.[5] Both of the Kress bells bear arms of Venetian families (the Boldu (?) and Moro respectively). The indications are, therefore, that the present bell is connected with the Veneto. These bells are generally dated to the first half of the sixteenth century, although production may have continued for some time.

Notes

1. Annotated copy of Christie's (Bardini) 1899, loc. cit. Museum records, Salting's Notebook, GS VII, p. 62, values the bell at £40, amended to £50 (date of notation unknown).
2. Bode 1910, I, p. 18, pl. XL.
3. Collection M. Piet-Lataudrie; see *Les Arts*, August 1909, p. 21 (as Riccio).
4. Photograph in Museum archive. The bell has the same form and turned handle, and virtually identical decoration to the crown and neck; identifiable with Bode (Beit) 1904, p. 64, 'bell, h. 15.8 with a coat of arms between dainty ornaments', given as Venetian, but not illustrated. The arms have not been identified.
5. For Kress, see Pope-Hennessy 1965, pp. 147–8, nos 540 and 541, figs 536 and 538; Washington 1994, pp. 230–1 (as probably Venetian, sixteenth-century). For Padua, see Cessi 1967, p. 111, pl. 38, where it is mistakenly associated with the Grandi due to the apparent inclusion of the Cles *impresa* (crossed branches of laurel and palm), subsequently corrected in Radcliffe 1992, p. 224; this is another example of arms applied to the shield after casting. These three bells are clearly from the same foundry and are discussed further under cat. no. 55.

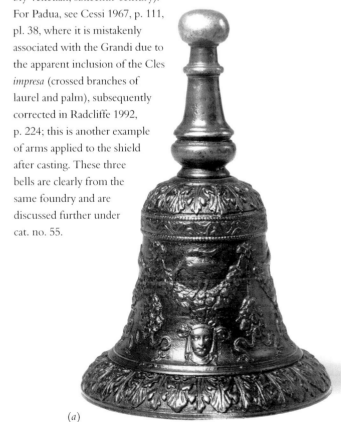

(a)

38. Hand bell with dancing putti and other figures

North Italian (probably Venice); 1500–50
Bell-metal
h. 12, 7.9 (without handle); diam. 9; wt 427.6 g.
M.676-1910

Provenance: Collection of Eugène Piot, Paris, until 1890 (Hotel Drouot (Piot) 1890, lot 29); collection of George Salting; bequeathed by Salting in 1910 (Salting Bequest, no. 2939).

Condition: Background irregular in places with small metal pimples; some areas have numerous blow-holes. Variation of colour and texture to the surface. Handle shows signs of repair.
Interior: rough interior surface with evidence of wear around the sound bow. Clapper and support wanting, with whitish metal in that area.
Dark brown applied patination.
Metal analysis: bell-metal with minimal lead.
The handle consistent, but with slightly more lead.

Hand bell with turned handle. Decorated around the crown with imbricated leaves. Below, a band of foliate decoration, from which are suspended garlands of laurel with a loop of ribbon at the centre. Around the waist, below the swags, is a blank shield flanked by cornucopiae and (to the right) a naked dancing female figure, three dancing putti and a naked male figure, truncated at the knees, blowing a horn; all resting on a fine, plain moulding wire. Around the sound bow, a row of downward-facing acanthus.

Both the imbricated leaf decoration on the crown and the acanthus around the rim are irregularly applied in the wax, perhaps indicating that they were prepared by an inexperienced workman. Despite this, and the surface pitting, the bell is of high quality. The acanthus around the sound bow is applied in eight groups of three leaves, with two additional leaves below and to the left of the shield.

Attributed to Padua in the fifteenth century in the Piot sale catalogue and amended by Salting to north Italy in his notebook, the bell was catalogued on acquisition as Italian, early sixteenth-century.[1] This was subsequently modified to 'Florentine?', late fifteenth-century, presumably due to the perceived similarity of the putti with those of Donatello.[2] However, north Italian bells are frequently given to Padua for a similar reason. The same group of putti appears in lower relief around the base of one of the Museum's mortars (cat. no. 6), which can be associated with Fabriano in the March of Ancona through comparison with signed mortars produced there. There is also a strong resemblance to the figures on the bronze relief of a *Baccanale* by Bertoldo di Giovanni (*c.*1440–91) in the Museo Nazionale del Bargello, Florence.[3] It is likely that such designs became quite widely disseminated and were used by more than one foundry. The putti also bear some relation to those flanking the shields of several mortars traditionally given to Venice or Padua (see cat. no. 20).

The figure blowing the horn appears on two other bells of related design, one in the Ashmolean Museum, Oxford, and the other in the Museum of Fine Arts in Richmond, Virginia, apparently produced by the same workshop.[4] The Oxford bell also has a similar, but not identical, dancing female figure with elongated, extended arms. A bell of similar shape and style in the Castello

(a)

Sforzesco, Milan, also has the swags with ribbon and cornucopiae seen on a large number of north Italian bells. A coat of arms identifiable as being that of the Surian family of Venice is prominently displayed.[5] The three bells examined (London, Oxford and Milan) all have an applied patination. Other related bells can be found in the Museo Castello del Buonconsiglio, Trento;[6] the Musée National de la Renaissance, Ecouen;[7] and a poorly cast bell in the Museo Correr, Venice, which is closely related in form.[8]

The overall form of the present bell, the style of the shield and the general decoration are north Italian of the early to mid-sixteenth century, although a later date cannot be ruled out. The relationship to bells with Venetian connections suggests that city as the probable centre of production.

Notes

1. See Hotel Drouot, loc. cit.; Salting Notebooks GSIV, noted as £40, 'worth 80', and GSVII, p. 62, valued initially at £80, amended to £120; Museum records.
2. Museum records.
3. See cat. no. 6 for a discussion.
4. The Oxford bell (inv. no. 1947.191.173, h. 12.9, 8.3 (without handle), diam. 9.2; see Warren, forthcoming) has a rough interior, with some minor chipping around the edge. The foliate decoration around the neck is applied in three sections, and the bell is turned behind the decoration. The Museum's bell is taller, narrower and more waisted, with only two layers of overlapping leaves around the crown, instead of three as at Oxford. The unpublished Richmond bell (inv. no. 37-11-23, given by Mrs John Kerr in memory of her husband, and

catalogued as unknown Italian) is apparently of poorer quality, judging from photographs. The author has not studied this bell.

5. Inv. no. Br.113, see cat. no. 55, n. 13 for details, see Coronelli 1694, p. 438, for the Surian arms (argent a bend checky of three sable and or; kindly blazoned by John Meriton).
6. Inv. no. 3203; h. 10.5, including the same shape and decoration around the neck, with similar swags; noted in the Castello records as workshop of Vincenzo and Gian Girolamo Grandi, but dated *c*.1500. The bell also bears a coat of arms (party per fess an eagle displayed, possibly identifiable with those of the Valier family, see Coronelli 1694, p. 451), and medallions containing profile portrait heads, including a man with a turban. Another bell in the Castello del Buonconsiglio (inv. no. 3207; h. 18.6, diam. 8.6; recorded as north Italian, second half of the sixteenth century) has the same shape and various elements of decoration as inv. no. 3203.
7. Inv. no. 15429, Wasset Bequest 1906, h. 15.5, diam. 8.3; *Objets d'art italiens de la Renaissance* (exh. cat.; Bordeaux, Nantes and Lyon), 1975, p. 42, cat. no. 59. It is of the same form as the present example and carries similar decoration to the crown, neck and sound bow. It also displays medallions with profile heads, related to those in Trento (see n. 6 above). The bell has the same handle figure as a different style of bell in the Museo Nazionale del Bargello, Florence (inv. no. 775). Similar putti supporters are seen on a bell in the Musée du Louvre, Paris, (inv. no. R.81), bearing the initials P. E. above a coat of arms (bendy; possibly identifiable with that of the Emo family of Venice, see Coronelli 1694, p. 161).
8. Inv. no. 1316, h. 9.9, diam. 9. Three plaster bell forms also survive in the Correr, including one which is closely related to the bell in that museum, possibly indicating that copies were reproduced at a later date. See also cat. no. 53, n. 23, for the Hermitage bell, which bears comparison in form and part of the decoration.

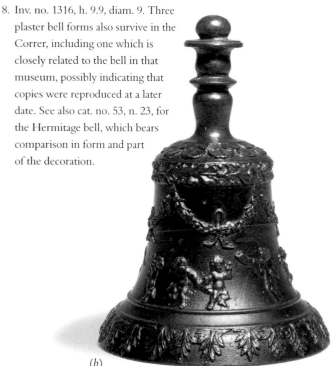

(b)

39. Hand bell with masks

North Italian (Padua or Venice); 1500–50
Bell-metal
h. 14.9, 8.2 (without handle); diam. 9; wt 523 g.
M.194-1938

Provenance: Collection of Dr W. L. Hildburgh, FSA, London, from 1913; on loan to the Victoria and Albert Museum from 31 May 1926 (no. 1468); given by Hildburgh in 1938.

Condition: Worked surface. The decorative medallions (see below) appear as though set in.
Interior: black lettering (WON or NOM); hand-written label marked 'Venice '13'; evidence of turning. Rusted where the handle was soldered on during a repair. Iron clapper and ring, possibly original. Remains of a foundry mark.
Silver-green patina, with brown patination applied to the handle; interior grey.
Metal analysis: bell-metal with some lead; handle brass with iron content.

A hand bell with turned handle, decorated with down-ward-facing overlapping acanthus around the crown and sound bow. On the waist, a moulding wire from which swags of leaves and fruit are suspended, with fluttering ribbons attaching pendants of garlands alternating with two medallions of a griffin, one of which faces forward and the other behind; below the swags, alternating grotesque masks of two different designs. The faint remains of a foundry mark inside: ⅄.

On acquisition, this bell was said to have been acquired in Venice, and this is substantiated by the hand-written descriptive label inside, marked 'Venice '13'.[1] It was dated to the first half of the sixteenth century. The bell bears a shape common to a vast number of north Italian examples; the grotesque masks are generic and therefore difficult to place with confidence, being widely used as decorative motifs (see also cat. no. 37, which is closely related). There are, however, virtually identical bells in the collection of Dr Anselm Lange,[2] and formerly in the Morgan Collection, London (now in the Pierpont Morgan Library, New York),[3] which bears the Strozzi arms, and the initials B. S. representing a member of the family.[4]

The Morgan bell is apparently crisper, has the same decoration and handle, but with a clearer division between the handle and the crown. A bell in the Virginia Museum of Fine Arts, Richmond, bears a similar mask.[5] The Virginia bell also has a relationship to one in the Kunstgewerbemuseum, Berlin.[6] The Lange, Morgan and the present bell were doubtless produced by the same workshop, possibly in Padua or Venice.

Another related variant

i. Museo Correr, Venice, inv. no. 1316 BIS; h. 7.1, diam. 8.1; two masks with cornucopiae and birds alternate with two rams' heads addorsed and bucrane with snakes emanating from the orbits and foliage decoration. This is a poor, squashy cast, with a roughish interior.

Notes

1. Museum records. The label suggests that Hildburgh bought the bell in Venice in 1913; no auction has been identified.
2. Pforzheim Reuchlinhaus and Hanau 1969, p. 16, and Lange 1981, p. 96, h. 15, as Italian Renaissance; it appears to bear only the foliate pendants and not the medallions.
3. See Bode 1910, I, p. 18, pl. XL; h. 6 in (15 cm.). There is apparently damage to some of the acanthus, the lower half of which is missing. The author has not examined the Lange and Morgan bells.
4. The painter Bernardo Strozzi (Genoa 1581–Venice 1644) may be a candidate, which would date the bell later than expected, to the first half of the seventeenth century; Enc. Ital., 32, p. 862; pp. 861–2 for the Strozzi family.
5. Inv. no. 37-11-31, h. *c.*11.5, diam. *c.*9; given by Mrs John Kerr Branch in memory of her husband.
6. Inv. no. 91,215, Pechstein 1968, no. 62. Here attributed to the Alberghetti foundry (see cat. no. 17 and Motture forthcoming).

(*a*)

40. Hand bell with arms of the Lippomani

North Italian (probably Veneto); 1530–70
Bell-metal
h. 9.8, 6.9 (without handle); diam. 9.4; wt 417.0 g.
587-1865

Provenance: Collection of Jules Soulages, Toulouse, until 1856; bought in 1865 for £3.

Condition: Granular surface; two large chips from the rim. Replacement pierced peg argent supports the clapper (consisting of brass ball attached by two interlocking wires) and swivels within the bell; lead residue indicates a repair. The crown possibly cast separately, dented at the rim and marked with a single fine line (possibly a decoration seam).
Interior: a foundry mark cast in relief, and evidence of turning.
Dark grey patination with greenish tinge, with worn areas appearing coppery in colour; grey patina on the interior.
Metal analysis: consistent high-tin bell-metal with some lead and minimal zinc.

Hand bell decorated with, on the flattened crown, fine foliate scrolls framed by rows of beads. On the return, egg and dart with dentils below. On the neck, a raised legend: PVLSV MEO SERV[O]S VOCO LIPO MANO TVOS ([with] my ring I call your servants, o Lippomano). A rope band separates the waist, which is decorated with a cartouche bearing a coat of arms (see below) with three grotesque masks, from which emanate ropes and swags of tied bundles of fruit; varying bunches of grapes, foliage and fruit are suspended from the beards; flanking the shield are two profile heads of classical figures, one an emperor facing to the left, the other Hercules wearing a lion skin facing to the right. On the sound bow, a row of downward-facing, overlapping acanthus.

The replacement peg argent is pierced for a tassel (missing) or possibly a leather handle. The clapper, consisting of a two-part shaft and brass ball, is a replacement. A foundry mark cast in relief appears just above the sound bow on the interior: ⚹

The exceptional high-tin content would have made the bell extremely brittle, and may have contributed to the damage.

This shape of bell is rare, and no other identical example has been found. The decoration around the crown differs from that of the body, and technical examination suggests that the upper section of the crown may be inserted. Taken with the replacement peg argent, it is possible that the top was replaced and the shape of the bell modified. It would, nevertheless, have had the unusual projecting shoulder. Apart from this distinctive feature, the bell bears a close resemblance in size and form to cat. no. 41. In addition to identical acanthus decoration around the rim, they have the same legend – here in relief, but incised on cat. no. 41 – which is found appropriately enough on a number of bells, including one formerly in the Piot Collection, Paris, described as being decorated with festoons and satyr masks, and therefore possibly close to the present example.[1] Despite the similarities with cat. no. 41, the overall treatment of the decoration varies, and the bells bear different foundry marks on the interior. The mark on this bell is also the symbol for 'Alpha', the first letter of the Greek alphabet (usually paired with 'Omega', the last letter, together denoting the beginning and end of all things), which is frequently seen on early bells.[2]

The inscription also refers to the owner of the bell, a member of the Lippomano family, whose arms (gules a bend between two lions' heads erased argent)[3] have also apparently been cast-in. Another bell with a similar legend (…SERV[O]S VOCO LIPO MANO), but with void shields, is in the Museo Civico, Bologna.[4] The Lippomani were a Venetian patrician family, who had several prominent members during the late fifteenth and, notably, the

(a)

(b)

sixteenth century.[5] The present bell was catalogued as Italian, about 1500, by Robinson and as first half of the sixteenth century by Fortnum.[6] Another in the National Gallery of Art, Washington (Kress Collection – without the projecting top and bearing arms possibly identifiable with the Aleardi), was similarly described by Pope-Hennessy as late fifteenth- or early sixteenth-century.[7] A third example (with the more usual rounded top) appeared in the 1899 Bardini sale catalogue, described as Venetian work of the school of Riccio, and said to be dated 1558.[8] All three were probably from the same workshop. Although the style and the decoration suggest an earlier date, the Bardini example indicates production in the mid-sixteenth century. It is, however, possible that the pattern continued in use over a long period. The Kress bell had previously been identified as north Italian,[9] and the evidence of the arms points to an origin in the Veneto.

(c)

Notes

1. Hotel Drouot (Piot) 1890, lot 27, as Paduan, beginning of the sixteenth century.
2. For example, Schilling 1988, p. 140, no. 250; p. 144, no. 269; p. 145, no. 273.
3. Spreti, IV, 1931, pp. 122–3.
4. Inv. no. 1408; the first part of the inscription is unclear (possibly + PVI [*sic*] SERVO MEO).
5. See Spreti, loc. cit. at n. 3. Three members of the family were bishops of Verona during the sixteenth century: Pietro 1543–8, Luigi 1548–58 and Agostino 1558–9 (Morando di Custoza 1980, Appendix).
6. Robinson and Fortnum, locc. citt.
7. Inv. no. 1957.14.113 (A.266.110C); Pope-Hennessy 1965, p. 147, no. 539, fig. 542, plus earlier literature; Washington 1994, p. 118 (as Italian, sixteenth-century). For the Aleardi arms (Lozengy argent and azure, on a chief or a crowned eagle displayed sable), see Morando di Custoza 1976, pl. VII, no. 59; for the Aleardi of Verona, see Crollalanza 1965, I, p. 27, although the arms for this branch appear to be different. The arms on this bell were previously said to have been identified as those of the Grimaldi (for which see Spreti, III, 1930, pp. 570–4).
8. Christie's (Bardini) 1899, lot 418 (no. 16, pl. 1); no specific date is given in the French version (*Catalogue des Objets d'Art Antiques, du Moyen Age et de la Renaissance provenant de la Collection Bardini de Florence dont la vente aura lieu à Londres chez Mr. Christie… Le 5 Juin 1899…*, p. 6, no. 16: 'Clochette. Manière de Riccio. Travail venitien, XVIème siècle'). Neither catalogue transcribes the inscription or describes the coat of arms.
9. Cott 1951, p. 139.

Bibliography

Robinson 1856, p. 118, no. 373; Ellacombe 1872, p. 312; Fortnum 1876, p. 76; *South Kensington Museum*, I, 1881, no. 83.

41. Hand bell inscribed 'A.M.'

North Italian (probably Venice); about 1550
Bell-metal
h. 9 (7 without handle); diam. 8.7; wt 398.5 g.
M.199-1938

Provenance: Collection of Dr W. L. Hildburgh, FSA, London; on loan to the Victoria and Albert Museum from 21 October 1930 (no. 4594); given by Hildburgh in 1938.

Exhibited: London 1975, p. 63, no. 118.

Condition: Lead solder from previous repair at top of handle, which has been cut down; chipped around the rim. Interior: a foundry mark, and evidence of turning. Worn, pale brown patination over dark grey metal. Metal analysis: a high-tin bell-metal with small amounts of lead and zinc. The tin content may be due to segregation, or possibly application of tin leaf or other surface treatments. The spectrum for the handle indicates comparable low copper and lead content, significant tin and very high iron. It was not easy to define this area, so the causes of the unusual reading are unclear.

Hand bell with ferrule and remains of handle. Decorated on the crown with fine filigree foliate scroll with two cartouches inscribed 'A.M.' On the body, between fine double mouldings, the inscription PVLSV MEO SERVOS VOCO ([with] my ring I call the servants); two coats of arms (party per pale five cinquefoils) supported by two putti and surmounted by a winged cherub head, with two vases below the cartouche, all flanked by outward-facing leaping dogs and inward-facing leaping antelopes; this design alternated with a complicated motif of a cherub head beneath a baldacchino flanked by foliated stems and vases containing plumes on which cranes (?) are mounted, all above a yoke-like scroll; below this motif are two snails (?) and a crab (?). On the sound bow (beneath a double moulding) is overlapping, downward-facing acanthus. The bell has an iron clapper, possibly original. A foundry mark appears just above the sound bow on the interior: ᴧ. The inscription has been cut into the metal, a difficult feat in light of the high tin content, and it may therefore be of later date.

Stated on acquisition to be sixteenth-century Venetian, the bell has been variously dated to the early part and middle of the century.[1] The initials in the cartouches are presumably those of the owner, as noted by Radcliffe, who considered that the unusual decoration was generally Venetian in character.[2] A similar bell was on the New York art market in 1974 (present whereabouts unknown).[3] On that bell some of the matching elements are arranged differently, including the dogs and antelopes, which have been transposed and all face the cartouche in imitation of supporters. An unidentified coat of arms has been inscribed on the shield, but there are no textual inscriptions. Another variation, closer to the New York example, is in the Museo Nazionale del Bargello, Florence.[4] On both these examples the winged cherub head appears to have a halo.

Animal motifs were very popular with bell-makers in both Italy and northern Europe (notably The Netherlands and Flanders),[5] but those on the present bell are smaller and more delicately modelled than the more common examples. The cartouche with putti and cherub heads is seen elsewhere,[6] but the overall decoration does not appear to relate to any of the other identifiable groups of bells, and the distinctive shape is also rarer. Not surprisingly, the inscription also appears on bells with a different decorative style.[7] It confirms that this was a household bell, used for summoning servants.

Radiography shows an impenetrable mass behind the coats of arms (pl. 41b), possibly the presence of solder, which would indicate that they were separately cast and applied. The bell was not therefore commissioned, but would have been a stock item with a blank shield, ready to be personalized. The arms have not yet been identified, but may provide some clues as to the origin of the bell in the future.

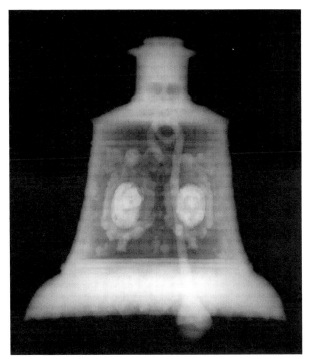

(b) X-ray of cat. no. 41.

Notes

1. Departmental records for the early dating; Radcliffe in London 1975 for the later.
2. In London 1975, loc. cit.
3. 'With Fioratti', according to a note in the departmental records. Nereo Fioratti was a collector and dealer, who operated in New York (L'Antiquaire Inc.), but was also based in Fiesole (information courtesy of Anthony Radcliffe).
4. Inv. no. 764 (Girard Gift, 1920); h. 14, 7.3 (without tassel); diam. 8.6. Very fine cast, but damaged; chipped badly around the rim and cracked; clapper missing.
5. For Flemish bells, see, for example, Lise 1978.
6. For example, Bargello, Florence, inv. no. 775 (Girard Gift, 1920); h. 16.5, 8.3 (without handle); diam. 9.6. This bell combines a variety of elements seen elsewhere: shape cf. cat. no. 52; leaf decoration cf. cat. no. 61; cartouche motif and 'heart' decoration cf. cat. no. 33. Another similar bell was at Sotheby's in Florence on 8 April 1974, lot 113, h. 12.5: it also bore a type of winged cherub head above a cartouche of different form, with a coat of arms (a castle) flanked by the initials F. and T. (possibly identifiable with the Tiepolo family, Venice, although the castle takes a different form from that shown in Coronelli 1694, p. 442). It was otherwise decorated with swags, rosettes and hanging trophies and arms, with acanthus decorating (but not covering) the sound bow; the crown was more rounded.
7. London 1975, loc. cit., and cat. no. 40.

(a)

42. Mortar with circular rope handle

North Italian; probably 1520–70
Copper and lead
h. 10.8; diam. 13.4 (rim), 8.5 (base); w. 14;
wt 2839.1 g.
Circ.383-1923

Provenance: Collection of Mrs Ellen Hearn,
Menton, France; given by Mrs Hearn in 1923
as part of the first instalment of the Alfred
Williams Hearn Gift in memory of her
late husband.

Condition: Some pitting on the surface,
with a few extrusions; traces of brown deposit
in the interstices of the decoration; a line incised
in the wax around the foot prior to casting,
and a suggestion of turning on the bowl.
Interior: green deposit.
Base: pitted, evidence of shrinkage where the pouring
sprue was attached.
Coppery patina.
Metal analysis: an unusual mix (not alloy) of largely copper and lead, with iron content. The iron reading may
indicate surface contamination.

A vase-shaped mortar with one handle in the form of a
rope, and a shallow recess inside the rim. Decorated
around the rim with a raised fillet and overlapping acanthus. On the body, between plain mouldings, anthemion
and palmette. Below, a gadrooned bowl and plain foot.

The acanthus appears to have been applied, somewhat
haphazardly, in three strips, and the decoration around the
body in four panels. The gadroons are unevenly arranged.
The quality of the casting is poor, but there is some evidence of use and therefore no real reason to doubt the
authenticity of the mortar. The metal is not technically an
alloy, but an unusual mixture of copper and lead. The
higher proportion of lead at the rim indicates that the
mortar was cast inverted in the normal way (as is evident
from the base), with more of the lead (which is heavier
than copper) having sunk to the lower portion of the
mould.

The mortar was acquired as Italian, sixteenth-century. It is
a common type of mortar in both shape and decorative
style and falls into Middeldorf's 'classical Renaissance'
category, usually given to Padua or Venice in the first half
of the sixteenth century.[1] The form relates to that of a
mortar signed by Pietro Partilori, who is listed by Wittop
Koning as having signed mortars dated 1520 and 1524.[2]
However, the Partilore were founders active from the late
eighteenth century in Verona, with a Pietro Partilora
(d. 1822) signing bells in the first part of the following
century.[3] In any event, this type of mortar was produced
from the early sixteenth century onwards.

Notes
1. See Middeldorf 1981, pp. 126–7, no. 34. The related variants
   are too numerous to list; see also cat. nos 43, 44 and 63.
2. See Wittop Koning 1975, pp. 32–3, for the mortar carrying
   a legend with the signature PIETRO PARTILORI FECE, also
   indicating that it was made for the apothecary G. A. ARDUINI;
   ibid., p. 30 for a note of dated mortars by Partilori.
3. Verona 1979, pp. 92, 94, p. 131, for bells signed by Pietro
   Partilora between 1802 and 1821. It is possible that a different
   founder with a similar name was active in the sixteenth century, but the source of Wittop Konig's notation (see n. 2
   above) is unknown.

43. Mortar with Malatesta arms

North Italian; 1550–1600
Bell-metal
h. 9.5; diam. 11.7 (rim), 7.9 (base); w. 12.8; wt 2162 g.
M.2682-1931

Provenance: Collection of Mrs Ellen Hearn, Menton, France, from September 1907; given by Mrs Hearn in 1931 as part of the second instalment of the Alfred Williams Hearn Gift in memory of her late husband.[1]

Condition: Some pitting and small extrusions of metal; evidence of turning; traces of brown deposit in interstices of decoration, with some green spots.
Interior: smooth with minor pitting, including a small round pit at the centre; green deposit.
Base: pitted, with remains of two sets of incised, parallel concentric circles.
Traces of black patination, notably inside, worn to reveal dark bronze surface.
Metal analysis: bell-metal, with tin content at the lower end of the range, on the base and rim; some lead. The reading for the body also indicates zinc and much higher tin levels, together with iron.

A vase-shaped mortar with two scroll handles and moulded rim. On each side of the body, a medallion containing a coat of arms (per pale quarterly three torteaux in the first and fourth bendy in the second and third bendy) with the legend IACOMO MALATESTA and cornucopiae supporting birds, with foliate scrolls terminating in a flower, flanked by acanthus leaves, with an astragal below. Gadrooned bowl and moulded foot.

On acquisition the mortar was described as eighteenth-century,[2] although its form relates to mortars usually associated with the sixteenth century (see, for example, cat. no. 42). Another example of similar form and handles, but with an additional flared rim, is in the Museo Correr, Venice.[3] The poorly cast legend presumably refers to the *condottiere* Giacomo Malatesta (1530–1600), a member of a branch of the family that had ruled Rimini during the fifteenth and early part of the sixteenth century.[4] The coat of arms appears to be a variation of the Malatesta arms, surmounted by a helm.

Notes

1. Museum records; noted in a copy of Mrs Hearn's notebook, p. 18, as 'Bronze mortar, Malatesta arms', bought for or valued at FF312.50.
2. Museum records.
3. Inv. no. 132; h. *c*.9.9, diam. 7.5 (base).
4. See Litta, X, part 1, 1874, pl. XXI, for details of his long and illustrious career in which he served the Colonna of Rome, the Dukes of Urbino and the Venetian Republic.

44. Mortar with swags and shields

North Italian; sixteenth or early seventeenth century
Leaded bronze
h. 13; diam. 15.2 (rim), 9.9 (base); w. 16; wt 4060.2 g.
M.27-1938

Provenance: Collection of Dr W. L. Hildburgh, FSA, London; from 1911(?); on loan to the Victoria and Albert Museum from 14 August 1934 (no. 4844); given by Hildburgh in 1938.

Condition: Various casting flaws, including those on the rim and base moulding; worn.
Interior: scratched, with deposit.
Base: smooth, with a few pits. Mottled appearance.
Bronze colour; traces of black patination on both exterior and interior.
Metal analysis: a leaded bronze of consistent alloy, with a higher reading of iron on the base, possibly due to local contamination.

A vase-shaped mortar with two plain scroll handles, separately cast and soldered on. On the flared rim, an astragal, below which is a row of overlapping veined leaf. Each side of the body decorated with a garland with fluttering ribbons flanked by blank cartouches. Trilobed gadrooning on the bowl, set at an angle. Concave foot with projecting, moulded base.

This is a common type of mortar, identified on acquisition as Italian, sixteenth-century, with the notation 'from Innsbruck 1911', presumably indicating when and where it was purchased by Hildburgh. It is closely related to an example categorized as 'classical Renaissance' by Middeldorf.[1] The decoration is unusually laid out with the isolated garland at the centre and marginalized blank cartouches. It bears some relation to a mortar in the Musée des Arts Décoratifs in Paris, which is similar in style and has an equally unusual arrangement of motifs.[2]

The leaf decoration appears to have been unevenly applied in seven strips. It is worn and the detail is difficult to distinguish. Variations of this leaf type appear on a number of functional bronzes, including a group attributed to Gaspare di Girolamo Macri of Brescia (see cat. nos

53–4), and others, less closely related, such as cat. no. 36 (dated to around 1535), which this mortar resembles in form.[3] Large mortars cast by Barborini of Parma are also similar in shape, although the foot moulding differs. Two examples are signed by Vincenzo Barborini and dated 1600 and 1636.[4] Based on its profile and evidence of wear, the present mortar is likely to be sixteenth- or possibly early seventeenth-century in origin, and produced in a north Italian centre.

Notes
1. Middeldorf 1981, pp. 126–7, no. 34.
2. Inv. no. 39250; h. 9.6, diam. 12 (rim), *c*.6.5 (base). See also Metman and Vaudoyer 1910, pl. IX, nos 103 (inv. no. Pe389) and 111 (inv. no. 6243) for mortars of the same basic form.
3. Compare also cat. nos 42 and 43.
4. See Launert 1990, pp. 71 and 206, fig. 231, for the mortar dated 1600 (then Kunsthaus Lempertz, Cologne); inscribed LUIGI GAMBARO FEGE [*sic*] FONDERE DA BARBORINI VINCENZO NEL ANNO MDC (as Venetian). See Radcliffe 1992, pp. 244–7, no. 44, for that dated 1636; at p. 246, n. 3, he questions Wittop Koning's citation (1975, p. 30) of a mortar signed by Vincenzo Barbarini (*sic*) and dated 1600, in view of the date span between the two examples. However, while Radcliffe demonstrated that the mortar is not Venetian (Barborini came from Parma but may have been active elsewhere), Launert's description, cited above, would appear to

confirm that a Vincenzo Barborini was active in 1600. It seems likely that it is the same mortar as cited by Wittop Koning, rather than another bearing the same date. The inscription 'F . F . BARBORINI . F . MDC' on a mortar cited by Radcliffe (loc. cit.) (Musée des Arts Décoratifs, Paris) could perhaps stand for 'Fonderia Fratelli Barborini Fece 1600' or 'Fonderia Famiglia Barborini…' rather than the initials of an individual member of the family. A mortar in the collection of Georg Laue, Munich, inscribed A . M . ET . A . V . F . GIO . STEFANO . PIAZA . 1698, can perhaps be attributed to the Barborini (Peter Dreyer, Julia Lachenmann and Georg Laue, *Wunder kann man sammeln*, Munich, 1999, p. 81, recognized the relationship with Barborini but identified Piaza as the founder. The legend suggests the mortar was a gift to Piaza. I am grateful to Norbert Jopek for this reference and for discussing the inscription). Another mortar formerly in the collection of Raoul Tolentino of Rome bore the legend in two panels GUARESCHI ANTONIUS FECIT FACER and DOMINICUS BARBORINI PARM . FECIT AN . 1729 (Tolentino 1925, lot 240). This demonstrates that the Barborini foundry continued to operate at least until the early eighteenth century.

45. Mortar with horse-head handles

North Italian, sixteenth century (probably 1550–1600)

Leaded bronze

h. 14.5; diam.15 (rim), 10.4 (base); w. 18.9; wt 4929.7 g.

343-1889

Provenance: Bought from Michelangelo Guggenheim, Venice, in 1889 (with 335 to 354-1889, £300).

Condition: Waxy cast. Masks worn; chipping around top and base (possible casting flaws); some surface cracking. One handle apparently failed in the casting and the head only was replaced (hollow-cast and loose-fitting; see below). Interior: reddish deposit around the bowl and indentation at the centre. Minor scratches and pits.

Base: apparent radial crack and casting flaws. Evidence of shrinkage where the pouring sprue was attached. Golden patina.

Metal analysis: leaded bronze. The repair to the handle of different composition with a higher tin and zinc content. The iron reading probably indicates surface contamination or treatment.

A bell-shaped mortar with two cast-in projecting handles in the form of horse heads terminating in foliage. Decorated around the rim with guilloche with, below, acanthus overlapping water leaf (?) on a cyma recta moulding. On the body, fleshy foliage scrolls springing from a single leaf, alternating with female masks with rosettes above. A gadrooned bowl and plain moulded foot.

The mortar was designated as 'Italian, 16th century' when it was bought from Michelangelo Guggenheim, and this broad attribution was retained by Launert.[1] It appears to have been cast in one piece. The repair to the damaged handle may have been carried out in Guggenheim's workshop.[2] The foliage bears some resemblance to cat. no. 30 and the related mortars, but here it is more fleshy. The form is also distinct, being closer to a vase, with a defined foot. Mortars with handles in the form of horse heads survive, for example, in the Museo Civico, Padua,[3] and the Boijmans Van Beuningen Museum, Rotterdam,[4] but these are otherwise unrelated.

The lack of comparative pieces makes it impossible to clarify the mortar's place of origin. The Venetian provenance and the style of the decoration suggest that it was made in north Italy.

Notes

1. Inventory and Launert, locc. citt.
2. See p. 16.
3. Banzato and Pellegrini 1989, pp. 118–19, no. 110.
4. Inv. no. L.36, h. 19.5, diam. 19.7, signed by Bartolommeo Pesenti of Verona; see Avery 1981 (1979), pp. 77–8, fig. 13; see cat. no. 48, n. 6, for further references to Pesenti.

Bibliography

Inventory 1890, p. 36; Launert 1990, pp. 70 and 207, no. 233.

46. Hand bell with Malabia arms

Attributed to Alessandro Bonaventurini
(c.1515–after 1570)
North Italian (Verona); dated 1561
Bell-metal
h. 11.9, 9.4 (without handle); diam. 10.2; wt 605.4 g.
586-1865

Provenance: Collection of Jules Soulages, Toulouse, until 1856; acquired in 1865 for £3.

Condition: Extremely crisp cast. Remaining handle knop apparently broken and soldered; remains of the handle missing. The decoration below the handle worn and distorted; smeared appearance around the edge of the crown. Large crack (repaired) adjacent to Malabia arms, and chipped around the mouth. Clapper rusted.
Interior: repair at the centre of the waist; evidence of turning (sharp) and wear on the sound bow from ringing. Greenish-grey patina.

Metal analysis: bell-metal with some zinc and lead; body and handle knop consistent. Iron reading probably due to surface treatment or contamination. Iron clapper.

Decorated around the crown with square billet with anthemion and palmette below. On the neck is the legend: IO IACOBVS MALHABIA MDLXI (Giovanni Jacobo Malabia, 1561) and a single vine leaf, bordered with two moulding wires. On the waist, two bands of ornament divided by two moulding wires: (i) foliate ornament *alla grottesca*, (ii) three different coats of arms supported by winged sea monsters. Two moulding wires separate the sound bow, which is decorated with downward-facing acanthus and foliage. The ferrule is surmounted by the moulded knop of a broken handle.

The consistency of the alloy analysis for the body and remaining knop of the bell suggests that it was probably the original, which was broken and repaired. A narrow band of decoration was possibly obliterated from around the edge of the crown. The lettering was applied in individual panels for each letter, with the exception of the IO, IA, MA and IA, which appear to share a panel. The arms were apparently made in a similar manner to cat. no. 49, with the standard shield being overlaid with the relevant arms in the wax before casting.[1]

The bell was described simply as Italian by both Robinson and Fortnum.[2] However, the coats of arms have recently been identified as those of Veronese families, including the Sarego (gules three swords or in bend bendwise sinister)[3] (pl. 46a), with a helm surmounted by a hawk or eagle displayed. Another is probably the Brenzoni (bendy or

and gules on a chief gules a lion passant-gardant argent)[4] with the initials M and B (pl. 46b). The third (argent in pale a fleur-de-lis and wagon or a base vert) belongs to the Malabia,[5] and the initials ZI (for Zuan Jacobo) and M flanking the shield are those of the Giovanni Jacobo Malabia noted in the legend (pl. 46). Robinson suggested that this inscription probably referred to the maker, in view of the custom of bell-founders to sign their work.[6] However, extensive research on Veronese founders confirms that there was no bell-maker by that name.[7] Taken with the appearance of his coat of arms being cast-in, this indicates that Malabia commissioned the bell. He can most likely be identified with the Giovanni Jacobo Malabia who, according to his will of 1593, was procurator of the convent of the Maddalene (or S. Maria delle Vergini) at Campo Marzio in Verona.[8]

The present bell is dated 1561, when Malabia would have been about forty-one years old. It belongs to a large group (see also cat. nos 47–8) that have been variously catalogued, sometimes as Venetian, but whose decoration and shape are similar to bells produced in Verona. Their form gives the appearance of miniature church bells with the 'moulding wires' and, in this case, a legend around the neck or mully groove (see fig. 3).

At that time, the most important Veronese bell-founder was Alessandro Bonaventurini, whose last known bell was dated 1562.[9] The de Levis family (see cat. nos 49–51) arrived in the city in the 1560s, their earliest known work being the church bell in the Santuario di Santa Maria della Pace, signed by Santo de Levis and dated 1567. The palmette design can also be seen on the Museum's Gagiona bell by Giuseppe de Levis, dated 1582 (?) (cat. no. 49), and elements of the decoration continued to be used over a long period of time by successive workshops. However, the combination of motifs and the date of facture leave little doubt that the bell was made by Alessandro Bonaventurini.

The attribution is supported by the connection with Giovanni Malabia, who lived near to the Bonaventurini. Malabia's son, Don Carlo, was the abbot of the monastery of Santa Maria in Organi, which was, at the time, run by the Benedictine monks of Monteoliveto. It was one of the richest abbeys in the territory and paid particular attention to artistic matters. This resulted in the abbey making purchases from the Bonaventurini foundry, both for itself and its dependants, throughout the sixteenth century.

(a)

(b)

It has been suggested that the bell may have been commissioned for Santa Maria in Organo by the abbot's father.[10] The personalized legend on the hand bell, however, suggests that it was more likely to have been made for Giovanni Malabia himself. Unlike the Sarego and Brenzoni, the Malabia were not patricians, but in the context of Verona at the time this is not particularly significant. The inclusion of the Sarego and Brenzoni arms possibly reflects a desire to be associated with two of the most powerful patrician families, but the inclusion of initials around the Brenzoni arms indicates that a specific relationship is more likely. It has not yet been possible, however, to establish a connection between Malabia and the two families.[11]

Very similar decoration can be seen on bells formerly with Bardini and in the Maurice Kann Collection.[12] Apart from the inscriptions, these differ only in the appearance of griffin supporters in place of the sea monsters, separated by distinctive sprouting foliage that also surmounts the oval cartouches. The same creatures appear on another hand bell in the Museum für Kunst und Gewerbe, Hamburg, bearing the Bonaventurini foundry mark.[13] Here the mark and initials B. B. are prominently displayed in place of a coat of arms, referring to Don Bonaventura Bonaventurini (c.1490–after 1555). The same mark appears on a large bell from Sommacampagna by Bonaventura dated 1539, and is similar in form to Alessandro Bonaventurini's personal mark, which varies primarily in the initials.[14] Another of these ragged staff marks can be seen (without flanking initials) set into a wreath on a mortar in the Fitzwilliam Museum, Cambridge, which bears a band of fine vine tendril, but with leaping dogs and dragons around the body.[15] This mortar can, therefore, also be attributed to the Bonaventurini foundry.

Notes

1. The X-ray is not entirely conclusive, but as the inscription was cast-in it is likely that the arms were also.
2. Robinson and Fortnum, locc. citt.
3. See Motture, loc. cit., for earlier discussion; for the Sarego arms, see Manara 1842, pp. 25–30; Crollalanza 1965, II, p. 492. Tentatively identified as Manelli of Florence by Fortnum, loc. cit.
4. Crollalanza 1965, I, p. 472; Morando di Custoza 1976, no. 508, pl. LVIII.
5. Morando di Custoza 1976, no. 1505, pl. CLXVIII.
6. Robinson, loc. cit.

7. See Verona 1979.
8. Archivio di Stato di Verona, *Anagrafi del Comune*, reg. 816 (anno 1593), contrada di S. Nazaro. I am grateful to Dott. Enrico Maria Guzzo of the Museo Canonicale for assisting me in the use of the archive and for translating part of the will.
9. For the Bonaventurini, see Verona 1979, pp. 9–10, 55–67, 129–30, and Padua 1986, pp. 391–9.
10. Luciano Rognini made this proposal in a letter to the author. I am grateful to him for his assistance in considering the context of the bell and for furnishing the background details outlined above. He agrees with the attribution to Bonaventurini, hinted at but not confirmed in Motture 1997. See Verona 1979, pp. 56–7, for Bonaventurini and S. Maria in Organo.
11. The possibility that the bell was made in connection with Malabia's role as procurator of S. Maddalene was put to Dott. Rognini, who advised that there is no evidence that the Brenzoni and Sarego had any connection with the church. Dott. Rognini favoured the connection with the Abbey of S. Maria in Organo, based on the arguments outlined above and as the families may have been patrons of the abbey.
12. Christie's (Bardini) 1899, lot 415 (no. 21, pl. 1) and Petit (Kann) 1910, lot 353.
13. Inv. no. 1873-321; h. 14.5. The condition is apparently similar to the present bell, with the presence of a crack and solder at the handle. This bell compares closely to another formerly with Bardini (Christie's (Bardini) 1902, lot 72, no. 13, pl. 2, as 'School of Riccio, early 16th century'), which is virtually identical to the bell signed by Bartolommeo Pesenti of Verona and dated 1676 (see Avery 1981 (1979), p. 77, fig. 12), and to one in the National Gallery of Art, Washington (Kress Collection) (Pope-Hennessy 1965, p. 147, no. 538, fig. 535; Washington 1994, p. 118), which also contains other motifs apparent on the Bonaventurini and de Levis bells. This clearly demonstrates the reuse of motifs by the different Veronese foundries over a long period.
14. Charles Avery recognized this relationship in 1997, and I am grateful to him for allowing me to publish his findings. The Hamburg bell was unavailable during my visit in 1996, but was noted from a photograph as relating to the present Veronese example. See Verona 1979, fig. 13, for Alessandro's mark; Sommacampagna 1989, pp. 6–7, for the Bonaventura bell (illus.).
15. Inv. no. M.14-1952, h. 12.4, diam. 15.5 (rim), 9.3 (base); given by E. Saville Peck. The decoration of this mortar provides additional links with other groups.

Bibliography
Robinson 1856, p. 118, no. 372; Ellacombe 1872, pp. 311–12 (illus.); Fortnum 1876, p. 77; Motture 1997, p. 101, fig. 6.4.

47. Hand bell with the arms of Pietro Moscaglia

Attributed to the Bonaventurini foundry
North Italian (Verona); 1540–70
Brass
h. 12.6, 9.8 (without peg argent); diam. 10.8; wt 788.7 g.
M.686-1910

Provenance: Capel Cure Collection, London, until 1905 (Christie's 1905, lot 169); collection of George Salting, London; bequeathed by Salting in 1910 (Salting Bequest, no. 2937).

Condition: Some damage to the upper decoration where the ferrule has been let in and soldered. Hairline cracks running inside and chipping around the mouth. Some green deposit in the interstices. Off-centre hole in peg argent.
Interior: iron clapper shank with ball attached, held in place by some form of composition, possibly dirty lead; evidence of turning; some green corrosion.
Coppery brown patina.
Metal analysis: body apparently a low-zinc brass with lead content. The peg argent is a quaternary alloy bronze. The iron content reflects either surface treatment or contamination. Analysis of the clapper ball indicates copper with high iron, lead and tin, indicating either a bronze ball with iron contamination or an iron ball with solder.

Decorated around the crown with shells and foliage. On the neck, ivy or vine (?) leaves, bordered with parallel moulding wires. On the waist, two bands of ornament, divided by a moulding wire: (i) bucrania with *vittae* hung with festoons supporting displayed birds; (ii) three identical coats of arms, surmounted by a helm, with the legend PETRVS MOSCALEA, supported by winged sea monsters. Around the sound bow, acanthus and foliage. Pierced replacement peg argent.

Although the metal has the appearance of bronze or bell-metal, the analysis indicates that it is a brass. This is surprising in view of the analysis of the comparative pieces, which are all bell-metal. However, as no specific tone was required for this type of bell, brass could have been used, as it is for modern handle bells. The vine leaf was applied in one strip and the frieze of bucrania in five, the pattern consisting of one bucranium and swag.

Catalogued as 'Florentine, 16th century' in the Capel Cure sale,[1] the bell was registered as 'Italian, early 16th century' on acquisition. It must have been made for a Pietro Moscaglia, whose name appears in the latinized form around his coat of arms (azure a chevron company counter-company of three rows argent and gules between three flies or).[2] The Moscaglia were an old illustrious family in Vicenza and Verona, who obtained entry to the *Nobile Consiglio* in 1546. There is no Pietro among those listed as members of the Council.[3] The context for which the bell was made is unknown, but the appearance of personal arms perhaps suggests that it was used by the owner for calling servants. The form of replacement handle could either take a tassel or would allow the bell to be suspended, suggesting that it may have been adapted for use in a different context at a later date. This adaptation has been achieved rather haphazardly, evidenced by the damage to the decoration of the bell and the off-centre placement of the piercing on the peg argent.

This bell, together with two others in the collection (cat. nos 46 and 48), belongs to a group related in shape and decoration to those produced in Verona by the Bonaventurini foundry. It is identical in pattern to cat. no. 48 but with a truncated body, as there is only a single moulding wire separating the second and third tiers of decoration. Virtually identical bells are in the Museo Correr, Venice, and formerly in the Figdor Collection.[4] All were probably made in the 1560s or the preceding decades, in light of the date of 1561 inscribed on cat. no. 46, although a later date is also possible due to the continuing use of the motifs.

Notes

1. Bought for £78 15s. (£78.75) by Fisk (?); unclear entry in annotated sale catalogue.
2. Crollalanza 1965, 2, p. 184; Morando di Custoza 1976, no. 1775, pl. CXCVIII; blazon translated by John Meriton. The coat of arms on the bell is slightly different, and radiography indicates that they were cast-in.
3. Cartolari 1854, part I, p. 181 (under Moscalea); part II, p. 70 (under Moscaglia). The will of Giovanni (?) Francesco, [son of?] Pietro Moscaglia (Nob. Jo^s. Francⁱ. [fglⁱ (?): illegible] Petri de Moscaleis) survives in the Verona Archive: Archivio di Stato di Verona, *Anagrafi del Comune*, 2 March 1556, (*atti Burann?*) Mo 148, Ao 99, p. 201.
4. See cat. no. 48 for details.

Bibliography

Motture 1997, p. 102, fig. 6.5.

48. Hand bell

Attributed to the Bonaventurini foundry
North Italian (Verona); 1540–70
Bell-metal
h. 18.3, 10.2 (without handle); diam. 11.3; wt 783.7 g.
470-1899

Provenance: Stefano Bardini, Florence; bought for £37 (Christie's (Bardini) 1899, lot 110; fig. 1, no. 19).[1]

Condition: Square section let into top of bell with replacement handle attached with modern screw extension and washer. Dented on the upper moulding wire and chipped around the mouth.
Interior: clapper missing; interior cracks and evidence of turning.
Variable patina from dark brown to greenish-grey.

Metal analysis: bell-metal with a small amount of zinc and lead. Copper handle.

Decorated around the crown with shells and foliage. On the neck, ivy or vine (?) stems and leaves bordered with two moulding wires. On the waist, two bands of ornament divided by two moulding wires: (i) bucrania with *vittae* hung with festoons supporting displayed birds; (ii) three (blank) shields (see below) supported by winged sea monsters. A single moulding wire separates the sound bow, which is decorated with downward-facing acanthus and foliage. Turned (replacement) handle.

The vine leaf was applied in one strip and the frieze of bucrania in five, the pattern consisting of one bucranium and swag; the primary decoration consists of three panels, one for each complete pattern.

At the time of the Bardini sale the bell was described as Florentine, but variously dated to the early eighteenth century in the English catalogue and to the end of the fifteenth century in the French.[2] It was entered in the Museum inventory, however, as 'Italian 16th century'.[3] The bell has since been identified as forming part of a group of bells related in shape and decoration to those produced by the Bonaventurini foundry in Verona, one of which is dated 1561 and inscribed with the name of the owner, Giovanni Jacobo Malabia (cat. no. 46).[4] Elements of the decoration continued to be used over a long period of time and can also be seen, for example, on bells by the de Levis and by Bartolommeo Pesenti in the Museo Nazionale del Bargello, Florence,[5] and the Louvre (dated 1676).[6] Only the ubiquitous acanthus on the Louvre bell (there poorly cast) is specifically related to the current example. Dating such bells securely is therefore difficult, but in this instance it seems most likely that the bell was produced around the middle of the sixteenth century in view of its close similarity to the dated Malabia bell.

The present bell is closely related to cat. no. 47, but is slightly larger in scale because of the additional moulding wires that separate the two tiers of decoration on the waist. The decoration is less distinctly cast; the joins where the wax strips were applied are not so clearly evident. The shields are blank, but appear unevenly cast, giving the impression of an indistinct image of a coat of arms, in a similar manner to those on a virtually identical bell in the Museo Correr, Venice, and another formerly in the Figdor Collection, Vienna.[7] These bells were doubtless produced in some numbers, either for general sale or to order. In each case the purchasers were able to attach their personal arms subsequent to casting. It is possible that the uneven surface is due to some form of preparation for attachment. An example survives in the Bargello, Florence, where applied silver shields with unidentified arms (a bend three trees) have been attached.[8]

Notes

1. With Durlacher apparently acting as agent; he is noted as the purchaser in the annotated sale catalogue.
2. For the French version, see *Catalogue des Objets d'Art Antiques, du Moyen Age et de la Renaissance provenant de la Collection Bardini de Florence dont la vente aura lieu à Londres chez Mr Christie... Le 5 Juin 1899...*, p. 7, no. 19: 'Clochette. Travail florentin, fin XVème siècle'.
3. Inventory, loc. cit.

4. For a discussion of interrelationships, see Motture 1997.
5. Inv. no. 754 (Girard Gift, 1920), h. 16.8 (9.2 without tassel), diam. 9.9. See Avery 1981 (1972), pp. 51–2, figs 16–17.
6. Inv. no. R.56 (Rothschild Collection), h. 8.8 (without replacement handle), diam. 9.6 (dimensions from Avery, loc. cit. below). See Avery 1981 (1977), pp. 77–8, fig. 12. See also Verona 1979, pp. 10–11 and 76–8 for Pesenti (or Pisenti; also called de Pesenti).
7. Correr, inv. no. 1312 (Richetti Gift), h. 13.5, with modern T-shaped handle (10.2 without handle), diam. 10.6. See Mariacher 1971, p. 31, cat. no. 90. The faint outline on one of the shields appears to represent a standing figure with a staff, but is probably just the uneven surface, as suggested. For the Figdor bell, see Planiscig (Figdor) 1930, no. 375, fig. CXLVI, as Venetian, from the workshop of Pietro Lombardo, *c.*1500. Both have the truncated bodies similar to cat. no. 47.
8. Inv. no. 753 (Girard Gift, 1920), h. 13.8 (8 without replacement handle), diam. 13.8. I am grateful to Jeremy Warren for drawing this to my attention.

Bibliography

Inventory 1903 (objects acquired in 1899), p. 77; Motture 1997, pp. 102–3.

49. Hand bell with the arms of the Gagiona family of Verona

By Giuseppe de Levis (1552–1611/14)
North Italian (Verona); initialled and dated 1582 (?)
Bell-metal
h. 9.5, 8.8 (without handle); diam. 10.3; wt 545.2 g.
A.16-1973

Provenance: Bought from Dr Anselm Lange, Hannover, in 1973 for £1,294.22.

Exhibited: New York 1989, no. 170.

Condition: Hole in knop, handle missing. Chipped and damaged on the upper rings of decoration and some areas masked by a compound; areas of wear. Large interconnected cracks to right of foundry mark.
Interior: evidence of turning; clapper missing.
Dark grey-brown patination, worn.
Metal analysis: bell-metal, with some zinc and lead content. The knop secured with a lead-tin solder.

Decorated around the crown with anthemion and palmette. On the waist, two bands of ornament bordered by two moulding wires: (i) displayed harpies separated by stylized foliage; (ii) three roundels containing coats of arms within a cartouche, each supported by two male figures and alternated with foliate decoration flanked by downward-facing dolphins intertwined with tridents. Around the rim, 'S' scrolls and fleurs-de-lis. Inside is a foundry mark with the initials I.D.L. (pl. 49a), for Giuseppe de Levis, together with a date in Arabic numerals, partially obliterated (pl. 49b). Pierced knop.

The foundry mark replaces the usual full signature of Giuseppe de Levis, a member of the dynasty of bell-founders active in Verona from the mid-sixteenth to the mid-seventeenth centuries.[1] The coat of arms, which is clearly cast-in, is that of the Gagiona family of Verona (azure, in pale an eight-pointed

(a) Foundry mark inside bell.

star or and a pineapple or stalked vert).[2] A standard design was adjusted in the wax prior to casting, as a shadow of the basic 'Tuscan' shield shape can be seen beneath the roundel containing the arms. Another bell, apparently of lower quality but with identical decoration and bearing the same *stemma*, is in the Virginia Museum of Fine Arts.

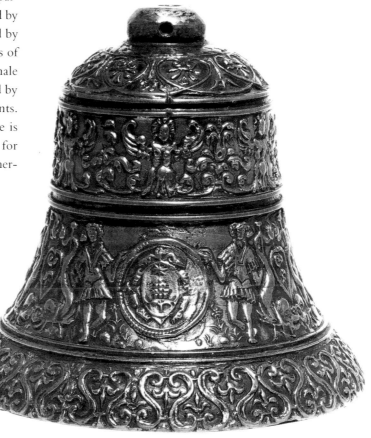

(b) Arabic numerals (1582?) inside bell.

However, a different trademark appears inside the Virginia bell, 'LCFV' – which Avery suggests probably stands for 'Levis Compagnia Fecit Veronae' – together with the date 1587.[3] It is not possible to distinguish with certainty the last two numbers of the date inside the present bell. It was given as '1590?' by Avery,[4] but is possibly 1582, which, if correct, would make this the earliest extant dated bell made by Giuseppe (see cat. no. 50).

Many of the motifs displayed on this bell are typical of the de Levis workshop, and some were used by various Veronese bell-makers over a long period of time.[5]

Notes

1. For details of the de Levis foundry, see Avery 1981, pp. 45–78; Verona 1979; Avery 1992; Motture 1997, pp. 101–3.
2. Previously identified by Ulrich Middledorf. See Crollalanza 1965, III, p. 62; translation of the blazon courtesy of John Meriton. Radiography confirmed that the arms were added in the wax.
3. Avery 1992, pp. 47–8, figs 18–20; inv. no. 37-11-24, h. 16.3, diam. 10.1. The Virginia bell has not been examined by the author.
4. Avery 1981 (1972), loc. cit.
5. Numerous bells survive from the de Levis workshop. See also cat. nos 46–8 for bells from the Bonaventurini foundry; cat. no. 46, n. 9, for further references. The successors to the de Levis were the Pesenti; for all these foundries see references at n. 1 above.

Bibliography

Pforzheim Reuchlinhaus and Hanau 1969, p. 19; Avery 1981 (1972), p. 50, figs 11, 12; Lange 1981, pp. 102–3; Avery 1992, p. 47; Motture 1997, pp. 101, 103, fig. 6.3.

50. Hand bell with sun motif

By Giuseppe de Levis (1552–1611/14)
Italian (Verona); signed and dated 1583
Bell-metal
h. 15.5, 8.5 (without handle); diam. 10.4; wt 687.4 g.
A.7-1987

Provenance: Given by Daniel Katz, London, in 1987 in memory of his father Peter Katz.[1]

Exhibited: New York 1989, no. 174.

Condition: Chipped around the mouth. The handle broken and repaired beneath the lower bead; it was possibly cast in three pieces (see pl. 50c).
Interior: evidence of turning.
Dark brown-black patination, worn to reveal dark grey-brown metal.
Metal analysis: high-tin bell-metal with low zinc and lead content, and some antimony. The handle similar, but with lead and predominantly tin at the joint. Iron clapper.

Decorated around the crown with acanthus and gadrooning. On the waist, two bands of ornament bordered with two moulding wires: (i) displayed harpies separated by stylized foliage; (ii) three shields (see below), each supported by two male figures and divided by foliate decoration flanked by downward-facing dolphins intertwined with tridents. Around the sound bow, 'S' scrolls with fleur-de-lis. Both the iron clapper and the foliate decorated handle appear to be original. Inside a raised inscription with the Arabic numerals '83' (pl. 50b).

The handle is possibly made in three separate sections, or was broken and repaired. The joins were made with an exceptionally high-tin bronze.

One of the shields bears the legend IOSEPH/DE LEV/IS VER/F, the usual signature of the Veronese founder Giuseppe de Levis.[2] The remaining shields are charged with a radiant sun within which is a human face, a motif that usually represents truth (the sun illuminating everything with its light). It is possible that the radiant sun was

(a) Detail of shield with signature.

Notes

1. The bell was bought by Katz from Robert O'Connor, a dealer of George Street, London, in the early 1980s; verbal advice from Daniel Katz.

2. See, for example, Avery 1981 (1972) p. 48, fig. 6; p. 49, fig. 9; Avery 1981 (1973) p. 57, fig. 6; p. 59, fig. 12; p. 61, fig. 16; p. 62, fig. 18; Avery 1981 (1979), p. 72, figs 3 and 6.

3. For example, the radiant sun was the *impresa* of the Marchese of Mantua, Ludovico Gonzaga (1422–81); see London 1982, no. 51. See New York 1989, no. 174, and Avery 1992, p. 47, for a discussion of the motif.

4. Amayden 1910–14, II, p. 228. I am grateful to Charles Avery for this suggestion and reference. See also Coronelli 1702 (no page numbers; contained in the chart on regions in Venice) for the arms of the Commune de Ifiria, Venice.

5. Morando di Custoza 1976, pl. IX, no. 81 (Altemani: azure, a sun or) and pl. XLVI, no. 409 (Bonenti: argent, a sun or).

Bibliography

Williamson 1991, p. 876; Avery 1992, pp. 45, 47, figs 15, 16; Motture 1997, p. 100, fig. 6.2.

the personal motif or the arms of the owner, whether this was an individual or a corporation.[3] The arms of the della Vetera family of Rome are particularly closely related (azure, a sun or, bordered gules and argent indented).[4] Also similar, and with a local connection, are the arms of the Altemani and Bonenti of Verona, both of which bear the radiant sun.[5] As with the Gagiona bell (cat. no. 49), the motif has been cast-in, the standard 'Tuscan' shield having been amended in the wax, indicating that the bell was specifically commissioned. Customizing the bell was simply a matter of adjusting a standard model, as is evident from the X-ray (pl. 50c).

(b) Arabic numerals '83' inside the bell.

The numerals on the interior are presumably an abbreviation for 1583, indicating the date of manufacture. This is therefore the earliest firmly dated bell produced by Giuseppe, although the unclear inscription inside the Gagiona bell might provide the slightly earlier date of 1582.

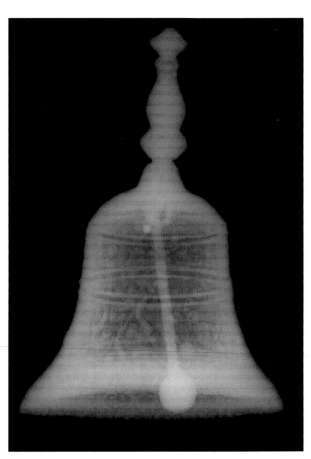

(c) X-ray of cat. no. 50.

51. Crucible

**By Paolo (1572–1635) and Francesco de Levis
(1573–1630)**
Italian (Verona); signed, *c*.1620–5
Bell-metal
h. 8.9; diam. 11.1; w. (including handle socket) 16;
wt 988.9 g.
M.26-1923

Provenance: Collection of Mrs Ellen Hearn, Menton,
France, from 1908;[1] given by Mrs Hearn in 1923 as part of
the first instalment of the Alfred Williams Hearn Gift in
memory of her late husband.

Exhibited: New York 1989, no. 182.

Condition: Wooden handle missing. Indentation and signs
of cracking in the bottom; repaired with small inset
section of bronze. Relief clogged with soft, pale red compound.
Interior: pitted and scratched.
Brassy patina with dark brown areas.
Metal analysis: consistent cast of bell-metal with zinc and
lead. The feet and handle have apparently a lower tin content and the feet higher lead.

Decorated around the rim with a band of ivy or vine-leaf
scroll; with a hollow projecting handle socket, decorated
with water leaf. Signed PAVLO/FRANC . /LEVI/VER . /F
in an oval cartouche at the front, and the initials . N . M .
appear below the handle. Supported by three feet comprising inverted 'wild man' masks, with flopping ears and
small horns.

The handle and feet were probably cast separately and
joined, as indicated by the different results of the metal
analysis.[2]

On acquisition, the crucible was initially referred to
as a 'stewpan', but entered in the Museum register as a
Veronese sixteenth-century saucepan, with handle wanting. The object was originally identified as the work of a
single member of the de Levis family of Veronese founders,
called Paolo Francesco de Levis.[3] However, Luciano
Rognini's research revealed that Paolo and Francesco
were the two sons of Giuseppe de Levis (1552–1611/14),[4]
enabling the crucible to be correctly catalogued for the
Gardens and Ghettos exhibition in New York in 1989.[5]

The crucible is an unusual piece, bearing none of the
motifs particularly associated with the de Levis foundry.
Without the inscription, therefore, it would have been
impossible to attribute with certainty. Both the shape and
the presence of a handle indicate that it was designed for

heating the contents over a flame. However, there is no evidence that the vessel was used in this way, and no other comparable example has come to light. A wooden extension would originally have been fitted to the handle socket. The repaired indentation inside suggests that the vessel was used for grinding. It is most likely originally to have been found in a scientific or pharmaceutical (rather than domestic) context and the letters NM probably refer to the owner.[6] An alchemical connection is suggested through the reversed image of the inverted wild man on the feet, and possibly also through the vine scroll.[7]

Two bells with the individual signatures of Paolo and Francesco are documented and were dated respectively 1611 and 1615 (both lost). Two other bells are known to have been signed jointly by the de Levis brothers: one for S. Anastasia, Verona (1622), now lost, and another for the church of the Madonna del Monte at Sommacampagna, near Verona (1624).[8] The crucible could, therefore, have been produced between about 1610 and 1630, but the joint signing pattern suggests that this utensil was produced in the first half of the 1620s.

Notes

1. The crucible is doubtless the 'bronze bowl on feet (Verona)' bought by Mrs Hearn from the dealer Thomas Sutton for FF450 in 1908, four years after her husband's death. Museum records: Hearn file, part II, for Mrs Hearn's notebooks p. 25; part III, RP 23/1053, for acquisition papers. See also pp. 16–17.
2. Physical examination of the object, surprisingly, does not indicate clearly that the feet were cast separately, but they were perhaps cast-on.
3. Avery 1981 (1974), loc. cit.
4. See Verona, loc. cit.

(a)

5. Avery in New York 1989, loc. cit. At this time the family was erroneously believed to be Jewish; subsequently corrected in Avery 1992, p. 52, n. 1, acknowledging Rognini's discovery that the family came from the village of Levo in the territory of Bergamo.
6. The high relief of the applied panels is matched by the prominent stops that separate and frame the letters.
7. See cat. no. 59 for discussion of the vine scroll.
8. See Verona 1979, pp. 73–4 and 130, for the four bells; Paolo was erroneously referred to as Pietro in the documentation for the S. Anastasia bell. The inscription on the Madonna del Monte bell also states that they are the sons of Giuseppe, who had died at least ten years earlier: PAVLVS ET FRANCISVS/ FILII Q. IOSEPH/DE LEVIS/VERONAE ME. FECERVT – MDCXXIIII; see Sommacompagna 1989, pp. 8–9 (and illus.) for the Madonna del Monte bell.

Bibliography

Avery 1981 (1974), p. 69, fig. 15; Verona 1979, p. 74; Avery 1992, p. 51; Motture 1997, p. 106.

52. Hand bell with displayed birds

North Italian (possibly Verona); 1560–1600
Bell-metal
h. 8; diam. 10; wt 404.1 g.
M.3-1947

Provenance: Given by Dr W. L. Hildburgh, FSA, London, in 1947 (earlier provenance unknown).

Condition: Tiny chip at the rim. On the waist, an incised line that runs around the bell but does not disturb the applied decoration. Handle missing.
Interior: smooth and shiny with turning marks. Clapper missing.
Dark brown-black patination; grey metal inside.
Metal analysis: bell-metal. The iron content is probably due to surface contamination or treatment.

Hand bell with handle missing, decorated around the crown with downward-facing acanthus, bordered by moulding wires. Around the neck, a row of bead. Around the waist, bordered by astragals or moulding wires, sprouting foliate scrolls supporting birds, between which are displayed eagles emanating from which are hanging beads. The sound bow divided into two bands of decoration: above, foliate and floral swags, below which are foliate motifs; vine decoration and a row of beads.

On acquisition the bell was identified as late sixteenth-century Italian, but with uncertain provenance.[1] A bell with identical applied decoration was in the collection of Anselm Lange, who described the eagles as those of the Borghese.[2] The handle of the Lange bell was formed by the figure of Mercury, examples of which are found on several bells sometimes attributed to the Paduan bronzist and sculptor Tiziano Aspetti (1557/9–1606) on the basis of the style of this figure. Examples of the same figure, but apparently representing David with the head of Goliath, exist in the Museo Correr, Venice, and in the Museo Civico, Padua; the bells to which they are attached bear a close relationship to each other and a resemblance in both form and decoration to the present example, although they are rather more crudely cast.[3] Two other bells in Padua are also similar; the first attributed to Padua in the second half of the sixteenth century,[4] and the second to the circle of Giambologna, late sixteenth or early seventeenth century. The attribution of the latter is also based on the style of its handle figure, which is said to relate to Giambologna's statuette of a bagpiper, although there is no direct connection.[5] The handle is perhaps a replacement.

A third example of the present model was in the Maurice Kann Collection, Paris, catalogued as Paduan, sixteenth-century.[6] The handle figure took the same form as that on a bell in the Museum für Angewandte Kunst, Cologne, consisting of a female holding her finger to her mouth, appropriate for calling meetings to order (fig. 12).[7] The Cologne bell itself, however, bears no direct relationship to this group, but was produced by the same workshop as cat. no. 53, identified as that of Gaspare di Girolamo Macri of Brescia. Again, the handle on the Cologne bell may be a replacement, as it is not stylistically related to the decoration of the bell itself. However, it fits well with the Kann Collection bell, and may therefore be original to that example. The figure style relates to that of works produced by Giuseppe de Levis in Verona, notably an allegorical figure that surmounted a hand bell convincingly attributed to him.[8]

The general form of the present bell, together with the use of moulding wires separating the bands of decoration and the clean casting, is also comparable to bells produced by the de Levis foundry, such as cat. no. 49. The bell is certainly north Italian and can possibly be associated with Verona in the second half of the sixteenth century.

(a)

Notes

1. Museum records.
2. Pforzheim Reuchlinhaus and Hanau 1969, p. 17, and Lange 1981, p. 99, as Italian, sixteenth-century.
3. Correr inv. nos 248, 436; for Padua inv. no. 263, see Banzato and Pellegrini 1989, pp. 102–3, no. 79. See above p. 64, n. 42 for details.
4. Inv. no. 264, Banzato and Pellegrini 1989, p. 105, no. 86.
5. Inv. no. 407, ibid., pp. 131–2, no. 129; see also p. 131, nos 127–8, for similar figures. See, for example, Berger and Krahn 1994, pp. 106–8, nos 65–6, for statuettes after the Giambologna model.
6. Petit (Kann) 1910, p. 56, lot 338, h. 12; present whereabouts unknown.
7. Inv. no. H457. See also p. 50 above. The Cologne bell has not been examined by the author.
8. Avery 1981 (1972), p. 51, fig. 15, from the Canessa Sale, New York 1924, lot 220.

53. Hand bell with the arms of the Rossi family (?)

Probably workshop of Gaspare di Girolamo Macri (documented 1548–9)

North Italian (Brescia); 1540–80

Bell-metal

h. 10.3, 8.3 (without peg argent); diam. 9.5; wt 5076 g.

M.28-1923

Provenance: Sangiorgi, Rome (Sangiorgi 1910, lot 68, pl. 19); collection of Mrs Ellen Hearn, Menton, France, from 1910; given by Mrs Hearn in 1923 as part of the first instalment of the Alfred Williams Hearn Gift in memory of her late husband.

Exhibited: London 1975, no. 117; Tulsa 1979, no. 52.

Condition: Fairly crisp cast; chipped around the mouth. Replacement peg argent.

Interior: scratchy surface, but evidence of turning; iron clapper removed since acquisition.

Dark brown patina.

Metal analysis: bell-metal, with some zinc and lead. The peg argent is leaded bronze, with some zinc. High iron reading on the surface of the bell may be due to surface contamination or treatment.

A hand or hanging bell with pierced peg argent and modern tassel. Decorated around the crown with overlapping rows of veined leaf. On the neck, arabesque ornament with rope borders. On the waist, festoons of cornucopiae with suspended bucrania, below which is a flowering foliage motif flanked by casts from an antique gem showing *Faustulus finding Romulus and Remus under a fig-tree*,[1] alternating with a coat of arms (a rampant lion, three bendlets sinister) overlapping a plain moulding, flanked by sprigs of flowers or thistles. Around the sound bow, another row of overlapping veined leaf.

The bell appears in the Sangiorgi catalogue without the tassel, which was therefore probably added by Mrs Hearn between 1910, when she acquired the bell, and 1923, when it was presented to the Museum.[2] It was considered at that time to be a late fifteenth-century Paduan cast, but was given to Venice and dated to about 1500 on acquisition, the arms being tentatively identified as those of the Rossi of Venice.[3]

The same distinctive, veined-leaf decoration is found on other bells, candlesticks and oil-lamps in various collections (some of which appear to be nineteenth-century casts). One such candlestick in the Museo Poldi-Pezzoli, Milan, signed 'Gaspar' and dated 1551, formed the basis of an attribution of the group by Planiscig to a founder named Gasparo, whom he assumed to be a Venetian.[4] Radcliffe had already associated the bell with Brescia by 1975,[5] and later convincingly identified Gaspare as the Brescian founder, Gaspare di Girolamo Macri, who appears in the city's records in 1548 and 1549. He supported this supposition by comparison with a bell with similar decoration, also in Milan (Castello Sforzesco), made for the Brescian Jurists and dated 1589.[6] The veined leaf, together with other decorative features, also appears on bells that can be associated with Venice.[7] The decoration sometimes consists of a single row of leaves, as on the Brescian Jurists' bell, but on other examples the tips of a second layer of leaves are visible, as on the two bells in the Museum (see also cat. no. 54) and the signed candlestick in the Museo Poldi-Pezzoli, Milan. A mortar in the Kunstgewerbemuseum, Berlin, combines the two, with a double layer around the top and a single at the bottom.[8]

The coat of arms is closely related to that on another similar bell in the Museum für Angewandte Kunst, Cologne (see fig. 12),[9] possibly representing the arms of the Rossi family of Brescia.[10] However, this blazon is common throughout Italy, and without the benefit of tincture is difficult to identify securely.[11] The arms of the Rossi, Badoer and Barozzi,[12] all of Venice, are also similar, though not identical to those on the present bell. The addition of bends sinister signifies illegitimacy or lack of

right to inherit, or it could be a sign of difference between one branch of a family and another.[13]

As has been noted, these bells have traditionally been ascribed to Venice (an important centre for bronze casting), as several examples bear Venetian arms. Bronzes from the foundries there certainly found their way to other centres within the Venetian *terraferma*. Equally, there was an active bronze industry in Brescia during the sixteenth century,[14] with Brescian bronzists also receiving commissions from Venice and other cities in its empire.[15] It is therefore quite likely that several foundries in different locations made use of the same decorative designs, with ideas being transmitted through patrons, the objects themselves and the movement of workshops or itinerant workers.[16] Lack of documentary evidence in respect of both commissions and workshop practice, however, makes it difficult to arrive at any firm conclusions regarding the grouping and relationships between many of the bells produced in northern Italy at this time.

Nevertheless, the close relationship between several of these bells makes it likely that they were produced by the same foundry. This is undoubtedly the case with the Museum's two examples and that in Cologne, which are so closely related to the Milan bronzes to suggest an attribution to Gaspare. Another one that is directly related in form to the Milan bell also bears the single-row leaf, and identical swags.[17] A hand bell in the Museo Civico, Brescia, has the same basic form as both the present example and the Cologne bell, but otherwise the decoration is different in character.[18] A further bell of similar form and sharing some of the decorative elements, including the double row of veined leaf, is in the Ashmolean Museum, Oxford.[19] The handling of the decoration is different from the Museum's example; the casting is considerably less crisp than either the signed candlestick or the bell in Milan. The decoration is neatly but unusually arranged with profile heads and plaquettes suspended from a rail.[20] The plaquettes have been identified by Warren as based on a design by the Brescian, Maffeo Olivieri (1484–1543/4).[21] While adding weight to the idea that they originated in Brescia, plaquettes of this kind were very portable, and Olivieri had connections with Venice, for example, having been given the commission for the candelabra presented to St Mark's in 1527.[22] Comparison of signed works from different periods of the Alberghetti foundry indicate that the forms and style can vary considerably over time. It is possible, therefore, that the Oxford bell was produced by the same foundry as the Brescian bronzes, but this remains open to question.[23]

Notes

1. See Walters 1926, no. 984, and Raspe-Tassie, II, 1791, no. 10508, for examples. Gem identified by Lucy Cullen.
2. Sangiorgi 1910, loc. cit. According to the transcript of Mrs Hearn's notebooks, a 'Small fine bronze bell Renaissance' was purchased by Thomas Sutton in 1910, and valued at FF1,625.
3. Museum records.
4. Planiscig 1932.
5. London 1975, loc. cit.
6. Castello Sforzesco, Milan; inv. no. 117; Radcliffe 1984, p. 761 and fig. 31.
7. See Motture, loc. cit. and cat. nos 54 and 55, for further discussion and comparisons.
8. Inv. no. 90,335, h. 12.9, diam. 16.5 (rim), 13.3 (base); see Pechstein 1968, no. 54, as Italian, end of the fifteenth century.
9. Inv. no. H457.
10. Argent, a rampant lion gules; Rietstap, V, 1921, pl. CXCIII; Crollalanza, II, 1965, p. 444.
11. The arms of the city of Brescia itself, for example (argent, a rampant lion azure). The Cologne bell is surmounted by a figure holding a finger to its lips, as though calling a meeting to order. This, combined with the rampant lion and the veined leaf, could suggest that it was made for the Brescian city council.
12. Argent, three bends or, a rampant lion gules; argent, three bendlets gules, a rampant lion or; argent, a rampant lion gules, a bend azure; Coronelli 1694, pp. 401, 8 and 40 respectively.
13. See Guelfi Camajani 1921, p. 95, for reference to illegitimacy; the alternative interpretation was proposed by John Meriton.
14. See Rossi 1977.
15. See Radcliffe 1984, p. 762, for example, and below.
16. The Venetian founder Tommaso di Conti, for example, also worked in Brescia, and Giulio Alberghetti had connections; see, for example, A. Fappani, *Enciclopedia Bresciana*, IV, Brescia, 1981, p. 225, 'Fonderie'; see also pp. 31–3.
17. Private collection, New York, in 1972, h. 9.8.
18. Inv. no. B9, h. 15, diam. 9.
19. Inv. no. 1888.CDEF.B1001, h. 11, 9.3 (without handle), diam. 9.5.
20. Another example of this arrangement is evident on a bell in the Kunsthistorisches Museum, Vienna; Planiscig 1924, p. 79, no. 143.
21. Warren (forthcoming); I am grateful to Jeremy Warren for providing me with a copy of his catalogue entry prior to publication. He attributes the Oxford bell, along with the two V&A examples, to Gaspare's workshop.
22. See n. 15.
23. Several examples of bells with potential relationships exist. Among these is one in the Hermitage, St Petersburg; see Berlin 1977, pp. 35–6, no. 19, as Venetian, end of the fifteenth/beginning of the sixteenth century. This bell has similar form and aspects of the decoration, notably the festoons and bucrania; it does not include the 'Gasparo' leaf. However, the Hermitage bell can also be compared in form to cat. no. 38; it bears similar acanthus around the sound bow (a common motif).

Bibliography

Radcliffe 1984, p. 762 and fig. 30; Motture 1997, p. 105.

(a)

54. Hand bell with the lion of St Mark and three coats of arms

**Probably workshop of Gaspare di Girolamo Macri
(documented 1548–9)**
North Italian (Brescia); 1540–80
Bell-metal
h. 18.8, 8.5 (without handle); diam. 8.8; wt 493.1 g.
715-1884

Provenance: Collection of Alessandro Castellani, Rome, until 1884 (Rome (Castellani) 1884, p. 255, no. 802); bought for £8.[1]

Condition: Crisply cast decoration, but poor condition; crack, breaks and repairs, partly with lead solder, and area of filler missing; several chips around the rim. Handle appears to be made of several components, with some solder evident.
Interior: scratchy, uneven surface, but evidence of turning. Lead solder, together with dark brown wax, is used to attach the handle; clapper missing.
Dark brown patina.
Metal analysis: high-tin bell-metal with some lead; iron reading probably due to surface contamination or treatment. Iron handle.

A hand bell with handle, decorated with acanthus knops and terminating in a fir cone.[2] Decorated around the crown with overlapping rows of veined leaf. On the neck, a band of foliate ornament with rope borders. On the waist, four swags with stars (?) above; vases of flowers are suspended from the swags with, below, casts from a Graeco-Roman gem of the Emperor Vespasian;[3] below the swags are three coats of arms (a chevron; party per pale indented; party per pale, a greyhound gorged saliant) and the lion of St Mark in a shouldered quatrefoil flanked by sprigs of flowers or thistles. The sound bow is delineated by a plain moulding and decorated with another row of overlapping veined leaf, with a plain area beneath.

The bell was identified as Italian, sixteenth-century, in the Castellani catalogue.[4] The same distinctive leaf ornament that appears around the top and bottom of the bell can be seen on a signed candlestick in the Museo Poldi-Pezzoli, Milan, which has been convincingly attributed to the workshop of the bell-founder, Gaspare di Girolamo

Macri, active in Brescia in the mid-sixteenth century.[5] The lion of St Mark (pl. 54) and the coats of arms indicate a Venetian context. Two of the *stemmi* can be identified as those of the patrician Pesaro family (party per pale indented azure and or; pl. 54a),[6] and the Zancani, a *cittadino* family (party per pale argent and gules, a greyhound

(a)

(b)

(c)

saliant argent, gorged sable, pl. 54b).[7] The third (a chevron; pl. 54c) could represent a number of noble Venetian families: the Canal, Cavalli, Pisani, Savorgnani (or Savorgnoni) or Trevisan (or Trivisan).[8] The arrangement of arms is reminiscent of the decoration found on panels made for the Arti dei Mistieri (or guilds) in Venice.[9] The combination of arms belonging to families of different social standing raises questions about the context for which the bell was created.[10] If made for a guild or confraternity, the bell could have been used to call meetings to order; or it may have been made for an ecclesiastical context, as it was the practice of such corporations to maintain an altar to their patron saint in one of the local churches. Similar combinations of a variety of arms, together with the lion of St Mark, decorated large bells produced for Verona, notably the *Rengo*.[11] The possibility that the bell was made for a council or committee of another centre in the Venetian empire cannot therefore be entirely ruled out, although the lack of other city arms alongside Venice's lion makes this less likely.

While technically it is not possible to confirm whether the bell was made in Brescia, Venice or another centre in the Veneto, the close relationship between this bell, cat. no. 53 and the works given to Gaspare permit a tentative attribution to his workshop.[12]

Notes

1. Drury Fortnum acted as the Museum's agent at this sale.
2. The handle is possibly a modern replacement, being cast in iron and of a different style from surviving sixteenth-century examples.
3. See Walters 1926, no. 1988, for a similar example of a Vespasian gem; see also Motture 1997, pp. 105–6, and p. 49 above for the use of gems in bell decoration.
4. Rome 1884, loc. cit.
5. Radcliffe 1984; see cat. no. 53 for a full discussion.
6. Coronelli 1694, p. 351.
7. Kindly identified by Jeremy Warren in the manuscript of *Cittadini originarii* in a private collection, London.
8. Coronelli 1694, pp. 91, 102, 360, 419, 443.
9. For examples of surviving panels, see Maria Santina Anzalone et al., *Le Insegne delle Arti Veneziane al Museo Correr*, Venice, 1980.
10. I am grateful to Irene Ariano, Nicholas Davidson, Peter Laven, Richard MacKenney and Jeremy Warren for discussing my ideas on the possible context. There was no firm opinion in this regard, but differing views as to the significance of the combination.
11. See Verona 1979, pp. 59–60, for a description of the combination of arms of officials of Verona and their Venetian overlords; see also pp. 34, 35 above for the *Rengo*.
12. See cat. nos 53 and 55, and especially Motture 1997, for a fuller discussion and references.

Bibliography
Radcliffe 1984, p. 761; Motture 1997, pp. 103–4.

55. Bell with the arms of the Bembo family of Venice

North Italian (Venice, or possibly Brescia); 1540–80
Bell-metal
h. 14.5, *c.*10.5 (without peg argent); diam. 13.2;
wt 1344.0 g.
M.1-1947

Provenance: Collection of Dr W. L. Hildburgh, FSA, London; on loan to the Victoria and Albert Museum from 13 June 1944 (no. 1468); given by Hildburgh in 1947.

Condition: A few chips around the rim. Two holes in the peg argent, which is soldered (?) into place, and with the clapper ring projecting through. The upper crown possibly let into the bell.
Interior: remains of clapper, apparently not original; clapper ring supported through two holes in top of bell. Two adjacent holes where the original clapper was attached (?). Wax filler.
Mid-brown patina.
Metal analysis: high-tin bell-metal, with minimal zinc and lead. Iron reading probably due to surface contamination or treatment.

Decorated around the shoulder of the crown with acanthus. On the neck, a band of foliate decoration within a rope border, from which are suspended festoons of cornucopiae and bucrania. Below are profile heads of *Apollo Pythius* and a bearded emperor and two coats of arms (a chevron between three roses) flanked by flowers or thistles, between which are small medallions with profile heads facing each other. Moulding wires and acanthus on the sound bow.

On the assumption that the peg argent is original, or an identical replacement, the bell was designed to be suspended. This is also suggested by its scale and weight compared to the hand bells. The imagery is more appropriate to a secular than a religious setting, and it was therefore probably a doorbell or, more likely, an interior hanging bell.

The bell was presented to the Museum as part of Hildburgh's New Year gift of 1947 as 'Italian, early 16th century'.[1] Elements of the decoration are identical to those found on cat. no. 53, including the reproduction of gems, the cornucopiae with intertwined ribbons, the suspended bucrania and the coat of arms flanked by sprigs of flowers.

(b)

(a)

The foliate decoration around the top is close to that on cat. no. 54 and the similarity of the mouldings and the shape of the bell also suggest that it belongs to the same group. However, it lacks the distinctive leaf decoration associated with the Brescian founder, Gaspare di Girolamo Macri, which appears on the other two bells.[2]

The present bell has been convincingly ascribed to the same workshop as three others in the National Gallery of Art (Kress Collection) in Washington.[3] These are assigned to Venice on the grounds that the arms of the Moro family are displayed on one of the bells.[4] The arms on the present bell can be identified as those of the Bembo family of Venice,[5] which would appear to support this view. It has not been possible to identify with certainty the arms on another of the Kress bells, which displays the letters 'BB' on either side of the shield, but it is possibly that of the Boldu family of Venice.[6] Nevertheless, as has already been demonstrated (cat. no. 53 and p. 33), it is possible that the bells were commissioned elsewhere within the Venetian empire.

The large emperor head is close to the *Septimius Severus* plaquette based on a cameo in the Hermitage, here cast in reverse.[7] The identities of the small profiles are unclear, but the female head is perhaps based on a Hellenistic gem, possibly representing an idealized portrait of Arsinoe II as Demeter,[8] and the left-hand portrait above the shield is similar to a Graeco-Roman gem of Vespasian.[9] Like the *Faustulus* gem on cat. no. 53, the *Apollo Pythius* is also known in an eighteenth-century cast made by James Tassie, a specialist in casting cameos and intaglios.[10] The original gem has not been located, but may assist in providing more secure parameters for dating the bell.

The cornucopiae with ribbons and bucrania also appear on a different style of bell in the Kunstgewerbemuseum, Berlin,[11] and on various vases and mortars, all associated with the Alberghetti foundry in Venice.[12] Close examination, however, indicates a slight difference in the arrangement of the ribbon. On this bell and cat. no. 53 the right-hand ribbon loops over then behind the cornucopia, while the left is reversed.[13] On the 'Alberghetti' pieces it is the opposite way around, with the left-hand ribbon loop-ing over and then behind, and the right reversed. This does not necessarily establish a separate group, including the present example and the Kress bells, as distinct from the 'Alberghetti' type presumably produced in Venice. The motif of hanging cornucopiae and bucrania in its various forms was doubtless quite common, and was probably produced by workshops in both Venice and Brescia.

A bell that provides a further link between the various groups is in the Museo di Castello di Buonconsiglio, Trento.[14] This also bears affronted medallions with profile heads, although different in character from those here, and similar laurel swags with ties and identical banding around the neck to cat. no. 38. Its form and style link it directly with the Bembo bell, and it can therefore be viewed as part of the extended group (along with cat. no. 37).

Notes

1. See p. 17.
2. See cat. no. 53 for references and discussion on Gaspare and bronze production in Brescia and Venice.
3. Inv. nos. 1957.14.112 (A.265.109C), 1957.14.115 (A.268.112C) and 1957.14.114 (A.267.111C); Pope-Hennessy 1965, pp. 147–8, no. 540–2 (figs 536, 538 and 537) under 'Italian (unlocated), late fifteenth and early sixteenth century'; Washington 1994, pp. 230, 231 and 160 respectively, the two former examples as probably Venetian, sixteenth-century, the latter as north Italian, sixteenth-century.
4. Pope-Hennessy 1965, p. 148, no. 541.
5. Azure, a chevron or between three roses of the same; Coronelli 1694, p. 54; Rizzi 1975, p. 55, fig. 31a, no. 3.
6. Pope-Hennessy 1965, no. 540. Boldu arms: party per bend azure and argent, the first part with a dove argent gorged with a ducal crown or; see Coronelli 1694, p. 14; Crollalanza 1965, I, p. 100.
7. See Rome 1982, p. 40, no. 7; also F. Rossi, 'Le gemme antiche e le origini della plaquetta', and N. Dacos, 'Le rôle des plaquettes dans la diffusion des gemmes antiques: Le case de la collection Médicis' in Luchs 1989, pp. 59–69 and 71–91 respectively.
8. Walters 1926, no. 1185.
9. Ibid., no. 1988.
10. See Raspe-Tassie 1791, p. 198, no. 2822. See Motture, loc. cit., esp. n. 40 for further discussion and references.
11. Pechstein 1968, no. 52; see cat. no. 17.
12. See cat. no. 26; for examples of mortars, see Pope-Hennessy 1965, pp. 154–5, nos 566 and 567, attributed to the Alberghetti in Radcliffe 1992, p. 225.
13. Similar swags (with large flowers over the joins) can be seen on a bell of high quality in the Castello Sforzesco, Milan; inv. no. Br.113; h. 17, 9.5 (without handle), diam. 8.8; Alberici 1976, pp. 26–7, fig. 20. The arrangement of the ribbons is not entirely clear, but apparently runs over on both sides. The bell is decorated with a coat of arms (identified as those of the Surian family of Venice; see Coronelli 1694, p. 438); see also cat. no. 38. Another example in the Walters Art Gallery, Baltimore, inv. no. 54.208 (as Italian, sixteenth-century), h. 14.3, has the right ribbon looped underneath – i.e. opposite to the present arrangement. It bears arms that are probably those of the Molini family (the arms could be blazoned in English as azure a catherine wheel or (spokes at the rim with moline ends); however, it probably represents a windmill, in view of the owner's name (*mulino* being Italian for mill; *mulino avento* translates as a windmill); see Coronelli 1694, p. 299; Rizzi 1987, p. 55, fig. 31a, no. 23). I am grateful to John Meriton for blazoning.
14. See cat. no. 38, n. 6, for details; cf. also the bell at Ecouen, cat. no. 38, n. 7.

Bibliography

Pope-Hennessy 1965, pp. 147–8, no. 540; Motture 1997, pp. 105–6, fig. 6.9.

56. Vase or mortar

North or central Italian (Florence or Venice?); 1550–1600

Bronze

h.12.2; diam. 11.7 (rim), 7.8 (base); w. 14; wt 1514.1 g.

M.670-1910

Provenance: Montgermont Collection, Paris;[1] collection of Martin Heckscher, Vienna, until 1898 (Christie's (Heckscher) 1898, lot 78); collection of George Salting, London; bequeathed by Salting in 1910 (Salting Bequest, no. 2949).

Condition: Finely cast. Minor indentations around the rim. Large pit, below one handle. The handles are possibly later additions.

Interior: minor indentations; circular indentation by middle, another irregular pit in the bowl.

Base: inscribed concentric circles; evident pour-rod and spindle hole. Worn and rubbed down around the edge.

Dark brown patina; light bronze where worn.

Metal analysis: a consistent low-tin bronze, with minimal zinc. Nickel appears in the spectrum for the top of the bowl, but is absent from the base.

Bell-shaped vase, with two rouged scrolled handles with projecting female busts. The projecting rim decorated with rosettes between two ovolos; with dentils below. The body decorated on each side with two cherubs supporting by a rouged ribbon a shield of arms (per pale confronting lions' heads), and holding in their hands labels respectively bearing the initials A and C. Alongside the shield smaller putti supporters; masks above and below the shield. Foliage and vine-scroll decoration emanates from a small rosette at the base of each handle. The large putti stand on an ovolo moulding, below which is a frieze of overlapping acanthus and a cove. On the bowl, eight gadroons forming the spine of acanthus. On the projecting foot, a band of downward-facing acanthus leaves, bead and reel and imbricated scales.

The handle forms are unusual and the casting is particularly fine.

The vase was attributed to sixteenth-century Milan in the Heckscher Collection sale catalogue, where the initials on the labels were identified as those of Ambrosio (*sic*) Caradosso.[2] The justification for this suggestion is not documented. The initials presumably refer to the owner of the vase, but the coat of arms has yet to be identified. Salting does not comment on the place of origin of the vase, but it was attributed to the School of Sansovino and dated to the early sixteenth century on acquisition.[3] This attribution reflects the stylistic relationship of the putti with those of the Florentine sculptor Jacopo Tatti, called Sansovino (1486–1570), who settled in Venice in 1527. Sansovino's bronze putti, however, have greater diversity and movement, avoiding the use of mirror images as seen on the present vase.[4] A variant of the vase without handles was formerly in the Pierpont Morgan Collection, London.[5]

A similarity of form and elements of the decoration can be seen on a vase in the National Gallery of Art (Widener Collection),[6] and another closely related to it (which utilized the same form of handle as the Widener example) was formerly on loan to the South Kensington Museum.[7] These vessels, which are less finely cast, are otherwise not closely related. The present vase bears features seen on mortars associated with sixteenth-century northern Italy,[8] but are comparatively common ornamental motifs.

Notes

1. See n. 2 below.
2. Christie's (Heckscher) 1898, loc. cit. The earlier provenance from the Montgermont Collection is mentioned here. Ambrogio Caradosso has not been identified, nor have the Caradosso arms.
3. The vase is noted by Salting as having cost £661 10s. (£661.50), but he valued it at £750; Salting Notebook, GSVII, p. 60. The Heckscher provenance is noted.
4. See, for example, Boucher 1991, II, pls 156, 160, 166.
5. Current whereabouts unknown; Bode 1910, I, p. xxxviii; II, p. 23, no. 190; formerly in the Pfungst Collection, London. The coats of arms apparently obliterated.
6. Inv. no. A.126; with mythological scenes and the arms of the Este family; given to north Italy, sixteenth-century. *Works of Art from the Widener Collection*, National Gallery of Art, Washington, 1942, p. 8, described as a mortar; Wilson 1983, p. 173, attributed to the Circle of Guglielmo della Porta (?), Lombard-Roman, *c*.1515?–77.
7. Photograph in the Sculpture Department archive (neg. no. 3552). Another version is at Anglesey Abbey, Cambridgeshire (The National Trust). The status of these vases requires further consideration.
8. The form of gadrooning, for example, relates to that on the mortar signed by Giulio Alberghetti (1536–72) in the Museo Nazionale del Bargello (see pp. 96–7, fig. 13, and cat. no. 24, n. 2, for details), which also bears rosettes and acanthus decoration.

57. Bowl with snake handles

North Italian (Milan); *c.*1560–80
Brass
h. 8.6; diam. 25.7; w. 40.1; wt 2890.8 g.
M.687-1910

Provenance: Collection of Charles Antiq, Paris, until 1895 (Antiq 1895, lot 348); collection of George Salting; bequeathed by Salting in 1910 (Salting Bequest, no. 2895).

Condition: Crisply cast. One initial 'R' partially obliterated (see pl. 57a).
Interior: two round patches inside, one at centre (pourhole), plus curved rectangular patch. Some pitting and scratches.
Dark brown patination.
Metal analysis: a low-zinc brass, with minimal lead. The high iron content is probably due to surface contamination or treatment.

Turned bowl with a moulded, indented rim, shallow foot and two handles in the form of intertwined snakes, below which are grotesque masks. Decorated on the body with two identical coats of arms (a lion rampant holding a six-pointed mullet) on a scalloped shield with draped and fluttering ribbon and a female mask below, flanked by the initials G . P . and . R ., and four different scenes: (i) bound grotesque figures supporting a vase on which sit addorsed male figures wearing Phrygian caps and holding stringed instruments (viole da gamba?), flanked by draped males holding cornucopiae, (ii) a squatting grotesque nude seated on paired cornucopiae and holding two others supporting tritons; in the centre a cloaked figure

with Oriental headdress, (iii) a cartouche containing a flower(?) and crown flanked by cornucopiae and with a mask, foliage and drapery above, supporting mermen, (iv) a mask flanked by small cornucopiae and grotesque beasts with, at the centre, flowers supporting addorsed beasts (apes?) holding cornucopiae, and with a brazier above.

The handles appear to be made of two components. They may have been derived from a life-cast and are possibly later additions. The base is probably an addition. The use of a low-zinc brass is unusual compared to the other decorative objects of this date in the catalogue, but brass was used at the time for making utensils.[1]

The bowl was described as 'a superb Italian bronze' of the beginning of the sixteenth century in the Antiq sale catalogue, where it is shown on a stand supported by three seated putti, subsequently lost or separated prior to its acquisition in 1910.[2] Salting, who had paid £200 for the bowl, but later valued it at £400, considered it to be Venetian.[3] On acquisition, however, it was designated simply as sixteenth-century Italian, although the arms were tentatively identified as being those of Perinelli of Ferrara.[4] Pope-Hennessy related it to a hemispherical bowl in the Kress Collection, which he considered to be Paduan or Venetian.[5] In fact, the Kress bowl bears no direct relationship, but is comparable to another example in the Kunstgewerbemuseum, Berlin, which has been convincingly attributed to the workshop of Alfonso Alberghetti.[6] There is another bowl with the same decoration in the Musée des Arts Décoratifs, Paris, but of poor quality, particularly in comparison to the crisp decoration on the present example.[7] The nature of the casting of the Paris bowl, notably the lack of definition of the applied

grotesques, suggests that it is an after-cast, or probably just a poor casting, particularly as it has a rectangular patch inside.

The Museum's bowl is closely related to another, larger example, known as the Visconti-Annoni marriage bowl, in the Ashmolean Museum, Oxford (formerly Cyril Humphris, London), which clearly came from the same workshop.[8] That bowl apparently celebrates the marriage of Silvia Visconti and Giovanni Battista Annoni, which is known to have taken place between 1571 and 1580, shortly after the death of Silvia's first husband, Alfonso Cicogna. According to one source, he died in 1567, leaving two daughters by his wife, who is noted as having remarried Giambattista Annoni.[9] The shield containing the coat of arms is identical in form, along with the shape of the vessel and the style of the decoration. This bowl was connected to the work of Leone Leoni (1509–90) and Annibale Fontana (1540–87) in the Humphris sale catalogue, and, although the comparisons cited are not particularly convincing, the relationship to these Milanese workshops is likely to be correct.[10] There is a close relationship, for example, between the triton figures on the present bowl and that below the bronze group of *Charles V and Fury* by Leone and Pompeo Leoni, dated 1564 (Museo del Prado, Madrid).[11] Similarly, the reverses of Leone's medals and others produced in his circle bear a stylistic relationship.[12] Warren has also made convincing connections between the Oxford bowl and the Leoni and other Milanese *botteghe* producing works in hardstone or rock crystal, among them the Sarachi brothers, who were active in Milan during the last quarter of the sixteenth century.[13] A rock-crystal bowl in New York, for example, illustrates a relationship in both form and decoration between the present bowl and products of the workshop.[14]

Notes

1. Biringuccio referred to his visits to the brass-makers of Milan (Biringuccio/Smith and Gnudi 1990, pp. 70–1; Biringuccio 1540, I, 19v).
2. Antiq, loc. cit.
3. Salting Notebook, GSVII, p. 58.
4. The initials possibly indicate a second name beginning with R., but the arms have yet to be securely identified. The arms of the Pinadelli of Venice are similar (party per fess azure and or, a lion rampant counter-changed, the raised dexter paw supporting a mullet gules; see Morandi di Custoza 1985, pl. CCLXXXVI). The seal of Nicolai Perotti (Migeon 1904, p. 299, no. 385) is also similar, but the Perotti family arms are not directly related (see Spreti, V, 1932, pp. 265–6). The bowl was later described as north Italian, first half of the sixteenth century, in the Museum records.
5. Pope-Hennessy, loc. cit.
6. Pechstein 1968, no. 89; see also Radcliffe 1992, pp. 228–9.
7. Metman and Vaudoyer 1910, p. 4, nos 123 and 124, and pl. XI (two views), as Italian, end of sixteenth century; h. 3.5 (erroneous measurement), w. 23.5.
8. See London 1988, no. 12; Sotheby's 1995, no. 14; and esp. London 1999, pp. 100–1, no. 33.
9. See L. Tettoni and F. Saladini, *Teatro Araldico*, II, Lodi, 1843 (no page ref.); the form of Silvia's name appears here as Livia Visconti. I am grateful to Timothy Wilson for this reference.
10. See Sotheby's 1995, loc. cit. at n. 8.
11. Madrid 1994, p. 104, fig. 1. The treatment of the ribbon is also identical to that found on north Italian bells of the mid- to late sixteenth century (see cat. nos 53 and 55).
12. See, for example, Philip Attwood in Washington/New York 1994, pp. 151–7, nos 49–52.
13. See London 1999, loc. cit. at n. 8 above.
14. See Olga Raggio 'Light and Line in Renaissance Crystal Engravings' in *Bulletin of the Metropolitan Museum*, vol. X, 1951/2, pp. 193–202; esp. pp. 199 (illus.) and 202.

Bibliography

Pope-Hennessy 1965, p. 145, no. 526.

(a)

58. Mortar with handles in the form of mermaids

North Italian (Milan?); *c*.1560–80
Bronze
h. 19.3; diam. 24.6 (rim),
16.5 (base); w. 25.3; wt 13 kg.
335-1889

Provenance: Bought from
Michelangelo Guggenheim,
Venice, in 1889
(with 335 to 354-1889, £300).

Condition: Poor-quality cast with rough surface; wear around decorative features and deposit in the interstices. Handles worn.
Interior: 'hammered' surface, dipped at the centre, with a deposit in places.
Base: smooth.
Mottled dark brown applied patination, worn to reveal yellow bronze.
Metal analysis: Bronze of virtually pure copper and tin. The lower tin content in the base may be explained by segregation of the elements during the casting, due to the size of the object.

Bell-shaped mortar with projecting, moulded rim and recessed lip with two handles in the form of nude female mermaids with scroll arms and bifurcate tail. The body decorated with two identical coats of arms (see below) in cartouches, the sides of which are formed by profile female figures similar to the handles and surmounted by a lion mask; the cartouches are flanked by foliate decoration (pampus or papyrus?) with rosettes in the upper spaces. Moulded foot.

Acquired as Italian, sixteenth-century, the mortar bears a coat of arms possibly identifiable as those of the Milani of Rovigo,[1] in north-eastern Italy. The decoration relates directly to that on the 'Annoni-Visconti' marriage bowl in the Ashmolean Museum, datable to about 1570–80, in both the foliate decoration and the handles, but is of notably inferior quality. By extension, it may have been produced in the same orbit as the Museum's bowl (cat. no. 57), which bears an obvious relationship to the larger Ashmolean example. The dating of the mortar to the same period as the bowls is supported by the shield type.[2]

Notes
1. Mirando di Custoza 1985, CCXLII (argent a triple-towered castle proper, a plume of smoke vert rising from the central tower, all beneath a scroll with motto DEFENDIT ET ARCET and a base vert).
2. See, for example, Goodall 1958–9, p. 211, fig. 3.

Bibliography
Inventory 1890, p. 35.

59. Mortar and pestle

North Italian(?);
probably sixteenth century

Brassy bronze mortar with brass pestle
h. 13.5; diam. 15.8 (rim), 9.3 (base); wt 3764.1 g.
pestle: l. 21.5; diam. (i) 3.2, (ii) 3.8; wt 796.3 g.
M.28 and A-1938

Provenance: Collection of Dr W. L. Hildburgh, FSA, London;
on loan to the Victoria and Albert Museum from 14 August
1934 (no. 4839); given by Hildburgh in 1938.

Exhibited: London 1975, p. 65, no. 119; Tulsa 1979, no. 44.

Condition: Crisp cast, but the joins of the pattern were
smoothed in the wax before casting. Porous appearance
in places and white deposit in the interstices;
tiny surface air bubbles (?).
Chipped around the rim.
Interior: pitted around the
bowl; evidence of turning
and faceted marks.
Base: pitted.
Mottled brassy patina;
variable patination inside, possibly removed in places
through use.
Metal analysis: brassy alloy of copper and zinc,
with low tin and lead content. Brass pestle.

(b)

Bell-shaped mortar, decorated around the rim with an
astragal. On the body, between narrow mouldings, a band
of vine tendrils and grapes emanating from acanthus, the
bowl slightly protruding. Moulded foot. Turned pestle.

The pattern is applied in two panels, consisting of one
complete pattern and a repeat of the left-hand section with
a fragment of acanthus scroll.

Acquired as Venetian, the attribution of this pestle and
mortar was subsequently broadened to 'Italian' and dated
to the first half of the sixteenth century.[1] It is one of the
best examples of the model, which is known in several
versions of varying quality and slightly different dimensions. Those in Florence (Corsi Collection),[2] Columbia,[3]
Milan[4] and the Royal Pharmaceutical Society, London,[5]
are all virtually identical in profile and closely related in
scale. Though variously attributed, these mortars may
have been produced by the same workshop. The present
version is slightly different and considerably finer in
facture. The pestle was clearly made for the mortar; the
diameters of the two ends vary slightly, and it is likely that
they were both used for grinding.

(a)

Vignette decoration was reproduced over a long period, sometimes in conjunction with other elements. This is exemplified by a mortar in the Musée Jacquemart-André de Chaalis,[6] and by a nineteenth-century mortar in the Museo Storico Nazionale dell'Arte Sanitaria, Rome, considered an after-cast of a sixteenth-century model by Lise and Bearzi.[7] Although the grape vine had alchemical associations,[8] it was a commonly used motif and does not necessarily have any particular significance in this instance. Consequently it is difficult firmly to assign the mortar to a specific place of production. On the basis of its form, it is likely to date from the sixteenth century, although a seventeenth-century date cannot be ruled out.

Another related variant

Sotheby's, London, 2 July 1997, lot 432; sold for £1,092 as north Italian, early sixteenth-century.

Notes

1. London, loc. cit.
2. Corsi Collection, h. 12.2, diam. 15; Middeldorf 1981, p. 100, no. 27, as 'classical Renaissance type', usually given to Venice or Padua, first half of sixteenth century.
3. Columbia Museum of Art (Columbia SC), inv. no. CMA1963.42, h. 12.4, diam. 13.6 (rim), 9.1 (base), wt 3146.8 g; Pope-Hennessy 1965, p. 156, no. 579, fig. 603, under Italian, middle and late sixteenth-century. Pope-Hennessy asserted that the Columbia mortar had a casting fault and was not therefore worked up, whereas the Museum's version was chased. However, there is no clear evidence of chasing.
4. Castello Sforzesco, h. 13, diam. 16; Lise 1983, p. 265, no. 14, as Lombardy (?), sixteenth-century.
5. Inv. no. OBI 20 (no details available).
6. Inv. no. 2068; h. 20, diam. 28 (rim), 15 (base), inscribed R . R . M . M . DI . S . ANNA D'ALBINO (catalogued as Italian, seventeenth-century). Catalogue details courtesy of R.-H. and Mme A.-M. Bautier.
7. H. 26, diam. 31; Lise and Bearzi 1975, pl. LXXVIII. See also cat. no. 67.
8. Grape juice represented the mercurial water that dissolved the 'dead' matter from which the new could be created; see Abraham 1998, p. 89.

Bibliography

Review 1938, p. 55 and pl. 22b; *Pharmaceutical Journal*, 26 March 1938, p. 329; Pope-Hennessy 1965, p. 156 (no. 179).

60. Altar bell

North Italian (Teglio); dated 1616
Bell-metal
h. 9.6, 8.7 (without ferrule); diam. 11.2; wt 637.9 g.
M.203-1925

Provenance: Said to have come from a church in Teglio (Valtellina, north Lombardy); given by Signora Ada Cardinale of London and Rome in 1925.

Condition: Severely chipped around the rim; long hairline crack from the rim; evidence of turning. Ferrule (or peg argent) replaced (?) and part missing; soldered into place.
Interior: turned, scratched, and with rubbed and flaking golden-brown patination.
Iron clapper with ball and large retaining ring.

(a)

(b)

(c)

Dark brown patination, worn in places. Both the interior and exterior have applied patinations, which have eroded to reveal the grey bell-metal.

Metal analysis: a high-tin bell-metal with minimal zinc and lead. The iron content on both the bell and ferrule (which is high) may be due to surface contamination.

Altar bell, delineated with moulding wires and decorated on the waist with a monogram above a bowl of fruit or flowers, a T (or Tau), a nude boy playing a drum and the date 1616.

On acquisition the bell was said to have come from 'the church of Teglio' in north Lombardy.[1] Although it may have been fitted with a tassel and used as a hand bell, the ferrule could equally have been suspended from a wooden framework.[2] It was, therefore, possibly a sancting bell that stood on an altar, or was attached to the chapel wall, and rung by a long cord. The monogram, variously transcribed in the museum records as FHC (?) and FAC, is not clear. The 'T' takes the form of the Greek letter Tau, which gave its name to the tau cross, a staff carried by a bishop or abbot.[3] The decoration combines religious and secular motifs in an unusual form.

This form of sancting bell is quite common at this period. The bell bears some similarity to another, larger example, bearing the Medici arms, formerly in the Pope-Hennessy Collection.[4] Both examples have similar banding and sparse decoration; the main difference is the profile, with the present bell having a more broadly splayed mouth. It can also be compared to a seventeenth-century loam-cast bell bearing the Messina arms.[5]

Notes

1. Museum records. It has not been possible to identify the specific church; see L. V. Bertarelli, *Guida d'Italia del Touring Club Italiano: Piedmonte, Lombardia, Canton Ticino*, Milan, 1916, p. 296. See also p. 35 for an alternative, though less likely, suggestion regarding the imagery of the tau cross.
2. See p. 35.
3. The T was described in the Museum records on acquisition as a tau cross; the suggestion that it perhaps stands for Teglio was made independently by both Paul Williamson and Anthony Radcliffe.
4. Sotheby's, New York, 10 January 1996, lot 70, Italian, seventeenth-century; h. 12.
5. Jennings 1989, p. 24. An interesting contrast is made between the Messina bell and a modern sand-cast hand bell, which – while having the same dimensions – weighs 0.9 kg. (2 lbs) less than the earlier example.

Bibliography
Review 1927, p. 54.

61. Hand bell

De Maria foundry
North Italian (Vicenza); *c*.1690–1700 (or possibly
a later cast)
Bell-metal
h. 8.7; diam. 10; wt 509.1 g.
M.78-1929

Provenance: Given by Dr W. L. Hildburgh, FSA, London
in 1929.

Condition: Handle missing. Poorly defined casting,
with large area of loss around the crown; chipped
around the edge; green deposit.
Interior: areas of green corrosion.
Mid-brown patina with areas of greyish metal.
Metal analysis: bell-metal with some lead and low
zinc content. The iron reading is presumably due to
surface contamination.

Hand bell with moulded crown decorated with flying
birds alternating with florid fleurs-de-lis in triangular panels. The body delineated by a cove above and scotia below,
and decorated with figures of the Virgin and Child: the
Virgin crowned with a halo standing on a crescent moon,
supporting the Christ Child (crowned with a halo, and
either blessing or holding an orb) in the right arm and

holding a sceptre in the left and flanked by fleurs-de-lis; St
John the Evangelist with arms crossed against the chest
and flanked by fleurs-de-lis; St Anthony Abbot with fore-
shortened halo, holding a book in the proper left hand and
a staff in the right, with a head of a pig to the left and a fire
to the right, a separate fleur-de-lis at the left; the figures
separated by arabesques containing genii of victory with
outstretched arms holding wreaths. Around the sound
bow, downward-facing elaborate fleurs-de-lis applied in
extended triangular panels. Around the rim, in relief, a
pointing hand, a cross, two fleurs-de-lis DA ... HON-
OREM ... DEO (to the honour of God) ... I – – O; each
word separated by a fleur-de-lis; two fleurs-de-lis precede
the I O; between these letters are two blank panels.

Designated Italian, seventeenth-century on acquisition,
the bell was noted in the Museum records as having been
acquired by Hildburgh in Venice. It relates to a group of
hand bells of distinctive shape, apparently signed by different members of the De Maria family, bell-founders of
Vicenza. The most notable is that in the Metropolitan
Museum of Art, New York, which bears virtually identical
decoration (pl. 61b). This is an extremely high-quality,
crisp cast, signed around the rim GIOVANNI BATTISTA
DE MARIA IN VICENZA MI FECE 1693, applied on

(a)

plaques rather than as individual letters as is normally the case, and with a florid R.[1] Another of the same date (Museo Correr, Venice) carries the signature OPVS FRANCISCI MARIÆ DE MARIA (without a florid R).[2] A third, high-quality, unsigned example is in the Museo Nazionale del Bargello, Florence.[3] The stamp of St Anthony (possibly accompanied by the other two stamps) can be seen on a bell signed 'Opus Antonio Mariae De Maria' and dated MDCLXXIV (1674) in a Paduan private collection.[4]

(b) The Metropolitan Museum of Art, inv. no. 1986.269.

The De Maria family moved to Vicenza from Valdobbiadene (Treviso) in the sixteenth century.[5] Only three members of the family, active from the seventeenth to the nineteenth centuries, are noted by name in the published accounts of the family history. Antonio Maria De Maria (d. before 1697)[6] apparently died without sons and the foundry passed to his (unnamed) brothers and nephews. Francesco was a later descendant, known to

have signed at least three works between 1788 and 1792.[7] The only other specifically noted family member is Francesco's son, Felice (d. 1854). The foundry production was divided into three main periods based on dated examples of its work. Objects produced in the first period (beginning in 1637) were signed 'Opus Antonii Mariae De Maria Vicentini'. The second period (beginning in 1707) was characterized by the signature 'Opus Fratrum De Maria Vicentini'. Bronzes cast in the third period (beginning in 1768) bore the signature 'Opus Felicis De Maria Vicentini).[8]

The signatures on the New York and Venice bells do not accord with the signing pattern outlined above, but the imagery can clearly be related to the foundry. The earliest bells bearing the signature of Antonio Maria date from 1637 to 1725, indicating that the name continued to be used long after his death. However, there is also a mortar dated 1595 in the Kunst und Gewerbe Museum, Hamburg, bearing an identical signature.[9] The date was either erroneous or, more likely, the inscription refers to a predecessor bearing the same name, perhaps the founder who moved to Vicenza. The Correr bell, signed Francesco Maria De Maria, was dated one hundred years earlier than those produced by his namesake Francesco De Maria. This again indicates an unknown predecessor, possibly one of Antonio Maria's brothers.

Similarly, there is no specific mention of Giovanni Battista (the founder responsible for the Metropolitan's hand bell). The Metropolitan's bell was produced when the foundry's products generally bore the signature of Antonio Maria. However, also from this period was a church bell (now in the Museo Civico, Pordenone) dated 1699 and signed 'Opus Martini Mariae De Maria', doubtless another brother or nephew of Antonio Maria.[10]

The four hand bells examined are made by the usual method; there is no evidence to suggest that they are aftercasts and no reason to question their authenticity on grounds of facture. The Museum's example is notably less defined in its casting, and there are slight variations in the dimensions of the group. The explanation for the inscriptions on the New York and Venice bells, therefore, must be that they were made by otherwise undocumented relatives of Antonio Maria's, who were signing small objects in their own right while the foundry was still under his control.[11] A parallel is suggested by the appearance of the signature of Giovanni Alberghetti on a hand bell cast while the workshop was presumably still under the control of his father (cat. no. 17). The close relationship between shape and decorative features of the present group suggests that they were all produced around the same time, dating the Museum's hand bell to around 1690–1700. However, the possibility that the De Maria or another imitative foundry were producing such works later on cannot be ruled out.

The Virgin is depicted as S. Maria della Vittoria, an image commonly found on bells. St Anthony Abbot (or Anthony the Great of Egypt) is shown with various attributes: a bell, here shown hanging from the staff (usually depicted in the form of a tau cross), a pig and a fire. A similar figure, but representing St Anthony of Padua, appears on a bell made by the De Maria brothers in 1714 for Santa Croce, Vicenza.[12] The third figure shows St John the Evangelist with his hands crossed on his chest as he is usually depicted when mourning, with the Virgin below the crucified Christ. The design of the bell is particularly appropriate for a hospital, with the inclusion of St Anthony Abbot, intercessor against epidemics; St John the Evangelist, whose faith protected him from the poisoned chalice and enabled him to restore life to two men killed by the poison; and the Virgin in her role against epidemics, famine and war, with her emblem, the lily, also prominently displayed. The presence of the genii emphasizes that faith can bring victory over illness and even death. This combination of imagery was perhaps originally connected with a foundation dedicated to S. Maria della Vittoria or St Anthony.

Other related variants

i. Kunstgewerbemuseum, Berlin, inv. no. 94,407, h. 12.5 (including ferrule of 3.5), diam. 10.2, also bought in Venice (from Guggenheim, 1894); Pechstein 1968, no. 98. An unsigned bell of the same form and bearing much of the same decorative elements, including the *Virgin and Child* relief, and the style of the foliate panels. Pechstein notes another dated 1676 in the Museum für Kunsthandwerk, Frankfurt (inv. no. WMG8). Ibid., no. 97, another unusual bell, shows some interrelationship with the De Maria examples and those of the Bonaventurini of Verona (see cat. nos 46–8).

ii. Museo Nazionale del Bargello, Florence, inv. no. 775 (Girard Gift, 1920), h. 16.5, 8.3 (without handle), diam. 9.6: bears the same 'fleurs-de-lis' decoration around the rim and crown, but is otherwise unrelated.

Notes

1. Inv. no. 1986.269, gift of Nathaniel Spear, Jr, 1986; h. 15.6, 9.1 (without turned handle), diam. 10.1. The absence of decoration around the crown on the Metropolitan's bell is unusual, and the upper section may have been reworked at a later date; the handle is possibly a replacement. However, cf. the Pesenti hand bell of 1676 in the Louvre (Avery 1981 (1977), p. 77, fig. 12).

2. Inv. no. 1317 (Richetti Gift); handle missing, h. 8.2, diam. 10.2.

3. Inv. no. 759 (Girard Gift, 1920); h. 17 inc. replacement handle in the form of a female saint (?), 10 (without handle), diam. 9.7.

4. Padua 1986, p. 324, no. 93; h. 15.5.

5. For the family, see DBI, 38, 1990, pp. 511–14; summary biographies in Padua 1986, p. 390, and Carollo and Sottil 1994, pp. 16–17. Details of their early history are unknown due to the destruction of the relevant archive at Valdobbiadene, but are based on S. Rumor, *Della famiglia De Maria e di alti fonditori di campane vicentini*, Vicenza, 1885, pp. 13–28 (quoted in DBI, 38, 1990, p. 513).

6. His date of death is unknown, but the date of 1697 appears on the tomb slab of Antonio Maria and his heirs in the church of San Giuliano, Vicenza (illus. Carollo and Sottil 1994, p. 107).

7. DBI, 38, 1990, p. 513.

8. See DBI and Carollo and Sottil 1994, locc. citt. at n. 5 above.

9. Inv. no. 1959.125, h. 13.4, diam. 16.2 (rim), base 12 (Launert 1990, pp. 206–7, no. 232); bearing the legend OPVS ANTONIO MAR\IAE DE MARIA; around the rim IOSEPH DE STOCHETIC PHARMACOPOLA AD SIGNUM VITIS AUREAE 1595. It also has the small hand and other motifs seen on the De Maria bells. A mortar formerly with Bardini and in the Figdor Collection was apparently signed OPVS/ANTONII . MAR/IAE . DE MARIA ., h. 16, diam. 18.8 (Planiscig (Figdor) 1930, no. 433), and another signed OPVS FRATRUM/DE MARIA/DE… (?) survives in the Museo Correr, Venice; inv. no. 1425, h. 14.2, diam. 16. All bear the distinctive large acanthus, which is also seen on mortars signed by Bartolommeo Pesenti of Verona (see Avery 1981 (1977), p. 78, figs 13 and 14).

10. Padua 1986, p. 252, no. 12.

11. An extension to the De Maria family tree can be suggested to include Antonio Maria I (active 1595, and possibly the source of the foundry signature of that name); a descendant, Antonio Maria II (documented 1665, 1682 and d. before 1697); Antonio's brothers and/or nephews Francesco Maria, Giovanni Battista and Martino (all active in the 1690s); a descendant, Francesco (active in the 1780s and 1790s) and Francesco's son Felice (d. 1854).

12. Carollo and Sottil 1994, pp. 38 and 115 (illus).

62. Mortar with plaquettes of the Virgin and Child, St Anthony of Padua and St John the Baptist

North Italian (possibly Padua or Venice); probably
***c*.1700–20**
Leaded high-tin bronze
h. 14.7; diam. 16.7 (rim), 8.8 (base); wt 2843.8 g.
M.1-1945

Provenance: Collection of Dr W. L. Hildburgh, FSA, London; given by Hildburgh in 1947.

Condition: Two rough indentations by the St John relief; smearing and evidence of surface working between the Virgin and Child and St Anthony reliefs, and around the moulding and foot. Some fine lines in relief, possibly where the mould cracked during casting. Evidence of turning.
Interior: pitted and scratched, with patchy appearance; chipped around the rim. Colour variation in the bowl (reddening) and a greenish deposit. Evidence of turning and signs of porosity.
Base: pitted through shrinkage where pouring cup was attached; smooth at edges.
Dark brown patination, worn; light bronze underneath.
Metal analysis: a high-tin bronze with significant added lead. The high iron content of the base reading may be due to contamination.

Conical mortar with wide-spreading rim and splayed base. An astragal around the lip, with three astragals separating the splayed rim from the body. The body decorated with three reliefs depicting half-figures of: (i) St John the Baptist holding a cross and banner in the right hand and pointing to it with the left, the banner bearing the legend ECCE AGNVS DEI (Here is the Lamb of God); (ii) the Virgin and Child, the Virgin crowned and holding a sceptre in the form of a fleur-de-lis in the right hand, with a star above, and supporting the Christ with the left hand; the Christ Child (a star above his head) holding out an orb surmounted by a cross in the extended left hand; (iii) St Anthony of Padua supporting the blessing (?) Christ Child on the right arm, and holding a lily in the left hand. The heads of the two saints have an outline of a halo in relief; the figures of the Christ Child each have a halo in the form of rays. The reliefs rest on an astragal and the foot is distinguished from the body by a torus moulding.

(a)

(b)

The mortar was registered on acquisition as Italian (provenance uncertain), late sixteenth-century. A larger but virtually identical mortar is in the Musei Civici, Brescia. It is of lower quality and lacks the large torus moulding, but is decorated with the same three plaquettes, additional leaf decoration and the legend ANTONIO ALBERTI 717.[1] The incomplete notation was accepted by Rizzini as referring to the date of 1717.[2] While unusual, it is difficult to speculate on the meaning of the numbers, if not a date.

The three applied wax reliefs were unevenly cut around the images, and are similar to those found on bells from the fifteenth century onwards, although no other precise examples have been identified. They do not relate to any known plaquettes that sometimes appear on these objects, such as those by Donatello and Moderno reproduced by the Veronese bell-foundries in the sixteenth and seventeenth centuries,[3] and are probably the founder's own models.[4] St Anthony of Padua, a Franciscan friar and priest, was Portuguese but settled eventually in Italy, dying in Padua at the age of 36. His relics are in the church dedicated to the saint in that city. He is shown here carrying the Christ Child, an iconography that possibly refers to his vision of the Virgin and Child. The addition of the Virgin and Child relief is therefore appropriate, as is St John the Baptist, who was venerated by the monastic orders and was portrayed as a guardian against the plague. He was also the precursor of Christ. The St John plaquette illustrates the passage from the gospel

(John 1: 29, 36) when John looked towards Jesus and said, 'This is the Lamb of God' – the words that appear on his banner. The iconography would have been particularly appropriate for a monastic hospital.

Mortars of similar basic shape, but with differently moulded feet, can be seen in the Museo del Castello Sforzesco, Milan, and in the Royal Pharmaceutical Society, London.[5] According to Lise,[6] this type was much imitated in the nineteenth century, and a variety of examples exist, notably those from the Canciani foundry of Venice, which have a more rounded spreading rim and moulded foot, together with projecting handles.[7] The type is, in fact, closer to the larger-scale examples in the engraving showing the preparation of theriac in Venice during the seventeenth century (fig. 10). The nature of the decoration on these mortars distinguishes them from the present example, which is, however, closely related to certain bell types and was most likely adapted from a bell mould.

Considering the examples of similar mortars made in Venice or Padua, the potential iconographic connection with Padua, and the survival of a related piece in Brescia, a north Italian provenance seems certain. An example of a St Anthony relief appears on a mortar of different form in the Museo Estense in Modena, described as Emilian or Lombard, sixteenth-century.[8] The present mortar could equally have been cast in the sixteenth or seventeenth centuries, but presumably originates from around the time of the example in Brescia, and therefore probably dates to the early eighteenth century.

Notes

1. Inv. no. 165; h. 19.5, diam. 22 (rim), 13 (base); the mortar has not been examined by the author; Rizzini 1915, p. 33, gives the legend as 'ANTONIO ALBERTI 1717' and suggests that Alberti is the name of the artist; it is more likely to represent the owner.

2. Rizzini, loc. cit. at n. 1 above.

3. See Franzoni in Verona 1979, p. 10; p. 68, no. 19 and fig. 17.

4. For similar German examples of the *Virgin and Child* relief, see Thurm 1967, e.g. p. 62, no. 1077, fig. 219, bell in Memmingen, cast by Arnold and Peter Brunckler in 1677.

5. Milan inv. no. Br.88, h. 13.5, diam. 16; Alberici 1976, p. 28, and Lise 1983, p. 273, fig. 21; decorated with sage leaves and inscribed D . I . C.; as seventeenth-century. London, for example, inv. no. OB17, h. 14, diam. 14.5 (rim), 8.5 (base), wt 2948.8 g. (undated in the museum's records); the profile of the foot is more defined.

6. Lise, loc. cit. at n. 5 above.

7. Pedrazzini 1934, p. 164; Farmacia Venzi, Camposampiero, dated 18—(?), and Lise and Bearzi 1975, fig. LXXIV, Museo Storico Nazionale dell'Arte Sanitaria, Rome, second half of the nineteenth century. For Canciani, see Sbarigia 1985, p. 94, signed CANCIANI VENETUS FUSORIS OPUS, as Paduan, 1803; Pedrazzini 1934, p. 163, Farmacia Mantovani, Venice; two mortars inscribed CANCIANI VENETI CUCORIS [FUSORIS(?)] OPUS, dated 1793 and 1806.

8. Barbolini Ferrari and Boccolari 1996, p. 125, no. 11.

63. Mortar with porpoise-head handles

North Italian; nineteenth century

Leaded bronze

h. 13.2; diam. 16.2 (rim), 10.7 (base); w. 19; wt 5038.7 g.

341-1889

Provenance: Bought from Michelangelo Guggenheim, Venice, in 1889 (with 335 to 354-1889, £300).

Condition: Waxy cast; pitted, chipped and cracked in places, one small 'split' apparently due to pressure inside; arm and upper foreleg missing from both centaurs; one handle miscast. Interior: some surface pitting and deposit; indented; evidence of repair/casting-in of miscast handle. Base: pitted; evidence of shrinkage where the pouring sprue was attached; a fine spindle hole at the centre. Mid-brown patina.

Metal analysis: a leaded bronze with low zinc content. The differentials in the readings are probably the result of segregation of the elements during casting (see below). Antimony present in the handle.

A modified vase-shaped mortar with projecting rim with recessed lip and two handles in the form of porpoise heads. On the body, two astragals with overlapping decoration on each side consisting of a grotesque mask flanked by different motifs of centaurs carrying women. On the bowl, six tapered ribs evenly spaced. A concave foot with narrow projecting base.

The mortar, which was designated as Italian, sixteenth-century on acquisition, has an unusual undulating shape combining elements of Middeldorf's 'Renaissance' and 'classical Renaissance' types.[1] The centaurs appear on a number of writing caskets (generally known as centaur caskets), some of which are genuine productions of the late fifteenth or early sixteenth century, while others are clearly later after-casts. In this instance, the reliefs vary from those that appear on the Museum's genuine centaur casket (inv. no. M.7-1933), which is crisply cast. The arrangement is, however, found on other caskets, including those in the National Gallery of Art, Washington (Kress Collection), the Skulpturensammlung, Berlin, and the Thyssen-Bornemisza Collection.[2] Generally, the arms of the centaurs support two cornucopiae conjoined to form a circle (see also cat. no. 64), which usually contains a clipeate bust. Beneath the centaurs are, to the left, pan pipes and, to the right, a stringed instrument. These details are missing from the present mortar. It appears that the central part of the mortar relief was cut in the wax prior to application and replaced by a foliated grotesque mask.

The foot has a smeary appearance, possibly suggesting that it was smoothed by using wet cloths rather than a strickle (see p. 25). Metal analysis indicates segregation of the elements during casting. However, as the mortar was apparently cast upside-down, it would be more normal to find a higher lead content at the rim, rather than the base, as in this instance. The dating of this piece, therefore, appears to be nineteenth-century in view of these questions, together with the odd arrangement of the decoration, and the known reproduction of the centaur design during that period. Nevertheless, there is apparent evidence of use, with the indentation inside causing a split to the outer surface of the mortar.

Notes
1. For example, Middeldorf 1981, pp. 88–99, nos 22–6, and pp. 126–7, no. 34.
2. Frankfurt 1985, pp. 522–3; nos 238 and 239; and see Radcliffe 1992, pp. 194–203, no. 31, for the Thyssen example and a full discussion of the caskets, including references to nineteenth-century examples and copies in terracotta by Manifattura di Signa.

Bibliography
Inventory 1890, p. 36; Launert 1990, p. 208, no. 234.

64. Mortar with centaur decoration

North Italian (?); nineteenth century
Leaded high-tin bronze
h.10.6; diam. 14.6 (rim), 10.2 (base); wt 4453.1 g.
347-1889

Provenance: Bought from Michelangelo Guggenheim, Venice, in 1889 (with 335 to 354-1889, £300).

Condition: Very waxy and ill-defined cast, but with some sharp undercutting; some dents, pits and scratches on the surface. Green corrosion spots and red deposit on the rim. Interior: porous appearance in bowl with minor pitting; rubbed in other areas.

Base: large hollow where the casting sprue was attached; smooth at edges; casting flaw on the rim.

Brassy colour with applied black patination.

Metal analysis: basically bell-metal with substantial added lead and minimal zinc.

Bell-shaped mortar with a moulded, spreading rim. On the body, delineated by two torus mouldings between astragals, a repeated relief of opposed galloping centaurs carrying nymphs on their backs and supporting two cornucopias that form a roundel, in the centre of which is the shadow of a shield. Heavy, moulded foot.

The hind legs of the centaurs overlap, creating a raised area of the motif.

The mortar was acquired as Italian, sixteenth-century. The reliefs are poor casts, after those that appear on a number of Italian writing caskets of the late fifteenth or early sixteenth century, generally known as 'centaur caskets'.[1] One such bronze relief was the source for a marble panel on the cathedral façade at Como, by the Ticinese sculptors Tommaso and Jacopo Rodari da Maroggia in 1480, so the design must originate before that date.[2] However, it was reproduced on the caskets over a long period of time. In addition to the notably squashy appearance, evidence of after-casting in this instance is confirmed by the pimple in the centre of the blank shield, reproducing the nail head affixing the shield on the original relief from which the cast was taken. Clipeate busts usually decorated the centre of the casket reliefs, but in some cases coats of arms replaced them. According to Radcliffe, all coats of arms that were separately attached are 'of questionable authenticity', and the Museum possesses one good casket onto which a shield has been added at a later date.[3] An elaborate mortar formerly in the Hommel Collection, Zurich, decorated with centaur casket reliefs (including clipeate busts) was also considered a fake by Radcliffe.[4]

The indications are, therefore, that the casts for the mortar's reliefs were probably made in the nineteenth century, from a centaur casket with an added (but missing) coat of arms. In addition, the combination of the squat shape, associated with fifteenth-century mortars, and heavy mouldings, commonly found on sixteenth-century types, adds to the suspicion that the mortar is a later concoction. This can be compared with a mortar in the Thyssen-Bornemisza Collection, Lugano, which was assigned to the nineteenth century by Radcliffe partly for this reason;[5] no exact parallel from the sixteenth century has been identified. However, a notable difference is that the present object was cast with a solid foot in the normal way, though not entirely successfully, as evidenced by the hollow caused either by insufficient metal being poured into the mould or, more probably, by shrinkage where the pouring cup was attached (see p. 29). It therefore varies from the fake, sand-cast mortars identified by Lockner.[6]

The provenance from Michelangelo Guggenheim leads one to question whether he was producing examples in his factory. However, the correspondence at the time of acquisition indicates that the object came from his personal collection, as a Renaissance cast. The quality is apparently lower than a bronze, miniature reproduction of the Alberghetti well-head in the courtyard of the Palazzo Ducale, Venice, stamped by the Guggenheim factory.[7]

Notes

1. For a comprehensive discussion of the caskets, see Radcliffe 1992, pp. 194–203.
2. Ibid., p. 200.
3. Ibid., p. 202, and see n. 33 for reference to V&A casket inv. no. M.7-1933, here incorrectly numbered M.73-1933.
4. Sale of A. Hommel Collection, Zurich (Oberer Parkring), 10–18 August 1909, lot 434, as by Donatello; Radcliffe's opinion noted in the departmental archives.
5. Radcliffe 1992, pp. 230–1, no. 39.
6. Lockner 1976b.
7. A photograph of a miniature well-head was submitted for opinion by the former owner. The bronze, which was not examined, was stamped into the rim 'STABILIMENTO GUGGENHEIM', and was apparently sold at Sotheby's, Billingshurst, between 1994 and 1999, but the records have not been located. See p. 16 for Guggenheim; it has not been possible to locate a catalogue of the foundry's production. Other nineteenth-century founders also produced variants of these miniature well-heads, including Angelo Giordani. See Howard Ricketts Limited, *Exhibition of Works of Art, Arms and Armour*, 4–15 December 1972, London, no. 4, signed by Giordani, the dating misinterpreted as 1556, being the date of the original inscribed on the model. Another similar miniature is in the Museum of Fine Arts, Springfield, Mass., inv. no. 66. Mel.24, gift of Susan Dwight Bliss.

Bibliography

Inventory 1890, p. 36.

65. Vase or mortar with grotesque masks

North Italian (?); nineteenth-century
Bell-metal with lead and zinc
h. 9.5; diam. 9.1 (rim), 8 (base); wt 1552.2 g.
M.692-1910

Provenance: Collection of George Salting, London, from 1891;[1] bequeathed by Salting in 1910 (Salting Bequest, no. 2948).

Condition: Waxy cast with wear on the high relief of the masks and decoration; some distortion in the pattern, and occasional excess material. Evidence of turning.
Interior: spindle hole visible at centre point; some green deposit.
Base: spindle hole at centre and concentric circles.
Metal analysis: quaternary alloy – effectively bell-metal with added zinc and lead. The base has a higher lead reading (see below).

Thistle-shaped vase or small mortar with flared rim decorated with 12 acanthus leaves. On the body, a band of grotesque masks with foliage emanating from their mouths, alternating with columns surmounted by cherub heads, from which two masks are suspended. On the bowl, two grotesque (or lion) masks alternating with acanthus leaves in groups of three. Flattened foot, decorated with downward-facing acanthus.

The foot may have been cast separately and affixed;[2] radiography was inconclusive, but indicates a density where the foot and body are joined. Analysis indicated a higher lead content in this area, possibly suggesting a lead filling or solder. The alloy is, however, otherwise consistent with the rest of the vase, and the increased lead may be due to segregation during casting. The evidence of a spindle hole both inside the bowl and under the foot perhaps indicates that they were cast together. The acanthus around the bowl was apparently applied as individual leaves; the central leaf of each group of three overlaps the flanking pair.

Although vase-shaped, this object was made in the same manner as a mortar and it is possible that it was used for that purpose. The vase was initially thought by Salting to be Paduan, fifteenth-century, possibly by Andrea Briosco, called Riccio (1470–1532), but was given to early sixteenth-century Venice on acquisition, later modified to north Italy, about 1500.[3] Stylistically it relates to products of the late fifteenth or early sixteenth century, but the masks suspended from the cherubs' heads are unusual, and the vase is doubtless a later cast.

Notes
1. See n. 3 below.
2. This suggestion was first made by Kenneth Turner during physical examination.
3. Salting Notebooks GSIV, as fifteenth-century, 'perh: by Riccio', apparently bought in 1891 for £55; GSVII, p. 60, as Paduan, valued at £85; see Museum records for acquisition details.

66. Mortar decorated with a female figure in a cart

Probably north or central Italian; *c*.1810–30 (?)
Bell-metal
h. 14.2; diam. 17.8 (rim), 11.9 (base); wt 7453.5 g.
340-1889

Provenance: Bought from Michelangelo Guggenheim, Venice, in 1889 (with 335 to 354-1889, £300).

Condition: Waxy, indistinct cast; visible turning marks; minor chips around the rim. Deposit (probably wax) around the decoration with possible corrosion beneath. Interior: faceted surface; patination worn around the bowl. Base: cut/smoothed at a slight angle; evidence of shrinkage around central pour-hole, and surrounding pitting. Dark brown patination.
Metal analysis: bell-metal with minimal lead content.

Conical mortar with projecting, recessed lip with interior moulding. Embossed around the rim with astragals, between which are concave beaded ovals separated by plates with radiating oak leaves; an additional small section of oval added to fill the field. On the body, a female figure seated in a two-wheeled cart drawn by lions and attended by two winged putti, one flying and holding the reins of the lions and the other walking ahead; the pattern repeated three times, the third pattern minus the leading putto. Mouldings delineate the foot, which is decorated with a frieze of vine leaf.

The iconography appears to combine two possible scenes: Cybele in a cart drawn by lions, or part of a Bacchic triumphal frieze, showing Ariadne in a chariot (although it would usually be drawn by leopards, tigers or goats, and less frequently by centaurs or horses). The use of lions would favour Cybele, but the lack of the turreted crown on her head, plus the inclusion of flying putti, makes the Bacchic scene more likely. Alternatively, it could be a triumphal procession, although the identifying attribute of the figure is unclear.[1]

The form of the mortar, though not the decoration, bears some relationship to two mortars in the Museo Storico Nazionale dell'Arte Sanitaria, Rome, both dated 1810 and presumably given to central Italy by Lise and Bearzi due to their location.[2] Similarly, the so-called 'Neoclassic?' mortar in the Corsi Collection in Florence is fairly close, but without the distinctively treated recessed rim.[3] The indistinct nature of the cast suggests that it was made from a mould of a bronze relief. However, the joins in the wax patterns are evident, though not sharply defined, and despite its poor quality there is no reason to believe that the mortar is not a genuine product of the early nineteenth century. The alloy indicates that it was probably made by a bell-foundry.

Notes
1. See van Marle 1932, pp. 111–51, for Triumphs; p. 150, fig. 173, illustrates a Netherlandish plaquette of the *Triumph of Justice*, on a chariot pulled by lions; see also Weber 1975, I, p. 297, no. 678,9 and II, pl. 187. The attribute is possibly a cornucopia, the attribute most commonly associated with Ceres or Abundance, but also a number of allegorical figures, including Peace.
2. Lise and Bearzi 1975, pls LVII and LVIII; Sbarigia 1985, pp. 100 and 95 respectively (the date of the former here given as 1870).
3. Middeldorf 1981, pp. 164–7, no. 44.

Bibliography
Inventory 1890, pp. 35–6.

67. Vase

**Signed by Pietro (1765–1838)
and Francesco (1795–1849) Cavadini
North Italian (Verona); probably
between 1824 and 1838**
Bell-metal
h. 25; diam. 8.2 (rim),
12.1 (base); w. *c.*17.3;
wt 3850.9 g.
M.703-1910

Provenance: Collection of George Salting, London,
from 1890; bequeathed by Salting in 1910 (Salting
Bequest, no. 2935).

Condition: Crisp casting, with minor pitting in places
and some extraneous metal, notably in the inscription.
Evidence of turning. Possibly missing a lid.
Interior: evidence of turning inside the neck; smooth and
undulating following the basic shape of the vessel.
Base: hollow, even casting, following the contour
of the basic exterior shape. Clear evidence of
turning. Green corrosion. Wax or resin in
a thin layer underneath and obscuring
the base of the bowl itself.
Applied dark brown patina, worn to
reveal brassy metal.
Metal analysis: bell-metal with low zinc
and lead content. Iron reading probably
due to surface contamination or treatment.

Vase with inverted pear-shaped body and handles in the form of grotesque female figures. The lip formed by an astragal, below which is a band of overlapping, downward-facing laurel leaves. Around the body: (i) a frieze of running vine pattern; (ii) festoons of fruit and flowers; (iii) a band of water leaf on a projecting moulding; (iv) gadrooned bowl. On the stem of the spreading foot are alternating large and small downward-facing leaves meeting an ogee moulding. Projecting base with bead and reel on the horizontal plane; a cock bead and, on the vertical plane, a band of water leaf, below which is a legend cast in relief: PETRUS EJUSQUE FILIUS FRANCISCUS CAVADINI FUSORES VERONENSES (Pietro and his son Francesco Cavadini, founders of Verona).

The legend is applied in four separate panels, with the words Petrus and Cavadini being larger than the two remaining panels, perhaps having been prepared for an earlier, independent signature. The form of the top suggests that it may originally have had a lid.

The vase was acquired as from the workshop of Pietro Cavadini of Verona and dated to the second half of the sixteenth century.[1] In fact, the Cavadini family ran what became the leading bell-foundry in Verona from 1794 until the 1980s, when it finally closed.[2] The signature on the present vase corresponds with the founding member of the family, Pietro, and his son Francesco; 19 bells, cast between 1824 and 1838, when Pietro died, are known to have carried their joint signatures – Rognini cites one with the identical form of inscription at Brentonico, Trento.[3] The family also used Pietro's name on bells made after his death,[4] but the joint signature indicates that the vase was made during the 1820s or 1830s. The foundry produced a variety of objects, as their advertisement suggests,[5] but they were primarily specialists in bell casting. This is reflected in the alloy used for the vase.

Although the decoration, which is particularly finely cast, is reminiscent of earlier, commonly used patterns – such as the vine leaf (cf. cat. no. 59) – the form is more complicated than that which would normally be associated with the sixteenth century.

Notes

1. Salting notebooks, GSIV, indicates that it was bought in 1890 (provenance unknown) as late sixteenth-century by Cavadini of Verona for £100; in GSVII, p. 60, it was valued at £120, amended to £160.
2. For the Cavadini, see Verona 1979, esp. pp. 96–120, inc. family tree; pp. 131–3 for listings of bells; see also Padua 1986, pp. 408–9. Other contemporary foundries were those of Antonio Selegari and Luigi Chiappani. I am grateful to Luigi Cavadini for allowing me to visit his house and foundry, and to Luciano Rognini and Massimo Granuzzo for arranging the visit. The foundry survives as it was on the day that work ceased, and Sig. Cavadini retains a collection of moulds and casts from his and other foundries. The present vase did not survive among the patterns.
3. Verona 1979, pp. 131–2, for the list of known signed bells, and pp. 98 and 109, n. 28; the legend cited uses the V-form instead of the U.
4. Ibid., pp. 98 and 109, n. 29.
5. Ibid., p. 111.

(a) Detail of the signature around the base.

SOUTH ITALIAN

෨෯

68. Mortar with projecting ribs and rosette decoration

Probably south Italian; *c*.1300–25
Leaded bronze
h. 12.5; diam. 15.7 (rim), 11.3 (base); w. 17; wt 3777.5 g.
346-1889

Provenance: Bought from Michelangelo Guggenheim, Venice, in 1889 (with 335 to 354-1889, £300).

Condition: Bowed near the handle; wear at ends of ribs. Handle cast separately.
Interior: bowl worn; white speckled deposit in bowl and green deposit near rim.
Base: smooth, but convex due to use.
Dark brown patination, worn to reveal brassy colour inside bowl and under base.
Metal analysis: bell-metal with lead. The handle analysis could not be computed.

A conical mortar with a single loop handle, embossed with ten upright ribs, between which are various cartouches, panels, medallions and rosettes representing (from the handle) a rampant griffin(?), an unidentifiable confronting beast with foliate stem terminating in a fleur-de-lis, a warrior on horseback with raised sword, a rosette, a displayed eagle, a rosette, a warrior, a displayed eagle, an elephant and castle. On the recessed foot, a star, a rosette in a square panel, a star, a rosette (square), a patera (rosette on a medallion), a fleur-de-lis, a patera, a star, a rosette (square), a rosette (round), a fleur-de-lis and bird(?).

The bowl has been noticeably worn and the base pushed out of shape through heavy grinding, indicating that a bronze or iron pestle was used to break down quite hard substances.

Acquired as part of the substantial purchase from the Venetian antiquarian and manufacturer of art works, Michelangelo Guggenheim, this mortar was initially catalogued as 'Italian, 14th century'. This broad attribution is accepted by Launert and refined by Buzinkay to the second half of the fourteenth century.[1] Ribs are a common feature of early mortars,[2] and they are here combined with applied motifs that relate in type and style to seals of the thirteenth century. The warrior on horseback, for example, is similar to that on a middle Rhenish wax seal of Count Henry III of Sayn, of *c*.1206–7.[3] The eagle equally bears comparison with seals of the Hohenstaufen emperors, who ruled in southern Italy for much of the thirteenth century.[4] The elephant and castle is also commonplace as a decorative device in the same period, and the rosette decoration could have been produced at that time. The mortar is probably later in date, utilizing motifs of an earlier style that would doubtless have been widely available. It is, therefore, a rare early example of its kind, datable probably to the early fourteenth century, and most likely south Italian in origin.

Notes
1. Launert and Buzinkay, locc. citt.
2. Known in numerous examples, such as Museo Storico Nazionale dell'Arte Sanitaria, Rome, Lise and Bearzi 1975, pl. III; as Italian, mid-fourteenth-century.
3. See, for example, *Die Zeit der Staufer. Geschichte, Kunst, Kultur* (exh. cat.), Stuttgart, 1977, I, p. 46, no. 70; II, fig. 18.
4. See, for example, ibid., I, pp. 50–1; II, fig. 25, for a similar (though not identical) eagle. I am grateful to Paul Williamson for these references and his suggestions on origin.

Bibliography
Inventory 1889, p. 36; Launert 1990, p. 193, fig. 212; Buzinkay 1996, p. 45, fig. 37.

(*a*)

69. Mortar with lion handles

South Italian (Melfi); dated 1555
Bell-metal
h. 10.3; diam. 13.2 (rim), 7.8 (base); w. 18; wt 2689 g.
318-1903

Provenance: Bought from N. Bear, London, in 1903 for £6.

Condition: Evidence of turning; squashy cast with scratched and mottled surface, the scratches of a dotted appearance; solder line where handles attached; chipped, cracked and pitted around base; white deposit in the interstices.
Interior: smooth, dark patina.
Base: smooth, with minor pitting.
Brassy mottled patina, darker inside and black around the recess of the rim.
Metal analysis: bell-metal, with some lead and zinc.

Conical mortar with two projecting handles supporting sejant lions, decorated on the moulded, projecting rim with a raised inscription: . 1555 (inverted) . + and the remains of an illegible inscription (- T (?) T A). On the body, three panels each side, with a border and fine central staff over which is foliate decoration. Moulded, recessed foot.

The decorative panels were cut from longer strips and are all different and haphazardly applied. The borders of the panels are worn, but the interior of the mortar shows no obvious sign of use.

The Italian origin and date were correctly noted at the time of acquisition, but the mortar was erroneously described in the recommendation for purchase as Flemish, fifteenth-century.[1] Launert suggested it may be Venetian.[2] At least four other closely similar mortars survive (listed below), two of which have inscriptions linking them to Melfi, a bronze-founding centre for the northern Basilicata region, south-east of Naples (see ii and iii below). Four of the mortars are dated between 1555 and 1558, the present example being the earliest.[3] Another mortar of basically the same form, but with couchant lions on the handles, is inscribed FECIT MAGISTER ANTONIUS DE NAVE MEFIERI . MCCCCLXXXVI (Antonio de' Navi caused me to be made, 1486).[4] Instead of panels, this example has fine, lobed ribs, similar to those in cat. no. 70, and bears an unidentified coat of arms, presumably that of the owner. It is given to Emilia in the second half of the fifteenth century, but was possibly also produced around Melfi.

One of the mortars in this group (no. iii below) was erroneously dated to 1228 by Lipinsky, the two number fives having been applied in reverse.[5] A similar mistake is evident on the present mortar, where the fives have been placed upside-down. The inscription on no. i below has been interpreted as possibly referring to Taranto, the principal port of the Basilicata region.[6] The inscribed names represent the different owners of the mortars. The founder is yet to be identified.

Other related variants
i. Location unknown, h. 10.4. Agnew's, November–December 1989, no. 66. Inscribed around the rim: MASTRONARDO . DOLCETO . DIAMATE (?) TARRANO (?) A.D. 1556. 'Tarrano' possibly to be read as 'Taranto'.

ii. Milan, Castello Sforzesco, inv. no. 100; signed FRATE ANTO-
NIO REGALE ARBANESE DE MELFI 1558; Alberici 1976, pp. 28
and 29, fig. 29; Lise and Bearzi 1975, p. 61.

iii. Private collection, Milan; inscribed CESARE CAVVOTO DE
MELFI A.D. 1558. Angelo Lipinsky, 'Fonditori in Bronzo nella
Melfi Medievale' in *Potenza*, I, no. 1, November–December
1967, pp. 40–6, esp. pp. 41–2 (illus.), the date wrongly transcribed as 1228. The cast is damaged.

iv. Corsi Collection, Florence; h. 11.4, diam. 13.5, w. 18.5.
Middeldorf 1981, pp. 58–63, no. 14, as early Renaissance type,
decorated with an unidentified coat of arms (a bull).

v. Metropolitan Museum of Art, New York (Untermyer
Collection). Hackenbroch 1962, p. 16, pls 42 and 43, figs 45 and
46; formerly R. Tolentino Collection, and possibly identifiable
with the mortar formerly in the collection of Horace Wright of
Edgware in 1954, illus. in *The Chemist and Druggist*, 2 January
1954. The mortar is of the same form, but with notably different
decoration. This mortar appears to be of questionable authenticity; it has not been examined in detail by the author (see also vi
below).

vi. Philadelphia College of Pharmacy and Science, Philadelophia,
Lawall and Lawall 1934, pp. 579–80, fig. 30. A similar model to v
above, with a more elaborately moulded base.

Notes

1. Museum records, Bear nominal file, Report dated 6 April
   1903 signed by W. W. Watts, Keeper of Metalwork.
2. Launert, loc. cit.
3. See Radcliffe 1992, p. 230, n. 3.
4. Museo Civico, Modena, h. 11; Barbolini Ferrari and Boccolari
   1996, p. 124, no. 7.
5. Lipinsky, loc. cit. at no. iii above. He also identified the mortar
   as the work of a thirteenth-century founder, Cesare Cavuoto
   of Melfi, based on the inscription around the rim.
6. Agnew's, loc. cit. at no. i. above.

Bibliography

Inventory 1907 (Acquisitions 1903), p. 52; Launert 1990, p. 205,
no. 229.

ITALIAN,
REGION UNSPECIFIED

ॐ

70. Mortar with ribs and a shield supported by putti

Italian; 1450–1500
Bronze
h. 12; diam. 15.8 (rim), 9 (base); w. 12.1, wt 3865.8 g.
349-1889

Provenance: Bought from Michelangelo Guggenheim, Venice, in 1889 (with 335 to 354-1889, £300).

Condition: Waxy appearance; worn. Several casting flaws on the rim.
Interior: scratched; pitted bowl with porous appearance.
Base: smooth, with some pitting.
Dark brown patination, with green and grey deposits on exterior and interior.
Metal analysis: bronze with zinc and tin; handle has higher tin content. Iron ring.

Conical mortar with corded handle and a plain iron ring. Moulded projecting rim with shallow recess. On the body, three pairs of cavorting winged putti supporting a blank *testa di cavallo* shield, between five projecting, tapered ribs, which terminate in a trefoil. Moulded foot.

The present mortar was acquired simply as Italian, sixteenth-century, and later modified to Florentine, fifteenth-century.[1] The basic form is similar to cat. no. 1, but the decorative features have been elaborated, and the addition of mouldings and figurative decoration places it later in date. It falls broadly into Middeldorf's 'early Renaissance' group.[2] Other examples include two from the Castelli Collection in Siena, both given to fifteenth-century central Italy,[3] and another, with additional figurative decoration, formerly in the Castiglioni Collection, Vienna, catalogued as Tuscan, mid-fifteenth-century.[4]

The form is apparently developed from a type exemplified by a mortar in the Castello Sforzesco, Milan, given to Lombardy in the fifteenth century by Lise, which has similar ribs and handle.[5] The present version has a moulded, shallow foot in comparison to the plain, deep recessed foot of the Milan example. The additional decorative features also support a later dating.

Notes

1 Inventory, loc. cit., and Museum records.

2. See, for example, Middeldorf 1981, p. 42, no. 10.

3. Lise and Bearzi 1975, p. 56, fig. 68, as central Italian, end of the fifteenth century; p. 57, fig. 69, as Umbrian, mid-fifteenth-century.

4. Muller (Castiglioni) 1925, p. 23, lot 100; with the legend in gothic lettering, transcribed as: SERE . NICOLOE DE SERE . BARTOLOMEO . (probably to be read: BARTOLOMEO SERE . NICOLOE DE SERE). See also ibid., lot 98, signed by Crescimbene of Perugia, dated 1440, which is an elaborate version of basically the same form.

5. Inv. no. Br.95, h. 17, diam. 18.8, also decorated with a shield charged with a cross in relief; Lise 1983, p. 249, no. 2; he refers also to the diffusion of this type in France and Spain as well as central Italy, although the rib types are more refined in the French and Spanish examples. See also Alberici 1976, p. 28 and fig. 21, as Italian, fifteenth-century. See also Lise 1983, p. 248, no. 1.

Bibliography

Inventory 1890, p. 36.

71. Mortar with female-headed dragons

Italian; 1450–1500, possibly nineteenth-century
Leaded bronze
h. 10.7; diam. 14.2 (rim), 9 (base); w. 14.4; wt 3151.6 g.
351-1889

Provenance: Bought from Michelangelo Guggenheim, Venice, in 1889 (with 335 to 354-1889, £300).

Condition: Casting flaws/chips at the rim; some pitting. Green deposit in interstices. Evidence of where the metal has run during casting.
Interior: recessed in the bowl; green deposit.
Base: some evidence of shrinkage where the pouring sprue was attached; smoothed at the edges.
Mottled patina on both exterior and interior.
Metal analysis: leaded bronze, with some zinc. Consistent cast, but higher tin content in the body than in the base.

A conical mortar with projecting moulded rim and small loop handle and recessed foot. The body decorated on each side with confronted dragons with female heads, between which are vases of flowers.

The recession inside the bowl is apparently due to wear through use.

The mortar was registered simply as Italian, sixteenth-century, on acquisition.[1] Similar, although not identical, dragons can be seen on a mortar in the Columbia Museum of Art, Columbia SC (formerly Kress Collection), which is otherwise of a different form.[2] The decoration gives no clues as to the place of origin of the object, but the dragons indicate a possible alchemical association.[3] The form compares with Middeldorf's 'early Renaissance type' and probably dates to the second half of the fifteenth century.[4] This form of mortar was, however, produced over a long period of time and with widely varying decoration.[5] In addition, the poor quality, odd arrangement of the decoration and the combination of early form and handle (compare cat. no. 68, for example) with more elaborate mouldings, suggest that this may be a nineteenth-century cast.

Notes

1. Inventory, loc. cit.
2. Pope-Hennessy 1965, pp. 156–7, no. 580.
3. See Cirlot/Sage 1971, p. 87.
4. See Middeldorf 1981, pp. 58–69.
5. See, for example, cat. nos 4–7 and 69.

Bibliography
Inventory 1890, p. 37.

72. Mortar with alchemical symbols

Italian; *c*.1480–1500
Bronze
h. 17.9; diam. 21 (rim), 11.6 (base);
wt 9943.9 g.
M.271-1923

Provenance: Collection of Mrs Ellen Hearn, Menton, France; given by Mrs Hearn in 1923 as part of the first instalment of the Alfred Williams Hearn Gift in memory of her late husband.[1]

Condition: Small casting flaw in the rim; waxy cast.
Interior: obscured by powdery residue.
Base: smoothed off; central pin-hole visible, with concentric circles; two large casting flaws at the edge.
Dark brown patina; worn at the edge and centre of the base to reveal brassy bronze.
Metal analysis: bronze, with zinc and low lead content.

Conical mortar with rounded, projecting lip. Around the top of the body, a vine leaf intertwined with a stem. On the body proper, delineated by two flattened astragals (the lower part slightly recessed), four truncated, grotesque masks of a horned beast or stylized lion with vine tendrils, leaf and bunches of grapes emanating from the mouths; inscribed in relief between each mask with the symbols: ⅍ Ⱥ ⱦ $.

All the decoration is highly stylized. Plain, recessed foot.

This large mortar was considered on acquisition to be probably Italian work of the fifteenth century.[2] It origins are uncertain, and the nature of the decoration is both unusual and enigmatic. The symbols can be interpreted as: ⅍ = aleph, the first letter of the Hebrew alphabet. ⱦ = daleth, the number four.[3] The stops adjacent to these symbols are contractions for vowels, and may modify their meaning. Ⱥ could represent an alchemical sign for calcination,[4] a process whereby substances were reduced by heat. This action was frequently described in alchemical literature as 'pulverizing over a fire', for which a metal mortar or similar utensil may well have been used.[5] On the other hand, it may simply be interpreted as *or*, the French for gold and Hebrew for light. $ may be another alchemical symbol for *sel des Pélerins* ('Pilgrim's salt').[6] Alternatively, it may symbolize silver; the dollar sign that it resembles having been derived from the silver mark. Another possibility is that it represents the initials of an owner.[7] Taken alongside the other motifs, scientific or

(a)

(b)

hermetic associations would be more likely than any personalization. Vines and grapes are common decorative forms, which are used to ornament both bells and mortars. However, in an alchemical context, they also had symbolic associations.[8] It is, therefore, probable that the decoration of the mortar carried a specific imagery, the meaning of which has been lost.[9]

The form corresponds most closely to Middeldorf's 'early Renaissance' type[10] and, coupled with the style of the decoration, indicates a date around the end of the fifteenth century.

Notes

1. Possibly the 'Bronze mortar, 15th century' bought by Mrs Hearn in August 1904 (Eastbourne) for FF237.50 (Museum records, Hearn nominal file, Mrs Hearn's notebook, p. 4).
2. Museum records (Hearn nominal file); a letter from W. W. Watts, Keeper of Metalwork, to the Director justifies acceptance of the gift: 'The mortar appears to be a good example, probably Italian work of the 15th century: we shall be glad to exhibit it.'
3. Aleth is equal to the number 1, and can be translated as ox or plough; daleth (4) means door and is linked with Venus (or possibly it is resh = 200, linked to the sun and meaning 'head')

The lettering is also reminiscent of gothic script used on German bells of the fourteenth century; see, for example, Schilling 1988, p. 143, nos 265–6; see p. 147, no. 283 for 𝕺𝕽 and ✴.

4. See Dom Pernety, *Dictionnaire Mytho-Hermetique 1787*, Paris, 1972, for lists of symbols and their meanings.
5. See Roberts 1994, pp. 101, 104 for an explanation, symbolic interpretation and references.
6. See Pernety, op. cit. at n. 4.
7. For example, the same conjunction of the letters S and I were used by the Lord of Rimini, Sigismondo Malatesta (1417–68), probably signifying the first letter of his name, plus that of his mistress, Isotta degli Atti (see Corrado Ricci, *Il Tempio Malatestiano*, Rimini, 1974, pp. 315–19).
8. See p. 180; they were symbolic of the *prima materia* from which it was believed all life sprang. The stylized vine leaf and stem on the mortar are virtually identical to those of a modern German mould; see Schilling 1988, fig. 432, model by Ulrich and Schilling at Apolda, between 1846 and 1952.
9. I am grateful to Alistair McFarlane, Michael Keen, Norbert Jopek and Jemma Street for helpful discussions and assistance in identifying the symbols and their associations.
10. Middeldorf 1981, pp. 58–69, nos 14–15, are basically conical with a flared rim and recessed foot, although the moulding and details differ from the present example.

73. Mortar decorated with monsters

Italian; sixteenth century
Bell-metal
h.13.8; diam. 18.5 (rim), 13 (base); w. *c.*20.7; wt 6936.6 g.
5427-1901

Provenance: Transferred from the Museum of Practical Geology, inv. no. 1045 (14 October 1901).

Condition: Casting fairly crisp, with little wear; rough background with greeny-grey deposit. Some extraneous metal remaining between the legs of one of the monsters. Evidence of turning on the rim, with a defined line where it joins the body of the mortar.
Interior: smooth, with green deposit and minor pitting.
Base: smoothed, but with evidence of shrinkage around the pour-hole.

Dark brown patination, brassy where worn underneath. Metal analysis: bell-metal with some zinc and lead. The body and handle are consistent; the base has a lower tin content reading, possibly due to surface wear abnormalities.

Cylindrical mortar with projecting lip, recessed inside, and two projecting, ribbed handles that terminate in rosettes, adjacent to which is a band of egg and dart. Moulded lip enriched with six winged cherubs' heads; each side of the body decorated with three winged monsters displayed, between which are (two) elliptical rosettes. The monsters wear stylized loin cloths; they have no arms and the legs of a goat, with cloven hooves and scrolls emanating from the knee; their distinctive Egyptian-style headdresses overlap the rim. The shallow moulded base is decorated with a band of riband-like ornament.

The handles were probably cast-in. It is unclear whether the rosettes were applied in the wax prior to casting or attached subsequently. They are deeply undercut, and would not, therefore, have been cast in wax in moulds as described on p. 27 (fig. 5), but would possibly have necessitated some form of piece-mould. The mortar is notably heavy compared to others of its size.

The object was described in the transfer papers as an 'ancient bronze mortar', but was registered as Italian, sixteenth-century. Another virtually identical version, but without the elliptical rosettes, appeared on the art market in New York in 1966, where it was similarly catalogued.[1] A group of mortars, attributed to Florence in the late sixteenth century, are also decorated with displayed harpy-like creatures, but the style, shape, scale and handling of the group vary considerably.[2]

The decorative arrangement leaves little doubt that the mortar had alchemical associations. The inclusion of the cherub heads around the rim probably relates to imagery of the heavenly sphere, and rosettes are frequently seen in conjunction with alchemical imagery.[3] The unusual form of the monsters fits no exact description of the usual beasts, as it combines the somewhat androgynous, but possibly female, head and winged torso with oddly modified goats' legs. There is insufficient evidence to assign the mortar to any particular region.

Notes

1. Bernard Black Gallery, New York, April 1966, no. 3; h. 13.5; black patination, as Italian, sixteenth-century.
2. Including: (i) formerly Cyril Humphris, London (formerly with Dollard, New York), see Sotheby's 1995, I, lot 30; (ii) Paris, Musée Jacquemart-André, inv. no. 1088 (*Catalogue Itinéraire* 1948, p. 95, as Venetian, beginning of the sixteenth century; (iii) private collection in Keswick, England.
3. Fantastic beasts are also connected to Cabalistic literature.

Bibliography

Inventory 1901, p. 96.

74. Mortar with lion's head handles

Italian; *c*.1530–40
Leaded bronze
h. 17.5; diam. 24.3 (rim), 15 (base); w. 24.8;
wt 11639.9 g.
M.683-1910

Provenance: Collection of George Salting, London, from 1896 (?);[1] on loan to the Victoria and Albert Museum from 15 March 1907; bequeathed by Salting in 1910 (Salting Bequest, no. 2521).

Condition: Several cracks in the rim; distortion and some repairs. Rough appearance to the bronze and greenish-brown deposits in the interstices. Minor dents on the surface; sage leaf worn; waxy decoration.
Interior: fairly even hammered appearance around the inside.
Base: smooth with wide ring indicating where pouring cup was attached; scratched in places.
Dark brown patina; bronze colour where worn under the base.
Metal analysis: leaded bronze with consistent alloy in the handle and body, but with lower lead and tin content reading at the base.

Bucket-shaped mortar with projecting moulded rim, recessed inside, and two projecting handles in the form of lions' heads with elongated necks. On the body (at the lower part), a band of anthemion and palmette-style decoration, above which the field is divided into eight spaces by panels of foliate scrolls. Set into these spaces are masks (under the handles); on one face, a coat of arms (out of three mounds three palm trees, two of them bowed)[2] flanked at the base by the initials A B and surmounted by a helm; on the other face, a lion mask with two sage leaves emanating from the jaw; each flanked by smaller lion masks with three smaller sage leaves emanating from the chin. A five-part moulding separates the recessed foot, decorated with a different anthemion and palmette frieze and projecting moulding.

The two anthemion and palmette friezes appear to be applied in one strip, the joint appearing below the central lion mask with sage, at what would be the back of the mortar. There is no obvious explanation for the lower lead

and tin readings at the base, although they may be due to segregation of the metal during casting.

The mortar was catalogued on acquisition as Italian (provenance uncertain), sixteenth-century.[3] The shape is basically similar to an example given by Middeldorf as 'early Renaissance type (Milan?)'.[4] It is most closely related to a smaller one in the Musée Jacquemart-André in Paris of similar form, decorated with an identical lion mask (without the sage), the same foliate scrolled panels (differently arranged), and an anthemion and palmette frieze.[5] The Paris mortar has a single rope handle with an iron ring. Again, there is a hammered appearance to the interior and a dark patina. Many of the same basic features are also shared by a mortar in the Metropolitan Museum of Art, New York.[6]

A key to the likely dating of the present mortar can be gained from another published piece, dated AD MDXXXVII (1537), bearing the same style of decoration and, apparently, identical arms, but flanked by the initials F and R (?).[7] The arms have yet to be securely identified.[8] A similar style of mortar, without handles, and with a broader band of decoration bears the sunburst IHS medallion and the legend SANCTA MARIA DI IESV MDLXXXXI (1591).[9] The sacred monogram is in the form used by the followers of S. Bernardino of Siena, and the date confirms that this basic form of mortar continued to be used over a long period of time. Another small but simpler mortar with decoration applied in panels (cat. no. 2) has the same symbol.

Notes

1. It can probably be identified with the 'Mortar, large 16th century' that Salting bought in 1896 for £90, and which he later valued at £120; Salting notebook GSVII, p. 61 (date uncertain).
2. The arms could alternatively be interpreted as: out of three mounds two palm trees bowed, a star in chief.
3. Museum records.
4. Middeldorf 1981, cat. no. 15, pp. 64–5.
5. Inv. no. 1103, h. 14.5, diam. 19.3 (rim), 10 (base); *Catalogue Itinéraire* 1948, p. 96, as Venice, *c*.1500.
6. Inv. no. 10.18.2, h. 19.7, diam. 26.7; Rogers Fund 1910 (bought in the Sangiorgi sale), catalogued as Venetian, first half of the sixteenth century.

7. *The Burlington Magazine*, CXVII, September 1975,
   p. 624; fig. 80.
8. They bear a similarity to those of Silvestro di Giovan Battista
   Baldoli da Foligno (Podestà of Florence in 1500) on a stone
   panel in the Museo Nazionale del Bargello, Florence
   (Francesca Fumi and Cambi Gado, *Stemmi nel Museo Nazionale
   del Bargello*, Florence, 1993, pp. 106–7). The identification
   with the Baldoli cannot be confirmed, however; other arms
   are equally close, and no exact match has yet been found.
9. Sotheby Parke Bernet, New York, 31 May 1974, lot 45. Another
   related piece was formerly in the Gramberg Collection (1920
   (?); photograph in departmental archive, no further details).

(*a*)

75. Mortar with dancing putti

Italian; 1550–1600 (?)
Leaded bronze
h. 20.8; diam. 27.8 (rim), 15.9 (base); w. 30.7; wt 16.5 kg.
7846-1861

Provenance: Bought for £5 in 1861 (provenance unknown).

Condition: One large and several minor chips and casting flaws around the rim. Some minor surface cracking and pitting; remains of flashing on the moulded bowl. Evidence of turning in the background. Putti and handles worn. White and green deposits in the interstices.
Interior: pitting and green deposit in the bowl and colour variation; apparent copper enrichment. Faceted marks, suggesting heavy use of the pestle(?), and remains of black patination(?).
Base: evidence of shrinkage and pitting on the base where cast; smoothed down.
Dark brown patination.
Metal analysis: a consistent leaded bronze. The iron reading probably reflects surface contamination or treatment.

Bell-shaped mortar with two handles in the form of curved herms with satyr head and scroll ends. Projecting moulded rim with recessed lip and moulded bowl and foot. On each side of the body, an identical frieze of five symmetrically arranged dancing putti holding hands, and beneath each handle, in mirror image, a putto playing a tambourine.

On acquisition the object was catalogued as Florentine, sixteenth-century, subsequently clarified on the label text as 'early sixteenth-century', while Launert settled for the broadest description of Italian, sixteenth-century.[1] Comparison can be made with a group of mortars, the form, mouldings and, in most cases, the handles of which are all similar to the present mortar. Each of these is divided into two main registers by an astragal between two fillets, with the upper register decorated with festoons of identical form, but variously arranged with other elements.

The first example from this group (Corsi Collection, Florence) is also decorated with dancing putti (arranged in three pairs on each side, each pair made from the same mould) and bears the legend 'D . M . ᴬ ANCILLA VIGLIE-GAS', which Middeldorf indicates may suggest a Spanish origin.[2] The inscription could be translated as 'Doña Maria Ancilla Vigliegas', presumably the name of the Spanish noblewoman for whom it was made, but the form favours an Italian origin.[3] The handles on the Museum's mortar, while appearing larger in proportion to the body of the mortar itself, may possibly be of the same scale as those on the smaller Florence example. Another related piece, formerly with Cyril Humphris, London, also has the herm handles and swags, here emanating from a blank shield, but bears no decoration around the lower register.[4] Linking these two is another in the Musée Jacquemart-André, Paris, which has the same putto frieze as the Florence mortar, and the swags and shield of the Humphris mortar, but with apparently less practical, small scroll handles.[5] The fourth object in the group also has the figurative handles and a variation on the festoon decoration, and bears grotesque figures, flanked by foliage and birds around the lower register, executed in the same flattened style of the putti on the Florence and Paris examples.[6] Lange illustrates a hand bell with identical putti, which he ascribed to Italy at the end of the seventeenth century.[7]

It is extremely likely that the four mortars of this group were produced in the same workshop. Despite the parallels in shape and handle type, however, it is difficult to conclude with certainty that the present mortar can be included within this group, due to the lack of the upper decorative division and the difference in style of the putto frieze. Here, the putti have shorter hair and are treated in a more three-dimensional manner, with rounded bodies and projecting knees. The legs are also differently arranged in some cases, with one depicted as kicking rather than resting on the lower moulding.

One other mortar, also from the Corsi Collection in Florence, is worth noting in this connection, as it highlights the difficulties of drawing firm conclusions, particularly when based on photographs alone.[8] With different handles and variations in the mouldings, it is basically the same shape as the mortars cited above, and has dancing putti of a similar type (but with crossed legs) to those on the other Corsi mortar and the one in Paris. The putti are apparently less worn and this, together with the different arrangement, gives the impression of more rounded figures closer to those on the Museum's mortar. The second Corsi mortar bears two coats of arms, one charged with a lion rampant and the other 'in chief a displayed eagle and a lion rampant'. The form of the shield is quite different from that on the Paris and Humphris mortars. Unfortunately, the charges are too common to determine the owners with certainty.

A mortar that bears some resemblance in shape, and in the form of its handles, has the legend 'I . S . R . F . 1764' on the body and 'GIVSEPPE FEDELI E FRATELLI' around the rim.[9] The related mortars discussed above are more heavily moulded and the basic form and style of the present example appears to indicate a date in the second half of the sixteenth century; the exact place of origin cannot be readily determined.

Notes

1. Inventory and Launert, locc. citt.
2. Middeldorf 1981, pp. 118–23, no. 32; h. 16.5, diam. 18.5, w. 19. The legend is transcribed as 'VIGLIEGAS . D . M . ANCILLA' in Lise and Bearzi 1975, XXXVII, colour plate (given as private collection, Milan), as Florentine style, second half of the sixteenth century.
3. While probably a name, the word *Ancilla* is also Latin for 'handmaiden'. I am grateful to Marjorie Trusted for pointing this out.
4. Sotheby's 1995, Part 2, lot 230, as Florentine, sixteenth-century; h. 15, with pestle of l. 19.
5. Inv. no. 996; *Catalogue Itinéraire* 1948, p. 85, attributed to Bartolomeo Bellano (Padua), *c.*1480.
6. See Launert 1990, p. 200, no. 221, as Italian, second half of the sixteenth century; h. 16, diam. 19.5; then Kunsthaus Lempertz, Cologne.
7. Lange 1981, p. 104.
8. Middeldorf 1981, pp. 110–15, no. 30; h. 19, diam. 22.7, w. 27.7; no place of origin specified.
9. Christie's, New York, 11 January 1994, lot 53. I . S . R . F . presumably refers to the founder (I. S. R. Fecit?), and the inscription on the rim to the owners, probably a pharmacy. Alternatively it is a pharmacy sign and the Fedeli were founders.

Bibliography

Inventory 1868 (objects acquired in the year 1861), p. 26; Launert 1990, p. 197, no. 217.

Appendices

൙ൟ

APPENDIX 1: Normalized EDXRF alloy analysis results[1]

Key

Cu = copper	Zn = zinc	Mn = manganese	T = trace
Sn = tin	Fe = iron	Sb = antimony	Matl = material
Pb = lead	Ni = nickel	As = arsenic	

Cat. no.	Inv. no.	Object type	Part	Cu	Sn	Pb	Zn	Fe	Ni	Mn	Sb	As
1	M.21-1938	Mortar	Base	71.6	6.6	9.1	1.5	10.9	0.2	0	T	–
1	M.21-1938	Mortar	Handle	74.2	7.1	6.2	1.3	11.1	0.3	-0.1	T	–
1	M.21-1938	Mortar	Ring	-7.7	-1	0.4	1	108.1	-0.7	-0.1	–	–
2	M.26-1938	Mortar	Base	84.3	7.1	3.8	1.8	3	0	0.1	–	–
2	M.26-1938	Mortar	Bowl	76.7	16.4	1.9	2.6	2.3	0.3	-0.1	T	–
2	M.26-1938	Mortar	Handle	52.6	19.3	16.9	3.8	7.2	0.1	0	–	–
2	M.26-1938	Mortar	White	69.1	12.4	7.4	3.4	7.7	0.1	-0.1	–	–
3	M.24-1938	Mortar	Base	78	10.4	8.5	2.5	-0.4	0.9	0.1	–	–
3	M.24-1938	Mortar	Bowl	77.6	12.3	5.9	2.9	0.2	1.2	-0.1	–	–
3	M.24-1938	Mortar	Handle	72.5	13.4	9.1	2.5	1.5	1.1	-0.1	–	–
4	M.684-1910[2]	Mortar dated 1465	Base	82	10	7	–	–	T	–	–	–
4	M.684-1910	Mortar dated 1465	Bowl	84	12	4	–	–	–	–	T	–
4	M.684-1910	Mortar dated 1465	Motif	85	12	4	–	–	–	–	–	–
5	11-1869	Mortar dated 1468	Motif	67.5	13.1	9.2	2.7	7.5	0.3	-0.3	–	T
5	11-1869	Mortar dated 1468	Base	90.7	5.8	3.7	0.7	-1.1	0.3	-0.1	–	T
6	M.29-1938	Mortar dated 1507	Black matl	75.6	12.3	10.3	2.3	-1.6	1.1	0	–	–
6	M.29-1938	Mortar dated 1507	Bowl	76.1	12	9.1	2.3	-0.8	1.4	0	–	–
7	344-1889	Mortar	Motif	71	20.1	4.3	1.9	2.3	0.1	0.2	–	–
7	344-1889	Mortar	Bowl	82.2	14	2.4	1.3	0.2	0.1	-0.1	–	–
7	344-1889	Mortar	Base	84.2	9.3	2.1	0.6	3.9	0.1	-0.1	–	–
7	344-1889	Mortar	Infill[3]	89.6	7.3	1.5	0.5	1.2	0	-0.1	–	–
8	7847-1861	Mortar dated 1480(?)	Base	85	9.8	2.1	0.6	2.5	0.1	-0.1	–	–
8	7847-1861	Mortar dated 1480(?)	Rim top	61.7	26.8	6.7	2.8	1.3	-0.2	0.9	–	–
8	7847-1861	Mortar dated 1480(?)	Handle	76.4	13.9	4	1.3	4.3	0.1	0	–	–
8	7847-1861[2]	Pestle	–	–	–	82.8	8.6	8.5	–	–	–	T	–
9	M.21-1923	Mortar dated 1490	Base	87.6	3.3	6.7	2.3	-0.1	0.2	-0.1	–	–
9	M.21-1923	Mortar dated 1490	Handle	68.3	7	19.6	2.9	2	0.2	-0.1	–	–
9	M.21-1923	Mortar dated 1490	Rim	68.8	4.4	19.3	1.6	5.8	0	-0.1	–	–
10	7848-1861	Mortar dated 1515	Base	91.2	4.3	3.4	-0.4	1.4	0.1	0.1	–	–
10	7848-1861	Mortar dated 1515	Bowl	89.8	6.3	4.2	-0.3	0	0.1	0	–	–

Cat. no.	Inv. no.	Object type	Part	Cu	Sn	Pb	Zn	Fe	Ni	Mn	Sb	As
10	7848-1861	Mortar dated 1515	Handle	76.7	7.6	8.8	0	6.4	0.1	0.2	–	–
10	7848-1861	Mortar dated 1515	Rim	81.9	5.5	8.8	0.8	2.7	0.1	0.1	–	–
11	M.685-1910	Mortar dated 1515	Rim	46.9	15.5	36.4	3	-2	0.2	0.1	–	–
11	M.685-1910	Mortar dated 1515	Solder	67.2	13.6	17.5	2.6	-1.2	0.4	-0.2	–	–
11	M.685-1910	Mortar dated 1515	Bowl	71.5	7.5	18.3	1.2	1.4	0.2	0	–	–
11	M.685-1910	Mortar dated 1515	Base	90.1	4.1	6.2	0.4	-0.9	0.1	0	–	–
11	M.685-1910	Mortar dated 1515	Top bowl[4]	84.4	7.8	8	0.3	-0.8	0.2	0.1	–	–
11	M.685-1910	Mortar dated 1515	Handle	68.5	10.1	18.4	2.1	1.2	0.3	-0.6	–	–
12	M.671-1910	Hand bell	Body	85.1	12.5	1.9	0.4	0	0.1	-0.1	–	–
12	M.671-1910	Hand bell	Handle	83.5	12.3	2.4	-0.4	2.2	0	0	–	–
13	M.996-1926	Mortar	Base	81.8	7.2	6.1	4.8	-0.1	0.2	0.1	–	–
13	M.996-1926	Mortar	Bowl	78.4	11.1	6.6	4.6	-0.5	0.1	-0.3	–	–
14	10-1869	Mortar	Base	62.3	15.3	18.7	2.7	0.7	0.4	-0.2	–	–
14	10-1869	Mortar	Lower rim	67.4	19.9	10	2.5	0	0.4	-0.2	–	–
14	10-1869	Mortar	Motif	45.7	36.5	9.7	4	3.1	0.7	0.2	–	–
15	A.2-1974	Mortar dated 1642	Top rim	74.4	21.7	4.1	1.5	-1.7	0.2	-0.1	–	–
15	A.2-1974	Mortar dated 1642	Handle	71.4	19.5	3.2	1.9	3.9	0.3	-0.2	–	–
16	M.2681-1931	Mortar dated 1647	Rim	89.5	3	6.9	0.2	0.2	0.3	-0.1	–	–
16	M.2681-1931	Mortar dated 1647	Handle	85.9	5	6.1	0.5	2.7	0.3	-0.5	–	–
16	M.2681-1931	Mortar dated 1647	Shield	73.2	6	21.9	3.7	-5	0.4	-0.2	–	–
16	M.2681-1931	Mortar dated 1647	Base	85.7	11.3	2.2	0.5	0.2	0.2	-0.1	–	–
17	335-1886	Hand bell	Body	43	32.5	4.1	2.7	17	0.6	0.2	–	–
17	335-1886	Hand bell	Top	87.3	-0.7	0.6	10.5	2.4	0.3	-0.4	–	–
18	736-1893	Footed bowl	Body	88.3	8.1	2.7	0.3	0.4	0.3	-0.1	–	–
18	736-1893	Footed bowl	Base	90.9	6.6	3	0.3	-1.2	0.5	0	–	–
18	736-1893	Footed bowl	Waist	85.1	9.4	4.7	0.3	0.1	0.3	0.1	–	–
18	736-1893	Footed bowl	White[5]	81.3	10.9	6.2	0.6	0.4	0.4	0.2	–	–
18	736-1893	Footed bowl	White[5]	41.5	27.2	30.9	2.9	-2.9	0.2	0.1	–	–
19	1581-1855	Footed bowl	Top rim	87.4	0.4	1.7	7.8	2.6	0	0	–	–
19	1581-1855	Footed bowl	Middle rim	82.2	0.8	3.5	8.7	5.1	-0.1	-0.2	–	–
19	1581-1855	Footed bowl	Bowl	82.9	1.4	3.7	8.5	3.5	-0.1	0	–	–
19	1581-1855	Footed bowl	Lower rim	73.1	0.6	2.6	14.4	9.3	0	-0.1	–	–
19	1581-1855	Footed bowl	Rim	79.8	0.3	2.2	16.2	1.5	0	0.1	–	–
20	350-1889	Mortar	Bowl	88.1	12.3	1	0.1	-1.5	-0.1	0.1	–	–
20	350-1889	Mortar	Base	88.2	11	1.7	0.1	-1	0	0	–	–
20	350-1889	Mortar	Handle	80.1	18.6	2.7	0.4	-1.8	-0.2	0.1	–	–
20	350-1889	Mortar	Infill	79.2	17.2	0.4	1.7	2.4	-0.1	-0.8	–	–
21	M.22-1923	Mortar	Body	87	12.7	1.3	-0.1	-0.7	-0.1	0	–	–
21	M.22-1923	Mortar	Handle	82.7	13.1	2.9	0.4	1	0	-0.1	–	–
21	M.22-1923	Mortar	Base	86.6	11.1	1.6	-0.1	1	0	-0.1	T	–
22	Circ.382-1923	Mortar	Body	86.5	11.6	2.3	-0.2	-0.4	0.1	-0.1	–	–

Cat. no.	Inv. no.	Object type	Part	Cu	Sn	Pb	Zn	Fe	Ni	Mn	Sb	As
22	Circ.382-1923	Mortar	Base	89.7	9	1.7	-0.3	-0.2	0.1	0	–	–
22	Circ.382-1923	Mortar	Handle	84.6	13.1	2.5	0.2	-0.4	0.1	0	–	–
23	M.25-1938	Mortar	Body	84.2	11.1	0.4	0.3	4.1	-0.1	0	–	–
23	M.25-1938	Mortar	Base	78.3	9.7	0.4	0.2	11.6	-0.1	-0.1	–	–
24	345-1889	Mortar	Body	94.3	7.2	0.5	-0.6	-1.7	0.3	0	–	–
24	345-1889	Mortar	Base	91.2	7.8	1	0.1	-0.5	0.5	-0.1	–	–
24	345-1889	Mortar	Handle	91.9	8.2	0.6	-0.1	-0.9	0.4	-0.1	–	–
25	342-1889	Mortar	Body	82	7.2	8.9	0.4	1.5	0	0	–	–
25	342-1889	Mortar	Base	89.7	4.3	3.5	0.1	2.3	0.1	0	–	–
26	35-1865	Vase	Body	94.6	5.7	0.5	-0.1	-0.8	-0.1	–	–	–
26	35-1865	Vase	Belly	94.9	4.9	0.3	0.3	-0.3	0	–	–	–
26	35-1865	Vase	Handle	85.1	4	4.6	4.7	1.5	0.4	–	–	–
26	35-1865	Vase	Base	92.3	6.8	0.7	0.3	-0.2	0.1	–	–	–
27	M.690-1910	Footed bowl	Body	86.5	8.1	5.6	0.4	-0.4	0.1	-0.1	–	–
27	M.690-1910	Footed bowl	Base A[6]	78	9.3	13.1	1	-1.6	0.2	0	–	–
27	M.690-1910	Footed bowl	Base B[6]	70.3	9.5	16.8	0.9	2.4	0.2	-0.1	–	–
27	M.690-1910	Footed bowl	Waist	85.9	7.1	7.3	-0.1	-0.2	-0.1	0	–	–
28	M.702-1910	Mortar	Body	84	4	0.6	1.4	10	-0.1	0.1	–	–
28	M.702-1910	Mortar	Inset[7]	95.5	3.1	0.2	-0.3	1.6	0	0	–	–
28	M.702-1910	Mortar	Infill[7]	94.8	3.2	0.9	0.4	0.6	0	0.1	–	–
29	M.701-1910	Mortar	Bowl	94.8	5.4	0.3	0	-0.4	0	0	–	–
29	M.701-1910	Mortar	Handle	91.5	7	1.1	0.2	0.2	0	-0.1	–	–
29	M.701-1910	Mortar	Base	95.6	4	0.4	-0.3	0.1	0.1	0.1	–	–
30	348-1889	Mortar	Body	95.9	4.5	0.4	0	-0.8	0.1	0	–	–
30	348-1889	Mortar	Base	93.4	5.2	0.8	1	-0.4	0	0	–	–
30	348-1889	Mortar	Infill	94	4.7	0.9	0.5	-0.2	0.1	0	–	–
30	348-1889	Mortar	Handle	88.8	8.4	1	0.7	0.9	0.1	0.2	–	–
31	336-1889	Mortar	Body	91.2	1.6	3.6	0.1	3.3	0.3	0	–	–
31	336-1889	Mortar	Handle	95.3	1.4	2.2	-0.9	1.6	0.3	0.1	–	–
31	336-1889	Mortar	Base	92.6	1.4	2.5	-0.3	3.3	0.4	0.1	–	–
32	354-1889[2]	Mortar	Bowl	95	3	1	–	–	–	–	T	–
33	339-1889	Mortar	Rim	92	6	1.6	-0.1	0.8	0	-0.2	–	–
33	339-1889	Mortar	Base	94.2	5	0.4	-0.4	0.7	0	0.1	–	–
34	M.23-1938	Mortar	Body	86.6	7	4.1	1.6	0.2	0.4	0	–	–
34	M.23-1938	Mortar	Base	86.7	4.2	6.5	2.6	-0.1	0.2	-0.1	–	–
35	352-1889	Mortar	Base	88.5	5.8	3	0.5	1.7	0.5	-0.1	–	–
35	352-1889	Mortar	Rim	70.3	9.5	10.2	1.8	7.7	0.6	-0.1	–	–
36	337-1889	Mortar	Body	69.3	27.7	2.2	2	-1.3	0.1	-0.1	–	–
36	337-1889	Mortar	Base	63.7	31.1	1.6	2.7	1.1	0	-0.2	–	–
37	M.675-1910	Hand bell	Body	56.6	33.5	0.3	1.5	7.8	0.1	0.2	–	–
37	M.675-1910	Hand bell	Handle	68.6	29.5	0.3	0.9	0.6	0.2	-0.1	–	–

Cat. no.	Inv. no.	Object type	Part	Cu	Sn	Pb	Zn	Fe	Ni	Mn	Sb	As
38	M.676-1910	Hand bell	Body	81	16.8	1.5	-0.1	0.9	-0.1	-0.1	–	–
38	M.676-1910	Hand bell	Handle	76.6	17.8	3.5	0.6	1.7	-0.1	-0.1	–	–
39	M.194-1938	Hand bell	Body	72.3	22	4.2	0.6	0.7	0.2	0	–	–
39	M.194-1938	Hand bell	Handle	79.5	-1	1.5	9.3	9.8	0.1	0.8	–	–
40	587-1865	Hand bell	Rim	63.1	33.7	2.6	1	-0.8	0.3	0.3	–	–
40	587-1865	Hand bell	Shield	63.5	32.5	2.9	1.9	-1.3	0.3	0.1	–	–
40	587-1865	Hand bell	Top	59.3	31.8	4.4	2.1	2.1	0.3	0	–	–
41	M.199-1938	Hand bell	Body	66.6	30.6	2.1	1.6	-1.2	0.4	0	–	–
41	M.199-1938	Hand bell	Top	5.2	11	4.8	1.2	78.1	-0.2	-0.2	–	–
42	Circ.383-1923	Mortar	Base	88.7	0.1	8	0.1	2.9	0.1	0	–	–
42	Circ.383-1923	Mortar	Rim	83.3	-0.2	12.6	0.2	4	0	0.1	–	–
42	Circ.383-1923	Mortar	Body	87.2	0.2	10	0.2	2.3	0.2	0	–	–
42	Circ.383-1923	Mortar	Handle	83.8	-0.2	12.9	0.1	3.2	0.1	0	–	–
43	M.2682-1931	Mortar	Base	83	14.6	2.5	0.2	-0.4	0.1	0	–	–
43	M.2682-1931	Mortar	Inner rim	79.1	16.7	3.4	0.8	0	0.1	-0.1	–	–
43	M.2682-1931	Mortar	Handle	74.1	19	4.3	0.9	1.5	0.2	-0.1	–	–
43	M.2682-1931	Mortar	Body	57.1	28.4	3.3	4.3	6.2	0.4	0.3	–	–
44	M.27-1938	Mortar	Base	85.4	4.2	4.9	0.1	4.6	1	-0.1	–	–
44	M.27-1938	Mortar	Bowl	86.3	5.3	5	0.3	1.6	1.5	0	–	–
44	M.27-1938	Mortar	Handle	83.5	7.4	9.5	0	-2.4	1.7	0.3	–	–
45	343-1889	Mortar	Bowl	81.3	6.6	4.3	0.6	6.8	0.5	0	–	–
45	343-1889	Mortar	Base	80.3	2.7	4.5	0.2	11.6	0.6	0.1	–	–
45	343-1889	Mortar	Head W[8]	84.9	5.4	5.6	0.7	2.8	0.5	0.1	–	–
45	343-1889	Mortar	Head R[8]	75.5	14.6	2.8	6.3	0.8	0.2	-0.2	–	–
46	586-1865	Hand bell dated 1561	Body	64.9	29	2.1	2.8	1.2	0.1	-0.1	–	–
46	586-1865	Hand bell dated 1561	Knop	65.8	25.5	3	2.7	2.9	0.1	0.1	–	–
46	586-1865	Hand bell dated 1561	Clapper	-5.6	-1	0	0.7	106.5	-0.5	-0.1	–	–
47	M.686-1910	Hand bell	Body	89.2	-3	4.2	2.5	7.1	0	0	–	–
47	M.686-1910	Hand bell	Handle	69.9	10.4	8.2	6.9	4.2	0.5	-0.1	–	–
47	M.686-1910	Hand bell	Ball	15.3	23.1	38.2	3.8	19.1	0.2	0.2	–	–
48	470-1899	Hand bell	Body	63.9	34.3	1.9	1.9	-2	0.3	-0.2	–	–
48	470-1899	Hand bell	Handle	101.3	-3.1	0.2	-0.1	1.4	0.1	0.3	–	–
49	A.16-1973	Hand bell dated 1582(?)	Body	63.7	32.9	2.5	2.5	-1.9	0.3	-0.1	–	–
49	A.16-1973	Hand bell dated 1582(?)	Shoulder	6	31.2	62.8	4.5	-4.4	0.1	-0.2	–	–
50	A.7-1987	Hand bell dated 1583	Body	59.2	32.7	4.8	1.7	1.3	0.3	0	T	–
50	A.7-1987	Hand bell dated 1583	Handle	32.8	60	10.7	2.6	-7.2	0.9	0.2	T	–
50	A.7-1987	Hand bell dated 1583	Handle 2	53.2	37.1	6.5	2.2	0.5	0.4	0	T	–
50	A.7-1987	Hand bell dated 1583	Ball	-9.4	-1.5	0	1.1	110.4	-0.6	0	–	–
51	M.26-1923	Crucible	Bowl	71.8	20.3	3.3	3.3	0.7	0.5	0	–	–
51	M.26-1923	Crucible	Foot	74.9	13.9	5.3	3.8	1.7	0.4	-0.2	–	–
51	M.26-1923	Crucible	Handle	73.1	15.5	3.2	3.7	4.1	0.4	0	–	–

Cat. no.	Inv. no.	Object type	Part	Cu	Sn	Pb	Zn	Fe	Ni	Mn	Sb	As
51	M.26-1923	Crucible	Plaque	69.2	22.7	3.3	3.3	1	0.5	0.1	–	–
51	M.26-1923	Crucible	Frieze	60.5	21.7	3.9	3.6	10	0.3	0.1	–	–
52	M.3-1947	Hand bell	Body	65.4	26.2	0.9	1.1	6.4	0.1	-0.1	–	–
53	M.28-1923	Hand bell	Body	48.6	34.9	1.6	2.2	12.8	-0.1	0	–	–
53	M.28-1923	Hand bell	Oval	58	27.2	1	1.5	12.2	0	0	–	–
53	M.28-1923	Hand bell	Handle	78.8	5.2	9.8	1.9	4.5	-0.1	-0.1	–	–
54	715-1884	Hand bell	Body	57.1	34.1	2.2	0.8	6	-0.1	0	–	–
54	715-1884	Hand bell	Handle	-5.8	-0.9	1.1	1.3	104.6	-0.4	0	–	–
55	M.1-1947	Bell	Body	59.3	35.5	1.1	1.9	2	0.1	0.1	–	–
56	M.670-1910	Vase or mortar	Top	89.6	5.9	0.8	1.1	2	0.5	0	–	–
56	M.670-1910	Vase or mortar	Base	90	5	0.7	1.8	2.1	0.6	-0.1	–	–
57	M.687-1910	Bowl	Top	86	-0.9	1.1	4.3	9.2	0.3	0	–	–
58	335-1889	Mortar	Base	94.1	6.5	0.2	-0.8	-0.1	0.3	-0.2	–	–
58	335-1889	Mortar	Bowl	82.9	14.9	0.5	0.5	0.6	0.5	0	–	–
59	M.28-1938	Mortar	Rim	82.4	2.9	1.3	7.6	5.4	0.4	0	–	–
59	M.28-1938	Mortar	Base	79.8	2.6	2.7	10.1	4.4	0.4	0	–	–
59	M.28A-1938	Pestle	End	80.2	-0.3	0.9	16.1	2.9	0.1	0	–	–
60	M.203-1925	Altar bell dated 1616	Body	58	30.4	1.5	1.7	8.4	0.1	-0.2	–	–
60	M.203-1925	Altar bell dated 1616	Handle	39.3	27.5	3.1	3	26.8	0	0.2	–	–
61	M.78-1929	Hand bell	Top	60.4	28.5	3.4	1.6	5.6	0.5	0	–	–
62	M.1-1945	Mortar	Base	59.9	12.9	11.1	0.8	15.3	0.1	0	–	–
62	M.1-1945	Mortar	Rim	66.2	18.4	14	1.1	0	0.3	-0.1	–	–
63	341-1889	Mortar	Rim	83.5	7.3	5.1	2.2	1.8	0.3	-0.1	–	–
63	341-1889	Mortar	Bowl	81.5	11.9	2.7	1.5	2.1	0.4	0	–	–
63	341-1889	Mortar	Base	74.9	8.4	8	2.8	4.7	0.4	0.8	–	–
63	341-1889	Mortar	Handle	78.9	9.4	7.7	2.1	1.6	0.3	-0.1	T	–
64	347-1889	Mortar	Body	63.2	17.7	18	1.9	-0.8	0.1	-0.1	–	–
64	347-1889	Mortar	Base	71.2	14.5	14.7	1.3	-1.8	0.1	0	–	–
65	M.692-1910	Vase or mortar	Body	71.4	24.1	3.3	5.8	-4.7	0.4	-0.4	–	–
65	M.692-1910	Vase or mortar	Base 1	75.7	13.7	3.7	5.6	1.2	0.1	-0.1	–	–
65	M.692-1910	Vase or mortar	Base 2	61.4	25.4	8.5	5.4	-0.9	0.3	-0.2	–	–
66	340-1889	Mortar	Body	79.5	19.3	1.9	0.6	-1.4	0.2	-0.1	–	–
66	340-1889	Mortar	Base	81.2	14.9	1.9	0.8	1.1	0.1	0	–	–
67	M.703-1910	Vase	Body	67	27.1	2.3	1.2	2.5	0.2	-0.2	–	–
67	M.703-1910	Vase	UBody[9]	66.7	24.2	0.9	2.6	5.4	0	0.1	–	–
67	M.703-1910	Vase	Top	67.4	30.5	2.5	1.2	-1.6	0	-0.1	–	–
68	346-1889	Mortar	Base	81.7	13.4	3.2	0.2	1	0.5	0	–	–
68	346-1889	Mortar	Body	81.6	12.9	4	0.8	0.2	0.7	-0.2	–	–
69	318-1903	Mortar dated 1555	Base	76.7	19.3	3.7	2.3	-2.1	0	0	–	–
69	318-1903	Mortar dated 1555	Body	85.7	15.8	1.3	0.1	-2.7	0	-0.2	–	–
70	349-1889	Mortar	Rim	89.3	5.3	1.7	2.2	1.3	0.1	0.1	–	–

Cat. no.	Inv. no.	Object type	Part	Cu	Sn	Pb	Zn	Fe	Ni	Mn	Sb	As
70	349-1889	Mortar	Base	89.9	5.4	2.5	2.9	-0.7	0	0	–	–
70	349-1889	Mortar	Handle	78.8	13	3.6	2.8	2	0.1	-0.2	–	–
70	349-1889	Mortar	Ring	-10.5	-1.4	0	1.1	111	-0.4	0.3	–	–
71	351-1889	Mortar	Body	81	10.1	7	1.8	-0.5	0.6	-0.1	–	–
71	351-1889	Mortar	Base	83.8	5.7	7.1	1.9	1.1	0.4	-0.2	–	–
72	M.271-1923	Mortar	Base	84.2	4.3	1.2	6.6	3.6	0.1	0	–	–
72	M.271-1923	Mortar	Rim	83.9	7.3	3.4	4	1.3	0	-0.1	–	–
73	5427-1901	Mortar	Body	70	19.4	2	5.1	2.8	0.4	0.4	–	–
73	5427-1901	Mortar	Handle	70	22.3	1.9	4.6	0.7	0.5	0	–	–
73	5427-1901	Mortar	Bottom	84.6	10.6	1	3.3	0.2	0.3	0	–	–
74	M.683-1910	Mortar	Body	79.8	10.2	9.4	0.8	-0.7	0.4	0.2	–	–
74	M.683-1910	Mortar	Base	93.6	3.9	2.6	0	-0.1	0.2	-0.1	–	–
74	M.683-1910	Mortar	Handle	79	10.7	6.7	-0.4	3.5	0.2	0.2	–	–
75	7846-1861	Mortar	Body	82.5	9.2	5.2	0.3	2.6	0.2	0	–	–
75	7846-1861	Mortar	Handle	78	8.6	7.2	0.7	5.4	0.1	-0.1	–	–
75	7846-1861	Mortar	Rim	82.7	7.9	6.8	0.4	2.1	0.1	0	–	–

Appendix 3

Cat. no.	Inv. no.	Object type	Part	Cu	Sn	Pb	Zn	Fe	Ni	Mn	Sb	As
1	4483-1858[10]	Hand bell	Bell	122	-15.6	6	-35.4	23.6	-0.3	-0.3	–	–
2	1210-1855	Hand bell	Top	57.9	9.2	31.4	0.5	1.1	-0.1	0	–	–
2	1210-1855	Hand bell	Handle	82.9	1.5	0.7	8.9	2.9	3.3	-0.3	–	–
3	353-1889	Mortar	Body	70.3	23.7	3.8	2.5	-0.6	0.2	0	T	–
3	353-1889	Mortar	Base	65.7	27.2	4.8	3.3	-1.5	0.5	0	–	–
4	M.22-1938	Mortar	Base	74.2	16.4	6.8	3.6	-1.2	0.2	-0.1	–	–
4	M.22-1938	Mortar	Body	57	32.3	7	4.7	-1	0.2	-0.2	–	–

Notes

1. The data has been 'normalized' to 100 per cent. The quantification of antimony and arsenic has not been completed as they are present in low concentrations, thereby potentially giving rise to high relative error, due to surface changes. There is also considerable difficulty in obtaining certified reference material for these elements in an appropriate matrix. Negative quantities arise due to the computational processes used. They are included for completeness. The analysis results and Dr Martin's observations have been summarized by the author under Metal Analysis in the individual catalogue entries.

2. This data was computed by comparison to one known standard only. The presence of nickel in the base and antimony in the bowl of cat. no. 4, and of antimony in cat. no. 32 and cat. no. 8 pestle, was identified by visual examination of the raw data. Silver was also present in cat. no. 8 pestle, similarly identified.

3. The infill in the base.

4. Top bowl, outer rim.

5. White material on the top rim.

6. Base A is the bulbous lower rim; base B is the straight section on the lower rim.

7. Inset is the central inset area; infill is the repair to this area.

8. Head W is the whole head; head R is the repair.

9. Upper part of the body.

10. Unable to quantify, due to mercury gilded surface.

APPENDIX 2: List of dated bells and mortars 1300–1850[1]

Type/date	Founder or inscription/legend	Location/bibliographical reference
Bell; 1321	Manfredino	Museo di Castelvecchio, Verona Verona 1979, fig. 2
Bell; 1329	Unknown foundry	Provenance, De Poli foundry of Vittorio Veneto Sommacampagna 1989, p. 15
Bell; 1358	Vivenco and Vittore of Venice	Museo di Castelvecchio, Verona Verona 1979, fig. 3
Bell; 1366	Jacopo	S. Pietro in Mavino, Sirmione Verona 1979, fig. 4
Bell; 25 July 1370	Jacopo	Museo di Castelvecchio, Verona Verona 1979, fig. 6
Bell; 1385	Jacopo	Museo di Castelvecchio, Verona Verona 1979, fig. 5
Bell; 1440	Crescimbene of Perugia	Formerly Castiglioni Collection Muller (Castiglioni) 1925, pl. XCVIII
Mortar; 1465	Attributed to the foundry of Guidoccio di Francesco of Fabriano	Cat. no. 4
Mortar; 1468	Guidoccio di Francesco of Fabriano	Cat. no. 5
Mortar; 1480(?)	Signed Giuliano de' Navi of Florence	Cat. no. 8
Mortar; 1480(?)	BARTOLOMEO DAVERRAZAON MCCCC .. XX	Private collection Cleveland 1975, no. 5
Mortar; 1490	Giuliano Mariotti de' Navi of Florence	Cat. no. 9
Mortar; 1490	Giuliano Mariotti de' Navi of Florence	Museo Nazionale del Bargello, Florence Lise and Bearzi 1975, p. 64, fig. 79; Rome 1982, p. 46, no. 16 See cat. no. 8, no. iv
Mortar; 1490	IOANNE BENTIVOLO SECVDO HANNIBALIS FI PP. ANO SALVTIS 1490 (inscribed around the base – an odd mortar of questionable status)	Formerly Dr Adolf Hommel Collection, Zurich J. M. Heberle, GMBH, 18 August 1909, Cologne lot 436; Hugo Benario Collection, Rud. Lepke's Kunst-Auctions-Haus, Berlin, 5 April 1927, lot 458
Mortar; dated 1491[2]	NICOLAVS.FABIANI.BOLNEOPECIEN.FECIT. A.D.MCCCCXCI (the inscription is false – see n. 2)	Musée des Arts Décoratifs, Paris Migeon 1907 (op. cit. at n. 2 below), cat. no. 6 Italian Art exhibition, Petit Palais, 1935, no. 1222, p. 350
Mortar; 1493	Unknown foundry	Alda Bergna Collection, Milan Lise and Bearzi 1975, p. 54, no. 66
Bell; 1494	Orlando of Verona	Verona 1979, fig. 7 (now lost)
Mortar; 1494	Giuliano Mariotto de' Navi of Florence	Museo Nazionale del Bargello, Florence Lise and Bearzi 1975, pl. XXX. See cat. no. 8, no. v
Mortar; 1500	Giuliano Mariotto de' Navi of Florence	Christie's, London, 30 November 1983, lot 171 See cat. no. 8, no. vi
Bell; 1501	Orlando of Verona	Cavadini Collection, Verona Verona 1979, fig. 8

Type/date	Founder or inscription/legend	Location/bibliographical reference
Mortar; 1502	Giuliano Mariotto de' Navi of Florence	Private collection, Germany Sotheby's, London, 22 April 1993, lot 205 See cat. no. 8, no. vii
Mortar; 1502	ANNO DOMINI 1502	Sotheby's, London, 8 July 1976, lot 178
Mortar; 1504	Giuliano Mariotto de' Navi of Florence	Private collection, London Sotheby Parke Bernet, New York, 29–30 May 1981, lot 205 See cat. no. 8, no. viii
Mortar; 1504	SI. DEVS PRONOBIS. QVIS. CHRONTRA NOS. MCCCCCIIII	Formerly Camillo Castiglioni Collection Muller (Castiglioni) 1925, pl. CII
Mortar; 1507	Attributed to Guidoccio di Francesco of Fabriano or a successor	Cat. no. 6
Mortar; 1507	IHS. MARIA.MDVII/A.M.	Civiche Raccolte d'Arte Applicata, Castello Sforzesco, Milan Lise and Bearzi 1975, pl. XXIII
Bell; 1508	Orlando Chercherle of Verona	Church of San Michelino, Sommacampagna Sommacampagna 1989, pp. 4–5
Mortar; 1510	PERMARCO. POLLASTRO. ADDI. PRIMO. DAVGVSTV. MCCCCCX. IVLIV. II. AVE.	Corsi Collection, Florence Formerly Johannes Jantzen Collection Middeldorf 1981, p. 46, no. 12
Mortar; 1514	QVESTO MORTARO E DE SARAFINO DE GVID AGNIOLE SPETIALE FRANCISCVS DE VRBINO TE FECIT MDXIIII	Sotheby's, London, 12 April 1990, lot 77
Mortar; 1515	Giuliano Mariotto de' Navi of Florence	Cat. no. 10
Mortar; 1515	Giuliano Mariotto de' Navi of Florence	Cat. no. 11
Mortar; 1520	LIBORIA BARAGLI L'ANNO 1520	*The Chemist and Druggist*, 9 January 1932, p. 25
Mortar; 1521	D. PETRVS ANTONIVS BEXVTIVS FE FI MDXXI	Formerly Camillo Castiglioni Collection Muller (Castiglioni) 1925, pl. CIII
Mortar; 1535	PINI GUSEPPE	Sothebys, Florence, 8 April 1974, lot 114
Bell; 1539	Bonaventura Bonaventurini of Verona	Parish of Sommacampagna Sommacampagna 1989, pp. 6–7
Bell; 1539	Alessandro Bonaventurini of Verona	Cavadini Collection, Verona Verona 1979, figs 10–13
Mortar; 1540	SIGISMUNDUS DE FRANCIONIBUS AROMATARIUS PPMDXXXX	Rijksmuseum, Amsterdam Launert 1990, p. 204
Mortar; 1543	ANCORA SPERO	M. Léon van der Hoeven Collection Hotel Drouot, 19–21 March 1906, lot 497
Mortar; 1553	SOLI DEO GLORIA 1553	Castelli Collection, Siena Lise and Bearzi 1975, p. 58, fig. 72
Mortar; 1555	1555 [inverted]. + and the remains of an illegible inscription (- T (?) T A)	Cat. no. 69
Mortar; 1558	FRATE ANTONIO REGALE ARBANESE DE MELFI 1558	Civiche Raccolte d'Arte Applicata, Castello Sforzesco, Milan Lise and Bearzi 1975, p. 61

Type/date	Founder or inscription/legend	Location/bibliographical reference
Hand bell; 1561	Attributed to Alessandro Bonaventurini of Verona	Cat. no. 46
Mortar; 1572	Alfonso Alberghetti of Venice	Museo Artistico Industriale, Rome Pettorelli 1926, fig. 195 See fig. 14
Mortar; 1580	HOC FACTVM EST AN DO	Sotheby Parke Bernet, New York, 26 November 1976, lot 46
Hand bell; 1582(?)	de Levis foundry of Verona	Cat. no. 49
Hand bell; 1583	Giuseppe de Levis of Verona	Cat. no. 50
Hand bell; 1585	Giuseppe de Levis of Verona	Formerly on the Berlin art market Avery 1981 (1972), p. 46, fig. 2
Mortar; 1589	Giuseppe de Levis of Verona	Private collection (on loan to Düsseldorf Kunstmuseum) Avery 1981 (1972), p. 48, figs 6–7
Bell; 1590	Giulio and Ludovico Bonaventurini of Verona	Museo di Castelvecchio, Verona Verona 1979, figs 21–6
Bell; 1590	Giuseppe de Levis of Verona	Cavadini Collection, Verona Verona 1979, fig. 27
Bell; 1590	Giuseppe de Levis of Verona	Verona 1979, figs 29 and 30
Bell; 1590	Servo de Levis of Verona	Comune, Sirmione Verona 1979, fig. 31
Mortar; 1591	SANCTA MARIA DI IESV MDLXXXXI	Sotheby Parke Bernet, New York, 31 May 1974, lot 45
Mortar; 1594	Stefano Parari	Formerly Figdor Collection, Vienna Lise and Bearzi 1975, p. 30, fig. 24
Mortar; 1595	Antonio Maria De Maria of Vicenza	Museum für Kunst und Gewerbe, Hamburg Launert 1990, pp. 206–7, no. 232
Mortar; 1598	ANTONIO DEL BR.. ANRDO 1598	Museo Storico Nazionale dell'Arte Sanitaria, Rome Lise and Bearzi 1975, pl. XXXVI; Sbarigia 1985, p. 89
Mortar; 1600	Vincenzo Barborini (from Parma)	Kunsthaus Lempertz, Cologne Launert 1990, p. 206, no. 231
Mortar; 1605	Giuseppe de Levis of Verona	Private collection (formerly on loan to the Victoria and Albert Museum) Avery 1981 (1977), p. 72, fig. 3
Mortar; 1606	GERONIMO GRAZIANO 1606	Civiche Raccolte d'Arte Applicata, Castello Sforzesco, Milan Lise and Bearzi 1975, pl. XLII
Mortar; 1608	PETRVS.BONVS.CANCS DOMINI.GNLIS. PERVSIE.ET.VMBRIE and ANNO MDCVIII	Sotheby's, London, 12 December 1991, lot 187
Bell; 1609	Ottavio de Levis of Verona	Museo di Castelvecchio, Verona Verona 1979, fig. 34
Mortar; 1611	CAESAR DE ISACHIS SIVE DE MECCHIONIS.F.F. ANNO DNI 16X1	Middeldorf 1981, p, 130, cat. no. 36, illus. p. 131
Bell; 1616	Unknown foundry	Cat. no. 60

Type/date	Founder or inscription/legend	Location/bibliographical reference
Bell; 1616	Servo de Levis of Verona	Museo di Castelvecchio, Verona Verona 1979, fig. 36
Bell; 1617	Servo de Levis of Verona	Church of San Michelino, Sommacampagna Sommacampagna 1989, pp. 8–9
Mortar; 1623	+ IN + FERMERIA – D – FULVIA – A – D – MDCXXIII	Middeldorf 1981, p. 146, cat. no. 40, illus. p. 145
Bell; 1624	Paolo and Francesco de Levis of Verona	Church of Madonna del Monte di Sommacampagna Sommacampagna 1989, pp. 8–9
Mortar; 1627	POMPEO VERGIGLIO 1627	Lise and Bearzi 1975, p. 59, fig. 74
Mortar; 1633	REGIO CUSTODE CRESCIT	Sotheby's, London, 6 July 1995, lot 173
Mortar; 1636	Vincenzo Barborini (from Parma)	Radcliffe 1992, pp. 244–6, cat. no. 44, illus. on p. 245
Mortar; 1637	SOLI DEO GLORIA 1637	Sotheby's, New York, 15 January 1992, lot 241
Mortar; 1642	Ambrogio Lucenti of Rome	Cat. no. 15
Mortar; 1647	Unknown, Rome (possibly Lucenti foundry)	Cat. no. 16
Bell; 1652	Paolo de Levis of Verona	Museo di Castelvecchio, Verona Verona 1979, fig. 35
Bell; 1666	Bartolommeo and Viviano Pesenti of Verona	Church of San Michelino in Sommacampagna Sommacampagna 1989, p. 11
Hand bell; 1676	Bartolommeo Pesenti of Verona	Musée du Louvre, Paris Avery 1981 (1977), p. 72, fig. 3
Mortar; 1689	Giuseppe de Polis	Sotheby Parke Bernet, New York, 26 November 1976, lot 47
Mortar; 1702	F. VINCENTIUS A SUBLAGO FECIT, 1702	Christie's, London, 7 July 1987, lot 45
Bell; 1709	Lucio de' Rossi (de Rubeis) of Padua (active at Verona)	Church of Madonna del Monte, Sommacampagna Sommacampagna 1989, p. 13
Bell; 1724	Lucio de' Rossi (de Rubeis) of Padua (active at Verona)	Private collection Verona 1979, fig. 39
Bell; 1734	Lucio de' Rossi (de Rubeis) of Padua (active in Verona)	Church of Madonna della Neve Sommacampagna 1989, pp. 12–13
Bell; 1734	Lucio de' Rossi (de Rubeis) of Padua (active in Verona)	Church of Cornodi Bussolengo Sommacampagna 1989, pp. 14–15
Mortar; 1738	Unknown foundry	Museo Storico Nazionale dell'Arte Sanitaria, Rome Lise and Bearzi 1975, pl. XLVIII
Bell; 1742	Angelo Poni of Verona	Chiesolina, Sommacampagna Sommacampagna 1989, pp. 16–17
Bell; 1743	Angelo Poni of Verona	Private collection Verona 1979, fig. 40
Bell; 1746	Angelo Poni of Verona	Archivio dell'Associazione Suonatori di Campane Sommacampagna 1989, pp. 16–17
Bell; 1746	Giuseppe Ruffini of Verona	Sommacampagna 1989, pp. 20–1

Type/date	Founder or inscription/legend	Location/bibliographical reference
Mortar; 1759	G.N.F.	Museo Storico Nazionale dell'Arte Sanitaria, Rome Lise and Bearzi 1975, pl. L; Sbarigia 1985, p. 89
Bell; 1760	Giuseppe Antonio Larducci of Verona	Museo di Castelvecchio, Verona Verona 1979, figs 41–3
Mortar; 1762	SANCTA MARIA LAURENTANA ORA PRO NOBIS. A.D.1762	Museo Storico Nazionale dell'Arte Sanitaria, Rome Lise and Bearzi 1975, pl. IL
Mortar; 1764	GIVSEPPE FEDELI, E FRATELLI	Christie's, London, 11 January 1994, lot 53
Mortar; 1764	FRANCISCUS XAVERIUS SAVIIOLI FUNDARE FECIT ANNO 1764	Museo Storico Nazionale dell'Arte Sanitaria, Rome Sbarigia 1985, p. 90
Bell; 1766	Giuseppe Antonio Larducci of Verona	Parish of Parona Sommacampagna 1989, pp. 18–19
Mortar; 1770	NICOLAUS MORETTI FUNDERE FECIT A D MDCCLXX/OPVS ANGELI ET FELICIS ERAT DE CASINIS ROM FUND SAC PAL APOST.	Sotheby Parke Bernet, New York, 26 November 1976, lot 48
Mortar; 1771	ADSM 1771	Museo Storico Nazionale dell'Arte Sanitaria, Rome Sbarigia 1985, pp. 90–1
Bell; 1772	Giuseppe Antonio Larducci of Verona	Museo di Castelvecchio, Verona Verona 1979, fig. 44
Bell; 1778	Giuseppe Ruffini of Verona	Private collection Verona 1979, figs 47 and 48
Mortar; 1781	DOMENICO GIUSEPPE PAUVESE IM NOVI	Formerly Raoul Tolentino Collection Tolentino sale cat., American Art Association, New York, 8–11 December 1926, lot 102
Mortar; 1797	NICASIO TORRES LO FUSE – PER FRANCESCO MARIA BIANCHINI A.D. MDCCLXXXXVII	*Italian Art Collection formed by Count Pepoli* (sale cat.), American Art Association, New York, 1929, p. 128, cat. no. 232
Mortar; 1799	P.USO.DEL SIG. CIPRIAN BREGAZNZE-1799	Museo Storico Nazionale dell'Arte Sanitaria, Rome Lise and Bearzi 1975, pl. LII
Mortar; 1803	Canciani foundry, Venice	Museo Storico Nazionale dell'Arte Sanitaria, Rome Lise and Bearzi 1975, pl. LIV; Sbarigia 1985, p. 94
Mortar; 1805	AD USUM ALOYSII FENICI PHARMACOPOLAE A.DNI MDCCCVA. Da Roma	Museo Storico Nazionale dell'Arte Sanitaria, Rome Lise and Bearzi 1975, pl. LV
Mortar; 1810	MARIANO MURATORI FARMACISTA 1810	Museo Storico Nazionale dell'Arte Sanitaria, Rome Lise and Bearzi 1975, pl. LVII
Mortar; 1810	MDCCCX	Museo Storico Nazionale dell'Arte Sanitaria, Rome Lise and Bearzi 1975, pl. LVIII; Sbarigia 1985, p. 95
Mortar; 1814	Andreas Muzzarelli and Antonio Montignani	Museo Storico Nazionale dell'Arte Sanitaria, Rome Sbarigia 1985, p. 95
Mortar; 1821	Unknown foundry	Giuliani Pharmacy Collection, Milan Lise and Bearzi 1975, pl. LXI
Bell; 1825	Antonio Salegari Partilora (signing Pietro Partilora)	Bussolengo Sommacampagna 1989, pp. 22–3

Type/date	Founder or inscription/legend	Location/bibliographical reference
Bell; 1825 (another)	Antonio Salegari Partilora (signing Pietro Partilora)	Bussolengo Sommacampagna 1989, pp. 22–3
Mortar; 1826	Daciano Colbacchini and sons of Padua	Museo Storico Nazionale dell'Arte Sanitaria, Rome Lise and Bearzi 1975, pl. LXII; Sbarigia 1985, pp. 98–9 (as about 1850, although the date, not visible, is cast-in; the author has not seen the mortar)
Bell; 1830	Antonio Salegari (or Selegari)	Museo di Castelvecchio, Verona Verona 1979, figs 49–51
Mortar; 1841	LUIGI.ROTA.F(ecit). B.C. COBIANCHI 1841.	Museo storico Nazionale dell'Arte Sanitaria, Rome Lise and Bearzi 1975, pl. LXVI (as 1844); Sbarigia 1985, p. 98 (as 1841)
Mortar; 1844	AUGUSTINUS FRESCAROLIS P.o. FECIT 1844	Museo Storico Nazionale dell'Arte Sanitaria, Rome Lise and Bearzi 1975, pl. LX; Sbarigia 1985, p. 98
Bell; 1844	Pietro, Francesco and Luigi Cavadini of Verona	From the Parish of Montechia di Crosara Sommacampagna 1989, pp. 24–5

Notes

1. The list provides examples of Italian dated bells with literature where images can be found, as a guide for comparison. Numerous other dated bells and mortars are, of course, cited in the literature and sale catalogues, with or without illustrations (e.g. Sbarigia 1985 contains further illustrated examples; several collections are unpublished: the Musée Jacquemart-André de Chaalis, for example, has several dated mortars for which published images are not available, including examples dated 1476, 1557, 1590 and 1698).

2. The form of this mortar (purportedly signed by a Nicolaus Fabiani in 1491) does not relate to mortars produced at this date, but bears an extremely close relationship to a mortar formerly on the art market in Rome (details and date unknown; a photograph is in the Sculpture Department archive) with a cast-in legend giving the name of the founder Eques Aloysius Valadier and the date 1781. This mortar and another attributed to Nicolaus Fabiani by comparison with that now in the Musée des Arts Décoratifs (see Gaston Migeon, *Catalogue raisonée de la collection Martin Le Roy...*, III, Paris, 1907, cat. no. 7) is doubtless a product of that foundry to which the punched signature has been added. Another potentially related mortar, though with less elaborate decoration, was formerly in the Tolentino Collection (Tolentino 1925, no. 29) and was on the New York art market (L'Antiquaire Inc.; Nereo Fioratti) in 1975.

APPENDIX 3
Pieces acquired as Italian and subsequently rejected as such

1. Hand bell with images of kings

German; *c.*1550
Gilt bronze
h. 12.7, 4.8 (without handle); diam. 9; wt 484.8 g.
4483-1858 (Metalwork Department)

Provenance: Bought in 1858 for £2 (provenance unknown).
Bibliography: Inventory 1868 (objects acquired in 1858), p. 1.
Metal analysis: unable to quantify due to mercury-gilded surface.

Described as 'Venetian, 16th century' on acquisition, the bell includes images of kings based on designs for plaquettes by Peter Flötner (*c.*1485–1546), who was active in Nuremberg from 1523. They represent four of the 13 ancient German kings portrayed in silver plaquettes in the Kunsthistorisches Museum, Vienna, which in turn closely resemble the wood-cuts of 12 kings executed by Flötner for *Ursprung und Herkummen der zwölff ersten alten Könige und Fürsten Deutscher Nation…*, published in 1543.

2. Hand bell with inscribed ornament

Origins unknown (Non-European)
Leaded bronze (?)
h. 12.3, 7 (without handle); diam. 8.7; wt 502.1 g.
1210-1855 (Metalwork Department)

Provenance: Bought for 12s. 1d. (60p) in 1855 (provenance unknown).
Bibliography: Inventory 1868 (objects acquired in 1855), p. 2.
Metal analysis: the abnormally high lead content may indicate solder and not reflect a true reading. The handle is basically brass, with minimal tin.

Acquired as Italian, fifteenth-century, in 1855, the bell bears no direct relationship to known European bells from the period, and the facture also differs, particularly regarding the incised decoration. Its origins and date are yet to be deter-mined, as no comparable works have so far come to light.

3. Mortar decorated with putti

French (Paris?); *c*.1550
Bell-metal
h. 7.9; diam. 11 (rim), 7 (base); w. 12; wt 1208 g.
353-1889

Provenance: Bought from Michelangelo Guggenheim, Venice, in 1889 (with 335 to 354-1889, £300).
Bibliography: Inventory 1890, p. 37; Pechstein 1968, no. 41.
Metal analysis: bell-metal with lead and zinc. Antimony present in the body.

Acquired as Italian, sixteenth-century, the mortar forms part of a group that was subsequently associated with Fontaine-bleau. These mortars were probably made in Paris around 1550. See also no. 4 below.

4. Mortar decorated with putti

After a French mortar of about 1550
Probably French; nineteenth-century
Bell-metal (quaternary alloy)
h. 7.9; diam. 10.8 (rim), 6.9 (base); w. 11.5; wt 1215.7 g.
M.22-1938

Provenance: Collection of Dr W. L. Hildburgh, FSA, London; on loan to the Victoria and Albert Museum from 14 August 1934; given by Hildburgh in 1938.
Metal analysis: basically bell-metal with added zinc and lead (also indentifiable as a high-tin quaternary alloy). The body has a much higher tin and lower copper reading than the base, which may be due to segregation or peculiarities of the molten metal in the crucible.

Acquired as Italian, fifteenth-century, this mortar is identical in pattern to no. 3 above. It has visible seamlines and lack of definition, indicating that the mortar is an after-cast. This would normally be smaller than the original from which the mould was taken, but the dimensions of the present example are commensurate with the remainder of the group, referred to under no. 3 above.

Glossary

ଔଔ

The terms in the glossary are defined for the context of this volume. Additional useful glossaries can be found in Penny 1993 and Bassett and Fogelman 1997. For the sculptural techniques, see in addition Rich 1947 and Baudry 1978; for heraldic terms, see Clark 1859 and Boutell/Brooke-Little 1970; for Italian heraldry, see Coronelli 1702, Guelfi Camajani 1921 and Goodall 1958–9; for terminology in connection with mouldings and ornament, see Harris and Lever 1966, Middeldorf 1981, p. 23 (diagram of mouldings), and Lewis and Darley 1986.

After-cast A replica cast from a mould taken from an existing sculpture or object. Bronze after-casts made by **lost-wax casting** are smaller than the original due to shrinkage of the wax and the metal as it solidifies. However, as the condition of the wax and metal is dependent on a variety of indeterminable factors, it is questionable whether accurate assessment of after-casts can be made on the basis of dimensions alone. Unless worked up in the wax prior to casting, details of an after-cast will usually be less defined than the original.

Antimony Brittle, grey metallic element, recommended in some sources to be added to **bell-metal** to improve the sound. Sometimes found as an element in **bronze**.

Argent See **canons** and **peg argent**. (Also an heraldic term for the colour silver.)

Arsenic Brittle, grey metallic element. Arsenic was often found close to copper deposits and was alloyed with copper from the end of the fourth millennium BC. Often found as a trace element in **bronze**.

Base In this context, the underside of a mortar.

Bell-metal High-tin **bronze**, which is usually defined as containing about 20–23 per cent tin and 77–80 per cent copper, but defined by some sources as a copper-tin alloy containing tin of more than 12 per cent. The high tin content makes the metal brittle, but provides the tone that is required for bells.

Body In this context, the central section of a mortar, between the **lip** (or rim) at the top and the **foot** at the bottom.

Brass A copper-zinc alloy, which can also contain other elements, including small amounts of tin. The term brass was also used for **bronze** sculpture, primarily in northern Europe (notably England) until about the seventeenth or eighteenth centuries. See pp. 19–20 for further detail.

Bronze Copper-tin alloy, often comprising various other elements, notably lead and zinc. The term is also used for copper alloys that do not contain tin, such as some modern bronzes, and also for brass, which is technically a copper-zinc alloy.

Canons The fittings at the crown of a large bell, usually taking the form of metal loops cast-in with the bell, from which it is suspended for ringing. The canons are grouped round a central loop or argent (see Jennings 1988, pp. 22–31, for details of fittings for large bells; see also **peg argent**).

Case See **'false bell' technique**.

Cast-on repair A technique whereby an area that has been damaged or has failed in the casting can be repaired by attaching a wax model of the missing area to the metal object and re-casting. For example, the casting-on of a foot onto a bronze sculpture: a wax foot would be attached to the bronze and nvested in moulding material, and would be cast following the **lost-wax** method, applied to the relevant area. On cooling, the new bronze foot would have fused with the existing bronze to which it was attached. A repair to the base of cat. no. 20 may have been cast-in, made using a similar method.

Cire-perdue See **lost-wax casting**.

Clapper A pendulum designed to strike a bell for producing the sound. It is suspended from a hook inside the bell. Bells can also be rung by hammers striking the exterior. (See also **shank**, **sound bow** and fig. 3, p. 25; Jennings 1988, p. 27, for clappers for large bells; Jennings 1989, p. 23, for clappers for English hand bells).

Cope The outer mould of a bell or related casting. The term doubtless derived from the liturgical over-garment of the same name. The material is the same or similar to that used for the **core** (see p. 24).

Copper A reddish metal used for making utensils and sculpture. Copper is comparatively soft and malleable, making it easy to hammer and shape, but less easy to cast. It becomes harder when alloyed with other metals, notably tin (to make **bronze**) or zinc (to make **brass**). These alloys frequently contain other elements, such as **lead**, and traces of **antimony**, **arsenic**, nickel, manganese, silver and others.

Core The internal part of a mould used for casting (also known as the *anima* – the Italian for 'soul'). In bell-making (and that of related utensils) the core represents the interior shape of the bell. Core material for small bells etc. is generally based on a mixture of clay with other ingredients. Due to the form of these objects, the core interlocks with the outer part of the mould (or **cope**) externally to form a secure unit (see pp. 24–9 for a full description of the process). In the production of hollow-cast lost-wax bronze figures, however, the core is encased inside the wax model and must be held in place by core-pins (or chaplets) to prevent movement in casting (see references under **lost-wax casting**).

Crown The top section of a bell (see fig. 3, p. 25).

'False bell' technique A method of making bells, mortars and other related utensils, by creating a model in clay of the object to be cast (that is, the 'false bell' or 'case'), from which the mould is made; see p. 28.

Ferrule The base of the handle of the bell, projecting from the **crown** (see fig. 3, p. 25).

Flashing Thin lines of metal, which are formed when metal runs into cracks and crevices in the mould during the casting process. Wax flashing is also formed when molten wax runs into joins in a piece-mould; these are removed prior to investment and casting (see **lost-wax casting** for further references to casts made in this way).

Foot The supporting section at the bottom of a mortar or bowl, which is usually moulded and/or projecting.

Gate The entry point for the metal to be poured into the mould; also known as the pouring **sprue,** pour-hole or cup.

Gilding The application of gold to the surface of an object. Different techniques can be used for gilding bronzes. Mercury or fire gilding involved the application of an amalgam of mercury and gold, which was then heated; the mercury evaporated and the gold fused to the surface of the bronze. Another method is known as mordant gilding, whereby gold leaf is applied using an adhesive, usually oil, size, bole or gesso. An object that has the gilding applied to selected areas only is referred to as 'parcel-gilt'. See also pp. 31, 58, nn. 49–51.

Hammer See **clapper**.

Hook See **strickle**.

Impresa Italian term for a device adopted by an individual, usually of some status, as a personal identifier. Relatives or close associates were also sometimes given permission to use an individual's *impresa* in order to mark their relationship. Plural: *imprese*.

Inscription Text that is applied to the surface of an object. Technically, the term refers to text that has been incised or punched into the surface, but it has taken on a broader meaning also covering texts that are applied. See the Catalogue Key on p. 60 for usage in this volume.

Investment The fire-resistant moulding material applied to a wax model in the casting process (see also **lost-wax casting**). The term can also be used for the moulding material used in the **'false bell' technique**.

Knop A section of the handle of a bell, or other decorative item, resembling a knob or bud (see fig. 3, p. 25).

Lead Dark grey, soft, heavy metal. Lead is frequently found in **bronze** (sometimes then called leaded bronze), although it does not technically alloy with the other elements, but remains in globules.

Legend In this context, text that has been applied to the surface in relief, rather than incised or punched. See also **inscription** and the Catalogue Key on p. 60 for usage.

Lip The area or edge around the opening at the top of a mortar, or of a bell. On mortars the lip is often projecting beyond the **body** of the mortar and can also be recessed on the interior. See also **mouth**.

Lost-wax casting A method of casting metal sculpture and utensils in which a model of the object to be cast is made in wax and covered in a mould of fire-resistant (or refractory) material, called the **investment**. As the mould is baked in preparation for casting, the wax melts and pours away through an outlet. The wax is therefore 'lost' from the mould, giving the process its name – also known by the French term, *cire-perdue*. The space created by the removal of the wax is filled with molten metal, which (when solidified) creates a replica of virtually the same size and detail as the original wax model. There are differences between the original wax and the finished metal object due to shrinkage in the metal as it cools, and any surface working. Bells and mortars can be made by this method, but may also be made by the '**false bell' technique** using clay (see p. 28). The method for casting bells and mortars is simple compared to the variations on the lost-wax method of producing sculpture (see, for example, Stone 1982; Penny 1993; Bewer 1996; Bassett and Fogelman 1997, pp. 54–6; Bewer in Amsterdam 1998).

Mould A negative form from which a positive can be cast. In this context, a mould takes three forms: 1. comprising the core and cope, which together form the mould from which the bell (or mortar, etc.) is cast (see fig. 4, p. 26); 2. the inscribed slabs from which wax impressions are taken for application to the bell as decoration (see figs 5 and 6, p. 27); 3. sand boxes in which simple bell forms are cast (see **sand casting** and fig. 1, p. 24). Moulds can take more complicated forms, particularly in the production of sculpture. They can also be made from a variety of materials, depending on their use, including clay mixes (which are then fired), plaster, wood and gelatine.

Moulding wires Projecting mouldings, usually taking the form of parallel astragals, although the term can equally apply to a single wire. Moulding wires provide frameworks for **legends** or other applied decoration, and delineate changes in the shape of the bell (see fig. 3, p. 25).

Mouth The opening at the bottom of a bell; also referred to as the 'rim' or 'lip', although the latter terms more properly refer to the edge of the opening itself (see fig. 3, p. 25).

Mully groove See **neck**.

Neck Area around the top of the bell, below the **crown** and above the **waist**, which is often decorated with a legend or band of ornament. Also known as the mully groove, particularly on large bells. It is often delineated by **moulding wires** (see fig. 3, p. 25).

Patina/patination The term patina refers to the surface finish of an object (including bronzes, furniture, and so on), and has come to mean both that which is naturally acquired over time (due to the effects of the environment, handling, cleaning, etc.) and a finish that is applied. Patination, however, is the more accurate term for an applied surface treatment. As it is not always possible to determine the status of the patina on the objects in this volume, no attempt has been made to apply these terms in their strictest sense. However, 'patination' has been used when an applied treatment is specifically referred to and 'patina' has been used in its more general sense; the use of this term does not necessarily indicate the absence of an applied surface treatment.

Peg argent An attachment from which a bell is suspended, taking the form of a rectangular projecting metal peg, usually pierced for fixing (a tassel sometimes being attached by this means) (see fig. 3, p. 25). Sometimes known as a git top. The argent forms the central loop of the **canons** for suspending large bells.

Porosity Porosity in a cast is due to gas bubbles being trapped in the metal as it cools. The causes for this can vary, but porosity often produces a spongy appearance to the cast, and dense areas can also be weak and easily damaged.

Pour-hole See **sprue**.

Quern A form of grinding bowl, or hand-mill. See also **saddle quern**.

Rib The outline of the cross-section of a bell, showing the undulating shape that allows for the reverberation of air inside the bell to create the tone (see fig. 3, p. 25).

Riser See **sprue**.

Runner See **sprue**.

Saddle quern A shallow form of grinding bowl, used with a rounded stone (instead of a pestle) for grinding grains, and so on. It doubtless took its name from its resemblance to a saddle in shape (see p. 37).

Sand casting A technique using fine moulding sand (also known as 'green' sand) impacted in a 'sand casting box' around a model of the object to be cast. The sand box usually consists of different sections, which can be removed intact with the impression of the object to be cast left in the sand.

The model is then removed and the space thus created filled with the molten metal. During the Renaissance this method was confined to simple objects, such as bells, lamps, plaquettes and medals. Sand casting was developed further in the nineteenth century and was subsequently used for a variety of sculptural castings.

Shank Part of a **clapper** (see fig. 3, p. 25).

Sound bow The area of the bell, just above the rim, where the clapper strikes. The sound bow is cast as the thickest part of the **rib** (or profile) of the bell in order to resist damage during ringing.

Spindle The central rod around which the mould for casting the bell is formed. It can be laid either horizontally or vertically (see figs 2 and 4, pp. 25 and 26).

Sprue A channel through which metal enters and runs through a mould (the runner), and air and gases escape from the mould (the riser or vent). Bells and mortars are poured by a comparatively simple spruing system, often with only one sprue (or **gate**) by which the metal enters, and perhaps one or two sprues allowing the air to escape (depending on the size of the object being cast). Evidence of the sprue for running the metal (also referred to as the 'pour-hole') can be seen on the bases of the majority of mortars in the collection (see also fig. 4, p. 26). Bronze sculptures require a more elaborate spruing system, consisting of several runners and risers, to enable the metal to run to the extremities of the mould.

Stemma Italian for coat of arms, the identifying device of an individual or family. Such devices are frequently found decorating bells and mortars to indicate ownership or other associations. Plural: *stemmi*.

Strickle The device for forming the outline of the interior and exterior of a bell-shaped form of casting. Also known as a 'hook' or 'sweepboard'; see fig. 4, p. 26.

Sweepboard See **strickle**.

Tin A grey, hard, metallic element, rare in comparison to copper and lead. When alloyed with copper it produces **bronze**, a harder and more easily cast material. Tin also adds the tonal quality to **bell-metal**.

Vent See **sprue**.

Waist The area of a bell, below the **neck** and above the **sound bow**; the name deriving from the shape.

Zinc A white metal, which alloyed with **copper** produces **brass**. See p. 19.

Bibliography

﷯

This bibliography is divided into two sections: books, articles, collection and sales catalogues, etc. (with primary sources indicated by an asterisk), in alphabetical order by author; and exhibition catalogues in date order (abbreviated by location). It includes relevant literature that is not quoted directly in the text. See also Notes and Summary Bibliographies on pp. 53–64 for additional specific bibliography.

Books, articles, collection and sales catalogues

Abraham 1998 Lyndy Abraham, *A Dictionary of Alchemical Imagery*, Cambridge, 1998.

Aitchison 1960 Leslie Aitchison, *A History of Metals*, London, 1960.

Alberici 1976 Clelia Alberici, 'I bronzi d'uso' in *Grandi Collezioni di Arte Decorativa nel Castello Sforzesco*, Milan, 1976, pp. 26–31.

Allison 1994 Ann Hersey Allison, 'The Bronzes of Pier Jacopo Alari-Bonacolsi, called Antico', *in Jahrbuch der Kunsthistorischen Sammlungen in Wien*, 89/90, 1993/4, pp. 37–310.

Allison and Pond 1983 A. H. Allison and R. B. Pond, Sr, 'On Copying Bronze Statuettes' in *Journal of the American Institute of Conservation*, 23, no. 1, 1983, pp. 32–46.

Amayden and Bertini 1910–14 T. Amayden and C. A. Bertini, *La Storia delle famiglie romane di Teodoro Amayden con note ed aggiunte del Comm. C. A. Bertini*, Rome, 1910–14 (reprint, 2 vols, 1930?).

Amico 1996 Leonard N. Amico, *Bernard Palissy in Search of Earthly Paradise*, Paris and New York, 1996.

Antiq 1895 *Catalogue des Faiences Anciennes…Porcelaines, Grès, Étains, Cuivres, Fers, Armes, Émaux cloisonnés…de la Collection de M. Charles Antiq*, (sale cat.) Hotel Drouet, Paris, 23–5 April 1895.

Arens 1971 Fritz Arens, 'Die ursprüngliche Verwendung gotischer Stein- und Tonmodel, mit einem Verzeichnis der Model in mittelrheinischen Museen, besonders in Frankfurt, Mainz und Worms' in *Mainzer Zeitschrift*, 66, 1971, pp. 106–11.

Avery 1981 Charles Avery, *Studies in European Sculpture*, London, 1981.

Avery 1981 (1972) Idem, 'Giuseppe de Levis of Verona – a bronze founder and sculptor of the later sixteenth century.

1 – Bells and mortars' in *The Connoisseur*, vol. 181, no. 729, November 1972, pp. 179–88; reprinted in Avery 1981, pp. 45–52.

Avery 1981 (1973) Idem, 'Giuseppe de Levis… 2 – Figure style' in *The Connoisseur*, vol. 182, no. 732, February 1973, pp. 87–97, reprinted in Avery 1981, pp. 53–62.

Avery 1981 (1974) Idem, 'Giuseppe de Levis… 3 – Decorative Utensils and Domestic Ornaments' in *The Connoisseur*, vol. 185, no. 744, February 1974, pp. 123–9; reprinted in Avery 1981, pp. 63–70.

Avery 1981 (1979) Idem, 'Giuseppe de Levis… 4 – New Discoveries' in *The Connoisseur*, February 1977, pp. 114–21; reprinted in Avery 1981, pp. 71–8.

Avery 1988 Idem, *Studies in European Sculpture II*, London, 1988.

Avery 1992 Idem, 'Giuseppe de Levis (1552–1611/14) and his relatives in the bronze casting industry in Verona' in *Verona Illustrata* (Rivista del Museo di Castelvecchio), no. 5, 1992, pp. 45–52.

Avery 1993 Idem, *Renaissance and Baroque Bronzes in the Frick Art Museum*, Pittsburgh, 1993.

Avery 1997 Idem, *Bernini: Genius of the Baroque*, London, 1997.

V. Avery 2002 Victoria Avery, 'Public and Private Bronze Foundries in Cinquecento Venice: New Light on the Alberghetti and di Conti Workshops' in Motture 2002 (forthcoming).

Bange 1923 E. F. Bange, *Staatliche Museen zu Berlin, Die Bildwerke des Deutschen Museums, II, Die Bildwerke in Bronze und in anderem Metallen. Arbeiten in Perlmutter und Wachs geschnittene Steine*, Berlin and Leipzig, 1923.

Barbolini Ferrari and Boccolari 1996 Elisabetta Barbolini Ferrari and Giorgio Boccolari, *L'Arte del Ferro nel Ducato Estense*, Modena, 1996.

Bassett and Fogelman 1997 Jane Bassett and Peggy Fogelman, *Looking at European Sculpture. A Guide to Technical Terms*, London, 1997.

Baudry 1978 Marie-Thérèse Baudry, et al., *La Sculpture. Méthode et Vocabulaire*, Paris, 1978 (esp. pp. 239–335, 'La technique de la fonte et les autres techniques de mise en forme des métaux').

Baxandall 1966 Michael Baxandall, 'Hubert Gerhard and the altar of Christoph Fugger: the sculpture and its making' in *Münchener Jahrbuch der bildenden Kunst*, 3rd series, 17, 1966, pp. 127–44.

Benedetti 1923 Maria Bendetti, 'Nuovi documenti sullo scultore Vincenzo de' Grandi' in *Studi Trentini*, IV, 1923, pp. 28–40.

Berger and Krahn 1994 Ursel Berger and Volker Krahn, *Bronzen der Renaissance und des Barock. Katalog der Sammlung*, Braunschweig, 1994.

Bertolotti 1890 A. Bertolotti, *Figuli, Fonditori e Scultori in relazione con la Corte di Mantova nei Secoli XV, XVI, XVII*, Milan, 1890.

Bewer 1985 Francesca Bewer, *The De La Pirotechnia of Vannoccio Biringucci (1480–1537) and Bronze Sculpture* (unpublished M.Phil. dissertation), University of London, Faculty of Arts, Warburg Institute, London, 1985.

Bewer 1993 Idem, *The Technological Investigation of Renaissance Bronze Sculpture. Including the Technical Reports of 14 Renaissance Bronze Statuettes from the Huntington Art Collection* (unpublished study), May 1993.

Bewer 1996 Idem, *A Study of the Technology of Renaissance Bronze Statuettes* (unpublished Ph.D. thesis), Department of Archaeological Conservation and Materials Science, University of London, University College, Institute of Archaeology, London, 1996.

Bewer 2002 Idem, 'The Sculptures of Adriaen de Vries; a technical study' in Debra Pincus (ed.), *Small Bronzes in the Renaissance* (CASVA Symposium Papers), *Studies in the History of Art*, Washington, 2002 (forthcoming).

*Biringuccio 1540 Vannoccio Biringuccio, *De la Pirotechnia*, Venice, 1540 (available in facsimile edition, ed. Adriano Carugo, Milan, 1977).

*Biringuccio/Smith and Gnudi 1990 *The Pirotechnia of Vannoccio Biringuccio. The Classic Sixteenth-Century Treatise on Metals and Metallurgy*, trans. and ed. Cyril Stanley Smith and Martha Teach Gnudi, New York, 1990.

Blackmore 1976 H. Blackmore, *The Armourers of the Tower of London. Vol 1. Ordnance*, London, 1976.

Blagg 1974 T. F. C. Blagg, 'The Archaeological Excavations' in T. F. C. Blagg, H. M. Blake and A. T. Luttrell, *An Umbrian Abbey: San Paolo di Valdiponte*, part ii, *Papers of the British School at Rome*, xlii, pp. 99–178.

Blagg 1978 Idem, 'Bell-founding in Italy: Archaeology and History' in H. McK. Blake, T. W. Potter, D. B. Whitehouse (eds), *Papers in Italian Archaeology I: the Lancaster Seminar*, BAR Supplementary Series 41, 1978, pp. 423–34.

Bober and Rubinstein 1986 Phyllis Pray Bober & Ruth Rubinstein, *Renaissance Artists & Antique Sculpture*, Oxford, 1986.

Bode (Beit) 1904 Wilhelm Bode, *The Art Collection of Mr Alfred Beit at his residence, 26 Park Lane, London*, Berlin, 1904.

Bode 1904 Idem, *Königliche Museen zu Berlin. Beschreibung der Bildwerke der Christlichen Epochen, II, Die Italienischen Bronzen*, Berlin, 1904.

Bode 1907, 1908 and 1912 Wilhelm Bode assisted by Murray Marks, *The Italian Bronze Statuettes of the Renaissance*, 3 vols, London, 1907, 1908 and 1912.

Bode 1908 See above, Bode 1907, 1908 and 1912.

Bode 1910 Idem, *Collection of J. Pierpont Morgan: Bronzes of the Renaissance and Subsequent Periods*, 2 vols, Paris, 1910.

Bode 1912 See above, Bode 1907, 1908 and 1912.

Bode and Friedländer 1912 Wilhelm Bode and Max J. Friedländer, *Die Gemälde-Sammlung des Herrn Carl von Hollitscher in Berlin*, Berlin, 1912.

Bode 1922 Wilhelm Bode, *Die Italienischen Bronzestatuetten der Renaissance*, Berlin, 1922.

Bode 1930 Wilhelm von Bode, *Die Italienischen Bildwerke der Renaissance und des Barock: Bronzestatuetten, Büsten und Gebrauchsgegenstände*, Berlin and Leipzig, 1930.

Bode/Draper 1980 Wilhem Bode, new edition, ed. and rev. by James David Draper, *The Italian Bronze Statuettes of the Renaissance*, New York, 1980.

Boström 1995 Antonia Boström, 'Daniele da Volterra and the equestrian monument to Henry II of France', *The Burlington Magazine*, CXXXVII, December 1995, pp. 809–20.

Boussel, Bonnemain and Bové 1983 Patrice Boussel, Henri Bonnemain and Frank J. Bové, *History of Pharmacy and Pharmaceutical Industry* (trans. James Desmond Newell), Paris/Lausanne, 1983.

Boutel/Brooke-Little 1970 J. P. Brooke-Little, *Boutell's Heraldry*, 1970.

Brizzi, Marini and Pombeni 1988 Gian Paolo Brizzi, Lino Marini and Paolo Pombeni, *L'Università a Bologna. Maestri, studenti e luoghi dal XVI al XX secolo*, Bologna, 1988.

Burton 1999 Anthony Burton, *Vision & Accident: the story of the Victoria and Albert Museum*, London, 1999.

Butterfield 1997 Andrew Butterfield, *The Sculptures of Andrea del Verrocchio*, New Haven and London, 1997.

Butters 1996 Suzanne B. Butters, *The Triumph of Vulcan. Sculptors' tools, porphyry, and the Prince in Ducal Florence*, 2 vols, Florence, 1996.

Buzinkay 1994 Péter Buzinkay, 'Mitteleuropäische Bronze-mörser des Mittelalters' in *Mitteleuropa. Kunst, Regionen, Beziehungen (2)*, (Student conference, 10–11 November 1994), Bratislava, 1994, pp. 20–38.

Buzinkay 1996 Idem., *Középkori bronzmozsarak. Középeurópai edénytÌpusok e reneszánsz elött (Medieval Mortars. Types of Vessel in Middle Europe before the Age of Renaissance)*, unpub. Ph.D. thesis, Eötvös Lóránd Tudományegyetem (ELTE) (Lóránd Eötvös University), Budapest, 1996.

Caglioti and Gasparotto 1997 Francesco Caglioti and David Gasparotto, 'Lorenzo Ghiberti, il "Sigillo di Nerone" e le origini della placchetta "antiquaria"' in *Prospettiva*, 85, January 1997, pp. 2–38.

Calvesi 1986 Maurizio Calvesi, 'Arte e Alchimia', *Art Dossier*, no. 4, Florence, 1986.

Caplow 1977 Harriet McNeal Caplow, *Michelozzo* (2 vols; Garland), New York and London, 1977.

Carollo and Sottil 1994 Alberto Carollo and Maria Cristina Sottil, *Vicenza, Città di Campane*, Vicenza, 1994.

Carregari and Mauli 1985 Mario Carregari and Gianni Mauli, *Arte Campanaria*, Verona, 1985.

Cartolari 1854 A. Cartolari, *Famiglie gia' ascritte al Nobile Consiglio di Verona*, Verona, 1854 (facsimile reprint, Bologna, 1969).

Catalogue Itinéraire **1948** Musée Jacquemart-André, *Catalogue Itinéraire*, 8th ed., Paris, 1948.

Cazala 1953 Madame Roger Cazala, *Les Mortier d'Apothicaires*, Grenoble, 1953.

⋆**Cellini/Bull 1956 (1979)** George Bull (trans. and intro), *The Autobiography of Benvenuto Cellini*, Harmondsworth, 1979 (first published 1956).

⋆**Cellini/Ashbee 1967** C. R. Ashbee (trans.), *The Treatises of Benvenuto Cellini on Goldsmithing and Sculpture*, New York, 1967.

⋆**Cennini/Thompson 1960** Daniel V. Thompson, Jr, (trans.), *Cennino d'Andrea Cennini, The Craftsman's Handbook. The Italian 'Il Libro dell'Arte'*, New York, 1960.

Cessi 1967 Francesco Cessi, *Vincenzo e gian Gerolamo Grandi. Scultori (secolo XVI°)*, Trento, 1967.

Champeaux 1886 A. de Champeaux, *Dictionnaire des Fondeurs, Ciseleurs, Modeleurs en Bronze et Doreurs depuis le moyen-âge jusqu'à l'époque actuelle*, Paris, 1886.

Christie's (Heckscher) 1898 Christie, Manson & Woods, *Catalogue of The Renowned Collection of Works of Art, Chiefly of the 16th, 17th & 18th Centuries, formed by the late Martin Heckscher, Esq. of Vienna…*, London, 4–6 May 1898.

Christie's (Bardini) 1899 Christie, Manson & Woods, *Catalogue of a choice collection of Pictures, Antiquities, Works of Art of the Middle Ages and Renaissance, from the collection of Signor Stephano Bardini, of Florence*, London, 5 June 1899 (French version cited in notes as relevant).

Christie's (Bardini) 1902 Christie, Manson & Woods, *Catalogue of a choice collection of Pictures and other Works of Art, Chiefly Italian, of Mediaeval and Renaissance Times. The property of Signor Stephano Bardini of Florence*, London, 26 May 1902 (and four following days).

Christie's (Gibson Carmichael) 1902 Christie, Manson & Woods, *Catalogue of the well-known collection of Works of Art of the Classic, Medieval and Renaissance Times, formed by Sir Thomas Gibson Carmichael, Bart*, London, 12/13 May 1902.

Christie's 1905 Christie, Manson & Woods, *Capel Cure Collection*, London, 4 May 1905.

Cicogna Emmanuele A. Cicogna, *Delle inscrizioni Veneziane*, 6 vols, Venice, 1824–53.

Cirlot/Sage 1971 J. E. Cirlot (trans. Jack Sage), *A Dictionary of Symbols*, London, 1971.

Cittadini Originarii Manuscript in a private collection, London: *Arme de Cittadini Originarii Veneti*, probably early sixteenth-century.

Clark 1859 Hugh Clark, *An Introduction to Heraldry*, London, 1859.

Cole 1999 Michael Cole, 'Cellini's Blood' in *The Art Bulletin*, LXXXI, 2 (June 1999), pp. 215–35

Cole 2002 Michael Cole, 'The Medici Mercury and the Breath of Bronze' in Motture 2002 (forthcoming).

Cole Ahl 1995 Diane Cole Ahl (ed.), *Leonardo da Vinci's Sforza Monument Horse: The Art of Engineering*, Bethlehem, Pa., 1995.

Conci 1934 G. Conci, *Pagine di Storia della farmacia*, Milan, 1934.

Coppel 1996 Stephen Coppel, 'George Salting (1835–1909)' in Antony Griffiths (ed.), *Landmarks in Print Collecting*, London, 1996, pp. 189–203.

Coronelli 1694 V. M. Coronelli, *Armi, ò Blasoni Dei Patritij Veneti, Co'Nomi Di quelli, che per l'Età si trovano capaci all' ingresso del Serenissimo Maggior Consiglio Nell'Anno corrente*, Venice, 1694.

Coronelli 1702 Idem, *Blasone veneto*, Venice, 1702.

Corvi 1997 Antonio Corvi (ed.), *La Farmacia Italiana dalle Origini all'età Moderna*, Pisa, 1997.

Cott 1951 Perry B. Cott, *Renaissance Bronzes. Statuettes, Reliefs and Plaquettes, Medals and Coins from the Kress Collection*, Washington, 1951.

Cowen and Helfand 1990 David L. Cowen and Wm H. Helfand, *Pharmacy, an Illustrated History*, New York, 1990.

Craddock 1990 P. T. Craddock (ed.), *2000 Years of Zinc and Brass*, London, 1990.

Crellin and Hutton 1973 J. K. Crellin and D. A. Hutton, 'Pharmaceutical History and its sources in the Wellcome Collection. V. Comminution and English Bell-Metal Mortars c. 1300–1850' in *Medical History*, XVII, 1973, pp. 266–87.

Crollanza 1965 G. B. di Crollanza, *Dizionario storico-blasonico delle Famiglie Nobili e Notabile Italiane…*, Bologna, (1886) 1965.

Davison 1906 D. Davison, 'Bell-Metal Mortars' in *Connoisseur*, XV, August 1906, pp. 229–34.

DBI *Dizionario Biografico degli Italiani*, Rome, 1960 ff.

d'espagnet 1972 Jean d'espagnet, *L'Oeuvre Secret de la Philosophie d'Hermès*, Paris, 1972.

de Jouy-Guitton 1876 Barbet de Jouy (pp. 314–22) and Gaston Guitton (pp. 323–35), 'La Porte de Cremone au Louvre' in *Gazette des Beaux Arts*, 18/1, 1876, pp. 314–35.

de Tolnay 1969 Charles de Tolnay, *The Youth of Michelangelo*, Princeton, 1969.

de Winter 1984 Patrick M. de Winter, 'A little-known creation of Renaissance decorative arts: the white lead pastiglia box' in *Saggi e Memorie di Storia dell'Arte*, 14, 1984, pp. 9–42.

Diderot Denis Diderot, *Encyclopédie, ou dictionnaire raisonné de sciences, des arts, et des métiers*, 17 vols, Paris, 1751–65.

Diderot *Planches* 1767 Idem, *Recueil de Planches, sur Les Sciences, Les Arts Libéraux, et Les Arts Méchaniques, avec Leur Explication*, V, Paris, 1767.

DNB *The Dictionary of National Biography*, New York and Oxford, 1903–96.

DNB Concise *The Dictionary of National Biography. The Concise Dictionary, Part II, 1901–1970*, Oxford, 1982.

Dolcetti 1968 Giovanni Dolcetti, *Il 'Libro d'Argento' dei Cittadini di Venezia e del Veneto*, 2 vols, Bologna, 1968 (reprint of Venice, 1922–8).

Draper 1992 James David Draper, *Bertoldo di Giovanni. Sculptor of the Medici Household*, Columbia and London, 1992.

Drescher 1992 H. Drescher, 'Glocken und Glockenguss im 11. und 12. Jahrhundert' in *Das Reich der Salier 1024–1125* (exh. cat.), Mainz, 1992.

Drey 1978 Rudolf E. A. Drey, *Apothecary Jars. Pharmaceutical Pottery and Porcelain in Europe and the East 1150–1850*, London and Boston, 1978.

Ellacombe 1872 The Rev. H. T. Ellacombe, *Bells of the Church: A Supplement to the 'Church Bells of Devon'*, Exeter, 1872.

Enc. Ital. *Enciclopedia Italiana di Scienze, Lettere ed Arti*, 36 vols and Appendix, Rome, 1936–45.

Engels and Sanderson-Engels 1996 Gerhard Engels and Susanne Sanderson-Engels, 'The Bell Tolls: Foundry Technology in the History of Culture' in *Foundry Management and Technology*, 124 (4), April 1996, pp. 46–56.

Fabriczy 1904 C. von Fabriczy, 'Michelozzo di Bartolomeo' in Jahrbuch der *Königlich Preussischen Kunstsammlungen*, XXV, Beiheft, 1904, pp. 34–110.

Fletcher and Rossing 1991 Neville H. Fletcher and Thomas D. Rossing, *The Physics of Musical Instruments*, New York, Berlin, etc., 1991.

Fortini Brown 1997 Patricia Fortini Brown, *The Renaissance in Venice*, London, 1997.

Fortnum 1876 C. Drury E. Fortnum, *A Descriptive Catalogue of the Bronzes of European Origin in the South Kensington Museum*, London, 1876.

Fortnum 1877 Idem, *Bronzes*, London, 1877 (South Kensington Museum Art Handbooks, ed. William Maskell).

Franceschini 1995 Adriano Franceschini, *Artisti a Ferrara in età umanistica e rinacimentale, Testimonianze archivistiche, Parte II, tomo I dal 1472 al 1492*, Ferrara and Rome, 1995.

Friedländer (Simon) 1929 M. J. Friedländer, et al., *Die Sammlung Dr Eduard Simon*, I, *Gemälde und Plastik* (sale cat., Paul Cassirer and Hugo Helbing), Berlin, 1929.

*****Gauricus/Chastel and Klein 1969** André Chastel and Robert Klein (eds and trans.), *Pomponius Gauricus, De Sculptura (1504)*, Geneva, 1969.

Giusti and Matteini 1998 Annamaria Giusti and Mauro Matteini, 'The Gilded Bronze Paradise Doors by Ghiberti in the Florence Baptistery. Scientific Investigation and Problems of Restoration' in *Metallrestaurierum. Metal Restoration* (paper of the International Conference on Metal Restoration organized by the Bavarian State Conservation Office and the German National Committee of ICOMOS, Munich, 23–5 October 1997), *Arbeitshefte des Bayerischen Landesamtes für Denkmalpflege*, 94 (1998), pp. 47–51.

Goldschmidt 1914 Fritz Goldschmidt, *Die Italienischen Bronzen der Renaissance und des Barock*, I, *Büsten, Statuetten und Gebrauchsgegenstände*, Berlin, 1914.

Goldschmidt and von Falke 1917 Fritz Goldschmidt and Otto von Falke, *Die Sammlung Richard von Kaufmann* (sale cat., Cassierer, Berlin/Helbing, Munich; foreword by Wilhelm von Bode), Berlin, 4 December 1917.

Goldthwaite 1980 Richard A. Goldthwaite, *The Building of Renaissance Florence. An Economic and Social History*, Baltimore, 1980.

Goldthwaite 1993 Idem, *Wealth and the Demand for Art in Italy 1300–1600*, Baltimore and London, 1993.

Goodall 1958–9 J. Goodall, 'Heraldry in Italy during the Middle Ages and the Renaissance', in *Coats of Arms*, 5, 1958–9, pp. 148–55, 209–12.

Guelfi Camajani 1921 Conte G. Guelfi Camajani, *Dizionario Araldico*, Milan, 1921.

Guilmartin 1980 J. F. Guilmartin, *Gunpowder and Galleys: Changing technology and Mediterranean warfare at sea in the Sixteenth Century*, London, 1980.

Gush 1978 G. Gush, *Renaissance Armies 1480–1650*, Cambridge, 1978.

Hackenbroch 1962 Yvonne Hackenbroch, *Bronzes, Other Metalwork and Sculpture in the Irwin Untermyer Collection*, London, 1962.

*****Hainhofer/Gobiet 1984** Ronald Gobiet, *Der Briefwechsel* *zwischen Philipp Hainhofer und Herzog August d.J. von Braunsweig-Lüneburg*, Munich, 1984.

Hall 1974 James Hall, *Dictionary of Subjects and Symbols in Art*, London, 1974.

Harris and Lever 1966 John Harris and Jill Lever, *Illustrated Glossary of Architecture 850–1830*, London, 1966.

Haskell and Penny 1981 Francis Haskell and Nicholas Penny, *Taste and the Antique*, New Haven and London, 1981.

Hay 1989 Denys Hay, *Europe in the Fourteenth and Fifteenth Centuries*, London and New York, 1989.

Hay and Law 1989 Denys Hay and John Law, *Italy in the Age of the Renaissance 1380–1530*, London and New York, 1989.

Helbing 1913 *Catalogue de la Collection de M. le Comm. M. Guggenheim Venise. Objets d'Art et de Haute Curiosité, Tableaux et Dessins de Maîtres anciens* (sale cat.), Hugo Helbing, Munich, 1913.

Hildburgh 1915 W. L. Hildburgh, 'Italian Wafering-Irons of the Fifteenth and Sixteenth Centuries', in *Proceedings of the Society of Antiquaries*, 2nd series, xxvii, 161 (1915), pp. 1–40.

Hildburgh 1946 Idem, 'On some Italian Renaissance Caskets with Pastiglia Decoration' in *The Antiquaries Journal*, XXVI, 1946, pp. 123–37.

Hotel Drouot (Piot) 1864 *Catalogue des Objets d'Art et d'Antiquités…de M. Eugène Piot* (sale cat.), Hotel Drouot, Paris, 25–30 April 1864.

Hotel Drouot (Piot) 1890 *Catalogue des Objets d'Art de la Renaissance, Composant la Collection de Feu M. Eugène Piot* (sale cat.), Hotel Drouot, Paris, 21–4 May 1890.

Impey and MacGregor 1985 Oliver Impey and Arthur MacGregor (eds), *The Origins of Museums. The Cabinet of Curiosities in Sixteenth- and Seventeenth-Century Europe*, Oxford, 1985.

Inventory *Inventory of the Objects in the Art Division of the Museum at South Kensington*, London, 1852–71; *List of the Objects in the Art Division, South Kensington Museum*, London, 1872–1908.

Jardine 1997 Lisa Jardine, *Worldly Goods. A New History of the Renaissance*, London and Basingstoke, 1997 (originally published 1996).

Jennings 1987 Trevor S. Jennings, *Master of My Art. The Taylor Bellfoundries 1784–1987*, Loughborough, 1987.

Jennings 1988 Idem, *Bellfounding*, Princes Risborough, 1988 (reprinted 1992).

Jennings 1989 Idem, *Handbells*, Princes Risborough, 1989.

Jestaz 1986 Bertrand Jestaz, *La Chapelle Zen à Saint-Marc de Venise*, Stuttgart, 1986.

Jopek 2002 (forthcoming) Norbert Jopek, *Catalogue of German Sculpture in the Victoria & Albert Museum, 1430–1540*, London, 2002 (forthcoming).

Kammel 1996 Frank Matthias Kammel, 'Die Glocken der Berliner Skulpturensammlung' in *Jahrbuch Preußischer Kulturbesitz*, XXXIII, 1996, pp. 173–97.

Kelly 1986 J. N. D. Kelly, *The Oxford Dictionary of Popes*, Oxford and New York, 1986.

Kris 1926 Ernst Kris, 'Der Stil "Rustique". Die Verwendung des Naturabgusses bei Wenzel Jamnitzer und Bernard Palissy' in *Jahrbuch der Kunsthistorischen Sammlungen in Wien*, 1926, pp. 137–208.

Kris (Weinberger) 1929 Idem in *Versteigerum der hinterlassenen Sammlung des Herrn Emil Weinberger, Wien* (sale cat.; Auktionshaus C. J. Wawra, Autktionshaus, Glückselig GMBH and Kunsthändler Richard Leitner), Vienna, 1929.

Lange 1981 Anselm Lange, *Europäische Tischglocken*, Kornwestheim, 1981.

Langedijk 1981 Karla Langedijk, *The Portraits of the Medici, 15th–18th Centuries*, 3 vols, Florence, 1981.

Launert 1990 Edmund Launert, *Der Mörser. Geschichte und Erscheinungsbild eines Apothekengerätes*, Munich, 1990.

Lawall and Lawall 1934 Charles H. and Millicent R. Lawall, 'An interesting collection of mortars' in *Journal of the American Pharmaceutical Association*, XXIII, no. 6, 1934, pp. 570–81.

LCI 1990 *Lexikon der christlichen Ikonographie*, 8 vols, Freiberg, 1990 (originally published 1968).

*Leonardo/Richter 1970 Jean Paul Richter (ed.), *The Notebooks of Leonardo da Vinci*, II, New York, 1970.

Lewis and Darley 1986 Philippa Lewis and Gillian Darley, *Dictionary of Ornament*, London, 1986.

Lise 1978 Giorgio Lise, 'Alcuni campanelli in bronzo di Jan Van Den Eynde (Johannes a Fine)' in *Rassegna di Studi e di Notizie*, VI, 1978, pp. 193–214.

Lise 1983 Idem, 'La collezione di mortai di bronzo del Castello Sforzesco' in *Rassegna di Studi e di Notizie*, XI, 1983, pp. 243–81.

Lise and Bearzi 1975 Giorgio Lise and Bruno Bearzi, *Antichi mortai di farmacia*, Milan, 1975.

Litta Count Pompeo Litta, *Famiglie celebri italiane*, 11 vols, Milan, 1819–95 (3 additional vols, 1903–13).

Lloyd 1934 J. T. Lloyd, 'Development of the Pharmaceutical Mortar' in *Practical Druggist*, 52 (January 1934), pp. 12–17.

Lockner 1976a H. P. Lockner, 'Mitteleuropäische Bronzemörser und ihre Hersteller' in *Kunst & Antiquitäten*, no. 2, 1976.

Lockner 1976b Idem, 'Mitteleuropäische Bronzemörser und ihre Fälscher' in *Kunst & Antiquitäten*, no. 3, 1976.

Lothian 1958 Agnes Lothian, 'Some English Bell Founders …and Their Mortars' in *The Chemist and Druggist*, Annual Special Issue, 28 June 1956, pp. 705–11.

Luchs 1989 Alison Luchs (ed.), *Italian Plaquettes, Studies in the*

History of Art, 22, (CASVA Symposium Papers IX), Washington, 1989.

Maclagan 1924 Eric Maclagan, *Victoria and Albert Museum. Department of Architecture and Sculpture. Catalogue of Italian Plaquettes*, London, 1924.

Maggioni 1952 Giuseppe Maggioni, 'Le Farmacie dei Monasteri di Padova e del territorio con particolare riguardo alle spezierie dei Benedettini' in *Il Farmacista*, 1952, pp. 492–4, 549–52.

Mann 1931 (1981) J. G. Mann, *Wallace Collection Catalogue. Sculpture: Marbles, terra-cottas and bronzes, carvings in ivory and wood, plaquettes, medals, coins, and wax-reliefs*, London, 1931, with supplement 1981.

Mannheim 1907 Jules Mannheim and Édouard Rahir, *The Rodolphe Kann Collection*, Paris, 1907.

Manni 1986 Graziano Manni, *Mobili in Emilia*, Modena, 1986.

Manni 1993 Idem, *Mobili Antichi in Emilia Romagna*, Modena, 1993.

Manora 1842 Giovanni Orti Manora, *Di alcuni antichi Veronesi Guerrieri che fiorirono a' tempi della Scaligeri*, Verona, 1842.

Mariacher 1971 Giovanni Mariacher, *Bronzetti Veneti del Rinascimento*, Vicenza, 1971.

Marquand 1972 Allan Marquand, *Robbia Heraldry*, New York, 1972 (originally published, Princeton, 1919).

Maskew 1926 W. Maskew, 'A Few Beautiful Mortars. From the Collection of Sir William Pope, F.R.S.' in *The Chemist and Druggist*, CV, July to December 1926, pp. 79–80.

Matthews 1971 Leslie G. Matthews, *Antiques of the Pharmacy*, London, 1971.

Menichetti 1974 Piero Luigi Menichetti, *Medici e Speziali in Gubbio* (ed. Dr Francesco Maria Pierotti), Gubbio, 1974.

Metman and Vaudoyer 1910 Louis Metman and J.-L. Vaudoyer, *Le Métal II: Le Bronze, Le Cuivre, L'Étain, Le Plomb. Premier Album du Moyen Age au milieu du XVIIIe Siècle*, Paris, 1910.

Meyer 1957 Franz Sales Meyer, *Handbook of Ornament*, New York, 1957.

Middeldorf 1981 Ulrich Middeldorf, *Fifty Mortars. A Catalogue*, Florence, 1981.

Migeon 1904 G. Migeon, *Catalogue des Bronzes & Cuivres du Moyen Age, de la Renaissance et des Temps Modernes*, Paris, 1904.

Miller 1999 Elizabeth Miller, *16th-Century Italian Ornament Prints in the Victoria and Albert Museum*, London, 1999.

Molinier 1886 Émile Molinier, *Les Bronzes de la Renaissance. Les Plaquettes. Catalogue Raisonné*, Paris, 1886.

Montagu 1985 Jennifer Montagu, *Alessandro Algardi*, 2 vols, New Haven and London, 1985.

Montagu 1989 Idem, *Roman Baroque Sculpture. The Industry of Art*, New Haven and London, 1989.

Montagu 1996 Idem, *Gold, Silver and Bronze. Metal Sculpture of the Roman Baroque*, New Haven and London, 1996.

Montevecchi and Vasco Rocca 1988 Benedetta Montevecchi and Sandra Vasco Rocca (eds), *Suppellettile ecclesiastica I (4. Dizionari terminologici)*, Florence, 1988.

Morando di Custoza 1976 Eugenio Morando di Custoza, *Armoriale Veronese*, Verona, 1976.

Morando di Custoza 1980 Idem, *Genealogie Veronesi*, Verona, 1980.

Morando di Custoza 1985 Idem, *Blasonario Veneto*, Verona, 1985

Motture 1997 Peta Motture, 'The decoration of Italian Renaissance hand-bells' in Stuart Currie and Peta Motture (eds), *The Sculpted Object 1400–1700*, Aldershot, 1997, pp. 99–116.

Motture forthcoming Idem, 'Functional bronzes from the Alberghetti and other North Italian foundries: attributions and inter-relationships' in *The Burlington Magazine* (forthcoming, 2001).

Motture 2002 (forthcoming) Idem (ed.), *Large Bronzes of the Renaissance, Studies in the History of Art* (CASVA Symposium Papers), Washington, 2002 (forthcoming).

Muller (Castiglione) 1925 Frederick Muller & Cie, *Collections Camillo Castiglioni de Vienne. Catalogue des Bronzes Antiques et de la Renaissance*, Amsterdam, 18 November 1925.

Nobili 1922 Riccardo Nobili, *The Gentle Art of Faking*, London, 1922.

Nutton 1993 Vivian Nutton, 'Greek Science in the Sixteenth-century Renaissance' in *Renaissance & Revolution. Humanists, scholars, craftsmen and natural philosophers in early modern Europe* (ed. and intro. J. V. Field and Frank A. J. L. James), Cambridge, 1993, pp. 15–28.

Nutton 1997 Idem, 'The rise of medical humanism: Ferrara, 1464–1555' in *Renaissance Studies*, 11/1, March 1997, pp. 2–19.

*★**Origo 1992** Iris Origo, *The Merchant of Prato. Francesco di Marco Datini. Daily Life in a Medieval Italian City*, Harmondsworth, 1992.

Pagel 1986 Walter Pagel (in collaboration with Pyarali Rattansi), 'Vesalius and Paracelsus' in *From Paracelsus to Van Helmont. Studies in Renaissance Medicine and Science* (ed. Marianne Winder), London, 1986, pp. 309–28.

*★**Paracelsus/Waite 1992** Arthur Edward Waite (ed.), *The Hermetic and Alchemical Writings of Paracelsus the Great*, Edmonds, Wa., 1992.

Parker 1988 G. Parker, *The Military Revolution: Military innovation and the rise of the West, 1500–1800*, Cambridge, 1988.

Peacock 1900 Florence Peacock, 'Metal Mortars' *in The Chemist and Druggist*, 1900, LVI, p. 128.

Peal 1974 C. A. Peal, 'English decorated bell metal mortars' in *The Chemist and Druggist*, 29 June 1974, 201, no. 4919, pp. 825–8.

Pechstein 1968 Klaus Pechstein, *Bronzen und Plaketten vom Ausgehenden 15.Jahrhundert bis zur Mitte des 17.Jahrhunderts. Kataloge des Kunstgewerbemuseums Berlin, Band III*, Berlin, 1968.

Peck 1932 E. Saville Peck, 'Notes upon a Cambridge Collection of Bell Metal Mortars' in *Proceedings of the Cambridge Antiquarian Society. October 1930–October 1931*, XXXII, 1932, pp. 24–32.

Pedrazzini 1934 Carlo Pedrazzini, *La Farmacia Storica ed Artistica Italiana*, Milan, 1934.

Penny 1993 Nicholas Penny, *The Materials of Sculpture*, New Haven and London, 1993.

Petit (Kann) 1910 *Catalogue des Objets d'Art et de Haute Curiosité du Moyen Age, de la Renaissance et autres…, Provenant de la Collection Maurice Kann* (sale cat.), Galerie George Petit, Paris, 5, 6, 7 and 8 December 1910.

Pettorelli 1926 A. Pettorelli, *Il Bronzo e il Rame nell'Arte Decorativa Italiana*, Milan, 1926.

Pharmaceutical Journal 1955 'History of Mortars. Address in Edinburgh' in *The Pharmaceutical Journal*, 7 May 1955, p. 354; 'Early mortars' p. 359; and 14 May 1955, p. 395 (letter from Edward Raynor on 'Early Mortars').

Planiscig 1924 L. Planiscig, *Die Bronzenplastiken. Statuetten, Reliefs, Geräte und Plaketten. Kunsthistorisches Museum in Wien*, Vienna, 1924.

Planiscig 1927 Idem, *Andrea Riccio*, Vienna, 1927.

Planiscig 1930 Idem, *Piccoli Bronzi Italiani del Rinascimento*, Milan, 1930.

Planiscig (Figdor) 1930 Idem in *Die Sammlung Dr Albert Figdor, Wien, I, 5, Kästchen und Schachteln des 14-16 Jahrhunderts, Kästchen aus Metall, Glocken, Mörser, Bronzegerät des Mittelalters, Bronzeplatten von Epitaphien, Wappen und Totenschilder* (sale cat., Paul Cassirer, Berlin; Artaria & Co., Glückselig GMBH, Vienna), Vienna, 1930.

Planiscig 1932 Idem, 'Gasparo, fonditore veneziano' in *Bolletino d'arte*, XXVI, 1932–3, pp. 345–51.

⋆Pliny/Rackham 1961 H. Rackham (trans.), *Pliny Natural History*, Vol. IX, books XXXIII–XXXV, Cambridge, Mass., 1961.

Pommeranz 1995 Johannes W. Pommeranz, *Pastigliakästchen. Ein Beitrag zur Kunst- und Kuturgeschichte der italienischen Renaissance*, Munster and New York, 1995.

Pope-Hennessy 1964 John Pope-Hennessy, assisted by Ronald Lightbown, *Catalogue of Italian Sculpture in the Victoria and Albert Museum*, 3 vols, London, 1964.

Pope-Hennessy 1965 John Pope-Hennessy, *Complete catalogue of the Samuel H. Kress Collection. Renaissance Bronzes*, London, 1965.

Pope-Hennessy 1993 Idem, *Donatello Sculptor*, New York, London and Paris, 1993.

Pope-Hennessy and Radcliffe 1970 John Pope-Hennessy, assisted by Anthony Radcliffe, *The Frick Collection. An illustrated catalogue. Volume III. Sculpture. Italian*, New York, 1970.

Précis 1864 *Précis of the Minutes of the Science and Art Department from 16th Feb. 1852 to 1st July 1863*, London, 1864.

Précis 1872 *Précis of the Minutes of the Science and Art Department from 8th July 1863 to 23rd December 1869*, London, 1872.

Précis 1878 *Précis of the Minutes of the Science and Art Department from 23rd December 1869 to 31st December 1877*, London, 1878.

Quarenghi 1870 Cesare Quarenghi, *Le Fonderie di Cannoni Bresciane ai tempi della Repubblica Veneta. Notizie Storiche con Documenti Inediti*, Brescia, 1870.

Radcliffe 1984 Anthony Radcliffe, 'Gaspare, fonditore bresciano' in *The Burlington Magazine*, CXXVI, no. 981, December 1984, pp. 761–3.

Radcliffe 1992 Anthony Radcliffe, Malcolm Baker and Michael Maek-Gérard, *The Thyssen-Bornemisza Collection. Renaissance and later sculpture with works of art in bronze*, London, 1992.

Radcliffe 1994 Anthony Radcliffe, *The Robert H. Smith Collection. Bronzes 1500–1650*, London, 1994.

Raspe-Tassie 1791 *A Descriptive catalogue of a general collection of Ancient and modern engraved gems, cameos as well as intaglios, taken from the most celebrated cabinets in Europe; …by James Tassie…arranged and described by R. E. Raspe*, London, 1791.

Ravanelli Guidotti 1990 Carmen Ravanelli Guidotti (ed.), *La Donazione Angiolo Fanfani: ceramiche dal Medioevo al XX secolo*, Museo Internazionale delle Ceramiche in Faenza, Faenza, 1990.

Ravanelli Guidotti 1994 Carmen Ravanelli Guidotti, *La Farmacia dei Gesuiti di Novellara*, Faenza, 1994.

Review *Victoria and Albert Museum Annual Review*, London, 1911–38.

Rich 1947 Jack C. Rich, *The Materials and Methods of Sculpture*, Oxford, 1974.

Rietstap 1921 J.-B. Rietstap, *Planches de l'Armorial Général*, Le Haye, 1921 (plates by H. V. Rolland).

⋆Ripa 1618 (1986) Cesare Ripa, *Nova iconologia di Cesare Ripa Perugino*, Turin, (2 vols), 1986 (facsimile edition of Ripa 1618).

Rizzi 1987 Alberto Rizzi, *Scultura Esterna a Venezia. Corpus delle Sculture Erratiche all'aperto di Venezia e della sua Laguna*, Venice, 1987.

Rizzini 1915 Dr P. Rizzini, *Illustrazione dei Civici Musei di Brescia*, Brescia, 1915.

Roberts 1994 Gareth Roberts, *The Mirror of Alchemy. Alchemical Ideas and Images in Manuscripts and Books from Antiquity to the Seventeenth Century*, London, 1994.

Robinson 1856 J. C. Robinson, *Catalogue of the Soulages Collection; being a descriptive inventory of a collection of works of decorative art, formerly in the possession of M. Jules Soulages of Toulouse, Now, by permission of the Committee of Privy Council for Trade, Exhibited to the Public at the Museum of Ornamental Art, Marlborough House*, London, 1856.

Robinson 1865 Idem, *Catalogue of the Works of Art forming the Collection of Robert Napier, of West Shandon, Dumbartonshire*, London, 1865.

Rome (Castellani) 1884 *Collection Alessandro Castellani. Objets d'Art Antiques du Moyen-Age et de la Renaissance* (sale cat.), Rome, 1884.

Rosenauer 1992 Artur Rosenauer, 'Proposte per il Verrocchio Giovane' in Steven Bule, Alan Phipps Darr and Fiorella Superbi Gioffredi (eds), *Verrocchio and Late Quattrocento Italian Sculpture*, Florence, 1992, pp. 101–5.

Rossi 1974 Francesco Rossi, *Placchette. Sec. XV–XIX*, Vicenza, 1974.

Rossi 1977 Idem, 'Maffeo Olivieri e la bronzistica bresciana del "500"' in *Arte Lombarda*, n.s. 47/48, 1977, pp. 115–34.

Rossing 1984 Thomas D. Rossing (ed.), *Acoustics of Bells*, New York, 1984.

Sangiorgi 1910 *Catalogue de la Vente des Objets D'Art* (sale cat.), Galerie Sangiorgi, Rome, 11–18 April 1910.

Sbarigia 1985 F. Sbarigia, L. Colapinto, G.B. Marini Bettòlo, C. De Vita, E. Cicconetti, O. Mazzucato, C. Sciorilli, *Universitas Aromatariorum. Storia e Documenti del Nobile Collegio Chimico Farmaceutico di Roma*, Rome, 1985.

Scalini 1988 Mario Scalini, *L'Arte Italiana del Bronzo 1000–1700. Toreutica Monumentale dall'alto Medioevo al Barocco*, Florence, 1988.

Schad and Warlimont 1972 C.-R. Schad and H. Warlimont, 'Werstoffeinflüsse auf die klanglichen Eigenschaften von Glockenbronzen' in *Metall*, 26, January 1972, 1, pp. 10–21.

Schofield 1992 Richard Schofield, 'Avoiding Rome: an Introduction to Lombard Sculptors and the Antique' in *Arte Lombarda*, 1992/1, pp. 29–44.

Schottmüller 1918 Dr Frida Schottmüller, *Bronze-Statuetten und Geräte*, Berlin, 1918.

Schottmüller 1921 Idem, *Bronze Statuetten und Geräte*, Berlin, 1921.

Somers Cocks 1980 Anna Somers Cocks, *The Victoria and Albert Museum*, London, 1980.

Sotheby's 1995 *The Cyril Humphris Collection of European Sculpture and Works of Art*, 2 parts (sale cat.), Sotheby's, New York, 10–11 January 1995.

Spreti Marquis Vittoria Spreti, *Enciclopedia storico-nobiliare italiana*, 6 vols, Milan, 1928–32.

Staley 1906 Edgcumbe Staley, *The Guilds of Florence*, London, 1906.

Stone 1982 Richard E. Stone, 'Antico and the Development of Bronze Casting in Italy at the End of the Quattrocento' in *Metropolitan Museum Journal*, 1982, 16, pp. 87–116.

TDA 1996 Jane Turner (ed.), *The Dictionary of Art*, 34 vols, London, 1996.

ter Kuile 1986 Onno ter Kuile, *Koper & Brons*, Amsterdam (Rijksmuseum, catalogue of the collection), 1986.

Tettoni and Saladini L. Tettoni and F. Saladini, *Teatro Araldico*, Lodi, 8 vols, 1841–8.

★Theophilus/Dodwell 1986 C. R. Dodwell (ed. and trans.), *Theophilus, The Various Arts, De Diversis Artibus*, Oxford, 1986.

★Theophilus/Hawthorne and Smith 1979 John G. Hawthorne and Cyril Stanley Smith (trans. and notes), *Theophilus On Divers Arts. The foremost medieval treatise on painting, glassmaking and metalwork*, New York, 1979.

Thieme-Becker 1992 Dr Ulrich Thieme and Dr Felix Becker, *Allgemeines Lexikon der bildenden Künstler von der Antike bis zur Gegenwart*, Munich and Leipzig, 1992.

Thorndike 1923–58 L. Thorndike, *A History of Magic and Experimental Science*, London and New York, 1923–58.

Thornton 1997 Dora Thornton, *The Scholar in his study. Ownership and Experience in Renaissance Italy*, New Haven and London, 1997.

Thurm 1967 S. Thurm, *Deutscher Glockenatlas, II, Bayerish-Schwaben*, Munich and Berlin, 1967.

Toderi and Toderi 1996 Giuseppe and Fiorenza Vannel Toderi, *Placchette secoli XV–XVIII nel Museo Nazionale del Bargello*, Florence, 1996.

Tolentino 1925 *The Collection of Raoul Tolentino* (sale cat.) American Art Association, Inc., New York, 29–31 December 1925.

Tranchini and Salvador 1983 E. Tranchini and R. Salvador, *Le autentiche fonderie di Campane e di Bronzi artistici a Ceneda (artigianato vittoriese tra il XV e il XX secolo)*, Vittorio Veneto, 1983.

van Marle 1931, 1932 Raimond van Marle, *Iconographie de l'art profane au Moyen-âge et à la Renaissance*, 2 vols, La Haye, 1931–2; I, *La vie quotidienne* (1931); II, *Allegories et symboles* (1932).

★Vasari/Maclehose 1960 Louisa S. Maclehose (trans.), *Vasari on Technique*, New York, 1960.

von Falke 1922 Otto von Falke, *The Bachstitz Gallery Collection. Vol. III. Objects of Art and Paintings*, Berlin, 1922.

von Falke 1940 Idem, 'Bronzemörser' in *Pantheon*, October 1940, XXVI, pp. 243–6.

Wackernagel 1981 M. Wackernagel, *The World of the Florentine Artist* (trans. A. Luchs), Princeton, 1981.

Wainwright 1988 Clive Wainwright, 'Models of Inspiration' in *Country Life*, CLXXXII (June 1988), pp. 266–7.

Wainwright 1989 Idem, *The Romantic Interior. The British Collector at Home*, New Haven and London, 1989.

Wainwright 1999 Idem, 'Shopping for South Kensington. Fortnum and Henry Cole in Florence 1858–1859' in *Journal of the History of Collections*, 11, 1999, pp. 171–85, reprinted in Ben Thomas and Timothy Wilson (eds), *C. D. E. Fortnum and the collecting and study of applied arts and sculpture in Victorian England*, Oxford, 1999, pp. 171–85.

Walters 1912 H. B. Walters, *Church Bells of England*, London, New York, Toronto and Melbourne, 1912.

Walters 1926 Idem, *Catalogue of the Engraved Gems and Cameos, Greek, Etruscan and Roman in the British Museum*, London, 1926.

Warren 1996 Jeremy Warren, 'Bode and the British' in Thomas W. Gaehtgens and Peter-Klaus Schuster (eds), *Kolloquium zum 150sten Geburtstage von Wilhelm von Bode*, *Jahrbuch der Berliner Museen*, 1996, pp. 121–42.

Warren (forthcoming) Jeremy Warren, *Catalogue of European Sculpture at the Ashmolean Museum: Before 1540*, Oxford (forthcoming).

Washington 1994 *Sculpture: An Illustrated Catalogue*, National Gallery of Art, Washington, 1994.

Weber 1975 Ingrid Weber, *Deutsche, Niederländische und Französische Renaissanceplaketten 1500–1650*, Munich, 1975.

Weinberger 1927 *Versteigerung der Hinterlassenen Sammlung des Herrn Emil Weinberger* (sale cat.), Vienna, 22–4 October 1927.

Weirauch 1967 Hans R. Weihrauch, *Europäische Bronzestatuetten*, Braunschweig, 1967.

Welch 1995 Evelyn S. Welch, *Art and Authority in Renaissance Milan*, New Haven and London, 1995.

Welch 1997 Idem, *Art and Society in Italy 1350–1500*, Oxford and New York, 1997.

Williamson 1991 P. Williamson, 'Acquisitions of Sculpture at the Victoria and Albert Museum 1986–1991' in *The Burlington Magazine*, CXXXIII, 1065, December 1991, pp. 876–80.

Williamson 1996 P. Williamson (ed.), *European Sculpture at the Victoria and Albert Museum*, London, 1996.

Wilson 1983 Carolyn C. Wilson, *Renaissance Small Bronze Sculpture and Associated Decorative Arts at the National Gallery of Art*, Washington, 1983.

Wittop Koning 1953 Dirk Arnold Wittop Koning, *Nederlandse vijzels*, Deventer, 1953.

Wittop Koning 1975 Idem, *Bronzemörser*, Frankfurt am Main, 1975.

Zanca 1987 Attilio Zanca (ed.), *Pharmacy through the ages: from the beginnings to modern times* (trans. Rudolf Carpanini and Gillian Mansfield), Parma, 1987.

Exhibition catalogues

London 1913 Burlington Fine Arts Club, *Catalogue of a Collection of Italian Sculpture and other Plastic Art of the Renaissance*, London, 1913.

Detroit 1958 *Decorative Arts of the Italian Renaissance 1400–1600* (The Detroit Institute of Arts), Detroit, 1958.

Amsterdam 1961 *Meesters van het Bronz der Italiaanse Renaissance* (Rijksmuseum), Amsterdam, 1961.

Hamburg 1961 *Sechs Sammler Stellen aus* (Museum für Kunst und Gewerbe), Hamburg, 1961.

London 1961 *Italian Bronze Statuettes* (Arts Council of Great Britain: Victoria and Albert Museum, London; Rijksmuseum, Amsterdam; and Palazzo Strozzi, Florence), London, 1961; see also Amsterdam 1961 and *Bronzetti Italiani del Rinascimento*, Florence, 1962.

Washington 1968 Giovanni Mariacher, *Venetian Bronzes from the Collections of the Correr Museum, Venice*, Washington, 1968.

Pforzheim Reuchlinhaus and Hanau 1969 Anselm Lange, *Klingende Kostbarkeiten. Tischglocken aus 5 Jahrhunderten in Bronze, Porzellan, Silber, Glas* (Schmuckmuseum, Pforzheim Reuchlinhaus and Deutsches Goldschmiedehaus, Hanau, 1969), Braunschweig, 1969.

Cleveland 1975 William D. Wixom, *Renaissance Bronzes from Ohio Collections* (The Cleveland Museum of Art), Cleveland, 1975.

London 1975 *Andrea Palladio 1508–1580. The portico and the farmyard* (Arts Council of Great Britain), London, 1975.

Vienna 1976 *Italienische Kleinplastiken, Zeichnungen und Musik der Renaissance, Waffen des 16. und 17. Jahrhunderts* (Schloss Schallaburg), Vienna, 1976.

Berlin 1977 *Italienische Bronzen der Renaissance (aus der Sammlung der Staatlichen Ermitage in Leningrad)* (Staatliche Museen), Berlin, 1977.

Tulsa 1979 *Gloria dell'Arte*, Tulsa, 1979.

Verona 1979 *Fonditori di Campane a Verona dal XI al XX Secolo*, ed. Lanfranco Franzoni (Museo di Castelvecchio), Verona, 1979.

London 1981 David Chambers and Jane Martineau (eds), *Splendours of the Gonzaga* (Victoria and Albert Museum), London, 1981.

Rome 1982 Pietro Cannata, *Rilievi e Placchette dal XV al XVIII secolo* (Museo di Palazzo Venezia), Rome, 1982.

Frankfurt 1985 *Natur und Antike in der Renaissance* (Liebieghaus), Frankfurt am Main, 1985.

Padua 1986 Gianfranco Cenghiaro and Pietro Giacomo Nonis (eds), *9 Secoli di Campane. Arte, Cultura, Storia, Simbolo nella Vita della Gente* (Oratorio della Santa Croce, Cervarese, Province of Padua), Monselice, 1986.

Ravenna 1986 *Piccoli Bronzi e Placchette del Museo Nazionale di Ravenna*, Ravenna, 1986.

Florence 1988 Loretta Dolcini (ed.), *Donatello e il restauro della Giuditta* (Palazzo Vecchio), Florence, 1988.

London 1988 Trinity Fine Art Ltd, *An Exhibition of European Sculpture and Works of Art* (Harari & Johns Ltd), London, 1988.

South Brisbane 1988 *Masterpieces from the Louvre* (Queensland Art Gallery), South Brisbane, 1988.

Venice 1988 Madile Gambier (ed.), *Una Città e il suo Museo* (Museo Correr), Venice, 1988.

New York 1989 Vivian B. Mann (ed.), *Gardens and Ghettos: The Art of Jewish Life in Italy* (The Jewish Museum), New York, 1989.

Sommacampagna 1989 Luciano Rognini and Giancarlo Tommasi (eds), *Documentazione di Antiche Campane delle nostre Comunità* (Scuola Materna 'Campostrini'), Sommacampagna, 1989.

London 1990 Mark Jones (ed.), *Fake? The Art of Deception* (British Museum), London, 1990.

Speyer 1992 *Das Reich der Salier 1024–1125* (Historischen Museum der Pfalz, Speyer), Sigmaringen, 1992.

Florence and New York 1993 Loretta Dolcini (ed.), *Verrocchio's Christ and St Thomas. A Masterpiece of Sculpture from Renaissance Florence* (Palazzo Vecchio, Florence, and the Metropolitan Museum of Art, New York), New York, 1993.

Trento 1993 Laura Dal Prà (ed.), *I Madruzzo e l'Europa 1539–1658. I principi vescovi di Trento tra Papato e Imperio* (Castello del Buonconsiglio), Trento, 1993.

Madrid 1994 *Los Leoni (1509–1608). Escultores del Renacimiento italiano al servicio de la corte de España*, Madrid, 1994.

Washington 1994 *see* main bibliography.

Washington/New York 1994 Stephen K. Scher (ed.), *The Currency of Fame: Portrait medals of the Renaissance* (The National Gallery of Art, Washington; The Frick Collection, New York; The National Gallery of Scotland, Edinburgh, 1994–5), New York, 1994.

Berlin 1995 Volker Krahn (ed*.), 'Von allen Seiten schön' Bronzen der Renaissance und des Barock* (Altes Museum, Berlin), Heidelberg, 1995.

Rosenheim 1995 Manfred Tremi, Rainhard Riepertinger and Evamaria Brockhoff (eds), *Salz macht Geschichte* (Zentrum Lokschuppen, Rosenheim), Augsburg, 1995.

Baltimore 1997 Brenda Richardson and Malcolm Baker (eds), *A Grand Design. The Art of the Victoria and Albert Museum* (The Baltimore Museum of Fine Art; Museum of Fine Arts, Boston; Toronto, Houston, San Francisco and V&A, London, 1997–2000), Baltimore and London, 1997.

Florence 1997 *Magnificenza all Corte dei Medici. Arte a Firenze alla fine del Cinquecento*, Florence, 1997.

Amsterdam 1998 Frits Scholten (ed.), *Adriaen de Vries 1556–1626* (Rijksmuseum, Amsterdam; Nationalmuseum, Stockholm; J. Paul Getty Museum, Los Angeles), Amsterdam, 1998.

London 1999 Jeremy Warren, *Renaissance Master Bronzes from the Ashmolean Museum, Oxford. The Fortnum Collection* (Daniel Katz Ltd), London, 1999.

Trento 1999 Andrea Bacchi, Lia Camerlengo and Manfred Leithe-Jasper (eds), *'La bellissima maniera': Alessandro Vittoria e la scultura veneta del Cinquecento* (Castello del Buonconsiglio), Trento, 1999.

Concordance

೧೦೩

Inv. no.	Catalogue entry
1210-1855	App. 3, no. 2
1581-1855	19
4483-1858	App. 3, no. 1
7846-1861	75
7847-1861	8
7848-1861	10
35-1865	26
586-1865	46
587-1865	40
10-1869	14
11-1869	5
715-1884	54
335-1886	17
335-1889	58
336-1889	31
337-1889	36
339-1889	33
340-1889	66
341-1889	63
342-1889	25
343-1889	45
344-1889	7
345-1889	24
346-1889	68
347-1889	64
348-1889	30
349-1889	70
350-1889	20
351-1889	71
352-1889	35
353-1889	App. 3, no. 3
354-1889	32
736-1893	18
470-1899	48
5427-1901	73
318-1903	69
M.670-1910	56
M.671-1910	12
M.675-1910	37
M.676-1910	38

Inv. no.	Catalogue entry
M.683-1910	74
M.684-1910	4
M.685-1910	11
M.686-1910	47
M.687-1910	57
M.690-1910	27
M.692-1910	65
M.701-1910	29
M.702-1910	28
M.703-1910	67
Circ.382-1923	22
Circ.383-1923	42
M.21-1923	9
M.22-1923	21
M.26-1923	51
M.28-1923	53
M.271-1923	72
M.203-1925	60
M.996-1926	13
M.78-1929	61
M.2681-1931	16
M.2682-1931	43
M.21-1938	1
M.22-1938	App. 3, no. 4
M.23-1938	34
M.24-1938	3
M.25-1938	23
M.26-1938	2
M.27-1938	44
M.28 & A-1938	59
M.29-1938	6
M.194-1938	39
M.199-1938	41
M.1-1945	62
M.1-1947	55
M.3-1947	52
A.16-1973	49
A.2-1974	15
A.7-1987	50

Index

Page numbers in *italics* refer to illustrations